# THE DEAD BUI
## THE DYI

For the Kellegher children of Annaghmacooleen, Cloone, County Leitrim: Saoirse, Tara, Tiarnán, Eirinn and Aoise

# THE
# DEAD
# BURIED
# BY
# THE
# DYING

## THE GREAT FAMINE IN LEITRIM

### GERARD MACATASNEY

MERRION

First published in 2014 by Merrion
an imprint of Irish Academic Press
8 Chapel Lane
Sallins
Co. Kildare
Ireland

© 2014 Gerard MacAtasney

British Library Cataloguing in Publication Data
An entry can be found on request

978-1-908928-50-4 (paper)
978-1-908928-49-8 (cloth)
978 1-908928-51-1 (PDF)

Library of Congress Cataloging in Publication Data
An entry can be found on request

Printed in Ireland by SPRINT-print Ltd

# CONTENTS

# ACKNOWLEDGEMENTS

I wish to thank the following for their assistance in the production of this book: the staff of the Catholic Diocesan Archives, Dublin; National Archives, Dublin; National Library, Dublin; Royal Irish Academy, Dublin; Public Records Office, Belfast; Paisley Central Library, Scotland; the National Archives of Scotland; the English National Archives, Kew, London.

A number of individuals did everything they could to assist me. I particularly want to thank Dolores Flynn, Kiltoghert Parish Office, Carrick-on-Shannon; Reverend Bill Atkins for access to Church of Ireland records; Debbie McCleary of the McClay Library, Queen's University, Belfast; Keith Nolan for photographing items in the Geraghty Collection in St George's Heritage Centre, Carrick-on-Shannon; Seán Gill for his expertise and patience in drawing the maps; to two students of RBAI, Conor Hamill for help with statistics and Matthew McClatchey for advising on computer programme safety; the librarians of the County Library in Ballinamore, especially Mary Conefrey. Sincere thanks go to Anna Mulvey, Cathy Mitchell Miceli and the members of the County Leitrim Society of New York for their donation towards my research costs. I am also indebted to Joe McManus and my cousin Anthony Flynn for their help. As always I wish to thank John Bredin for his support, interest and assistance and for allowing me access to the transcribed minute books of the Carrick-on-Shannon board of guardians. I also want to pay tribute to those individuals employed under the MRD Carrick-on-Shannon Fás scheme in the 1990s to transcribe these minute books – their hours of torture were not in vain.

I thank Lorna McCarthy for making me aware of the famine memorial in Mullaghgarve. Thanks to my sister and brother-in-law, Mary and Eamonn Kellegher, Annaghmacooleen, Cloone for affording me a regular bed and breakfast, often at short notice, during many research trips to the county. This book is dedicated to their five wonderful children who are all too familiar with the sites of famine graves throughout the county. To my mother and father for their constant support and advice. To my great friend Proinnsios Ó Duigneáin and Father Liam Kelly for willingly agreeing to read drafts of this book. Their time and expertise was greatly appreciated. Finally, I wish to thank Conor Graham (Publisher) and Lisa Hyde (Commissioning Editor) of Merrion Press for their faith in this book and patience in bringing it to fruition.

# LIST OF MAPS

# LIST OF TABLES

# INTRODUCTION

The Great Famine/An Gorta Mór resonates with the people of Leitrim and dotted throughout the county are famine memorials and graveyards. Monuments and plaques have been erected on the site of the former workhouse at Manorhamilton while the Carrick-on-Shannon and District Historical Society was behind an initiative which saw the construction of a memorial garden in the midst of the original workhouse cemetery. This group also oversaw the restoration of one of the original attics in the workhouse – a stark reminder of the grim reality of such places. In Drumshanbo, a famine graveyard, believed to hold 500 bodies, is signposted while the people of Mullaghgarve in the parish of Kiltubrid unveiled a monument on the side of Sliabh an Iariann to their local dead. At the same time, in the parish of Ardcarne, originally part of the Carrick-on-Shannon poor law union, victims are remembered on a plaque in the local graveyard which recalls how 'in the first 50 days of 1847 alone one hundred and ten victims were buried in this cemetery'.

Given this propensity for remembrance, it is somewhat surprising, then, that little has been written about arguably the most important event in the history of the county. T. M. O'Flynn's *History of County Leitrim* (published in 1938 and republished in 2013) does not mention the events of 1845 onwards while the highly-regarded *Breifne Journal* contains two articles on the famine in County Cavan, but nothing on Leitrim.[1] While local periodicals produced snippets of information it was not until 1987 that the first publication on the famine in the county appeared. Proinnsios O Duigneain's *North Leitrim in Famine Times* was one of a series of booklets on the history of the northern part of the county and as such it concentrated on the Manorhamilton workhouse. While revealing much new information on the experience of this establishment and the poor law union it served during the famine, the writer confined his sources to the board of guardians' minute books and local newspapers.

In 1996 the present author was commissioned by the Carrick-on-Shannon and District Historical Society to research and write a history of the famine in Leitrim. Given that this was to be published the following year the research period was rather restricted and although original material was uncovered it was essentially an overview of the poor law and the operations of relief committees formed under the auspices of the British government.

This new volume is a detailed work which attempts to understand the complexities of the period and to place Leitrim in its regional context as a county in the north-east of Connacht sharing substantial borders with Leinster and Ulster. Thus, a wide variety of documentary evidence has been utilised in the process. Most local histories of the famine have concentrated on two main sources: boards of guardians' minute books and the papers of the Relief Commission established by the British government. In this way much knowledge has been uncovered for the period 1845 to 1847 but the Relief Commission terminated operations in May/June of the latter year and correspondence to it ended shortly afterwards. In order to continue relating the effects of famine in the period thereafter historians have been left with no option but to rely largely on guardians' minute books and although these are a valuable source of statistics they lack the humanity of letters written by local correspondents.

In this work two major sources serve both to increase the depth of our understanding, by means of multiple letters written throughout 1846 and 1847, and demonstrate the extent to which the ravages of famine continued to affect the population until 1850 and beyond. The first are the records of the Irish Relief Association, located in the Royal Irish Academy and consisting of hundreds of printed questionnaires returned from applicants throughout the country. However, the second and most significant collection is that of the Society of Friends Relief of Distress Papers, held in the National Archives, Dublin. This vast archive contains thousands of letters and application forms covering the period 1846 to 1850 and enables us to examine at townland level the effects of the catastrophic events which engulfed the county during these years.

Although the minute books of the three workhouses in the county – Carrick-on-Shannon, Manorhamilton and Mohill – are incomplete, those that remain, used in conjunction with relevant British Parliamentary Papers, have been analysed in order to examine the workings of the poor law in these vital years. Other major collections accessed include the Outrage Papers, in the National Archives, Treasury Papers, in the English National Archives in Kew and the records of the Irish Reproductive Loan Fund, also in Kew. The work is supplemented throughout by reports from various local and national newspapers, together with material accessed in landed estate archives and is completed with an in-depth analysis of the census returns for 1851 and 1861.

In this way it is hoped that this work will make a contribution to understanding the complexities and nuances of the famine years at a local level in County Leitrim.

# Chapter 1

# A NATION OF PAUPERS

Measures taken to counter violence in the parishes of Mohill and Cloone,
November 1838. Courtesy of Seamus Geraghty Collection, St George's
Heritage Centre, Carrick-on-Shannon, County Leitrim.

# THE EMIGRATING TENANT'S Address To His Landlord

*I'm going to a country, where*
*From Poor rates I'll be free,*
*For Ireland is going to the dogs,*
*As fast as it can be..*
*I knew you'd like to stop me,*
*So I do it on the sly –*
*And with me take a half year's rent*
*So your honour, don't you cry!*

*Now that the Corn Laws are quite gone,*
*The grain's so mighty cheap,*
*I hardly find it worth my while*
*My plot of oats to reap;*
*But when its cut and all sold off,*
*To Yankee land I'll fly –*
*But sure I'll leave you all your land,*
*So your honour need not cry*

*I do not think I paid the rent*
*Within the last three years,*
*And so I owe your honour*
*Some trifle of arrears,*
*I mention this, because, perhaps,*
*You'd wish to say good bye,*
*But these arrears, I have them snug,*
*Your honour don't you cry*

*I hope your honour may have luck,*
*When all the country's waste,*
*And if they give out-door relief,*
*May your honour get a taste.*
*And if they build a workhouse,*
*For the landlords then to fly –*
*And you get in, why then I think,*
*Your honour need not cry.*

–Published in the *Roscommon and
Leitrim Gazette*, 6 April 1850

In 1835, French sociologist and traveller Gustave de Beaumont wrote of Ireland:

> I have seen the Indian in his forests, and the Negro in his chains, and thought, as I contemplated their pitiable condition that I saw the very extreme of human wretchedness; but I did not then know the condition of the unfortunate Ireland … In all countries, more or less, paupers may be discovered; but an entire nation of paupers is what was never seen until it was shown in Ireland.[1]

Such poverty permeated almost every aspect of society in Leitrim and featured prominently in any analysis of the county. For example, in 1832, in an application to the education commissioners from a school committee in Mohervogue, in the parish of Kiltubrid, it was stated that:

> The poor in this neighbourhood are unable to provide an adequate sum (however anxious for education) for their support being a poor naked destitute peasantry unable to even clothe their children decently or even to afford them the decent necessaries of life.[2]

In July of the same year the inhabitants of Glenade, in appealing for funds for a school in Caraduff, outlined some of the reasons for such poverty. They claimed that they were 'exceedingly poor, ground down by rackrents, tithes and other imposts' and consequently had been denied the means of affording their children 'the blessing of a liberal education'. Until now all they had was 'a poor hedge school about three miles from them' and now they were living 'in gross ignorance'.[3]

Poverty, together with 'the Catholic question', had remained in the forefront of British politics since the Act of Union (1801). With the granting of Catholic Emancipation in 1829 attention turned to the increasingly urgent matter of Irish poverty and in 1833 the British government established the Inquiry into the Condition of the Poorer Classes in Ireland. As well as sending questionnaires to various influential individuals throughout the country they also held public meetings in order, presumably, to obtain evidence as to standards of living from as wide a variety of sources as possible. In Leitrim gatherings were convened in the baronies of Dromahaire and Mohill and contributors commented on a variety of aspects of society. Local parish priest Fr Thomas Maguire

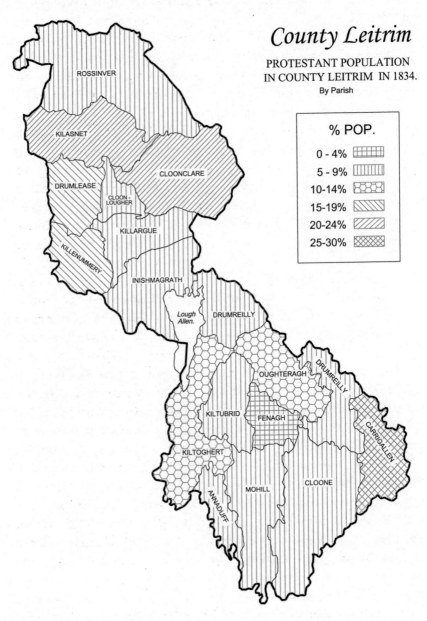

### County Leitrim

PROTESTANT POPULATION
IN COUNTY LEITRIM IN 1834.
By Parish

**% POP.**

0 - 4%
5 - 9%
10-14%
15-19%
20-24%
25-30%

Protestant Population in County Leitrim in 1834. Drawn by Sean Gill.

remarked that 'the labouring man … is accustomed to live entirely on potatoes … if he can by any contrivance add milk, salt and a few herrings when they are to be had cheap, he endeavours to be contented'. If meat was consumed at all 'it is on the two great festivals of the year, when he procures some pork at 2*d* per lb., or else some inferior beef'.[4] As to the quantity of potatoes necessary to sustain a labourer's family, it was agreed that for a family of five about one stone of potatoes was boiled for each of their daily meals.[5] At periods of distress, with his stock of potatoes consumed, the labourer was stated to be 'placed completely at the mercy of the dealers in meal and potatoes who are willing to supply him with food on credit, but always exact an exorbitant interest for the accommodation which they afford'. Circumstances such as this occurred at the beginning of summer, when employment opportunities were reduced, and this accentuated the reliance on such dealers. Thus, for example, when meal was available in the market at ten or twelve shillings 'the poor man is obliged to promise £1 for it, on four or five months' credit'. Interestingly, this applied more so to meal than potatoes simply because the latter were of a perishable nature.[6] In the meeting at Dromahaire a discussion took place as to the merits or otherwise of potatoes and meal. Simon Armstrong argued that if corn were substituted for the former 'there would be little or no chance of distress' and added that, in a year of surplus, corn could be kept over 'so as to meet the deficiency in the harvest of the three of four succeeding years'.[7] James Nixon stated that a hundred weight of potatoes was sufficient for a labouring man for at least eight days while Phelim Rooneen remarked that a similar weight of meal would maintain him for 'upwards of a month'.[8]

The assistant commissioners present at the meeting maintained that 'the general use of potatoes as food does not arise from any preference on the part of the peasantry for it'.[9] This view was corroborated by local men who remarked that 'a man that had his bellyful of either bread or potatoes ought not to complain; but what we'd like would be to have our dinner of potatoes and have bread to work upon in the morning'. In the opinion of Father Maguire:

> The true reason of it is that as the population and rents have alone increased, while wages and the demand for labour have decreased, the people have gradually been obliged to restrict themselves to that kind of food which can be raised in the greatest quantity from a given portion of land.[10]

This point was added to by Messrs John O'Donnell, Simon Armstrong and James Nixon who stated:

> Corn can never become the main article of food whilst holdings remain of their present size, even were the rents reduced; a man who occupies three acres considers himself very fortunate if the entire of the grain which his exertions can extract from it suffices to pay his rent: from the portion of land not devoted to corn he must feed himself; and that he cannot manage through any other crop than potatoes.[11]

In relation to rents it was stated that for a cabin and one rood of land a labourer 'would gladly' pay from £2/5 to £2/10. Father McGauran, noting that 'it seldom happens that the labourer rents merely the land on which his cabin stands', nevertheless stated that he had known of cases 'where five shillings a year ground rent was paid for 20 feet of land by 13'.[12] He also claimed that the farmer always obtained a profit, never less than one-fifth, of land he rented to a cottier and gave the following example:

> There are instances about Lurganboy where the difficulty of procuring land is extreme and where the cottier pays double and treble what the head landlord receives; if the farmer get £1 an acre, he will readily get £3 for a cabin and one rood of it, or about £1 for the cabin, and £2 for the quarter acre; the landlord undertakes to keep the cabin in repair and it is his interest to fulfil his engagement, which, however, he seldom does, and, as the cottier does not like to expend his money on a place from which he may at any time be removed, the whole house, and particularly the roof, is often in a wretched condition.[13]

Joshua Kell, agent on the Lane-Fox estate in Dromahaire commented that he always attempted to ensure the cottier would not pay a higher rent to the farmer than the latter would pay to the landlord, 'but very seldom with success'.[14]

A similar situation pertained in the barony of Mohill where it was claimed that farmers 'contrived' to make cottiers pay 'fully four times the rent for portions of bad land that he himself pays for the best on his holding'.[15] The precarious position of cottiers was illustrated in two ways.

First, if the landlord reneged on a promise to keep the latter's cabin in repair 'the tenant has no redress as his tenure is yearly and can easily be replaced if he complain'.[16] Second:

> The cottier is placed on the worst piece of land the farmer has; if any bog adjoins, he places the cottier there and the land which the latter has improved he takes into his own hands sooner or later.[17]

These comments are reflected in the following table from the Waldron estate in the parish of Annaduff which demonstrates both the small size of plots allocated and the high rent of each:

**Table 1.1: Return of Lismoyle 'Potato Soil', 1845**

| Occupier | Acres | Roods | Perches | Rent |
|----------|-------|-------|---------|------|
| Willy Shanly | | 2 | 18 | £2 7s 10½d |
| James Lenaghan | | | 22½ | 15s 0d |
| Frank Geeheran | | | 14 | £2 3s 0d |
| Michael Honan | | | 34 | £1 1s 9d |
| Patt Carroll | | 1 | 12 | £2 2s 9d |
| Dennis Currin | | 1 | 28 | £2 15s 9d |
| Frank Geeheran | | 1 | 9 | £1 19s 3d |
| Owen McGee | | | 35 | £1 16s 0d |
| Michael Honan | | | 31½ | £1 5s 3d |
| Patt Campbell | | 1 | 24 | £2 4s 6d |
| Thomas Boylan | | 1 | 27 | £2 9s 7d |
| Michael Egan | | 1 | 11 | £2 5s 1½d |
| Patt Gormly | | | 31 | £1 7s 8d |
| Frank Geeheran | | 1 | 5 | £1 19s 10½d |
| Michael Beirne | | 2 | 24 | £4 5s 0d |
| Willy Shanly | | 1 | 2 | £1 17s 6d |
| Mick Daly | | | 38 | £1 11s 4d |
| Patt Gormley | | 1 | 11 | £1 18s 9d |
| Barny Farrell | | | 35 | £1 6s 3d |

*Source*: National Library of Ireland, Waldron Papers (uncatalogued).

Hence, this field in the townland of Lismoyle, known as the Avenue Field, consisting of 5 acres, three roods and 10 perches brought in £38/12/2½ in conacre rent. Given that these men were earning around four shillings a week, such plots were costing their occupants half a year's earnings and in some cases much more. Not surprisingly, therefore, there was little expense on other items and consequently clothing in all areas was described as being 'very miserable'.[18] In Dromahaire, James Nixon commented that:

> There is a great deal of nakedness, partly through sloth and partly through necessity: a man has, perhaps, one good suit, which he wears on the 52 Sundays, and on a few holidays, but all the rest of his time he is in rags, both summer and winter. I don't think a labourer spends £1 a year in clothes for all his family.[19]

Local farmer, Phelim Rooneen claimed that:

> We generally reckon on a coat once in two years, and that costs 15s; and as for the wife and children, their little rags do not come to 10s a year; its seldom we buy anything for the young ones.[20]

In Mohill, the assistant commissioners found the comfortable appearance of those assembled at market or attending Mass to be 'in a great measure deceptive' as these clothes which were 'destined to serve on similar occasions for several years' were replaced at home by 'scanty coverings of rags'.[21] Father Smith related how he was aware of people who came to first Mass 'in decent clothes' and then ran home and exchanged with family members to enable them to appear at late prayers.[22] Children, almost everywhere, were 'scarcely protected from the weather', especially boys who were 'often without trowsers [*sic*] and were sometimes removed but by a shirt from a state of even indecent nudity'.[23] Both in Dromahaire and Mohill it was noted that homemade frieze was 'little worn' as coarse English cloth was cheaper to buy.[24] While the wearing of shoes in Mohill had increased compared to forty years previous, still it was less than it had been during the Napoleonic Wars.[25]

The prices paid for clothes, land and food can only be understood in the context of wages. Witnesses to the Poor Inquiry all agreed that the average daily wage for a labourer was 8d. It is difficult to obtain specific contemporary examples of wage levels but one excellent source is the Lough Rynn Weekly Return which catalogued all the works carried out, and the labourers employed at such, on the Clements estate just outside Mohill. For example, in September 1839 Pat Farrelly was appointed foreman on the estate and his wages varied from 10d to 1s per day. Beneath him worked a variety of men and women carrying out a huge range of tasks at various times of the year. The men were engaged in harrowing, ploughing, carting and spreading stones and clay, taking in hay and usually numbered about twelve alongside a mason and carpenter. The latter, Garret Beggs, was paid 2/6 per day for one week in June 1842 working at the schoolhouse. However, his work was not as regular as that of the labourers who were employed most of the year at 8d per day (4s per week). The women were employed at sewing, washing the exterior of the house, planting – and later picking – potatoes, spreading manure, pulling straw for thatching, cutting the tops off turnips, weeding quicks and drawing wood from the plantation. For this work they received 6d each day, while those employed within the house received 4d. However in the week 27 December 1841–1 January 1842 Agnes Reynolds received 8d for such work. The number employed was dependent on the time of year. For example, from 12–19 September 1842 ten women were employed but from 17–23 October none were required. A couple of weeks later fifteen were engaged in potato picking. Rose Boyle seems to have been a favourite worker as her name occurs regularly throughout the early 1840s engaged in a variety of occupations. One boy, Hugh Reynolds, was employed at a weekly wage of 1s and usually worked in the stable. The return records that those employed had to work on Christmas Day in 1843 and 1844.[26]

Of course, wages also dictated living conditions and in Dromahaire the assistant commissioners noted:

> The majority of cabins ... contained at least one bed-stead, or a substitute for it, formed often of some boards, supported by either stones or empty butter firkins; the bedding was universally wretched, consisting in general of little more than a sack stuffed with hay or chaff and a quilt or blanket, all in a state of great filth; the man and wife alone enjoy the accommodation of a bed raised above the floor; the other inhabitants sleep on straw, laid on the ground naked; and where the cabins are small and do not extend to a second apartment, but little space can be allowed between male and female. In addition it often happens that a vagrant and two or three children

are permitted 'to lay down their straw', to use Phelim Rooneen's words, with the usual inmates.[27]

In Mohill the 'stock of furniture' in such abodes 'seldom exceeded a dresser for plates, a few chairs, and a wooden chest'.[28]

In relation to the consumption of alcohol, it was agreed that while the number of licensed public houses had decreased in the barony of Mohill 'it is feared that the contrary is the case with the unlicensed'. To illustrate the point, Father McKiernan, parish priest of Cloone, suggested that about five years previous there had been six licensed houses and very few 'shebeen shops'. However, by the mid-1830s there were 'but two of the former description and I verily believe there are 400 of the latter'.[29] One of his colleagues, Father O'Farrell added:

> I have observed that instances of extreme intoxification are decidedly of more frequent occurrence among the most destitute class of my parishioners. When one of them has the opportunity of drinking at another's expense, or is disposed to spend any small extra earnings of his own, he seems to have lost all sense of shame, and keeps it up in many cases until he is perfectly senseless. Females are not often seen intoxicated. One is not surprised that labourers are unable to resist the temptation of the open whiskey shop, when they stand in the wet and cold, waiting in vain for an employer to engage them.[30]

However, attempts were being made to improve the condition of the people. One of the corollaries of the relief effort mounted during the 1822 famine was the creation of the Irish Reproductive Loan Fund. This London-based organisation attempted to create a network of local loan societies which would be funded to enable them to make small loans to local farmers, thereby allowing them to purchase seed and other agricultural goods. In this way they hoped that, eventually, Irish rural society would be improved.

The evidence from Leitrim would appear to suggest that the loan system made a significant difference to many in the county and if nothing else it offered an alternative to the expropriatory practices of moneylenders. The first fund to be formed was that in Cloone on 7 March 1834, and the following year Protestant curate, Rev Andrew Hogg related to Berry Norris of Mohill how the money had been

... impartially shared to every recommended industrious person, thus at the same time encouraging industry and rewarding morality by withholding loans from those who are in the habit of selling illegal spirits and striking off the names of others from our books who were in the habit of frequenting such establishments.[31]

Revelling in the practical effectiveness of the fund he rejoiced in the fact that it had 'enabled some to purchase cows who never had one before'.[32] Encouraged by a scheme which appeared to have 'succeeded admirably' the first meeting of the trustees of the Mohill fund took place on 12 December 1834. Members agreed to employ a sum of £1,000 in loans up to £5 to be repaid in weekly instalments of one shilling in the pound.[33] In the opinion of Berry Norris:

> From my personal knowledge of what has been effected by the Mohill loan and from the intimate intercourse I have had with the peasantry of this country for the last forty years I can confidently pronounce the loan system to be one peculiarly well fitted for ameliorating their condition and improving their habits. The very great anxiety with which the loans are sought, the punctuality with which the repayments are made, the gratitude expressed and the benefits acknowledged to have been derived are all strongly corroborative of this.[34]

Writing in similar vein Robert Jones of Manorhamilton enthusiastically added that 'such as heretofore could spend a portion of their money in the whiskey shops are not now found to enter those demoralising receptacles'.[35] Between 7 March 1834 and 3 February 1836 ten districts witnessed the emergence of loan funds:

**Table 1.2: Emergence of Loan Funds in County Leitrim**

| Area | Date of Establishment |
| --- | --- |
| Cloone | 7 March 1834 |
| Mohill | September 1834 |
| Drumshanbo | 13 April 1835 |
| Glebe (Mohill) | 2 January 1835 |
| Aughavas | 24 March 1835 |

| | |
|---|---|
| Manorhamilton | 1 May 1835 |
| Carrick-on-Shannon | 15 May 1835 |
| Drumsna | 22 June 1835 |
| Cashcarrigan | 18 November 1835 |
| Drumod | 3 February 1836 |

*Source*: The National Archives, Kew, London, Treasury Papers, 91/199.

By 1839 the number of local funds had increased to thirteen and although the Drumshanbo institution had been temporarily suspended for some months in 1836 they continued to play a role in helping the county's small farmers.[36] The following table illustrates the number of loans made in 1839 and their value:

**Table 1.3: Accounts of Charitable Loan Societies in County Leitrim, 1839**

| Society | Loans Made | Value (£) |
|---|---|---|
| Annaduff | 1,344 | 5,135 |
| Aughavas | 1,319 | 3,216 |
| Carrick-on-Shannon | 1,415 | 3,690 |
| Cloone | 2,633 | 7,216 |
| Clooncumber | 1,736 | 3,548 |
| Drumod | 497 | 1,698 |
| Drumshanbo | 1,193 | 2,331 |
| Glebe | 709 | 1,889 |
| Kiltubrid | 1,438 | 3,141 |
| Lakefield | 902 | 1,867 |
| Manorhamilton | 1,782 | 6,280 |
| Mohill | 3,145 | 8,854 |
| Willsbrooke | 162 | 950 |
| **Total:** | **18,305** | **49,815** |

*Source*: The National Archives, Kew, London, Treasury Papers, 91/199, Abstract from the accounts of the several charitable loan societies, 1839.

All those involved in the running of the funds commented on how they had induced a sense of responsibility amongst the people. Reflecting on its effects in Drumshanbo, Richard Clifford remarked that, as well as reducing drunkenness, it aided those who had previously been exploited by moneylenders:

> Exorbitant and illegal interests on small loans of money prevailed here to a frightful extent and the system has been completely put down. Starving families were periodically obliged to undertake the payment of twenty shillings for value to the amount perhaps of twelve but this ruinous evil is also dying away...[37]

R. Tate of Manorhamilton remarked on the same beneficial effects as regards alcohol and also noted that of 650 people who had received money from the fund only two had fallen behind with their payments.[38]

There is also evidence that some landlords were interested in improving the standard of their estates and trying to encourage tenants to develop holdings and agricultural practices. Foremost amongst these was Lord Leitrim of Lough Rynn and in the late 1830s he commissioned a detailed townland survey of his estate. The following examples, which echo many of the sentiments expressed at the poor inquiry meetings and by those overseeing loan funds, offer an insight into the thoughts of an Irish landlord in the mid-nineteenth century, his relationship with his tenants and the lives led by those living on his estate.

### Gortletteragh
Shebeen-selling should be done away with if possible. This townland is not in a creditable state considering that it is of tolerably good quality and has a high-road passing through it. The divisions must be much improved and every occasion should be seized to break leases so that eventually it may be some day or other remodelled.

### Rooskey
The tenants here should be forced to straighten their mearings immediately or the abatement be withdrawn. Conboy is still living at Rooskey notwithstanding the arrangement that he was to go to America. This is very disagreeable indeed and is a late instance of an able-bodied man getting a house and garden free, which I particularly object to. He ought to be put out or if that is not possible

he should be compelled to pay rent to his brother and the brother be compelled to provide him a better cabin.

## Farnaght

Each of the holdings must now be sub-divided and the occupants forced to leave their old ditches and follow a regular rotation which I hope they will be induced to do. Peter Reynolds' farm must be reduced. He is not improving it and the only excuse he gave ...was his new house which he has never finished. Suppose Creegan be shifted down to Peter Reynolds and gets five acres and Casson be given the 2½ acres now held by Creegan – reducing Peter to six. Let them be told that there will be a similar course pursued whenever a man is industrious. Watch Pat Mulligen – he has a great many fences to level and seems disinclined to do it but he must be forced to do so.

## Gortnalaugh

I am rather disappointed about Gort. I thought they would have got on better. They must all understand the facility of growing green crops by this time but they show no signs of improvement in their means.

## Clooncarn

The appearance of the houses has decidedly improved here which is very satisfactory and we must try to continue the improvement. The divisions must also be improved – this has been hanging on much too long. I was sorry to find that the extent of green crops does not seem to have increased materially in this townland.

## Drumrahoo and Drumhanay

One man to be picked out of the rest and every encouragement and threat held out to him to make a pattern for the rest (£10).

## Errew

I am very much annoyed at the state of Errew. It is so very near me and the land is so good that I regret very much that I cannot get any model farmers from among them. Some exertion should be used to improve the divisions.

### Currycramph

The holdings here are very much intermixed and as the tenants here promise so well, we ought to try to square their farms better; for this purpose one house must be re-built, another great object here ought to be to insist upon the farmers making their cottiers' houses less discreditable. Some of the cottiers are sitting rent-free. These should be ejected and put out immediately and let them make what bargain they please for a new house elsewhere. I do not want to turn them off the estate or off the townland but I think it desirable to break off their free right and let them pay some rent to the farmers.

### Breanross

This townland is in a very unsatisfactory state. I can see no improvement whatever here except perhaps Brian Donnelly and that is very trifling. The Gallaghers ought to be obliged to divide their farm and forced to make some improvement. Hugh Mulvey ought also to be spoken very stiffly to – and Brian Murray.

### Carrowbeagh

This also is very bad. The leases ought to be all broken, whether now or next year signifies little, but it would seem as well to break the lease at once for the farms must be altered some time or other and there may be some delay in getting possession of some of the holdings. I propose taking some one man and forcing him and encouraging him to set an example to his neighbours. Bruce proposes McGarty.[39]

These notes reveal the strategy employed by Clements on his estate – one of coercion and reward. For those who agreed to implement his proposals, especially on matters of crop planting, there were many benefits to be had, including enhanced security of tenure. For those who hesitated, the penalties were severe. For example, in the same papers it is noted that on 27 December 1838 all the tenants of the townland of Anaghadary were summoned to the agent's office and 'they all promised to make such improvements as Mr Bruce shall point out and Mr Norris explained that every person who shall fail in doing so will be made pay their rent to the day'.[40]

A few years later, in August 1843, David Stewart drew up a similarly detailed report on the condition of the Lane-Fox estate in Dromahaire. He noted how, thanks to the building of new roads and an extensive system of drainage, both of which had been initiated since 1830, hundreds of acres of mountain, moor and bogland on the estate were now accessible. However, the estate contained a 'very considerable number of tenants … whose holdings or farms as they are called are so small and the lands so poor and who at the same time have such large families of small children that they cannot pay any rent and cannot keep their families from starving without help from their landlord or from the poor rates'.[41]

One of the endemic problems in Irish society at this time was sub-division of land and Stewart alluded to the problem in 1831:

> For under the pretence of building a new cattle house or barn they put up a mud hovel and no sooner is it up than either the new or the old is occupied by a married son or a married daughter or some other undertenant who gets a portion of the land and who cannot again be dispossessed without the greatest difficulty.[42]

Twelve years later little had changed:

> At this time there are upwards of 200 young men upon the Dromahaire estate who have no land and if these young men are allowed to marry and bring their wives and families into their fathers', mothers' and brothers' houses they will divide and sub-divide the farms into such small patches as will in the end, and speedily too, render it impossible for the land to support the people, even without paying any rent.[43]

Thus, Stewart suggested that those of this particular area who could not be settled on the newly reclaimed land should be assisted to emigrate to Canada 'or some other country' as 'if they remain at home it will be found next to impossible to prevent their dividing the farms'.[44] In a subsequent report in May 1845 Joshua Kell revealed that the total arrears on Fox's estates amounted to £34,925. Of this £29,937 was due on the County

Waterford estate while the remainder, just over £4,907, had accumulated on the Dromahaire estate in the two years from May 1842 to May 1844. After several discussions with David Stewart it emerged that the lands had been 'much overlet' and it was decided that as there was 'no possibility' of recovering the rent arrears, they should be wiped clean. In this way it was hoped that 'this boon offered to the tenants may be the inducement to them to manage their farms well'. In Dromahaire about 500 tenants were to be granted new leases not exceeding twenty-one years while occupiers of cottages holding two to three acres received agreements by which they held their land from year-to-year with a stipulation that 'they shall not subdivide and to forfeit if they do'. Finally, the lands immediately around the town of Dromahaire 'heading to the river's mouth' including Stone Park and Stone Park Mountain, were to be reserved for building and not let on farm leases.[45]

The difficulty for those landlords who actually took an interest in their estates and attempted to introduce improvements was that they faced outright opposition from those in situ. For example, Joshua Kell, received the following threatening notice:

> I am necessitated to write to you in consequence of your inhumanity to those tenantry who are under your stewardship on the estate of the Right Hon. David Stewart who was at all times a good patron to his tenantry. I am informed that you are depriving part of the poor tenants of this little holding and giving them to others. I am greatly surprised that your honour would do anything so mean as to be the instigator of those poor persons to become paupers when you should be their patron as you were in the time past. I therefore desire you without further hesitation ... to leave them as they were in the past ... I will end your existence and send your soul to eternity before the month is expired which will leave your lady and family desolate ... spare me the trouble if you want to spare your life.[46]

Such notices were only a part of the attempts to intimidate those who were employed by landlords, and statistics from the 1841 census offer an explanation as to why possession of land, even tiny strips of conacre, was so vital. Apart from a small domestic spinning industry, which offered some employment to over 21,000 females, the overwhelming majority of the population was dependent on agriculture for its livelihood. Of 27,192 families in the county, 21,633 (75.3 per cent) were reported as being 'chiefly employed' in agriculture, 13,506 were categorised as 'farmers' while a further 25,124 were deemed as 'servants/labourers'. The fact that all but 625 of these were males strongly suggests that the majority of the working population were labourers.[47] Significantly the majority, 9,373 (50.1 per cent), lived on plots of one to five acres while a further 7,971 (43 per cent) survived on holdings up to fifteen acres.[48]

The main urban centres in the county were Carrick-on-Shannon, Manorhamilton, Mohill, Ballinamore and Drumshanbo. However, few of the population lived in such towns and the majority occupied land in all parts of the county. The first Ordnance Survey, compiled in the 1830s, indicated that there may have been as many as 200 clachans in the county, with an average of between eight and fifteen families in each. Clachans were clusters of houses, varying in number from six to thirty and they differed from standard villages in that they did not have shops, pubs or churches and were essentially self-sufficient. Often those living in such settlements were related while their farms were leased in common with the various members working together at different times of the year. Examples of clachans were those at Gorteendaragh, near Kiltyclogher; Kilroosky, at the foot of Knocknagapple Mountain; Slievenakilla, just north of the Yellow River; and Lugganammer, near the village of Cloone.[49]

Given the close proximity of families, both friends and rivals, it comes as no surprise that land disputes constituted the bulk of recorded rural conflict in the pre-famine period. Neighbours and families arguing over houses and land inevitably turned violent and a number of methods were engaged in to intimidate, threaten or take revenge on various parties. The typical pattern appears to have been firstly to cause damage to crops, then animals, then property such as gates and fences, escalating to attacks on the home and finally physical attacks on the person. The following examples are representative of many hundreds which occurred throughout the 1830s.

In April 1836 'some malicious person' entered the byre of Patrick Reilly in the townland of Drimhollow in the parish of Cloone and 'drove some instrument into the fundamental part of a bull and let him loose in the byre'. The reason ascribed for this action was that Reilly's landlord had been 'more accommodating' to him than another family, the McEnires, who lived in the same townland. The police revealed that this family appeared to have 'a bad feeling' to Reilly and had previously committed 'various petty acts' such as damaging his gates.[50]

In November of the same year three tons of hay which had been saved in large cocks was scattered in Stracreghan in the parish of Killasnet. Half the amount had been carried and thrown into a river leading to Glancar Lake while he rest had been flung throughout the meadow.[51] A similar event occurred in Wardhouse in the parish of Rosinver when five small cocks of hay were 'maliciously scattered' and twenty-five heads of cabbage were pulled up by the root. Hugh McGovern subsequently swore information against three Connolly brothers and Bryan Feely, all of whom lived in the same townland.[52]

While these attacks involved neighbours there were also causes of rival members of the same family in conflict. For example, in June 1839 the house of Bryan Monaghan in Edenbawn, parish of Cloone, was set on fire by his nephew. Monaghan's brother Michael had taken all his land and left him only the house. Bryan believed the arson was an attempt to remove him from the area and the police reported that the families had 'been at variance for years'.[53] Later that year, in Ardmeena in the parish of Oughteragh, a cow belonging to a local farmer was found in a ditch with its skull fractured, the second time such an attack had been made on the same individual. It emerged that he had taken a holding from which the previous occupier had been evicted. The constabulary noted how 'at the last Cloon fair he was followed by a group and feared that he would have been killed only that he took refuge in a house'.[54]

Such attempts to control where people lived were also reflected in the sphere of employment, as family and local loyalties proved the source of regular disputes. What appeared to generate particular animosity was work being given to an outsider. For example, throughout 1838 and 1839 attempts were made to both disrupt the employment of Michael McGlinn of Drumlish, County Longford, who was engaged in making a road in Cloone, and force him to relinquish his contract. In October 1838 a group of men broke into the house of Michael Donnolly in Bohey and swore him not to break any more stones for McGlinn. They also took the harness of a cart, belonging to the latter, which was later found destroyed. On the same night two pipes which McGlinn had marked on the road leading from Clooncumbra Chapel of Ease to Drumlish were 'completely demolished' and shots fired.[55] A similar attack was made in the same townland the following September when Hugh O'Neill underwent a similar ordeal. The police stated that this was 'merely a continuation of a system of intimidation against McGlinn who lives in County Longford...'[56]

Of course the level of wages was of crucial importance and efforts were made to ensure that nobody worked for less than the average wage. In the townland of Cloonbony, parish of Mohill, the following note was left on a pile of broken stones where William Shanly was in the habit of walking: 'Mr Corly (alias Shanly) I don't main to have your work for nothing, quit the job as soon as possible, for if not you will be maid quit it with sorrow and a cut head.' Apparently Shanly had been breaking stones for his employer, John Nesbitt, at low wages.[57] Similarly, a general notice was posted in Drumsna in March 1838 warning people not to work for less than 8 pence per day until 1 May and no less than 1/11 from then until St John's Day. In addition, 'anyone who digs an acre of ground under 17 shillings will be most severely punished'.[58]

Employers who attempted to dismiss workers also faced danger and in Half Cartron, in the parish of Mohill, in March 1837 four men, with their faces blackened, one armed with a knife, entered the house of Francis O'Brien and after punching him made him swear to immediately pay a maid servant he had recently dismissed.[59]

In Gubadoris, in the same parish, attempts were made to force a farmer both to employ only local people and pay higher wages. In April 1839 a party of men travelled around various farms and swore those labourers in the employment of John Halfpenny not to work for him unless he discharged a man he had lately employed. When the police arrived to interview the labourers they all 'doggedly refused any information' claiming they knew none of the men involved.[60] Two months later the intimidation of Halfpenny developed a more sinister aspect when one of his heifers was found with its skull broken in pieces by a stone hammer. This act had been the result of his refusal to pay higher wages.[61]

In January 1839, in Derrinlanaher in the parish of Innismagrath, a cart belonging to Terence O'Donnell was smashed to pieces. It was believed this act had been carried out because O'Donnell had 'recently started trafficking oats at a better price than others in the same trade'.[62] In Kiltyclogher a threatening notice was posted on the market house warning people not to buy bread from John Nixon. The police reported that Nixon had just opened a bakery in the town and his loaves were larger than those of his rivals.[63]

On 31 October 1833 a group of between 300–500 men, some armed with guns, pistols and pitchforks, marched in 'military order' to the Lodge House near Dromahaire. They attempted to break in and challenge

David Stewart about proposed changes to be implemented on the Lane-Fox estate. Specifically, they had been made aware of the intention of the landlord to unite a number of holdings into one large farm, thereby necessitating the eviction of sitting tenants.[64] Joshua Kell informed his brother that as a consequence, and to prevent a recurrence, 'we have since been guarded by a party of police and the yeomanry who are principally Mr Fox's Protestant tenants'.[65] This latter reference, introducing religious dissension into land issues, was reflected in the following comments made by the editor of the *Roscommon and Leitrim Gazette*:

> With regards to Ribbonism in Leitrim the combination seems to be of an entirely agrarian nature, its political character being most entirely kept out of sight, Still, an agrarian conspiracy is (in Ireland at least) intrinsically political, the landlords, being with few exceptions, Protestant and the members of the ribbon society, to a man, papist. The whole of Connaught is infected with it.[66]

In the mid-1830s the Protestant proportion of the county was 11 per cent although in the parish of Carrigallen it was 28 per cent, in Cloonclare, 21 per cent, and in Killasnet 20 per cent. In other areas it was almost negligible and in the parishes of Cloone and Kiltubrid it totalled 5 per cent while in Fenagh it was just 3 per cent (see Appendix One and Map One). Nevertheless, it was the Protestant gentry, and their families, many of them descended from those who had been granted land confiscated from the native population in the 1600s, who dominated life in the county.

The issue of paying tithes to Protestant gentry was an incendiary one in Irish society and exploded into life with the Tithe War of the 1830s. Although this did not impact to any great extent on Leitrim, the early months of 1832 witnessed reports in the local press which suggested serious opposition in certain districts. In January the *Roscommon and Leitrim Gazette* announced that the 'anti-tithe leaven has worked its way' into the parishes of Cloone and Mohill. The paper lamented how:

> Notwithstanding the liberal offer of the esteemed rector of 25 per cent as a bonus to his tenants to pay the tithe hardly any persons have come forward and as a last resort his agent's collector was last week obliged to distrain some cattle which were instantly rescued.[67]

To the disgust of the *Gazette* it appeared that local Catholic churches were being used as centres of opposition and it reported how 'Joseph Pilkington spoke at Mass in Cloone and from the altar urged the people not to pay tithes.' Further, it was alleged that he reassured them that he would free them from 'this pocket-picking system in the parish'.[68] It was also claimed that some tithe collectors about to enforce payment in the same parish on 30 January 1832 were threatened by a group of men and forced to leave. The paper urged the authorities to 'crush the insinuating viper of sedition'[69] and was supported in its demand by the Leitrim Auxiliary Bible Society which had been founded in 1824.[70] The latter, in a reference to Catholic Emancipation, argued that such developments were evidence that 'indifference and infidel liberality have polluted the sources of power and learning and cut off the stream of pure Gospel knowledge which has heretofore been so happily fertilizing our land'.[71]

Antipathy was increased further with the introduction of the National System of Education in 1831. By this means the British government hoped to introduce non-denominational education and provided finance both for the building of new schools and the improvement of those already in operation but prepared to come under the umbrella of the new system. However, in an effort to ensure cross-community support, all application forms were intended to be signed by clergymen of different denominations, a task which sometimes proved difficult. For example, although local Protestants signed the form in support of the proposed Cashcarrigan female national school the Protestant clergyman refused to do so.[72]

In Mohill the Catholic Free School had been established some years before and until 1832 had been supported by the 'principal Catholics of the town'. An application sought to obtain payment for the teacher and various books. However, the committee reported that:

The Protestant vicar has been waited upon this day by Edward McCabe the teacher for the purpose of getting his signature and received for answer that he would be most happy to serve him but that the measure of the Government or administration did not accord with the sentiments of the Protestant Clergy as regarded the new Education system and that on their principles he must decline giving his signature.[73]

The latter part of that year witnessed a very public example of anti-establishment feeling and a manifestation of a breakdown in the previous moral economy of the county. When supporters of Colonel Clements attempted to gain access to the hustings in Carrick in order to vote at the general election, they were faced by what the local paper referred to as 'an infatuated and Priest-ridden mob' throwing stones and hurling abuse. As a consequence the customary post-election chairing and public dinner had to be abandoned.[74]

From the mid-1830s onwards such events became a regular part of the outrage reports filled out by the local constabulary. For example, in November 1836 a large fire was started at the home of Reverend Andrew Hogg, Rector of Cloone. Writing to Dublin Castle 'in great agitation of mind' Hogg outlined how all the outhouses were burned to the ground and an attempt was made to set fire to his dwelling house 'and burn us in our beds'. When he went out to confront the attackers they attempted to kill his wife but he fired on them and in order to save his own life was forced to swim the river at the rear of his house to reach the safety of Claudius West. However, he was twice fired upon and received a small wound to his left knee. Relating that his wife was 'in a dreadful state of mind', Hogg demanded the establishment of a police barrack 'at the end of the lawn'.[75]

This particular attack was mentioned in a debate in the British House of Commons and received extensive coverage in the press. The latter hoped that the conviction and punishment of those found guilty would 'arrest the progress of the contagion of rebellion and insubordination which, having its baneful influence in the counties more immediately under the control of the Demagogue [Daniel O'Connell] seems now directing its destructive course to places hitherto comparatively tranquil'.[76] This perspective was reflected in the comments of Justice Foster at the assizes earlier in the year when he had noted there were fifty-eight persons for trial, a figure 'nearly double the number that I have at any time met in your county'. Included in this number were twenty-three offences of an 'insurrectionary character'.[77]

While Hogg had escaped, the man from whom he had sought assistance, Claudius West, was not so lucky. On 27 April 1840, as he was returning from his farm near Cattan, he was approached by two men who shot and fatally wounded him.[78] West was a member of the most high-profile family in the Cloone area. His brother, John Beatty West, had been an MP for Dublin while another, George Beatty West, was a magistrate in Leitrim.[79]

Such acts only reinforced the demands of people like Hogg for further protection. For example, in January 1836 Rev G. Montgomery of Inishmagrath Glebe believed that arrangements to strengthen the constabulary at Grouse Lodge and Drumshanbo would be 'the means of checking, at least for a time, the spirit of insubordination prevailing in the district of Ballinaglera'.[80] This letter was written two days after the police had destroyed two illicit distilleries in Coraleebber and Tullinalack. However, in attempting to take two prisoners they had been followed and shot at by 'the Steel Boys or night marauders', while one of the prisoners, Hugh Reynolds, had said 'he would have them all murdered before they could leave the spot'.[81] After an attack on the home of Michael Ward in Drumbrennan, in which a gun was stolen, and the posting of a threatening notice by 'Fire Brand' on a mill in Annaghearly, it was remarked that the townland was in the vicinity of Gowel 'where outrages of a similar nature occurred some time ago'. Hence the police considered it 'very necessary' that a new station be built in the latter area.[82]

At this time, in the absence of large-scale building of new barracks, the constabulary were billeted in the homes of those deemed to be at risk. However, this policy had consequences for those with whom they lived. In the townland of Currowna in Cloone a heifer belonging to James Byrne was 'houghed' (its hamstrings were severed), the motive ascribed being the fact he had two men from Cloone police station in his house each night.[83] When Thomas Brown of Corduff in Cloone prosecuted some of those who had attacked his house in search of arms he required the presence of two policemen in his home until 8 October 1839. The following March he received a threatening notice in which he was warned to give up his land 'or have his place consumed in ashes'.[84] In the same parish, this time in the townland of Killiveagh, a pig belonging to Bernard Cunnion was 'maliciously stabbed with some sharp instrument' the reason being that he, like the others, had allowed his house to be used as a police barracks.[85] Again in Cloone, this time in Annagh, a stack of turf belonging to Thomas Moran was set on fire. The police reported that Moran had just moved into the neighbourhood 'and is suspected by the locals of being brother to a man who became an informer in Longford'. Offering a reward of £5 they noted that 'any person connected with an informer is so cordially hated by the people that they are always in danger'.[86]

However, some people were evidently prepared to take the risk and, as the following letter from William Lynam in Mohill shows, both the state and the informer profited:

> I beg to bring under your consideration the name of John Gilroy who has from time to time afforded me much valuable information and as I deem it expedient to keep him on hands I would respectfully suggest the propriety of his being granted a small remuneration for his services. Around twelve months ago he received £11 for information which led to the conviction of the persons who attacked the house of John Leslie in this district. In October last he gave to Head Constable McManus information which led to the arrest of Patt McCormick, identified as one of the persons concerned in taking arms from the house of Thomas Dowler in County Longford. He also gave considerable information relative to the outrage committed in September last at the house of Mr Goslinn near Newtownforbes. I consider a small reward of £3 would have a very good effect such at present.[87]

It has been noted how threatening notices were widely used during land disputes. However, they also appeared in disagreements of a religious nature. For example, in Killivaghan in the parish of Cloone the following notice was placed on a house previously used as a police barracks:

> Important
> This is desiring all Protestants, Brunswickers and Orangemen to clear off the lands of Killiveghan – thee will share the same fate of Brock. Signed Capt. Rock.[88]

While this notice was targeted at a general audience the following, posted in Dromahaire in September 1837, was much more specific:

> To the County Leitrim and Neighbouring counties. Take notice that any person or persons calling with any of Jones in Dromahaire as the shopkeeper, smith or shoemaker or any other tradesman of any description shall meet with the most severe punishment I can inflict

on them. NB Let no person dare take this down.
Signed Captain Day Lights.[89]

A similar campaign was undertaken in Kinlough where the locals were warned to avoid communication 'with any of the Tory factions, particularly in Kinlough and its vicinity'. Specifically named were 'William Conolly Esq. of Mount Prospect; John Dickson, Esq. Woodville, [and] Barrister Johnston's family of Oakfield' as it was alleged that 'it is well known they do all they can to keep situations from Roman Catholics'. However, an exception was made for 'Torys such as William McSharry of Kinlough'.[90]

While it is questionable as to the effect these notices had on men enjoying such elevated positions in society there is little doubt that similar campaigns directed against local tradesmen did have an impact. In 1838 the parish of Kiltoghert witnessed a sustained effort to prevent work being carried out by one man. The following examples represent only two of many recorded. In August the house of Frank Rorke of Kilnagross was entered by a group who demanded that a recently-repaired wheel be given to them. On receiving it they broke it and told Rorke not to give any more work to John Crieg.[91] Some months later windows were broken in houses in the townlands of Drumgoola and Annaghasna, while all implements made or repaired by Crieg were destroyed. The reason for this campaign was that Crieg had attended an Orange meeting on the previous 12 July.[92]

Perhaps the most sustained campaign was that directed against John Stretton who lived in the parish of Cloone. In January 1832 the *Roscommon and Leitrim Gazette* reported how the following notice had been left on Stretton's door: 'Stretton you have got many warnings and this is the last so if you do not leave that before one month you may prepare your coffin.' The paper revealed that he was the only Protestant living in the townland of Glebe and two attempts on his life had already been made by what it called 'these midnight legislators'.[93] Later that month, a notice was placed on the bridge of Cloone: 'If anybody takes John Stretton's holding – woe be to him – I will call to see him. Anybody who takes this sign down before 24 hours shall be punished accordingly. Captain Rock.'[94]

Eventually Stretton was fatally attacked. Whilst returning from a visit in Cloone on 25 October 1838 he was shot and his head beaten in with the butts of the guns He died two weeks later.[95] In attempting to explain the killing to his superiors Constable J. Stuart noted how: 'Stretton had made himself obnoxious to the "boys" particularly by being a Tithe bailiff and an Orangeman and he had been often attacked before so that he was cautious about going out after night.'[96] Another policeman, James Perrin, was rather more blunt in his assessment of the death: 'Stretton was a well-known Orangeman and had often behaved with foolish and indeed reprehensible indiscretion.'[97]

A less significant event, but one which epitomised the sectarianism of the times, was the breaking of windows in a female school in the townland of Kivey in Carrigallen. The school was controlled by the London Hibernain Society and was presumably attacked because of its role in trying to convert local Catholics.[98]

The *Roscommon and Leitrim Gazette* had no doubt that blame for these events lay with 'the spiritual guides of those ill-advised people – the priests'.[99] Referring to the latter as 'surpliced ruffians' and to those carrying out such acts as 'O'Connell's police'[100] it maintained that 'to them [priests] may be attended all the evils which have afflicted this unhappy country since the cry of "Agitation" first sounded in our ears'.[101]

However, despite the fact that the vast majority of such occurrences were directed against Protestants there were similar anti-Catholic threats in areas containing substantial numbers of Protestants. Hence, John Maguire paid a heavy price for giving evidence against Orangemen who had assembled illegally in Manorhamilton on 12 July 1839. Shortly afterwards the following notice was placed on his door:

> Maguire I could not meet my maker and not tell you to keep in doors, you will meet, if you do not, Lord Norberry's fate, so leave town. A friend to religion 3 March 1840.[102]

The constabulary noted how, as a result of taking the prosecution Maguire had 'lost considerably in trade and was now in terror of his life'. He eventually asked for government assistance to leave the neighbourhood.[103]

Violence was also resorted to in domestic cases involving children and marriage. For example in Drumhall in the parish of Kiltoghert the local national school was burned to the ground in March 1837. The police ascertained that the former schoolmaster, Pat McDonogh, had been dismissed for getting a girl pregnant and they believed that it was either the girl herself or her relations who carried out the arson.[104] In January of the same year, a group of men broke into the house of John Mackin in Drumgoola, parish of Cloone. When they found Mackin was not there they dragged his wife out of bed and 'beat her severely with a blackthorn bush'. According to the official police report:

> She had been married the previous night and the suspicion is that the brother of her former husband opposed the marriage given that her land would now not pass to the children of her first marriage.[105]

In Cornulla, again in the parish of Cloone, stacks of oats and straw belonging to Edward Kilkenny were 'totally consumed by fire' in May 1838. The main suspect was Winifred McGarty, the mother of Kilkenny's children, to whom he had refused any support.[106] Similarly, when Pat Fowley refused to marry the mother of his child his house in Toomrod, parish of Killasnet, was attacked while oats and hay were destroyed in a nearby field.[107]

While attempts were made to force men to marry the mothers of their children, the women themselves occasionally resorted to extreme measures to deal with their situation. Either due to the shame of producing a child out of wedlock or the inability to cope with another mouth to feed, or a combination of both, the killing of children in the county was by no means uncommon. Indeed, in his evidence to a parliamentary committee in 1825 the assistant barrister for the county, Theophilus Jones, agreed that the law in relation to 'the maintenance of illegitimate children' was 'imperfect' and the cause of 'frequent infanticide'.[108] The following list represents some of the cases of this phenomenon reported by the constabulary in the pre-famine era:

> 7 April 1838
> The body of a female child tied in an apron was found in a drain on the roadside by the lake of Creenagh in a very decomposed state.

The constabulary reported:

> I have not been able to discover any woman who has lately been delivered of an illegitimate child in this neighbourhood but am making a diligent enquiry. The soldiers of the 33rd Regiment and John Stuart, Chief Constable, Mohill, subscribed for a coffin to be made and buried in the church yard. The child had been murdered two to three weeks before then drowned by its unnatural parents.

20 February 1838, townland of Cloughla, Carrigallen parish
The body of a one-week-old female was found dead and in a state of perfect nudity, having the left arm and part of the left leg eaten by a pig. An inquest found that the child was born alive.

30 November 1839, townland of Edenville, Rossinver parish
A boy who was fishing in the Drouse River found the body of an infant about two months old. The perpetrator must have come from some distant quarter as there is no person in the neighbourhood on whom the slightest suspicion could rest.

14 October 1839, townland of Blasthille, Killenummery parish
Two men hunting in a bog saw a bulk in a drain. It was found to be the body of an infant sown up in the bottom of an old sack. The child was a day or two old. From its decomposed state the body had been in the sack for the last month.

14 June 1840, townland of Drumheany, Kiltoghert parish
A man discovered the body of a female infant in the Shannon covered with coarse sacking cloth and weighed down by a stone of about 5 lb.[109]

The murder of children represented an aspect of society rarely mentioned in the local press which invariably noted such occurrences with a comment that the particulars were too gruesome for their readers. However, the contemporary constabulary reports often contained graphic descriptions of all outrages, and revealed the dark side of life in this period, none more so than the rape of women and children.

For example, on 31 August 1836 Michael McAndrew broke into the house of Bridget Finlay in the townland of Boyannagh parish of Rossinver. He 'attempted to violate her person' and a warrant was subsequently issued for his arrest.[110] In November that year Ellen Gorman (alias Martin) of Tullaghan alleged that Rodger Drurey of Dugarberry (Rossinver) raped her.[111] However, making an allegation and actually proving it was difficult in an environment of male-only juries. The following excerpt from the Carrick-on-Shannon assizes of February 1836 reflects this difficulty. John

McNama was indicted for 'violating the person' of Ann McAweeny, who worked in his house and slept in the same room as the rest of his family. The defence case was stated as follows:

Cross-examined by Counsellor Blekeney: Come over here, my pretty modest little girl. How long were you in McNama's employment?

Witness: I was six months living with him.

Counsellor: And you slept in the same room with him all that time?

Witness: Yes

Counsellor: In the same bed?

Witness: No

Counsellor: Were the beds very close?

Witness: They were

Counsellor: Your toes used to be touching?

Witness: No, they weren't

Counsellor: Oh, you used to be playing toey, toey (laughter)

Witness: What a chance!

Counsellor: Well it was heel and toe you used to be playing. Do you dance?

Witness: Yes

Counsellor: Then I'll engage you could foot it heel and toe?

Witness: Not a foot.

Counsellor: Now, look round at the prisoner and tell me, is he not what the girls call a *loughy* boy?

Witness: He's well enough

Counsellor: Would he not make a fine husband for modest Nancy?

Witness: He would not. I would not marry him at all.

Counsellor: Why, Nancy?

Witness: Because he done what he did.

Counsellor: Were you and he ever alone before?

Witness: Yes, we were.

Counsellor: And he never did such a thing before?

Witness: No, he never did.

Counsellor: Well, this affair took place before breakfast?

Witness: Yes

Counsellor: No doubt but you were terribly disturbed?

Witness: Yes

Counsellor: An tattered and torn, and all forlorn?

Witness: Yes

Counsellor: How long was it before breakfast?

Witness: About half an hour

Counsellor: Now, on your oath, who boiled the potatoes that morning?

Witness: It was the fire.

Counsellor: Well done, modest Nancy. Who washed them?

Witness: I did

Counsellor: Who put them in the pot?

Witness: I did

Counsellor: Who put it on the fire?

Witness: I did.

Counsellor: And yet it was the fire that boiled them (laughter). And you sat down and eat your breakfast with the man who treated you so badly, and supped out of the same noggin with him?

Witness: No, you're out there; we had noggins apiece.

Counsellor: Oh, I see; but you washed and put down the potatoes, got ready the breakfast, and eat your breakfast along with him every day that week and your father and mother within three miles of you, without ever saying a word about it. Gentlemen of the jury, did you ever hear of such a thing?

Witness: I did it to blindfold him.

Counsellor: Oh, but you won't blindfold the jury...[112]

After the jury returned a verdict of 'not guilty', there immediately followed another rape case; the *Roscommon and Leitrim Gazette* reported as follows:

Honor Fox, a respectable-looking female, came on the table, and on the swearing book being handed, said if she had to undergo the same ordeal as her predecessor, Ann McAweeny, she would give up the prosecution. Counsellor Blakeney raised his spectacles, and looked at her with a peculiar expression of countenance, as much as to say 'try me'. It was enough; she made a speedy retreat and the prisoner was liberated.[113]

As well as being humiliated in public alleged rape victims also had to deal with the consequences of having the courage to name their attackers.

On 5 July 1837 in the townland of Menacull (Oughteragh) 161 young
ash trees belonging to James Mulvey were cut down. Mulvey had given
protection to a woman named Mary Rorke who had sworn information
against Thomas Nailer for 'violating her person'. Mulvey maintained that
he saw Nailer's brother running away from his garden.[114]

Such family loyalty to somebody accused of a base crime was evident
in the case of seventeen-year-old Michael Sheridan of Dromod. On
the testimony of Dr Dunn, Sheridan had been committed for trial for
'feloniously assaulting' Emily Lynch, an illegitimate child of seven years of
age, 'with intent to commit rape'. Significantly, the police report noted how:

> Due to the reluctance of those with whom the child was placed to
> give evidence the police found it necessary to place her under the
> charge of Constable Owens at Dromod to sustain and support her
> as a crown witness.[115]

Such reports of child abuse were by no means unusual. For example in
July 1838 Michael McGuire, described as 'a poor travelling man from Sligo'
together with his young four-year-old daughter, lodged at the house of
Richard Crofton of Tawnleymore, Cloone. When he awoke the following
morning he was alerted by the screams of his daughter in a nearby field as
she was being assaulted by the family's seventeen-year-old son.[116]

Even groups which appeared to concentrate on agrarian matters
were involved in sexual impropriety. In Derrinurn townland, parish of
Inishmagrath, James Flynn received a threatening notice signed by Captain
Rock stating that if he were 'caught on the Sligo Road' his horse would
be 'houghed' while his wife would be 'left a widow and your children
orphans'. The only reason ascribed for this threat was that Flynn had
informed the local parish priest of the existence of 'a house of ill-fame' in
the neighbourhood.[117]

A most unusual occurrence, and one that emphasised the influence
and violence of such groups, was demonstrated in a report from the
townlands of Mohercreggy and Mullaghcullen in the parish of Kiltubrid
in February 1840. A group of between thirty and fifty men, some armed
with flintlocks, attacked two houses in which dances were being held. In
Mohercreggy they surrounded the house of Paul Geehan, a tactic also
used at the house of John Campbell in Mullaghcullen. The police report
read as follows:

At Geehans they dragged the fiddler out on the road, beat him unmercifully with sticks and compelled him to play several tunes to which they danced and they desired him to get into the house and for every person there to give him a 'silver ball and drink a shilling with Paul Geehan'. They then went to Campbells about one mile away and beat the fiddler and directed him never to be caught playing in that neighbourhood again and they who employed him would be scarred worse than him.[118]

Constable Meredith of Ballinamore believed that the object of these attacks was to deter 'certain musicians, and those employing them from playing in that neighbourhood'.[119]

To modern eyes such incidences appear highly unusual and inexplicable. However, the events at Mohergregg emphasised the importance of territoriality in pre-Famine Irish society. The vast majority of offences committed during this period centred around two inter-linked concepts: wages and land. Given the lack of an industrial infrastructure, work was extremely limited and therefore had to be carefully safeguarded; hence the attacks on, and intimidation of, those seen as outsiders. Without wages many people could not obtain ground on which to plant potatoes. As evident in Lismoyle, survival depended not on acres but on roods and perches of ground – enough to ensure a healthy crop of potatoes. However, this dependence, just managing to guarantee survival, meant that tens of thousands in the county lived in dire poverty and this long-standing issue was to be addressed by the British government in a manner which would have enormous ramification for the people of Leitrim.

# Chapter 2

# A CRUEL MOCKERY
# OF RELIEF

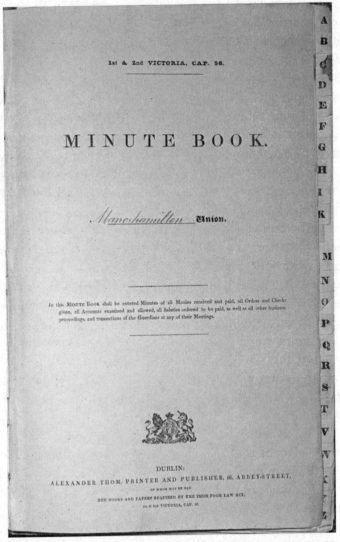

1st & 2nd VICTORIA, CAP. 56.

# MINUTE BOOK.

*Manorhamilton* Union.

In this MINUTE BOOK shall be entered Minutes of all Monies received and paid, all Orders and Checks given, all Accounts examined and allowed, all Salaries ordered to be paid, as well as all other business, proceedings, and transactions of the Guardians at any of their Meetings.

DUBLIN:
ALEXANDER THOM, PRINTER AND PUBLISHER, 86, ABBEY-STREET,
OF WHOM MAY BE HAD
THE BOOKS AND PAPERS REQUIRED BY THE IRISH POOR LAW ACT,
1st & 2nd VICTORIA, CAP. 56.

Manorhamilton Poor Law Union minute book, October 1839. Courtesy of Leitrim County Library, Ballinamore, County Leitrim.

FROM AT LEAST the early 1760s the parishes of Leitrim were caring for foundling children. For example, in July 1763 Mohill spent 17*s* 6*d* on the support of a foundling child while in 1788 £3 15*s* was expended on maintaining two foundlings.[1] However, the Dublin Foundling Hospital (established in 1704) offered an alternative and there is evidence that from 1780 the neighbouring parish of Cloone was availing of its services.[2] As the population increased the demands on local resources followed suit. In 1831 the Cloone vestry levied £5 for pauper coffins and £10 for nursing and burying foundlings,[3] but when it was proposed to levy more than £45 off the parish for these same causes the 1834 vestry was adjourned and at a subsequent meeting 'the several sums were not agreed to' and therefore not levied.[4]

Aside from vestries the poor relied on voluntary ad hoc contributions. For example, in that same year £71/7/3 was left as a bequest to the rector of Cloone 'for the benefit of the very poor of the said parish ... professing the Protestant religion for ever'. However, the rector, Andrew Hogg, appears to have ignored this stipulation and instead had the money placed in the accounts of the Aughavas Loan Fund.[5] The Cloone vestry minutes also contain references to 'poor money accounts' of Duke Crofton of Lakefield and Thomas Huston of Drumboher.[6]

As has been noted earlier, the question of Irish poverty was debated throughout the early decades of the nineteenth century, culminating in the establishment of the Enquiry into the Condition of the Poorer Classes of 1833–6. Despite outlining detailed proposals to counteract the problems of Irish society, the government decided to ignore the thoughts of the commissioners and instead to pursue a policy of poor law enforcement based on the amended English poor law of 1834. Under this system 130 poor law unions were to be established throughout Ireland, each served by a workhouse and administered by a board of guardians, some elected and some ex-officio. The maintenance of such institutions, and those forced to repair to them for relief, was to be met from the imposition of a new levy – the poor rate – paid by all occupiers of land. However, in August 1843 the law stipulated that only those in possession of land of value greater than £4 were to be rated. The ethos of the workhouse system was evident in what was termed the workhouse 'test' – there was to be no right to relief and all applicants had to prove they were destitute and without any possessions before being considered for admission.

On 16 December 1837 the *Roscommon and Leitrim Gazette* carried the first reports of the proposed Poor Law Bill. It noted that it contained 117 clauses 'many of which are very objectionable' while others were 'so unconstitutional as to be utterly inadmissible and wholly unworthy of a free nation valuing personal liberty'. The accompanying editorial, while acknowledging that 'something of this kind is required', castigated the measure as representing relief to 'that faction who are to be appointed to places of emolument as assistant commissioners and salaried officers and to extend the patronage of those men whose business it is to select the most notorious agitators and willing partisans to places of authority'. Pointing to the exclusion of able-bodied labourers, who, with their families, were 'in a state bordering on famine', it maintained that the poor were 'almost in a constant state of hunger and nakedness'. Thus, it referred to the measure as a 'cruel mockery of relief' in that it would only give aid to 120,000 out of a total of 2,500,000 'who compose the destitute poor of that country'. It argued that it failed to tackle the root causes of poverty which it pinpointed as 'miseries which are the consequence of absenteeism and a total disregard of the common duties of humanity in those landlords who ought to act as the guardians of the poor, and of the agricultural labourers especially'. Unable to avoid a descent into party politics it labelled Prime Minister Lord John Russell as 'the nominee of the Agitator' and referred to O'Connell as 'his employer'. Continuing in similar vein it argued that, due to the lack of relief for the able-bodied labourer:

> This class is therefore to be left in their present state of wretchedness, as if to be kept ready to obey the signal of any unprincipled agitator who might choose to employ them in the vilest and most lawless manner to promote his own mean and dishonest purposes.[7]

Even local MP, Viscount Clements, in offering the bill his support, realised that 'he did not speak the wishes of his constituents,' adding that 'an Irish member who supported this bill could not be accused of aiming at popularity, as he was bound to say the measure was most unpopular'.[8] In a House of Commons speech he acknowledged that the bill contained flaws and he believed that the proposed size of poor law unions at 400 square miles was 'much too extensive for practical purposes'. Similarly, he objected to the power vested in the poor law commissioners and believed that the 'worst part of the bill' was the fact that the commissioners could appoint others, in place of locally-elected guardians, 'at their will and pleasure'. In a prophetic statement he voiced his fear that 'they would have to exercise their power more frequently than perhaps they had anticipated'. Nevertheless, he rejected the claim that Ireland was too poor for the new law and while admitting that the gentry, farmers and clergy were against the proposal 'there was a class whose opinions had not been consulted and for which he pleaded – the destitute, unemployed poor, the aged, the infirm and the helpless'.[9]

By April 1838 opposition had moved from the pages of the press to the streets and the *Roscommon and Leitrim Gazette* was delighted to perceive that 'on this neutral ground Whig and Tory, Conservative and Radical, sinking all political animosity in the oblivion of the past, here stand forward in united strength to resist the measures with which heartless legislation would overwhelm an impoverished land'.[10] Hence, on 26 April, a meeting was held in the local court house in Carrick-on-Shannon with Charles Manners St George in the chair. Speakers focussed on a number of reasons for opposing the measure. For his part, St George examined the position of Ireland vis-à-vis Britain:

> She is a curious anomaly in the history of nations, a devoted, starring satellite to a neighbouring plethoric sister lagging behind for half a century in civilization and prosperity to whom she exports the bulk of her own produce while the most of her own population can scarcely purchase with the proceeds of that export their daily potato. Time will not allow me to enter into the source of this natural starvation in the midst of plenty … Tardy legislation has, hitherto, been the bane of Ireland – let us now avoid the contrary extreme and let the voice of the Irish people have, almost for the first time, some check on the disposal of their own means.[11]

Further, St George argued that destitution and poverty had arisen as a result of 'absenteeism, ostentation, utter want of adult education in the way of mechanics institutions, etc deficiency of infant and youthful education and neglect of improved systems of agriculture even by the landlords themselves'.[12] He also maintained that if existing institutions such as hospitals or lunatic asylums were extended this would suffice for the wants of the poor.[13]

# BALLYSHANNON UNION.

Ballyshannon Poor Law Union. Drawn by Sean Gill.

# CK-ON-SHANNON UNION.

Carrick-on-Shannon Poor Law Union. Drawn by Sean Gill.

Manorhamilton Poor Law Union. Drawn by Sean Gill.

# MOHILL UNION.

County Longford

COUNTY LEITRIM

Mohill Poor Law Union. Drawn by Sean Gill.

To cheers, Francis O'Beirne described the bill as 'vague, meaningless and injurious' and took exception to the clause which allowed government-appointed commissioners, 'strangers to the means and resources of the people', to take the place of locally-elected guardians. He lambasted Viscount Clements for voting for the measure and maintained that he had done so 'in ignorance', claiming:

> ...for there was never introduced a measure so pregnant with ruin and horrible consequences. It was no reply to him to assert that England had submitted to such a law. If the bad laws of England required it, the Irish did not want it – if the wealthy opulent manufacturing English can bear the burden does it follow that the pauper starving agricultural Irish with no other sustenance than the dry potato could support the overwhelming load of taxation.[14]

Thus, O'Beirne, in arguing for local taxation to be responsible for local poverty, maintained that the proposed law would prove to be 'a measure which would only inflict ruin on an already pauperised country'.[15]

Viscount Clements was unable, or unwilling, to attend the meeting but he sent a letter to John D. Brady (future MP for the county) which was read to the audience. Clements acknowledged the unpopular nature of the bill, and the fact that the district in which he lived was 'reckoned the poorest in the country' but hoped that opposition would pass when the details were better known. The letter continued:

> Great and heart-rending as is the poverty in this parish I feel fully convinced from the character of the poor cottiers that they would never consent to be deprived of the society of their families and submit to unpaid work and the other restraints of a poor house, however wholesome the diet and lodging might be, unless they were reduced to intense want.[16]

However, having finished reading the letter, Brady, to loud cheers, immediately announced his dissent from its contents. He went on to voice his own concerns and, in an insightful contribution, raised the prospect of evictions of small tenants on land under the value of £5 and the subsequent emergence of consolidated holdings by landlords otherwise unable to pay the poor rate. The meeting concluded with a series of resolutions which, amongst other things, criticised the 'enormous expenditure' consequent on its introduction; the fact that the mode of relief proposed would be 'at variance with the habits and feelings of the Irish people'; the law would give 'unlimited and uncontrolled power vested in the commissioners'; and finally, a suggestion that a 'better form of relief' would be to commence 'those great national improvements so manifestly required' and to employ people on these rather than confining them in workhouses 'a system prejudicial to habits and morals and inflicting punishment on want of employment as if it were a crime'.[17] Having digested these comments the *Roscommon and Leitrim Gazette* penned the following editorial:

> The consequence of the Poor Law Bill has at length become apparent and it is really frightful to peruse its clauses and ascertain the enormous expenses with which it would crush our pauper land – millions of pounds are to be dragged from a people to whom the same amount of pence would be an inconvenience.[18]

Significantly, it criticised the lack of an early and effective local response:

> Unfortunately this question did not possess enough party importance to awaken the energies of a people who are callous to every feeling that is not spurred forward by party rancour and animosity and they allowed a measure alike destructive to their morals and worldly comforts to progress slowly but surely through the legislature until at last frightfully aroused by signs of imminent danger they struggle, when almost too late, to remedy the evil, which has gained strength with its age but might have been easily crushed in its infancy, had proper measures been taken.[19]

In early June the same organ informed its readers that the bill had gone into committee in the House of Lords. More in hope than expectation it stated that in the upper chamber 'it will be shorn of its evils and given to the country in a revised and corrected form'.[20] However, by the end of July the bill became law and, leaving its political bias to one side, the paper made a salient point as to the importance of the new measure:

> It will form one of the most crucial tests of legislation ever applied to Ireland; and the consequences will be a total revolution, not only in

the social and moral character of the country, but a very formidable one as regards the present possession of landed property which may happen to be in any way encumbered.[21]

While the press and politicians debated the merits or otherwise of compulsory maintenance of the poor, the majority of the population in Leitrim continued to face serious hardship. In June 1839 it was reported that Morgan Crofton had purchased £400 worth of meal to be distributed amongst the 'industrious poor' around Mohill. Similarly, F. McKeon bought fifty tons of potatoes which were to be sold to 'poor housekeepers' at a reduced price by a committee in Drumshanbo.[22] Not to be outdone, George Manners St George contributed £50 towards a relief effort in Carrick-on-Shannon and also initiated the building of a road through part of his estate in order to provide work for the poor.[23] Similarly, Colonel Samuel White donated £25 as he 'did not wish to see want of food amongst the people on his estates'.[24]

The distress had been caused by the sudden increase in the price of meal and potatoes. By June meal was selling at sixteen shillings per cwt in Drumshanbo while in Carrick it reached twenty shillings, more than double the usual rate. However, the actions of the local landed gentry succeeded in significantly reducing them. When a number of men including Colonel Armstrong and Simon Armstrong of Hollymount purchased sixteen tons in Sligo they sold it at cost price in Manorhamilton and forced the price down to between three and four shillings per cwt. The latter also initiated a subscription in order to obtain a supply of food at less than cost to those in acute distress.[25]

Such was the level of distress in the parishes of Mohill and Cloone that each was subdivided in order to ensure an effective relief effort. In Mohill, each committee member assumed responsibility for one district and undertook to visit persons seeking relief. The relief committee also arranged for the purchase of several tons of meal in counties Sligo and Longford in order to reduce local prices. In addition, the managers of the Mohill Loan Fund agreed to lend sums of £1 and £2 to be repaid at the beginning of the harvest.[26]

Meanwhile, in Cloone it was decided to divide the parish into three districts for each of which a committee was established to collect and distribute subscriptions. Lord Leitrim contributed £25 while, like their counterparts in Mohill, the local loan fund made a donation. The press stated that the Rev. Andrew Hogg, 'the zealous and active secretary' of the latter was 'now busily employed in ascertaining those most deserving of, and most needing, loans'. It also noted that 'the greatest cordiality' prevailed between 'the Protestant and Roman Catholic clergymen' and by the middle of July subscriptions totalled almost £96.[27] Similarly in nearby Annaduff a fund to support the poor was organised by the Rev. George Shaw.[28]

As the distress continued the reaction of the gentry varied. Lord Leitrim contributed £50 to the Manorhamilton committee and gave a similar amount to the Cloone effort. However, what was described as a 'resident proprietor' of the latter parish refused to make any subscription 'on account of the lawless state of the peasantry there for the last two or three years'.[29]

In the parish of Inishmagrath there were only four contributors to the fund but the sum realised was £200. By this means the local committee supplied 200 families (about 1,000 individuals) for most of June and July with meal, all of whom 'had been obliged to sell either more or less of their cattle, or household articles at an immense loss' and were on the verge of starvation.[30] Meanwhile, a correspondent to the local paper lambasted George St George and the 'wealthy inhabitants' of the neighbourhood of Carrick for 'having evinced such fatal apathy to the state of our starving brethren' and contrasted this to the efforts made by landlords in other areas who had 'so nobly come forward to the relief of their distressed neighbours'. The writer noted this inactivity and compared it to the alacrity with which a meeting of 120 people had been held in the local grand jury room for the purpose of 'addressing the Queen on the subject of the late changes in her Majesty's Council'.[31]

While some preferred to restrict their frustration to print others took direct action and on 5 June Thomas Howard, chief constable at Carrick-on-Shannon, reported the theft and killing of a sheep in the townland of Aughintubber, parish of Annaduff. He deemed this action to be 'solely attributable to the high prices and want of provisions and that hunger alone caused this outrage to be perpetrated'.[32] In Lismoyle, in the same parish, the stable door of Thomas Waldron Esq. was forced open and a sheep killed. In his report Howard noted:

> Great distress prevails in this district at present in consequence of the unusually high prices of provisions and several persons with I have conversed are of opinion that dire necessity caused the perpetration of this outrage.[33]

In another audacious raid a 'fat sheep' belonging to Duke Crofton of Larkfield was killed and the carcass, minus the head and entrails, carried away.[34]

Meal was another target of those in need. On 9 June the oat mill of William Crawford in the townland of Drumherriff, parish of Kiltoghert, was broken into and seventeen stones of oatmeal stolen. In relating how he had instructed the constabulary to pay particular attention to mills and stores containing flour and meal, Howard cautioned against 'doing so in any manner that might create or excite alarm as to a scarcity of provision in the country'.[35] At the end of June it was reported in the press that a group of around thirty men broke into a house in Cloone and stole one ton of meal.[36]

Given that the crisis had resulted from the huge increase in the price of provisions some people decided to ensure that the market would remain accessible to people in their area. Hence, on 6 June a number of men attacked the house of Pat Foley in the townland of Aughrim in the parish of Kiltoghert, and after shooting his dog they ordered him not to charge any more than 2/6 per cwt for potatoes. The police stated that similar events occurred at neighbouring houses but Foley was the only one to report it.[37] In the townland of Drumcree in the parish of Annaduff a group of between twenty and thirty men attacked the house of Michael McDermott and stole 6 cwt of potatoes. As they left they handed him the following note: 'I solemnly do promise to pay Michael McDermott at the rate of 2/6 per cwt for your potatoes again New Years Day. July 7th 1839.'[38] However, a more direct approach was taken by a party of twenty men, their faces blackened and four of whom were armed, in an attack on Michael Cox in nearby Fargrim. They made him swear at gunpoint not to charge more than 2/6 per cwt for potatoes and then went to the houses of his neighbours informing them that potatoes were available from him at that price.[39]

The figures released by the Mohill relief committee offer some idea of the numbers relieved throughout the county. There, almost 900 families consisting of around 4,300 individuals were supplied on a weekly basis with meal at eight shillings per cwt. Those living on the land of landlords who refused to contribute were not discriminated against and received the same as every other family. The total amount subscribed was £207/5 and the first purchase of meal was made on 20 June. The last occurred just over a month later on 23 July and this (a value of £23/16/6) was distributed free of charge to those in need. A cash balance of £3/16/9 was distributed by committee members to those regarded as being in particular need.[40]

It was perhaps more than a little ironic that in the midst of such distress the assistant poor law commissioner, William John Hancock, toured the towns designated as centres for the establishment of workhouses. On 2 July he visited Manorhamilton while on 19 July he was in Carrick and Mohill. On each occasion he outlined the estimated costs of the poor law to local landed proprietors and gentry and explained that the expense of building workhouses would be met by instalments over a twenty-year period. The statistics were as follows:

**Table 2.1: Estimated Cost of Poor Law in County Leitrim, July 1839**

| Workhouse | Building Cost (£) | Annual Instalment (£) | Paupers Per Annum (£) | Total (£) |
|---|---|---|---|---|
| Carrick | 7,000 | 350 | 700 | 4,036 |
| M'hampton | 5,000 | 250 | 400 | 2,407 |
| Mohill | 6,000 | 300 | 600 | 3,460 |

*Source: Roscommon and Leitrim Gazette, 6 July 1839 and 20 July 1839.*

The question of the efficacy of a poor law, and the accompanying opposition, elicited a pamphlet on the subject from John Robert Godley of Killigar. Godley had been educated at Harrow and Christ Church, Oxford, graduating in Classics and in 1843 he turned his attention to the great debate of the times with *A letter on the subject of poor rates addressed to the landholders of the County of Leitrim*. The essence of Godley's argument was that the new measure could not be properly judged until it had received the 'full and cordial support' of the population. However:

> Far from this being the case I hear an [*sic*] universal outcry of complaint before anybody can possibly have reason to know that there is ground for it. I find among the rate-payers opposition to the collectors – among the guardians opposition to the commissioners and the very principle of the act – among the whole population a disposition not to make the best of the law, but as in them lies, to embarrass its working.[41]

He attempted to reassure his readers by explaining that the sums advanced by government for building the houses would be paid 'without interest' over ten years. In his opinion the alternative which had existed prior to the new enactment meant that 'small farmers, cottiers, clergy and a few resident landlords supported the whole of the pauperized population'. Hence:

> I maintain, without fear of contradiction that far more than all the expense contracted for the poor law machinery is paid, and would be so, were it ten times as heavy, by those who formerly contributed nothing at all.[42]

In this way, 'absentees and niggards, a large proportion, must now pay their full share'. In his judgment the object of a workhouse was 'to serve as a test by which we may distinguish true from pretended destitution'. Hence, 'if the machinery is paid by those who did not pay before you cannot be losers by this change and if one single individual is induced by the workhouse test to earn his own bread you are so far gainers'. He appealed to guardians to open the workhouses 'freely to all proper objects as long as there is room in them', warning that there must be no 'paltry attempt' to keep down the rates 'at the expense of the principle of the law'. Appealing to his readers he urged:

> [Do not] join in the unjust and unreasoning clamour which has been raised against this law, but ... do your best to make it work easily and successfully; this you can do by refusing relief to vagrants of whose claims and circumstances you know nothing; by offering no vexatious opposition to the collectors of the rates; and by electing as guardians honest men, men of business and above all men who are inclined favourably to the law.[43]

Despite these reassuring overtures, David Stewart was much less sanguine in his assessment of the new measure. He revealed that prior to the introduction of the poor law George Lane-Fox had employed tenants on his Dromahaire estate at task work and also supported the 'many widows' either by offering them work or giving food. Now, he was adamant that the 'weight of the Poor Law will bring this to a stop'.[44]

It is difficult to know whether or not the imminent introduction of the Poor Law was the catalyst for the establishment of the County Leitrim Protestant Orphan Society which came into existence in July 1839. As has been noted, in the decades prior to the new legislation abandoned and orphaned children were regularly cared for by people chosen and subsidised by the local Church of Ireland vestry. The new law ensured that the voluntary contributions on which such a system depended was now ended and it may be that this acted as an incentive for the organisers of the new group. Its aim was 'to provide diet, lodging and scriptural education for poor Protestant children [under twelve years] who have had one parent a Protestant and who by the death of either father or mother or both have been left in circumstances of destitution'. All persons engaged as nurses by the society had to be 'Protestant, of good character [and] recommended by the Parochial Clergy'.[45]

However, the emergence of this new body was overshadowed by developments within the poor law and a few weeks later, on 18 September 1839 the unions of Carrick, Manorhamilton and Mohill had all been declared. Carrick was to consist of fifteen electoral divisions, seven in County Leitrim and eight in County Roscommon; in Mohill there were thirteen divisions, all in Leitrim, while in Manorhamilton the union was made up of ten Leitrim-based divisions. Meanwhile, two divisions situated in the north-east of the county, Glenade and Kinlough, became part of the Ballyshannon union (see Appendix Two and Maps Two–Five).[46] In that same month the election of the first board of guardians to the Carrick union had taken place. Of the fifteen electoral divisions eight were disposed of without a contest. As it soon emerged that the remaining seven would become a sectarian battleground, the *Roscommon and Leitrim Gazette* condemned the 'mobocracy' which was 'trying to usurp authority', aided in their efforts 'by the clergy of the Church of Rome':

> Liberal Protestants who have subscribed largely for the erection of these political houses of worship will not believe the unholy purposes to which they have been turned. Voting-houses for preliminary political meetings were not taken into account when they thoughtlessly gave their money. It was not expected that these Roman Catholic *Churches* would be made training houses to introduce the vote by ballot, annual parliaments and universal suffrage.[47]

The paper alleged that meetings were held in almost every Catholic church in the union to elect guardians. It further commented that, in some, Protestants were 'held up to the scorn and contempt of the meeting', while in others 'drunkenness and rioting were the order of the day'.[48] The following is typical of the editorial stance of the paper:

> In this division [Leitrim] the Priests, the Very Revd. Dr Slavin, Vicar General and Dean of the Roman Catholic Diocese of Ardagh, went through the district armed capapie sword in hand – no, we beg his pardon, whip in hand, accompanied by Mr Evers, the big Priest from the neighbourhood of Longford who assisted, with a simple weapon, in dragooning the poor people to vote against Hugheen Walsh, as they called him, why we cannot for the life of us tell, except that Mr Walsh stood forward as the representative of Mr La Touche, the largest proprietor in the district.[49]

The paper also sought to denigrate those who stood for the Catholic vote. Hence, it noted that such candidates in Carrick were merely 'a yarn buyer of the name of McGan, who usually attends our Boyle market and Smith, a small shopkeeper in Carrick'.[50]

However, the influence of the clergy in the Carrick union seemed to have been somewhat overstated by the paper as, apart from Drumshanbo (which elected Farrell McKeon and James Reynolds), the candidates they were alleged to have endorsed failed to be elected. The paper put the defeat of the Conservative candidate in Drumshanbo down to 'the shameful neglect of the constabulary who left twelve townlands not served with voting papers, and those principally Mr Birchall's friends and supporters'.[51] Overall, though, the paper was pleased with the results and, somewhat ironically given its earlier comments, stated that 'we are glad to find the Priests losing a portion of that influence which they exercised with such a baneful effect in times gone by'.[52]

On the other hand, its worst fears were realised when the results of the Mohill union emerged. Only two contests took place, in the divisions of Mohill and Annaveagh, but each returned Catholic guardians 'by great majorities'. Thus, of the twenty-two elected guardians in the union only three were Protestant and the paper commented that, in relation to the Catholic clergy, 'though their influence may have been somewhat shaken by the results of the election in the Carrick-on-Shannon union, it is in Mohill as powerful as it is pernicious'.[53]

Indeed, it later transpired that there had occurred instances of intimidation during the Mohill election. On 21 September the house of Michael Reynolds in Drumbeighra was broken into by a party of armed men who threatened to 'roast him on the fire' if he would not swear to vote for the priest's candidate. Other houses in the area received similar visits.[54] In Manorhamilton union seven of the ten divisions were settled without a contest. However:

> As soon as the boundaries of the various electoral divisions were ascertained the Priests set to work, having resolved to take the matter entirely into their own hands. They made it the subject of their text, from which to harangue the people at the different chapels on the following Sundays, saying 'we have got the hold, let us keep it'.[55]

Once again the local paper's comments appeared to reflect a sense of paranoia than actual reality as it was only in the division of Rossinver that 'the priest's candidate' was successful. In both Manorhamilton 'the stronghold of Protestantism' and Lurganboy 'the priests could not be managed'.[56] The one successful candidate apparently sanctioned by the clergy was Hugh Roarke, a publican from Rossinver, and it was remarked that even he would have failed 'if Mr Wynne of Hazlewood had taken the same trouble in the Rossinver division that he took in Lurganboy'.[57]

As in Mohill, there was a case of attempted manipulation of voting papers. It was reported how a party of men, including one armed with a bayonet, broke into several houses in the townland of Brackeramore in the parish of Kilasnett. In fourteen cases they took voting papers for the Manorhamilton election by force and men were dragged from their beds and threatened with burning until they handed them over.[58] A similar attempt was made in Drummons, parish of Rossinver, for the election of the guardians of Glenade electoral division in the Ballyshannon union. Several houses were entered and voting papers stolen only to be later returned with alterations. Thus, where votes had been cast for James Ellis and Thomas Lipsett their initials had been erased and placed instead opposite the names of Patt Connolly and Terence Clancy.[59]

In the meantime, on 4 August 1840, the foundation stone of the Mohill workhouse was laid. It was remarked upon that upwards of 150 men were in daily employment on the site at an expenditure of almost £100 per week 'which in a season like the present, was attended with the happiest results'.[60] The *Roscommon and Leitrim Gazette* gave the following glowing report on progress:

> From the style of architecture, the site chosen (at the base of the hill entering the town, the crown of which is planted) and the front building finished with cut stone, which the contractor volunteered to accomplish at his own expense, it will form a very picturesque object, and give the traveller a very different idea of what the term *Poor-house* hitherto implied.[61]

One group not so enamoured with the progress of the workhouse was the County Leitrim Protestant Orphan Society. At its first annual meeting held in Carrick-on-Shannon court house on 30 June 1840 it revealed that it had received £117 in subscriptions by which it had been enabled to support twenty-seven orphans, while at the same time being forced to reject a further thirty for want of funds. As an example of its endeavour it revealed that one of its first successful applicants was 'the child of a poor unoffending Protestant who was brutally murdered in a remote part of the County Leitrim, leaving his family utterly destitute'.[62] Significantly, in relation to the progress of the Poor Law, members commented:

> The great object of the society is to rescue them from the dangers of error both in faith and viciousness in practice, to which they are in their unprotected state peculiarly exposed – dangers from which a workhouse would afford them, to say the least, a very questionable security.[63]

By 1841 the society's subscriptions had increased to £140, boosted by £20 from Lord Leitrim[64] with a similar increase in the number under its care to thirty-nine orphans.[65]

In that year's election of guardians there appears to have been much less controversy than before. The local paper noted that in the Mohill 'elections' there had been no contests while the elected board contained only one Protestant. However, it did carry a typical anti-clerical report:

> From enquiries made, we find that the Priests have been everywhere indefatigable in opposing the election of every man whose vote in the board room they could not command for whatever purpose they

thought proper. Most disgraceful scenes, we hear, have been acted in the chapel of Fenagh parish the last two Sundays but we are happy to learn the good sense of the Roman Catholics themselves rejected the Priest's candidate and re-elected a very worthy man (Mr Heeran) who had filled the situation the preceding year. We have heard, with great disgust, that torrents of abuse were poured on Mr Heeran by a man who professes to be a minister of the meek and lowly Jesus but the *impotent* malice of his Reverence can only excite feelings of contempt and abhorrence in every independent mind.[66]

By mid-1842 the Protestant Orphan society was catering for forty-five children, with almost as many turned away due to lack of funds. At their annual meeting in Carrick members concluded that 'experience has proved that the workhouse is a most unfit asylum for Protestant orphans'.[67] Such experience was not confined to one sect and the early years of the poor law in the county demonstrated that it would prove a test, not only for the poor, but also for those elected to manage it.

## WORKHOUSES

### Manorhamilton

The first meeting of the Manorhamilton board of guardians took place on 14 October 1839 and saw twenty-two members elect Cairncross Cullen as chairman and Simon Armstrong as vice–chair.[68] On 21 May 1840 the three guardians present noted that the erection of the workhouse buildings had not started although 'the salary of the clerk of works is accruing since the 13th of last month'.[69] Nothing of note occurred until a meeting held in the first week of June 1841 when the board made known its disapproval of the way in which the union had been valued. They claimed that this was 'not by any means uniform', given that some townlands and farms had been valued too high and similar properties too low.[70] A few days later an extraordinary meeting objected to the fact that the loan to pay for the workhouse construction was to be delivered in two amounts. In the opinion of the board this would simply necessitate expense as well as requiring two deeds.[71] Whilst such important meetings attracted large attendances the union business was usually conducted by guardians ranging from four to eight in number and as time went on the same names appeared in attendance: James Conolly, John E. Cullen, Colonel Armstrong, Simon Armstrong, Allan Nixon and Robert Davies.[72] On 6 June 1842, with the house reported as being 'close to opening' the guardians reported that the union, from its 'continual distress', was now 'suffering much' due to the fact that the establishment was not available 'when it long since should have been'. In addition they complained of 'an influx of paupers' from Sligo and surrounding unions.[73] As was the trend in other unions the largest attendances of guardians was reserved for important matters of finance and, arguably, local patronage. Hence on 20 June nineteen met to establish the salaries of the workhouse officers; two weeks later the largest attendance to date – twenty-three – congregated to appoint the officers, select a dietary and assign warders to the various electoral divisions.[74] However, their propensity to pay the lowest wage they could to rate collectors caused problems and having originally agreed an 'inadequate' wage of 4*d* in the pound they agreed to raise this to 5*d*.[75]

Having earlier expressed their annoyance at the fact that the workhouse loan was in two parts the guardians again felt compelled to voice their opposition to an order from the poor law commissioners. On 1 September, eighteen guardians heard 'with surprise and regret' of the unwillingness of the commissioners to sanction the appointment of James Dundass as medical officer of the workhouse. They cited his 'many years service in the navy and as medical attendant of our dispensary' and remarked that 'however anxious we may be and ever have been to meet the views of the commissioners we cannot willingly be a party to his removal from the situation to which he has been elected'.[76]

This sense of grievance was palpable in the midst of an ongoing dispute with the commissioners over the salary of the clerk. The guardians wished to raise his wage from £24 to £40 per year but the commissioners objected, much to the great annoyance of the board who commented:

> That we cannot look upon the bearing of the Poor Law Commissioners in this transaction as dignified and becoming. We conceive that they should be actuated by other motives than that of merely exhibiting their authority over us and giving us to understand that they are our Rulers. Or are we to suppose that they are acting under some secret influence? ... But the Commissioners have throughout manifested a total disregard for our feelings and wishes and seem to be desirous of using us as mere instruments

for recording their decisions without any regard to our own will
... After this expostulation, if the Commissioners think proper to
persevere in their opposition they may as well prepare to take the
whole management of the establishment into their hands as they
show little deference to our labour and services.[77]

Again, when the board ordered an increase in the diet of female paupers
engaged in hard labour, with an extra six ounces of bread and one half pint
of sweet milk for supper, they were rebuked by the commissioners and
had to rescind their resolution. The commissioners suggested that instead
of increasing the food available they should instead either employ more
paupers to do the work or simply not undertake extra work. They argued
that this was preferable to any departure from 'the essential principle that
the union is entitled to the full benefit of the services of the paupers'
maintenance in the workhouse without any remuneration or allowance
beyond the ordinary diet of the establishment'. In their judgment 'any
departure' from this 'will become the source of jealousy, discontent and
insubordination; beside holding out an inducement beyond what would
otherwise exist to persons to apply for admission as paupers'.[78]

The commissioners again intervened once more on 27 April 1843,
this time on a matter which was to cause severe problems for the board
throughout the next decade. They urged the board to 'use every exertion'
in having the balance of the rates collected and informed them that it
was illegal to pay interest to their treasurer on advances.[79] They had felt
compelled to comment as collecting sufficient rates to run the workhouse
was proving difficult. Indeed, in the eight months from 20 April to 28
December 1843 only £166/14 was collected while in twenty-three weeks
no money had been remitted.[80] As in other unions the collectors were
threatened by the guardians and in light of this communication from the
commissioners. Hence the collectors were warned that unless they paid in
their balances before 1 June their sureties would be proceeded against.[81]
Similar threats were made on 3 August, 14 September and 5 October
but these were to no avail.[82] The difficulty appeared to be once again the
terms of remuneration offered to the collectors and was highlighted by the
resignations of those for the districts of Manorhamilton/Kiltyclogher and
Dromahaire/Killenummery at the beginning of November.[83]

Of course, problems with the rates meant that the guardians could
not efficiently run the union and this was highlighted in September 1843

when the workhouse contractor demanded more than £75 for extra work carried out on the building. The board declared that they had not at present any funds to pay him and were in debt to their treasurer. Consequently, they asked the commissioners to include the amount in a further sum to be borrowed from the Exchequer Loan Commissioners.[84]

Throughout this year increased numbers in the house meant increased costs. For example, by late February there were more than twenty children which necessitated the appointments of a schoolmaster and mistress.[85] The workhouse pump regularly gave problems and subsequently required repairs. For example, on 17 August the master reported that, although there was sufficient water the pump was not working. Just over one month later it was stated to be 'perfect' but by 2 November it was once more out of order and at the end of that month the master consequently complained that 'a great portion of the time of the working paupers is occupied in conveying water from the well'.[86] Further cost was involved in an order to fence the boundary of the workhouse plot with an earthen ditch six feet wide and five feet deep with a double row of thorn quicks.[87]

In November the first workhouse death was noted when Ann Lee from the Dromahaire electoral division was reported to have died of dropsy.[88] In February 1844 an infant died of croup and he was interred in Cloonclare. The fact that a graveyard adjacent to the workhouse was not yet in existence is demonstrated by the fact that the master stated that after the death of Patt McManus they were 'waiting for his friends to carry him away'.[89] However, by March this appears to have been rectified as when a pauper died of croup while in one of the receiving rooms the minutes read: 'That a coffin be provided at the expense of the union at large and that he be buried in the ground lately set apart as a cemetery in the workhouse plot.'[90] As the reports of deaths became more common in the minute books they offered an insight into the type of people therein and the attitude of the public to the institution. When Peter Ward died it was reported that the symptoms were 'general disease visceral and ulcer of the lung' which the medical officer stated 'he had on entering the workhouse'.[91] Similarly, when an infant called Patt McNulty was admitted to the house he had 'scrofulous ulcers over the whole body' and died on the same day.[92] In a report on the death of the pauper in the receiving room it was remarked that 'the man was in a dying state and that his death was accelerated by the indecent hurry with which he was carried forward on horseback by two individuals who brought him here'.[93] The evidence in each of these deaths suggests that relatives regarded the workhouse as a last resort and somewhere they hoped that their kin would be looked after until they died and then be buried at the expense of the union.

In spite of their financial difficulties the guardians ordered that one hundredweight of beef be purchased and used in the inmates' dinner on Christmas Day 1843.[94] However, in order to save money they decided to buy two pigs and have them fed on the workhouse offal to enable inmates to have future meat dinners at Easter and Christmas.[95]

The continuing financial problems were highlighted when the board received an order to pay the first and second instalments (total of £640) on the workhouse loan in August 1844. The reply of the board was blunt: 'the union has not money at present to pay this'.[96] In an attempt to save money they voted 'as a measure of economy' to employ a tailor at an annual salary for the purpose both of making pauper male clothing and instructing some boys in his trade.[97] However, as in 1843, there were major problems in the collection of the poor rate. For example, from 31 October to 26 December, a total of eight weeks, there was only one (12 December) in which a payment (£10) was made.[98]

In their anxiety to raise funds the guardians decided to boost the remuneration of rate collectors. Hence, the wage for the Killenummery and Dromahaire collector was increased from $2\frac{1}{2}d$ in the pound to one shilling while that for Manorhamilton and Kiltyclogher rose by three pence to eight pence in the pound.[99] At a subsequent meeting of the board held on 2 January 1845 one of the guardians, James Fawcett, announced that he would be proposing a motion that any paupers in the house charged to the Drumkeerin division should be dismissed, 'the rate payers of such division having entered into resolution to maintain the poor by affording them voluntary outdoor relief'. The total rate to be collected in Drumkeerin was £151/13 and was second only to Manorhamilton (£281/4/8) in terms of expense consequent on paupers being maintained in the workhouse.[100] However, in stating that such action would be contrary to the law, Colonel Armstrong proposed an amendment to instead discharge Thomas and Jane Gilhooly, both from the Drumkeerin division, as they were deemed by the board to be 'competent to earn their bread'. The amendment was carried by nine votes to nil.[101]

In January and February 1845 the board received demands from the commissioners for repayment of a loan of £500. However, it was outlined how the union was in debt to the treasurer, owing more than £362, and therefore the board stated their inability to pay the instalment, adding that they were not aware 'of when they may be in a condition to meet the demand'. Nevertheless, they ensured that paupers received beef for their dinner at Easter.[102]

In April, a dispute amongst staff in the workhouse served to reinforce how the guardians' role was subservient to that of the commissioners. On 24 April it was announced that the master and matron, who did not enjoy a good working relationship, had resigned. However, while the board maintained that the matron was 'inactive' they asked the master to retain his position. In the opinion of the guardians, it was due to his supervision that the inmates were in a 'happy and healthy state'. They also argued that his dismissal would result in destitution for his family and himself and therefore requested a six-month trial period. In spite of their criticism of her they also requested a similar trial period for the matron.[103] However, the commissioners stated that they wanted to see new appointments to both positions.[104] In response the board maintained that both would become paupers and asked the commissioners to 'exercise … a laudable compassion'.[105] In spite of such appeals the board received a sealed order from the commissioners on 12 June but then instead of complying they asked them to explain their reasons, regarding their conduct as 'arbitrary in the extreme'. Hence, they insisted on re-electing both officers 'until such investigation take place'.[106] However, within one week, and 'reluctant to push the matter further', the guardians capitulated to the order of the commissioners, expressing their regret that 'greater deference has not been shewn to the expressed wishes of the board on the subject'.[107]

## Mohill

The first meeting of the newly-constituted Mohill board of guardians took place on 11 October 1839 at which it was agreed to rent a room from Catherine Knott at a cost of five shillings for each monthly meeting for one year.[108]

At a meeting on 9 July 1840 they resolved to pay £27/2/6 to those tenants who had previously resided on land designated as the site for the new workhouse. This land belonged to Sir Morgan Crofton and was to be rented from him at a cost of £15/10 per annum.[109] They also opted to borrow £8,000 from the Exchequer Loan Commissioners to finance the construction of a workhouse.[110]

On 10 March 1842, in the first of many interventions, the poor law commissioners stated their objection to the appointment of Farrell Kiernan as a poor rate collector for the electoral divisions of Carrigallen and Newtowngore as documents they had seen indicated he had been prosecuted 'for being connected with a secret illegal society'.[111] In fact, Kiernan, along with his brother, had been arrested in October 1839 and charged with offences in the Cloone area.[112]

An indication of the numbers the guardians expected to utilise the workhouse is offered by their initial tenders for clothing for seventy-five men and women and fifty boys and girls in March.[113] However, a suggestion of future financial difficulties was revealed in the same month when the union treasurer, the Longford-based National Bank of Ireland, informed the board that they could not make any further advances available until the present overdue balance was cleared.[114] On 25 May the board announced to the commissioners that it was ready to admit paupers but that 'the workhouse is unfit almost in every particular, especially the probationary wards which are in a very backward state'.[115]

However, at this time fever was reported as being 'very general' in the Mohill area and the local dispensary, 'although destitute of beds, bedding or furniture' was fully occupied with reports of deaths therein.[116] Consequently, and regardless of the unfinished state of the house, sixty-one paupers were admitted on 15 June 1842 and in the following week a further 133 entered.[117] The board justified such large numbers due to 'the state of great destitution which at present exists in the union' and they felt it incumbent on them to 'admit such paupers as shall appear totally destitute notwithstanding our not having a supply of clothing for them'.[118] By the end of the first week of July a further 269 had been admitted, leaving a total in the house of 453 paupers.[119] At the end of that month the figure peaked at 543 and this in spite of the fact that the house was 'still not in a perfect state'.[120] However, this move was deemed essential in order to save large numbers from 'actual starvation'.[121] Similar distress appears to have been evident in Carrick-on-Shannon but the local workhouse was not then complete. However, a rumour that the house would be opened at the end of June meant that 'a vast number of poor persons crowded into the town for the purpose of obtaining admission'.[122]

The running of the fledgling institution cannot have been helped by the resignation of the master and matron (Mr and Mrs Brady) in August and that month also witnessed the first non-attendance by guardians at a weekly meeting (3 August 1842) while on 11 August the first reference was made to a death in the house.[123] In September the union treasurer stated its willingness to advance the union £200 free of charge. However, this proposal was swiftly rebutted by the commissioners who stated that the poor rates were 'the only source from which funds can be obtained for that purpose'.[124]

On 15 September the board agreed to re-appoint the resigned master and matron but the commissioners only agreed to this in the short term and commented that there needed to be a 'decided and satisfactory improvement in the workhouse'.[125] However, within weeks the master had declared himself 'unequal to the duties of the workhouse' and resigned once more.[126] By this stage, the number of inmates had dropped significantly to 217 and an indication of the regime they had to endure was evident in the materials ordered to be given to women and young girls which included twelve spades, twelve shovels and two loys.[127]

An early sign of poor administration was revealed when the medical officer was admonished for not keeping a register of the infirmary nor of sickness and mortality levels.[128] By the end of the year the number in the house had fallen to 186 and weekly admission levels ranged from none to six.[129]

In February 1843, in an attempt to restrict costs, the board unanimously resolved to refuse any further admissions until all the various contractors had been paid. They also substituted meal and potatoes for bread in the house diet and wrote to the commissioners requesting their assistance in forcing poor rate collectors to pay in their collections.[130]

If it had proved possible to collect the entire poor rate this would have raised a sum in excess of £1,203 at a rate of 5*d* in the pound.[131] However, by the middle of that month it was revealed that the expenses of the union up to the end of September 1842 had exceeded income by just over £42 and it was in debt to several contractors. The clerk was therefore ordered to summon the poor rate collectors for 'wilfully disobeying the legal and reasonable orders of the board'.[132] Indicative of the problem was an allegation by one of the guardians, Thomas Brady, that the collector for Carrigallen and Newtowngore had 'misapplied' more than £20, 'the property of the union', since 30 January 1842.[133]

As it emerged that one creditor had been owed almost £66 since June 1842 the board was informed on 16 March that the first instalment of £400 due on the £8,000 workhouse loan was due.[134] The commissioners demanded to know why the union was 'considerably indebted to the contractors' and sought an explanation for the reticence in striking a new poor rate.[135] The problem actually stemmed from the poverty of those from whom the rate was supposed to be collected: they simply could not afford it, and the returns reflected this. For example, on 20 April £4/19/2 was paid in while on 4 May the total was just over seventeen shillings.[136]

The difficulty for the guardians was that the collection of the poor rate was proving problematic, as the *Roscommon and Leitrim Gazette* reported:

> We hear a very general and determined opposition to the payment of the poor rate has shown itself in a part of the Mohill union where the rate collector, named Moran, has been rescued by a numerous mob of cattle he had distrained under the usual warrant. It is supposed that the country people concluded the collection of the rate was altogether illegal and might therefore be opposed.[137]

By July it was being reported that rate collectors were facing intimidation. In Fenagh division the collector 'has been unable to progress in the collection' while the collector for Cloone and Aughavas had his house broken into by a party of armed men who 'broke his windows, swore him not to collect the rates and threatened to put him to death if he disobeyed'.[138] Not surprisingly he subsequently tendered his resignation to the board of guardians but this was rejected amid promises of assistance.[139] Criticising those 'evil-minded persons' who were 'stirring up the peasantry against the payment of the poor rate' the local paper sought to seek the source of opposition:

> Those who assist in misleading these poor people have much to answer for; we believe that the Roman Catholic clergy have *generally* done their duty in exhorting their flocks to pay the rates but we cannot help thinking if the landed proprietors, their agents and bailiffs would do the same, it would greatly diminish this senseless opposition.[140]

It suggested that as a means of tackling the problem local loan funds should refuse to aid anybody not in possession of a poor rate receipt, arguing that this 'would greatly tend to break down the conspiracy against payment'.[141] However, opposition was not confined to areas within Leitrim and the paper, in noting similar feelings in nearby Boyle, County Roscommon, commented:

> The entire peasantry seem opposed to it and there appears a unison of purpose in their resistance to the Poor Law system in this country which has not shown itself towards any measure enacted for Ireland, within our recollection.[142]

Despite these difficulties the Mohill board voted £1 to be used to purchase meat for the paupers' dinner on Easter Sunday.[143]

By April Pat Dolan, collector for Carrigallen and Newtowngore, had been convicted of withholding money he had collected and was dismissed from his post.[144] Perhaps desperate, the guardians appointed a new collector, in spite of opposition from the commissioners that he was a labourer 'not accustomed to writing' and having only a 'middling knowledge' of accounts, while another collector was dismissed from his post on 15 June.[145]

The corollary of non-collection of rates was increased hardship for the workhouse inmates and this was reflected in a remark made by the master when he noted a 'want of brogues' for some of the men who were otherwise forced to work barefoot.[146] Matters were not helped by what appeared to be an increasing level of indifference by the board of guardians. On 26 October none of them attended for a scheduled weekly meeting and the same thing happened on 7 December while two weeks later only two appeared.[147] In effect, this meant that the workhouse was not being properly managed and this was reflected in a report made by the board chairman, Lord Clements, who visited on 8 January 1844. He found the porter absent from his post, every door on the ground floor opened, including that of the infirmary, and girls present on the male side of the house. Thus, there existed 'the greatest possible confusion throughout the establishment' and as a consequence the master was reprimanded.[148]

In the meantime, problems with rate collection persisted and the minutes of 11 January 1844 noted that no money had been paid in, while on 15 February the total was just £5. No rate was paid on 22 February, 21 March, 11 April, 25 April, 16 May, and 23 May. By 9 May 1844 the total amount of uncollected rates was £1,396/16/3 and, compounding the problem, the board uncovered dishonest rate collectors.[149] On 23 May the collector for Cloone division, Edward Donnelly of Gortnaraw, was summoned to appear before the magistrates for 'detaining the poor rate and turning it to his own use'.[150] He was subsequently fined.[151] While the case against Donnelly seemed to elicit an immediate response from the collectors (£39/19 collected by 30 May, and £15 on 6 June), this was only temporary.[152] The collector for Eslin and Annaduff, James Moran, was ordered by the clerk to pay £8 into his hands after his accounts had been examined. When he refused to do so the clerk enquired of the board as to the course of action to be taken.[153] He also informed the members who bothered to attend that the collectors were not regularly presenting themselves to have their accounts examined.[154] On 25 July all collectors were ordered to collect and pay in their rate within sixty-two days. However, such problems did not seem to greatly trouble the vast majority of guardians as on 27 June, 11 July, 15 and 22 August meetings were adjourned due to insufficient numbers attending.[155]

By 10 October the union had received a demand from the Public Works Loan Fund for the first and second instalments (totalling £65) on a loan of £650 for providing the workhouse.[156] This was in addition to a demand for both instalments of the original workhouse to be repaid to the Bank of Ireland before 15 April 1844.[157] Incredible as it may seem Edward Donnelly had retained his position as rate collector for Cloone and on 24 October he was ordered to pay all monies due and produce his books before the board within thirty days.[158] Suddenly, money from Cloone started to emerge: on 7 November £11 was handed in while three weeks later a further £12 was deposited. By 12 December the division still had £93 uncollected, the next worst being Mohill with just over £59.[159]

Problems with poor board attendance persisted and on 31 October and 19 December only two guardians appeared.[160] At an 'extraordinary' meeting held on 23 December to discuss allowing the paupers a Christmas dinner five were present and they agreed to provide such.[161] The final board meeting of 1844 ended as many others had throughout the year with an order that all collectors collect their rates within six weeks.[162]

Various established trends were repeated in 1845 and due to lack of attendance board meetings had to be adjourned on 9 January, 30 January, 6 February, 13 February and 27 February. Indicative of the lack of co-ordination was the fact that on 13 February William Smyth had appeared and waited and then left before two other guardians arrived.[163] Similarly on 20 March only one guardian appeared and further meetings were adjourned on 15 May and 29 May while in the weeks of 13 March, 3

April and 10 April no poor rates were paid in to the union clerk.[164] As in previous years, the problems with collecting sufficient rates to run the workhouse, together with dishonest and inefficient collectors, continued. By the beginning of May £1,307 remained to be collected while the clerk had been instructed to prosecute James Moran, the collector for Eslin and Annaduff, who had retained more than £14 for his own use. At the same time the collectors for Fenagh, Newtowngore and Carrigallen resigned.[165]

However, the workhouse seemed to meet the demands placed on it simply because it was only ever about one-third filled. For example, in the first six months of 1845 the maximum number in the house was 245 (in the week ending 10 May).[166] Apart from this they varied between 200 and 245. Indicative of this lack of pressure was a request from the 34th Regiment of Foot of the British army to allow one of their companies to use a vacant part of the workhouse as a store. This appeal met with the unanimous approval of the board and they were allowed to utilise the male probationary wards at the 'usual remuneration'.[167] This lack of pressure appears to have led to a measure of complacency on the part of the guardians and there were no board meetings on 26 June, 3 July and 17 July, due to the attendance of only one, two or no guardians.[168] Consequently, and not surprisingly, given the supposed supervisory role played by the guardians, certain aspects of the administration were not up to standard. In August, the medical officer's books, especially those detailing sickness and mortality, were maintained in a 'negligent manner' while in September the guardians expressed their 'disapprobation' of the manner in which the clerk kept his books.[169]

Financially, things began to improve from July onwards when weekly rate collections ranged from £27 to £45, a significant improvement on earlier totals.[170] No doubt this was a consequence of the guardians prosecuting those collectors who failed to produce their books to the clerk.[171]

## Carrick-on-Shannon

On 3 October 1839 the election of chairman to the Carrick union took place in the local court house. With John Duckworth declining to accept any votes the contest involved Hugh Walsh and John Reynolds Peyton, 'two Roman Catholics', with the latter gaining the chair by one vote.[172] One of the first acts of the Carrick board was to come to a unanimous resolution that the site of the workhouse 'is very much exposed and badly situated for water' and thus it would prove difficult to obtain a water supply for the workhouse.[173] In noting this, the local paper commented that, nevertheless, 'the commissioners have determined on retaining the objectionable site'.[174] However, events were to prove the guardians correct in their assessment and the lack of a proper water supply continued as a major difficulty for a decade.

Due to the loss of the first minute book it is difficult to determine events in the union from 1839 onwards but by the early months of 1843 the workhouse was under pressure. The collection of poor rates had been proving extremely problematic with no money paid in for the weeks of 15 and 22 June; in addition, the collectors for the divisions of Drumreilly/ Drumshanbo and Gillstown had resigned while that for Kilglass had been suspended.[175] Thus, by the beginning of July, £1,487 remained uncollected.[176] Reflecting the difficulties that this caused was the fact that a committee of guardians had been established by the board to ascertain the viability of discharging those paupers deemed able-bodied. However, by the end of June no report had been received.[177] To exacerbate the situation there had been a long-running dispute between the guardians and the contractor over the condition of the workhouse, the former maintaining that the latter had not completed the building to a satisfactory standard. Their complaints to the commissioners were met with the order that they borrow £1,200 to complete the works, an order which they would 'refuse to entertain'.[178]

On 20 July 1843 the board remarked on the 'very gross negligence on the part of the contractor' due to his unwillingness to complete the pump.[179] This had caused a 'serious inconvenience' in the establishment and while eventually agreeing to borrow the £1,200 they wanted to employ an architect of their choosing to meet with the commissioners' architect to agree upon the changes which the commissioners argued were actually extra works outside the original contract. As far as the board was concerned such works should not have been regarded as extra, being, as they saw it, part of the original contract. However, the commissioners refused to accede to this request arguing that their accounts had already been subjected to a 'rigid examination' by their own architect. Therefore, the arbitration proposed 'would be useless'.[180]

In the meantime, the guardians decided to limit the number of admissions to the house. On 26 June there were none while throughout the month of July only one person was admitted. With solicitor's letters coming in from those contractors remaining unpaid (a figure in excess of £295) the board was forced to seek the aid of the military in collecting the poor rates in the Drumreilly division.[181] They argued that the 'great deficiency' in the area was due to 'a desire to insult the law rather than from a want of means'.[182]

It appears that the commissioners' architect, Wilkinson, after visiting the house, disagreed with the guardians' version of events as they criticised him for 'seeking to justify and excuse the unpardonable negligence of the contractor regarding the pump'. Re-enforcing their argument they noted that the master had requested the necessity for a second cart to convey water to the house as one was proving inadequate.[183] However, the commissioners, in expressing their 'regret' at the inconvenience caused, informed the board that they had sent an engineer to 'put the pump in order'. They also agreed to allow the board to employ someone to complete the unfinished works, the fee to be deducted from the contractor's accounts.[184] Despite this, the board still felt compelled to remind the commissioners of their resolution of 28 November 1839 which encapsulated their objections to the chosen site. If this had been listened to and acted upon 'the great additional expenditure for foundations, levelling, filling and providing water would have been obviated and a great saving effected for the poor rate payers of this union'.[185]

The financial situation of the union continued to deteriorate. In early November the board was served with summonses for sums in excess of £880 due to contractors and they requested an extension from the latter's legal representatives in order to obtain more money from rates. Thus, the rate collectors were ordered to collect all outstanding monies within ten days.[186] However, one week later, on 16 November, with only £40 paid in the board resolved that 'the funds of this union are in such a depressed state, we have not sufficient funds to meet any further increase in the number of paupers'.[187] In an attempt to obviate such difficulties John Duckworth proposed that a third rate be struck solely to pay off the debts of the union.[188] The guardians also sought the intercession of their solicitor who was asked to write to the 'several law agents now carrying on proceedings against them' in an attempt to gain more time to collect sufficient rates to pay the debts.[189]

At a subsequent meeting of the board on 30 November, attended by nineteen guardians and assistant poor law commissioner, Caesar Otway,

John Duckworth proposed that the third rate should be levied off each division according to its level of debt – a total of £1,300. However, his proposal was countered by an amendment which called for a further period to allow for collection of the original rate and this was carried by fourteen votes to four.[190]

The same meeting heard from a committee appointed to examine the various rate collectors' books and concluded that in the majority of cases 'due diligence has not been made by the collectors'.[191] Therefore, the members agreed to instigate legal proceedings against them and their sureties. Throughout October, November and December the number of weekly admissions to the house was restricted to single figures and from 16 November to 14 December there were no admissions and twenty-one rejections.[192] While some guardians were inclined to close the house, the board eventually chose to meet in the first week of January 1844 to discuss 'turning out all that appear strong and able-bodied'.[193] However, the commissioners urged caution in removing paupers when there appeared adequate room in the house.[194] While this communication may have discommoded the guardians their anger was ignited when a proposed visit to the site by one of the commissioners to hear the grievances of the board was cancelled. They learned of this with 'astonishment' and maintained that it was 'in accordance with the typical conduct adopted toward this board from the commencement of its operation by the said commissioners'.[195] In spite of their financial difficulties the board resolved that the inmates should receive a 'meat dinner' on Christmas Day.[196]

The financial problems came to a head towards the end of January 1844 when the sheriff laid an execution on the workhouse goods at the suite of businessman Pat Cosgrove. The latter was asked to delay proceedings until the board could find some means to settle his account but while members struggled to meet the demands of various creditors their decision to refuse to address the needs of the poor of the union were highlighted by the death of a local man, Darby Gormly.[197] The latter had applied for admission to the workhouse on 14 and 21 December but on the former date, when none were admitted, he was one of five rejected. On the latter date six people had been admitted but he failed to satisfy the criteria of being destitute. Three days later he died 'in circumstances of extreme destitution … at the door of a cabin near Carrick-on-Shannon'.[198]

In a further attempt to alleviate the position the board unanimously resolved to obtain an advance of £1,200 from the union treasurer, the

London and Dublin Bank, 'for the purpose of discharging certain pressing liabilities which if not liquidated will be the occasion of heavy expenses to the union'. In the event of the bank agreeing to their request they promised to lodge all rates with it until the debt was paid.[199] Before committing itself the bank informed the board that any loan would be predicated on the sanction of the poor law commissioners, who were asked to provide the board with an answer 'with the least possible delay'.[200] The commissioners, as requested, replied swiftly and whilst expressing 'regret' at the difficulties being encountered by the board opined that a loan with interest was not legal 'in the present state of the law'.[201] The board countered that unless money was forthcoming, either by means of a government loan or through the bank, it would be impracticable to keep the house open. A 'large sum' was already due to contractors and with current contracts ending on 25 March it would prove 'impossible' to find anyone to supply the house. Therefore, a loan was an 'absolute necessity'.[202] At a meeting attended by eighteen guardians on 21 March the board asserted that the commissioners were authorised to sanction a loan under the 35th and 89th sections of the Poor Law Act, which stated that the guardians could borrow money from any persons willing to advance it on security of the rates. They continued:

> If they persist in refusing, the only alternative left us is to discharge the paupers and close the house and upon them let the responsibility of such a course rest and not with the guardians who are most anxious by every means in their power to discharge their liabilities with the least expense.[203]

In stating that they were willing to allow the board to borrow money 'in every legal manner' the commissioners requested a statement of the sums due to creditors.[204] Evidently irked by this request, and the constant communication back and forward, the board impressed on the commissioners the 'absolute necessity' of their sanction for the contemplated loan. They outlined how, as a consequence of debts due to contractors, they were forced to purchase goods in the market on a weekly basis. Thus, the requested loan was required 'in order to save this union from utter ruin' and if refused the board stated that the house would have to be closed on the next board day.[205]

The apparent desperation of the board to acquire funds was highlighted by the fact that it was prepared to continue employing rate collectors who had failed to lodge substantial amounts of rate they had already collected. Thus, Pat Beattie was re-appointed to the Leitrim and Drumsna divisions on the understanding that he pay the sum of £31/13/9 due by him; William Beattie was hired for the Drumshanbo division on the basis that he pay £5/6/5 'remaining in his hands' while John McDermott who owed £30/15/11, was appointed collector for the divisions of Killukin and Creeve.[206] To add to the confusion it emerged that the union clerk had obtained money from one of the rate collectors as a loan to 'remove a pecuniary embarrassment'.[207] With contractors refusing to supply goods Pat Dockery, one of the guardians, was forced to spend around £13 each week in purchasing oatmeal and potatoes in the market.[208]

Having been refused a loan from either the bank or the government the guardians finally resorted to requesting an overdraft from the bank for £1,200. This was acceded to by the commissioners 'as a means of relieving them from immediate embarrassment'.[209] No sooner had this overdraft been obtained than the board was asked to repay the first and second instalments (£840) of the £8,400 to build the workhouse. However, they had more pressing debts and at the same meeting on 8 June it was revealed that, due to the overdraft, they had been able to pay more than £517 to contractors and workhouse staff.[210]

On 15 June it emerged that James Reynolds had been paid £31/6/8 for supplying water to the workhouse up to 19 September 1843.[211] Due to the fact that the recently repaired pump had broken down after three weeks the guardians suggested that the commissioners should pay any such further costs and maintained that the pump was 'altogether useless for the purpose of this institution'.[212] Not surprisingly, and emphasising their belief that boards of guardians were responsible for all their own costs, the commissioners refused to accede to this request.[213] Emphasising the woeful lack of provision for water on the site was a resolution from the board that two vessels be purchased 'for receiving the water from the down pipes in the male ward'.[214]

On 10 August the union was reported as being more than £1,000 in credit.[215] Given the severe financial difficulties of a couple of months previous this statement appeared to surprise the commissioners who presumed it was 'an error'.[216] By the 28 September this figure had increased to just over £1,295 but the board were quick to apprise the commissioners of the reality of the situation. Some of this money had accrued from improved rate collections (for example £127/5/3 on 22

June; £136/9/1 on 29 June and £157/10/8 on 6 July). However, £1,200 of the total resulted from the overdraft agreed with the bank and by the time it was repaid there would remain little more than £100 in their account. Consequently, far from being in a better financial situation, the board again applied to their treasurer for a six months loan of £500.[217]

Given their regular jousting with the commissioners, insult was added to injury when Caesar Otway revealed to the board that a mistake had been detected in the accounts of the contractor who had constructed the workhouse and money would have to be borrowed by the board to meet the shortfall. However, the indignant board members refused to accede to such a demand highlighting that, amongst other things, the union had been put to the expense of more than £113 to ensure a supply of water due to the fact that the contractor had not finished the pump. Voicing their unanimity in not wishing to borrow any money to pay the contractor they stated that they considered the conduct of the commissioners' architect 'highly improper' as he had taken the workhouse, which included the defective pump, from the contractors 'in an unfinished state'.[218] Poor attendance was one charge that could not be levelled at the Carrick board where meetings attracting double figures were by no means uncommon; their obvious disgust at this turn of events, however, was reflected in the appearance of only one guardian at the next board meeting on 19 October.[219]

Another conflict with the commissioners developed when the board voted to increase workhouse officers' salaries instead of augmenting their rations. This was objected to by the commissioners who requested that the board rescind the order. However, members refused to do so and argued that 'from our local knowledge and experience' they believed the union would benefit from such a move.[220] At a meeting on 7 December, attended by thirteen guardians, they announced their intention to petition parliament for an enquiry into the present state of the poor law in Ireland. They also demanded remission of the charge for construction of the workhouse which they regarded as an 'unwarrantable and extravagant expenditure'. In direct criticism of the poor law commissioners they lambasted their 'want of due consultation' with the board, especially in relation to the site chosen for the workhouse,

> ...which has in consequence of their obstinacy in persisting in their
> choice of site caused an enormous additional outlay of money and

by means of which also we are now without even a prospect of our ever being able to obtain within the precincts of the workhouse any supply of that most indispensible requisite.[221]

Nevertheless, the power of the commissioners was evident at a board meeting held on 21 December when the guardians were compelled to rescind their decision to enhance the officers' wages instead of their rations.[222]

The reality of their predicament was shown after they had repaid their £1,200 overdraft on 16 November.[223] On 30 November they had just over £9 in the bank and for three weeks in December they were in debt, only managing to scrape back into the black before the new year with £6/14 in the bank.[224] Despite there being more than £703 of poor rates uncollected they voted to allow the paupers a meat dinner on Christmas day 'similar to the scale given on last festival'.[225]

It is evident that the problems encountered by the Carrick board were not unique and throughout 1845 twelve unions also indicated their desire to seek a remission of the cost of building workhouses. They ranged from various parts of the country, Middleton (Co. Cork) to Letterkenny (Co. Donegal) and Ballymena (Co. Antrim) to Enniscorthy (Co. Wexford).[226] The Downpatrick board argued that the cost of their workhouse should be paid out of the government's consolidated fund and the Carrick guardians agreed to adopt a similar memorial 'as far as it is applicable to our union'.[227]

However, the constant strain in relations between the board and commissioners seems to have had an impact on the attitude of the guardians to their role in administering the affairs of the union. Hence, more adjournments of meetings occurred in 1845 than in any period since the workhouse had been completed. Thus, on eight occasions, the guardians failed to carry out their duty under the law to meet at least once each week. Invariably, when only two guardians met they were those based in Carrick – usually Dockery and Browne.[228] When they did meet they faced the same problems as before. On 29 March they were informed water was coming in through the walls of the female infirm ward due to damp as a result of 'the bad and imperfect state of the building'.[229] In an attempt to extend the workhouse test and thereby discourage applications to the house the board stipulated on 24 May that all able-bodied paupers then in the house could be hired out to the contractor currently engaged in the Shannon works in the town 'or any other individual who may be desirous to employ them'.[230] However, they were rebuked by the poor law commissioners who informed them that such action was not allowed under the law and therefore the board was unable to act on the resolution.[231] They had more success with the policy of removing those who had been in the house for one year from 1 September 1844 and in this way twenty-seven adults and eighteen children were discharged.[232] This action was justified on the basis that employment was available in the neighbourhood while it occurred at a period of the year 'when the new provisions will be had in abundance'.[233]

Within the house it was reported in July that the master had not maintained 'proper discipline' for a considerable time with the guardians describing the house and premises as being in a 'very unsatisfactory state'. It also emerged that he had been allowing paupers 'to go at large into the street of Carrick' and when this had been objected to by the chairman the master had used 'disrespectful language' to him. After an investigation by the commissioners the porter was forced to resign.[234]

Of course, one of the main difficulties remained that of the union finances. On 22 March the board called on the commissioners to dismiss the collectors for the divisions of Leitrim and Drumsna (Pat Beattie) and Keshcarrigan (Michael Tighe) due to the fact that Beattie owed £108 and Tighe £40. The guardians believed that both men had collected the money and not paid it in and they were subsequently dismissed.[235] With arrears of more than £1,300 the guardians expressed their regret at the 'apathy exhibited by our several collectors in the discharge of their duty and the embarrassed circumstances of this union'. As a consequence they were forced to once more apply to the bank for a loan of £750.[236] However, they received some respite when the Public Works Loan Commissioners decided to reduce the debt due on the workhouse loan of £8,400 by £475.[237] The application to the bank appears to have failed as the minutes record a further application for a loan, this time of £1,000. This was deemed essential for discharging certain pressing liabilities which if not liquidated 'will be the occasion of heavy expenses to the union'.[238] As before, the commissioners wrote to the board informing them that there was 'no provision in law' to contract a loan to meet current expenditure.[239] Despite this advice the board agreed a loan with the bank: £1,000 for six months at 6 per cent interest. In an attempt to animate the rate collectors the board promised to pay one shilling in the pound to collectors remitting the full rate within four months of receiving their warrant books. Those returning later would only receive sixpence in the pound.[240] However, by the end of November the usual complaint was voiced of collectors 'still not doing their duty' and being given twenty days to collect the rate.[241] As in previous years, despite such difficulties the board voted to give the inmates a beef dinner for Christmas but this would be the last such indulgence for years to come.[242]

The enactment of the poor law introduced major changes into Irish society with support for the poor now becoming compulsory. The embodiment of this legislation was the poor house and three of these dominated the towns of Carrick-on-Shannon, Manorhamilton and Mohill. Just as dominant was the role of the poor law commissioners and by mid-1845 the poor law unions in the county had all experienced similar problems. They had discovered that the word of the commissioners was, quite literally, law, and each board had been forced to acquiesce in a variety of instances to the dictate of the central authority. In addition, there had been significant problems in enforcing collection of the poor rate, the essence of the law, due, in many cases, to the poverty of a huge number of those liable and the intimidation of those appointed by the boards to collect rates. However, what the early years of the law also illustrated was that in times of crisis, as during the fever outbreak of 1842, those in need had nowhere to go except the workhouse due to the fact that voluntary committees were not going to be initiated by people already paying a compulsory tax. On average, there was a least one failure of the potato crop each decade in Ireland. With the workhouses already struggling in their infancy, and little demand for relief, the test would come when another inevitable failure of the staple diet of the people occurred.

# Chapter 3

# A DISEASE AFFECTING THE POTATO

## COUNTY OF LEITRIM.

By the Authority of the Lord Lieutenant of the County of Leitrim, I hereby nominate and appoint the following Gentlemen to form a Committee of Relief, for the CARRICK-ON-SHANNON District, for the purpose of affording Assistance to the Labouring Population, either by way of Labour or Alms, as they may think proper; and also, that they may communicate with the Commissioners appointed by Her Majesty's Government, in reference to the apprehended Scarcity: and I have the honor to request their attendance in the COURT-HOUSE of CARRICK-ON-SHANNON, on THURSDAY, the 9th day of APRIL, 1846, at the hour of 12 o'Clock, noon :—

| | |
|---|---|
| JOHN H. PEYTON, Esq. | The Rev. R. S. CLIFFORD, |
| FRANCIS LA TOUCHE, Esq. | The Rev. R. SLEVIN, |
| FRANCIS WALDRON, Esq. | The Rev. FRANCIS KEANE, |
| HUGH BYRNE, Esq. | JOHN KEANE, Esq. |
| CAPTAIN COX, | WILLIAM I. PEYTON, Esq. |
| WILLIAM PEYTON, Esq. | WM. HUTCHINSON, Esq. Surgeon, |
| GEORGE H. C. PEYTON, Esq. | ALEXANDER FARIS, Esq. |
| VERY REV. DOCTOR SLEVIN, | The Rev. THOMAS FITZGERALD, |
| The Rev. W. A. PERCY, | The Rev. Mr. MULROONEY, |
| The Rev. G. SHAW, | JOHN DUNNE, Esq. M.D. |
| The Rev. G. GEARTY, | Mr. COSBY W. IRELAND. |

And I appoint, as a District for the Relief of the abovenamed Committee, to consist of that part of the Parish of ANNADUFF, which is in the Barony of LEITRIM, and the Southern Division of the Parish of KILTOGHART, not included in the District of DRUMSHANBO.

*Given under my hand, in Carrick-on-Shannon, the 3rd day of April, 1846.*

## CLEMENTS,
### Deputy Lieutenant.

Appointment of a relief committee for the Carrick-on-Shannon district, April 1846. Courtesy of Seamus Geraghty Collection, St George's Heritage Centre, Carrick-on-Shannon, County Leitrim.

THE AUTUMN OF 1845 approached, as in other years, with the expectation of a good harvest. The *Roscommon and Leitrim Gazette* of 8 August reported that the crops had 'a most promising appearance' with farmers anticipating 'an abundant harvest'. September witnessed the annual agricultural society shows in Manorhamilton and Carrick at which were exhibited fine breeds of cattle, together with butter, potatoes, turnips and fowl.[1]

In Carrick, the Drumsna Amateur Band played 'several enlivening airs' while after the show the competitors dined at Churches' Hotel on beef, mutton, lamb and fowls, washed down with ale. In an after-dinner speech, Lord Leitrim informed the audience, amid great cheering, that the South Leitrim Agricultural Society had become affiliated to the Royal Agricultural Improvement Society of Ireland. However, in a short speech, almost enveloped by toasts to Queen Victoria, Prince Albert, the Lord Lieutenant, etc., William Smith of Mohill attempted to address the realities of life for those living in poverty. He argued that tenants should be regarded as fellow-men, not slaves, and treated with humanity. He also appealed for compassion as it appeared that, alongside distemper in cattle and disease amongst pigs, there was the possibility of a failure of the potato crop. Smyth's words, lost in a sea of self-indulgence, would prove to be the most significant of the evening.[2]

By October the local paper was reporting a 'disease affecting the potato' in the Netherlands and in the same month commented:

> When it is considered that millions of our poor countrymen wholly subsist upon the potato and that the present failure has extended itself all over Europe, we cannot shut our eyes upon the consequences which may follow a general failure of the staple food of this Kingdom.[3]

The sense of panic in this article was justified as, in the weeks that followed, reports from throughout the county confirmed that damage to the potato crop had occurred. John Veevers, writing from Mohill, stated that rot had developed amongst all types of potatoes and forecast that approximately one-sixth of the crop would be lost.[4] William Wray disagreed but shortly afterwards revised his opinion, commenting that 'the injury is discovered to be much greater than previously thought' as the late heavy rains have accelerated the disease with between one-sixth and one-quarter of the general crop unfit for use.[5]

Subsequent reports varied to a great extent and whilst agreeing that a portion of the crop had been lost, many commentators felt that a situation bordering on panic had been engendered by exaggeration on the part of speculators. Thus, in Manorhamilton, Drumkeerin and Ballinamore 'an abundant crop perfectly free from disease' was forecast. Indeed Denis Booth, writing from Lavagh, near Drumsna, at the end of November, reported that there would be plenty of food available until next summer and hence 'the panic that had been created in this county has in a great measure subsided'.[6] Similarly, Joshua Kell noted that in Dromahaire 'the potatoes are not so much injured as they were considered and represented to be some time ago', adding rather tentatively how 'we trust there will be no scarcity of food in this country'.[7]

However, later analysis of returns from the thirty-eight electoral divisions in the county confirmed the varied nature of the impact of the failure. In three there had been a loss of 20 per cent; in eight 30 per cent; in fifteen 40 per cent and in a further eleven the blight had damaged the crop to the extent of 50 per cent. In one division (unfortunately unnamed) the loss amounted to 80 per cent.[8]

The consequence was immediately apparent in the county's workhouses. On 9 October 1845 the potato contractor for the Manorhamilton union was informed that after that week pink potatoes would no longer be received in the house.[9] One month later the guardians, together with their counterparts in Carrick and Mohill, received a circular from the poor law commissioners in relation to the manufacture of potato flour or starch from diseased potatoes. Consequently, the master was ordered to purchase a few hundredweight of diseased potatoes and have them manufactured in accordance with the circular.[10] In early December James Nixon was contracted to supply the house with one hundredweight of potato meal on a trial basis and the guardians informed him that 'if it answers as an article of food' they would prepare a contract for it.[11] In November the guardians of Carrick and Mohill received an order from the poor law commissioners recommending that they depart from the established dietary of the workhouse by substituting oatmeal, rice bread or other food in lieu of potatoes.[12] In a subsequent resolution the Mohill board ordered the master to employ inmates of the house 'in turning the diseased potatoes as far as possible to profitable account' in accordance with directions recently issued by the government.

The shortage of potatoes was evident in the price for such in Carrick. On 13 December the guardians there agreed a contract for potatoes for three months from 1 January 1846 – with cups (the best quality of potato) at 2s 10½d and lumpers (the cheapest variety) at 2s 4d per cwt. Two weeks later the contractor had not perfected his bond so the guardians agreed a new deal with another provider. By this stage cups had increased to 3/3 while lumpers were selling at 2/7 per cwt.[13] For an institution which used thousands of pounds of potatoes each week this was a significant increase, but it was merely a taste of things to come. In the markets of Carrick, Jamestown and Manorhamilton, meanwhile, prices had increased within three months by one penny per hundredweight while in Drumshanbo they had advanced by one-and-a-half pence.[14]

One of the first areas to exhibit signs of distress was Annaduff and local protestant clergyman, Rev. George Shaw, outlined how 'the distress of the population of this district is great from the failure in the potato crop, not alone during the past season, but five or six years previously'. He reported that he had engaged many men in draining his glebe lands, in order to give them work and money, but was finding it impossible to employ all those who applied. Rev. King of Kilmore, near Drumsna, commented on the 'unspeakable distress prevailing in this neighbourhood' while Fr Henry Brennan, parish priest of Rooskey, told how he was being appealed to on a daily basis by hundreds of starving people many of whom were reduced to one meal of potatoes per day. In Carrick, distress was said to prevail to 'a considerable extent' with many people being in 'actual want' due to the 'markets' having been 'artificially raised'.[15] However, it was not only individuals who were revealing details of distress.

## WORKHOUSES

### Mohill

On 19 March, the Mohill guardians sent the following resolution to the poor law commissioners in Dublin:

> We entertain serious apprehensions as to the means within reach of the poor to provide for their families; that there can be no doubt of the extensive failure of the potato crop existing in the southern part of the parish of Mohill and that in that vicinity they are exporting such as are good and that there is every reason to fear that the people will not have potatoes for seeding their land. Cottiers at present are almost destitute and very shortly will be absolutely so. There are many families who are said to have provisions to last until the month of May but no longer and even farmers holding six or seven acres are said in some instances to be in great want. We are of opinion that the best mode of

meeting the emergency will be by public works for immediate money repayment and establishing a depot of Indian corn in the principal towns in the union, to be sold at the lowest possible rate.[16]

Despite the apparent concern manifested by this petition the attendance of guardians at weekly meetings did not engender confidence in their conviction, or ability, to alleviate distress. Indeed, it was rare for a month to pass without at least one adjournment due to non-attendance. Thus, on 28 August, 25 September, 13 November, and 18 December meetings had to be cancelled due to there not being sufficient guardians present to conduct business.[17] On the occasions on which they did convene business was usually carried out by only a few members. Indeed, on 11 September, 2 October, 9 October and 27 November there were only four guardians in attendance while on 11 December the total was three, the minimum required to conduct business.[18] At Christmas 1845, as in previous years, the inmates received a 'meat dinner' after a proposal made by John R. Godley to supply them with such.[19]

The new year began with summonses being issued against rate collectors George Crofton, James Moran and Edward Donnelly for 'wilfully detaining' monies collected by them. Donnelly was eventually prosecuted for withholding the sum of £10/5/5 and received a warning from the magistrates that a similar offence would result in him being 'severely punished'. In that same month another rate collector, who owed more than £43, tendered his resignation.[20] A request from the Audit Fund for payment of £9/10 was met with the response that funds at the disposal of the board had already been disposed of 'to meet their pressing demands'. A subsequent letter from the poor law commissioners ordering them to pay the debt was rejected as the board argued that their priority was to pay the accounts of contractors.[21]

On 29 January a meeting was adjourned as only two guardians attended and the same happened on 26 February and 5 March when no one appeared.[22] As before, meetings which did take place were usually attended by half a dozen guardians who conducted the business of the union. Exceptions occurred when important appointments had to be made such as on 19 February when nine attended in order to elect a new schoolmistress.[23] Often this was to make sure that the 'right person' obtained the position and guardians who never otherwise attended turned up to make sure the person they wished to see appointed was successful. In the meantime, the union debts were continuing to get larger and on 19 March the board received an order to pay the fourth instalment (£400) of the workhouse loan (£8,000) before 15 April together with £775 due from 22 May 1845.[24]

However, the effects of the potato failure were starting to make themselves felt. Although the master ordered 300 stones of potatoes in March a week later he reported that it was necessary to increase the allowance of oatmeal in the diet as potatoes were no longer being given to the paupers. Hence, dinner now consisted of eight ounces of oatmeal for adults and four ounces for children. At the same time the board commented on 'a vast number of representations of distress and seeking for relief' having been laid before them.[25]

## Carrick-on-Shannon

By late 1845 the Carrick board had been successful in removing long-term inmates from the house and perhaps mindful of the anticipated demand consequent on the potato failure members attempted to make entry even more difficult. In justifying such action they argued there had been 'frequent imposition practised by persons seeking admission' and so they decided that in future all applicants would have to procure the signature of four rate-payers in the same townland in which they resided, together with the usual ticket of recommendation from the local warden.[26] However, the commissioners swiftly reminded them of the regulations regarding admission of paupers and the idea was subsequently shelved.[27] Given the rapidly increasing price of potatoes it was no surprise to find that by the end of January 1846 the lumper was the only variety being used in the workhouse diet and by that stage almost 8,000 lbs were being consumed each week.[28]

As in Mohill, oatmeal was soon introduced into the diet with adults and children aged nine to fourteen receiving nine ounces made into stirabout for dinner, while the younger children 6½ ounces. This new dietary started on 16 February and was used on each Monday, Wednesday and Friday in the week.[29] However, oatmeal, just like potatoes, was in great demand and consequently witnessed a significant increase in price. By 24 January the lowest tender received by the board was 16/4 per cwt but two months later this had jumped to 18/10 per cwt. At the same time lumper potatoes were now 3/4 per cwt while cups were selling at 4/3 per cwt.[30]

In May 1845 the poor law commissioners had given their sanction to the guardians' intention to build a fever hospital on the workhouse site. However, they expressed doubt as to their obtaining the necessary funds by means of a loan from the Public Works Loan Commissioners and on 14 June the board decided to postpone discussion of the matter for a further six months.[31] Having examined tenders for the construction of the hospital, on 21 March 1846, they discovered that the new building would cost £1,000, exclusive of furnishing. The possibility of striking another rate solely to meet this cost was discussed but 'from the very distressed state of the union at this present season' it was considered 'impossible to collect any rate we would lay on for that purpose in addition to the rate lately struck … which will not be sufficient to discharge our present liabilities'. As an alternative they considered the possibility of borrowing from the Consolidated Fund.[32] By May, with typhus fever present in the workhouse and neighbourhood, the guardians requested the 'immediate attention' of the commissioners to the need for a fever hospital and enquired about the possibility of a loan from the Exchequer Loan Commissioners.[33] (They even considered renovating and utilising a temporary office which had been built by the contractor during construction of the workhouse.[34])

An indication of increased hardship in the union was reflected in comments made by the board on 6 June when they decided to postpone collection of the poor rate from the first week of October by one month 'in consequence of the general distress of the rate payers at present…'[35] However, the guardians were always keen to reduce costs in the house and from 14 June they introduced the cheapest food available – Indian meal. Thus, the adult dinner consisted of 4 oz of oatmeal and 5 oz of Indian meal made into stirabout. This item was also introduced into the children's diet. Consequently, potatoes were now to be used only on two days in the week, probably due to the fact that lumpers were selling at 3/11 per cwt. Thus, by this date only 1,120 lbs of this variety were being consumed each week in the house compared to almost 8,000 lbs less than six months earlier. One week later, the level of Indian meal in the diet was further increased so that an adult dinner consisted of 3 oz of oatmeal and 6 oz of Indian meal.[36] Obviously, the guardians were delighted with the saving to be made by using this cheap alternative and on 8 August they sanctioned it as the sole food for the inmates on five days of the week; hence, breakfast and dinner consisted of 8 oz of Indian meal stirabout for adults; 4½ ounces for those aged between 9 and 14; and 4 oz for children between the ages of 2 and 9.[37] However, the commissioners urged 'caution' in relation to the proportion of such meal in the diet, 'especially amongst children'.[38]

Nevertheless, Relief Commission member Sir Randolph Routh, in a letter to assistant secretary to the Treasury, Sir Charles Trevelyan, referred to the fact that 'great calamity' had been prevented in the country by the introduction of Indian corn meal 'which has become so popular that even the potatoes have been sold to procure the means of procuring it'. This was in spite of the fact that officials acknowledged that it was referred to as 'flint stone' due to its hardness.[39]

In the midst of further demands for payment of loan instalments the Manorhamilton board received a slight boost with the news that Lord Leitrim had offered to plant the workhouse grounds 'and otherwise ornament the ground connected with the workhouse at his own expense'. Needless to say this 'liberal offer' was 'gratefully accepted'.[40] However, this was an all together rare source of pleasure for the guardians at a period when the first potato failure was beginning to have an impact in a variety of ways. First and foremost the supply of potatoes was proving problematic. On 26 March 1846 and evidently due to a shortage in the house, the guardians resolved to employ somebody to buy one week's potatoes in the Sligo market and a few days later a tender for a month's supply at 3/8½ per cwt was accepted despite this being an increase of 3½d on the price negotiated four months previously.[41] In May the guardians deemed the price of bread 'too high' and instructed the master to erect an oven in order to bake bread in the house, believing that 'a saving would thereby accrue to the union'.[42] Given both the extra expense and subsequent attempts to save money the collection of rates became ever more important. However, as always, this proved a problem and in early April the collectors were ordered to present themselves at the next board meeting with all their account books settled. As was by now customary, they all ignored this command and their sureties were ordered to be proceeded against.[43] This appeared to make little difference as in the period from 14 May to 20 August, there were seven weeks in which no money was paid into the account of the union treasurer.[44] The porter, Michael Walsh, resigned, and his appointed replacement left the house only three months later 'under a charge of immorality'.[45] However, perhaps of more long-term significance was the fact that on 20 August, as in Carrick, the board authorised the clerk to purchase one ton of Indian meal for the workhouse 'by way of experiment'.

With the impact of the potato failure being felt throughout the country the British government established a Temporary Relief Commission in

November 1845. The main role of this body was to organise food depots and co-ordinate the efforts of local relief committees. The latter were to act as a medium for the purchase and re-selling of Indian corn imported by the government from America and to oversee the provision of employment on small local works-schemes. It was recommended that the committees consist of resident gentry – landlords, agents, magistrates etc. – together with clergymen of all persuasions and local poor law guardians. However, such stipulations proved difficult to enact in an area where many of the landed gentry were absentee proprietors. This problem was addressed by Lord Leitrim, writing from Lough Rynn, near Mohill who, having received a copy of 'The Instructions to Committees of Relief' replied that they were 'totally inapplicable to this district where landlords are almost unknown, the rector of Cloone absent, and agents frequently non-resident'.[46]

Further to this, it is evident that gentlemen such as Clements were experiencing teething problems in establishing committees. On several occasions he wrote to Dublin enquiring as to whether they were to be established on a county or baronial basis and if they could act independently of each other. Gradually, however, relief committees emerged in Mohill, Carrick, Carrigallen and Manorhamilton. They were chiefly concerned with obtaining Indian meal and selling it at as low a price as possible. Despite repeated requests to establish meal depots throughout the county, the government refused to furnish Leitrim with such an outlet and the nearest were sited in the towns of Longford and Sligo.[47]

The situation was exacerbated by the further refusal of the government to deviate from its policy of non-interference in the market. Hence, they would not encourage the release of large amounts of meal for fear it would lower the prices then being obtained by private traders. For example, on 22 April Rev. St George of the Carrigallen Relief Committee wrote to Captain Kennedy in Dublin enquiring about the price to be paid for Indian meal from the government depots. The reply he received reflected the opinion of the administration that supplies should be released at as late a date as possible, in order to avoid any price reduction. Therefore, he was informed that Indian meal was not even being distributed at present as 'it is thought that early June will be time enough in that part of the country'.[48] Similarly, when Rev. James Franks of Manorhamilton reported that money had been collected in Kinlough for the purchase of four or five tons of Indian meal at Sligo, he was informed that 'the state of that area does not require such assistance from the depot before the first of June'.[49] In this way, procedure often took precedence over provision, and when private suppliers eventually ran out of stock, the government released large quantities of meal onto the market when demand was high and people were willing to pay inflated prices. Indeed, meal increased to such an extent that relief committees, attempting to sell as cheaply as possible, were actually incurring losses on food purchased. Rev. C.S. Montgomery of Inishmagrath, writing on behalf of the Drumkeerin relief fund, stated that the local committee was selling at £10 per ton which represented a loss to them of £4. He also gave the following account of the aid they were affording to the poor:

> We distributed three tons, 13 cwt of meal to one hundred and eighty-eight families and were obliged to reject from fifty to sixty – there not being sufficient meal from the great and unexpected number of applicants. If we are not afforded further pecuniary aid, we must cease from affording any relief whatsoever in the course of two or three weeks.[50]

In Ballinamore, the local committee was selling oatmeal and Indian meal twice a week to around 600 families. The former was retailed at less than half price – 1s per stone – with the latter at 6d per stone and in cases of severe hardship, families were supplied free of charge.[51] However, this course of action was frowned upon by the commissioners who reminded the committee that:

> No relief is to be given gratuitously to able-bodied persons and no such relief should be given even to the aged and infirm so long as there is room for them in the workhouse of the district.[52]

Thus, in spite of the reports of distress, hardship and even starvation, the commissioners adhered to the principle that food had to be paid for.

The first government donation in aid of subscriptions to local relief committees was £75 given to Lismore in County Waterford on 25 March 1846.[53] However, it was not until 9 May that such money made its way to Leitrim. On that date the barony of Mohill received £170 to support its subscriptions of £252/12 and in the following weeks grants were made to the 'south division' of the barony of Leitrim

(£70); Carrigallen (£85); Ballinamore (£150); Drumshanbo (£80) and Drumkeerin (£70).[54] However, such grants were the minimum the government could do and their non-interventionist approach was epitomised in the following comments by Charles Trevelyan on 4 August 1846 who argued that in order to 'carry the people safe through the coming year':

> There cannot be a doubt that *our present operations* ought to cease with the harvest labour and the new crop.
>
> It has been proved by experience that the *immediate* effect of the prevalence of the potato disease is to force large supplies prematurely into the market, and that there is no period when relief is so little required as at the commencement of such a season.
>
> During the season which has just elapsed, we firmly refused to open our depots while the disease was making progress, and forcing the crop into the market, and reserved our supplies until they were imperatively called for *in consequence of the actual exhaustion of the crop in April, May, June and July*; the early issues being to a very moderate extent, and increasing as the year advanced. It was solely owing to this prudent reserve, that we were able to supply the void caused by the partial destruction of the crop over such a great extent of country, and if, with the prospects before us we were to begin our issues in August before the new crop is well out of the ground, I do not hesitate to say that it would be utterly impossible for us to meet the demands upon us throughout the ensuing year, in all the parts of Ireland in which the potato crop may fail; and the consequences would be likely to be extremely disastrous.[55]

While British politicians mused on theoretical approaches to need, the reality of grinding poverty was evident in a document which was posted in the townland of Moyglass in the parish of Kilglass, 'very poor country', in the Carrick union on 6 July:

> To the Honourable and Committee of Public Works
>
> We the indigent and needy and distressed class of Workmen of this part of the Vicinity having no means to procure a subsistence, can no longer bear the merciless pangs of hunger, humbly deprecates the Committee will take into consideration and commiserate the

awful and melancholy state of these humble and peaceful People, and give them Employment, according to every other part of the Country, before they are exposed to the impending danger of present famine which has neither shame nor honesty and before We violate the ties of honesty which we were bred to. We desire Work and nothing but Work, and hope the committee and Gentlemen of the Vicinity will find that for us, and hopes the honourable Gentlemen will not be offended at this Notice, because we are no Mollys. We distain it.[56]

In light of such, the government, alongside establishing and part-funding local relief committees, introduced the tried and trusted format of public works. Under this system the local grand jury applied to the Lord Lieutenant through a special presentment session for a work of public utility to be introduced to the area. In Leitrim the overwhelming number of presentments related to the construction and maintenance of roads, regarded by the government as the most useful way of providing simple, yet extensive, employment. Such works were to be financed by local taxation in the form of the county cess, although in the first instance it was usually provided by the Treasury in the form of a loan. Interest was charged on the latter at 5 per cent per annum, payable in half-yearly instalments of not less than four and not more than twenty payments. 217,851 people were being employed on relief works throughout the country by 4 July 1846. However it appears that although there were more than 7,000 in Roscommon and just under 3,000 in Sligo no such works had commenced in Leitrim or Donegal at this time.

This was in spite of the fact that, in April 1846, applications for works involving the construction of new, and improvement of present, roads had been made by the baronies of Carrigallen, Leitrim and Mohill. However, of the £24,300 applied for, none was made available and due to the inevitable bureaucratic delays it was not until May, when £6,000 was allocated to the county, that public works could be sanctioned. Thus, on 10 May the first works commenced in the barony of Leitrim, followed soon after by those in Carrigallen, Dromahaire and Mohill.[57] The end of July saw further enhancement of numbers employed so that, as the following table illustrates, they increased dramatically to stand at almost 11,000 at the beginning of August:

## Table 3.1: Employment on Relief Works in County Leitrim, July/ August 1846

| Date | Number Employed |
|------|-----------------|
| 11 July | 5,408 |
| 18 July | 6,405 |
| 25 July | 7,998 |
| 1 August | 10,702 |

*Source*: HC 1846, volume xxxvii, Correspondence explanatory of the measures adopted by her majesty's government for the Relief of Distress arising from the failure of the potato crop in Ireland. p.400–401.

By the latter date the numbers employed in neighbouring counties were: Cavan, 1,344; Donegal, 160, Roscommon, 34,223 and Sligo 9,285. The largest number in the country was 102,728 in County Clare.[58] The Leitrim figure for 1 August consisted of 3,538 in the barony of Rossclogher; 3,523 in Dromahaire; 1,610 in Carrigallen; 1,356 in Mohill, and 675 in Leitrim.[59] One of the officers of the Board of Works, Lieutenant-Colonel Jones, in submitting such figures to Charles Trevelyan lamented how 'our numbers are greatly increased'. He added, rather forlornly, 'what I foresaw early in the year is now verified; every man in the country who wants works, is forced upon us; we cannot help ourselves'.[60] In his figures Jones noted a total of 2,896 men employed on the roads in Leitrim for the week ending 18 July. Given that the total number employed for that week was 6,405, this would suggest that the majority employed in Leitrim, 3,509, consisted of women and children.[61] The number of road works in the county, with associated costs, was as follows:

## Table 3.2: Public (Road) Works in County Leitrim

| Barony | Cost | No. Improvements | New Roads |
|--------|------|------------------|-----------|
| Carrigallen | £2,900 | – | 4 |
| Mohill | £1,475 | 3 | 5 |
| Leitrim | £1,600 | – | 1 |
| Dromahaire | £2,550 | 2 | 2 |
| Rossclogher | £1,400 | 1 | 2 |

*Source*: HC 1846, volume xxxvii, Correspondence explanatory of the measures adopted by her majesty's government for the Relief of Distress arising from the failure of the potato crop in Ireland, p.419–427.

At the same time a further 2,410 people from counties Cavan, Fermanagh and Leitrim were employed on the Ballinamore and Ballyconell Canal[62] while, as the following table illustrates, significant numbers were employed on the Shannon Navigation works:

**Table 3.3: Numbers Employed in Improvement of the Shannon Navigation, September 1846**

| District | Numbers Employed | | | |
|---|---|---|---|---|
| | 6 September | 13 September | 20 September | 27 September |
| Jamestown | 1,813 | 3,352 | 4,121 | 4,477 |
| Ck–on–Shannon | 497 | 577 | 407 | 432 |
| Coothall | 1,000 | 1,956 | 2,039 | 2,252 |
| Knockvicar | 752 | 1,162 | 1,767 | 2,197 |

Source: British Parliamentary Papers, volume 6, Correspondence from July 1846 to January 1847 relating to the measures adopted for the relief of distress in Ireland, Board of Works series, p.135.

Of course, the intention of such works was to enable people to work in order to purchase provisions. Such a scheme was therefore dependent on the ability of the employees of the Board of Works to guarantee work was carried out according to schedule while at the same time ensuring labourers were promptly paid. On 7 August Fr Felix MacHugh, parish priest of Killargue, informed the relief commissioners that men employed on two roads in his neighbourhood – Greaghnafarna to Seanadagh Bridge and Tawnyleagh to Cloonagh – had not been paid for sixteen days. He stated that as a consequence many would have been in a state of 'extreme distress' save that the Killargue relief committee had given them meal on credit to be accounted for when they were paid. With 90 per cent of potatoes in the area 'unsound and unfit for use' he revealed that there had already been 'violent cases of sickness' due to people eating them. He therefore requested that the relief commissioners would 'speedily adopt some means of addressing such grievances'.[63]

MacHugh's correspondence was important in two respects; firstly, it revealed the dichotomy between those responsible for administering official policy and those supposed to benefit by it. It is likely that the non-payment of workers would have been regarded as a mere clerical oversight which may, or may not, have resulted in a reprimand to the person or persons concerned. However, the devastating consequences of such mistakes were evident in that those not paid were reduced to starvation. Secondly, his reference to the almost total annihilation of the crop in the district held out the prospect of a second successive failure of the staple diet of the people, much more devastating than that of 1845. The prospects for the future were grim.

# Chapter 4

# A TEMPORARY INCONVENIENCE

Letter from George Keppel, Downing Street, London, to his agent, William Lawder, 18 December 1848. Public Record Office, Belfast, D 4123/5/1/21, Turner Papers. Courtesy of Deputy Keeper of Records, PRONI.

IN SEPTEMBER 1846, believing that 'some change of scene and air was necessary' as he had been 'sinking body and soul in London all summer', antiquarian and music-collector William Forde arrived in Leitrim. He had been invited by 'Capt Pratt of the 41st' and during his visit he stayed at Letterfyne House where his hostess, Mrs MacNamara – an evicting landlord – was 'hospitality personified'. On 21 September he informed John Windele that:

> The piper Hugh Beirne has been dying for the last two or three years but while ensuring the life of the airs that would have perished with him I do believe I am the means of giving him life also. Stirabout and bad potatoes were working fatally on a sinking frame – but a mutton chop, twice a day, had changed Hugh's face wonderfully.[1]

In a further letter, written on 10 October, Forde, noting the 'many places of antiquity' in the area, complained that 'there is no-one about the place who knows or cares about these things'.[2] One of the possible reasons for such indifference, apparently ignored by Forde, was the prevailing social and economic conditions consequent upon a new, and much more comprehensive, failure of the potato crop.

In the autumn of 1846 the Relief Commissioners sent questionnaires to members of the police constabulary throughout the country. The intention was to obtain an accurate picture of the condition of the new potato crop. Each reply contained details of the crop sown from 1844 to 1846; the area planted in con-acre; other crops grown, and finally the extent of damage by blight in August and September of that year.

While reports varied according to locality they did so only in relation to the extent of devastation caused. Thus, in Ballinamore the crop was said to be blighted to 'an alarming extent' with around 80 per cent lost, the reporter commenting that, 'the state of the crop is deplorable – there is scarcely a sound potato to be had in the district and the decay is rapidly progressing'.[3] Around Manorhamilton the loss was in the region of 75 per cent with barely a field escaping the blight and 'the leaves and stalks which ought to be green are now black and withered'.[4] Carrick's crop was said to be 'totally destroyed' while Mohill had a deficit of around three quarters.[5] In Dromahaire the potatoes had been 'blighted very considerably' with many found to be 'utterly unfit for use'.[6] From Drumkeerin one observer maintained that 'if the disease continues for one month, there will be no potatoes in this locality'.[7] Later in the year these reports were collated and statistics produced which compared the acreage of potatoes for the previous three years with that for 1846. The results were stark: the national average yield per acre in the pre-famine years had been 159 cwt 98 lbs but in 1846 had fallen to 7 cwt 37 lbs. In County Leitrim the figures were even worse with the average falling from 157 cwt 42 lbs to just 2 cwt 28 lbs per acre.[8]

Such devastation meant that the relief efforts of the previous year would have to be greatly enhanced in order to cope with the huge numbers who had seen their sole means of survival wiped out. Three methods were adopted by the government: public works; the workhouse test and support of officially-sanctioned relief committees.

## PUBLIC WORKS

Given the heightened demand for work consequent upon the new crop failure, local relief committees experienced great difficulties through their inability to cope with demand; competing local rivalries; vested interests and ineptitude. For example, on 20 October government inspector, T. Sarcker attended the committee at Kinlough expecting to issue tickets to those ready for work but the lists were not prepared. The same situation pertained at Dromahaire a couple of days later.[9] Other inspectors complained of inactivity in Fenagh, Drumshanbo and Carrigallen and when the lists were eventually completed in Fenagh and Ballinamore they largely consisted of those holding three to five and in some cases, up to ten, acres. Captain Layard, in remarking that 'some glaring instances of improper names being submitted for tickets have come to light' stated his intention to strike off land holders, or those possessing oats or cows, in favour of 'indigent poor'.[10] In Ballinamore he encountered 'a vast number of improper names sent to me for tickets' and condemned the interference of clergymen and priests who were 'directing the clerks to take men in unknown to me'. He threatened to stop the works if this persisted 'but in consequence of the starving state of the people I have not hitherto done so'. He was also pressurised by clergymen on the Carrigallen committee 'in a most inconsiderate way' to increase the numbers on the works and reported that he did so 'as far as prudence would admit' but warned that 'unless a check is given to the course pursued' the works would run out in less than three weeks.[11]

On 31 October 1846 Captain Lardner stated that distress in parishes in the barony of Dromahaire was 'very great'. In particular he cited those of Inishmagrath and that part of Drumreilly within the barony. The number of people demanding work was in the region of 2,000 but only 700, 'with a great deal of difficulty' had been engaged on new roads. In the meantime, 'the remainder traverse the country in columns of 200 and 300 interfering with the works now in progress and threatening to disturb the peace of society'. In Mohill, parish priest Father Evers called for an increase of men employed and when he was informed that this could not be done he replied that 'if any death takes place he would swear that he applied to the Government officer for relief and was refused'.[12] Such demand for labour was occasioned by what was termed the 'extravagantly high' price of provisions both in Dromahaire and the neighbouring barony of Rossclogher.[13] As the following table illustrates the price of essentials more than doubled in some areas between January 1846 and January 1847:

**Table 4.1: Comparison of Commodity Prices (per ton), 1846–7**

| Location | Oatmeal | | Indian Meal | | Rice | |
|---|---|---|---|---|---|---|
| | 1846 | 1847 | 1846 | 1847 | 1846 | 1847 |
| Fenagh | £10 | £24 | – | £19 | – | – |
| Kinlough | £14 | £25 | £11 | £20 | – | – |
| Ballinamore | £11 | £26 | £9 | £21 | £19 | £32 |
| Drumod | £13 | £24 | – | £21 | £23 | £30 |
| Drumsna | £16 | £28 | £12 | £21 | – | – |
| Drumshanbo | £15 | £26 | £9 | £20 | £25 | £25 |
| Lurganboy | £16 | £26 | £10 | £20 | – | – |
| Manorhamilton | £12 | £27 | £10 | £20 | £28 | – |

*Source*: National Archives, Dublin, Society of Friends Relief of Distress Papers; information collated from applications to Society of Friends, 1846–7.

With food beyond the reach of a huge number of people and men reported as working 'by moonlight' for one shilling a day it was evident that visits by inspecting officers created tension. Captain Lardner reported on one such visit:

On Friday I attended the meeting of the Drumahaire Relief Committee when a scrutiny was commenced into some of the lists which produced such a manifestation of temper on the part of some of the gentlemen present that it had to be deferred to the next day.[14]

Similarly, in Manorhamilton the relief committee refused to allow scrutiny of the labour lists and Captain Layard was forced to rely on information from 'poor people' in his attempts to ascertain who was of independent means and employed on the works. In this way he was able to strike fifty-seven names off the list.[15] At the same time the parish priest of Ballinaglera refused to send in lists to the Dromahaire committee as 'no attention has been paid by the committee to the people of his parish'.[16] However, people who came forward to expose those gaining work on the roads were 'ill-treated or driven from the country' while for others, such as landlords, it was in their best interests to ensure certain individuals were employed so that rents could be paid. Therefore, as one inspecting officer commented, 'the employment of the really destitute seems to be set aside'.[17] After a couple of months the pressure of the job appeared to take its toll on Lardner and on 12 December 1846 he requested to be relieved from his duty as inspecting officer for Leitrim 'with as little delay as possible'.[18]

In mid-December, Captain Lagard complained there were more members in the Ballinamore relief committee 'than are desirable'. However, in stating that the Carrick-on-Shannon committee was 'well conducted' he added:

> The lower orders feel most uneasy at the continued rise in the markets and I deem it absolutely necessary that Government depots of corn be established, if only to quiet the public mind.[19]

The conditions which had to be endured by the men, women and boys employed on the public works was alluded to by Captain Layard in a letter written on 19 December when he stated that the snow had prevented him getting to both Ballinamore and Fenagh.[20]

In contrast to Lagard's appraisal of the Carrick committee's efforts Layard reported, just one week later, that the chairman had left, the secretary was 'away' and 'in short there is scarcely anybody left but the several relief committee clergymen and the Rev. Mr Percy'.[21] Besides difficulties with relief committees there were also bureaucratic hurdles to be overcome.

For example, in some cases men were left without employment for up to twenty-one days due to 'want of measurement' on the works. At the same time, the bank in Carrick was unable to furnish more than £80 in small change to workers which led the inspector to ask local loan funds and meal committees to retain the small change they received. It was also suggested, but not agreed to, that between £500 and £700 should be placed in the local bank, 'otherwise I fear it will be impossible for the payments to be made punctually to the men'.[22] In the meantime, Layard maintained that unless the relief committee in Carrick was allowed to sell meal at one or two pence lower than the market price purchases of meal would be 'of little use' given that 'the markets are so exorbitant in their demands'.[23]

Again, on 9 January 1847, Layard, in remarking that 'the lower orders are sinking fast from disease', articulated the 'absolute necessity which exists for the establishment of provision depots' in the barony of Carrigallen. Consequently, he urged the Board of Works to lose no time in bringing the matter before the 'proper authorities'.[24] Lardner's replacement, Captain Bull, soon experienced scenes that had driven his predecessor to leave the county:

> Every possible invention of imposition, forgery, and tampering with the check-clerks have brought this evil [fraud on the works] to such a pitch it is almost impossible to check it, and quite impossible to correct it without great assistance. I have none. Many persons of the Committees are the very persons implicated and the Committees are so divided among themselves, and their time taken up with violent personal altercations, that is impracticable to get through business or obtain any assistance from them.[25]

With distress continuing to persist increasing numbers sought employment on public works. On 20 February, Bull outlined the demand:

> At one committee application was made for upwards of 600 people to be received on the lists; and on my representing the total impracticability of such being done, I was told by one of the committee, 'that he should send the starving and dead bodies in carts to my house'. I consider it right to mention this, in order that the Board may see the difficulties and annoyances that the inspecting Officers are exposed to by the admission of improper persons upon committees.[26]

In similar fashion, Captain Layard complained that in the barony of Mohill great difficulty was faced in ascertaining 'improper parties' on the works. He also blamed some members of the Mohill committee 'for the injudicious and inconsiderate manner' in which names were brought forward for inclusion. However, unlike his colleague he was not afraid to name those he thought responsible and specifically singled out Father Evers and Father Fanning as the main culprits.[27]

The panic to obtain employment persisted despite the meagre remuneration on offer. For example, in Fenagh, where the public works employed around 500 people, it was remarked that the wages, typically 8–10$d$ per day, were not sufficient given that only one member of each family was permitted to work.[28] Similarly, in Cloone the number was almost 5,000 yet at least another 1,300 able-bodied labourers were unable to obtain work. In addition, Andrew Hogg commented that the wages available were 'by no means sufficient to preserve them and their families'.[29]

In total there were 203 works recommended in the county, amounting to an expenditure of £84,776. They were dispersed between each of the five baronies with forty-three in Carrigallen, thirty-five in Dromahaire, twenty-six in Leitrim, thirty-nine in Mohill and sixty in Rossclogher. Alongside road-building the other major source of relief work was land drainage. Unlike the former, the costs were made a charge on each electoral division concerned, rather than the larger baronial unit. This method was regarded as a way of encouraging landlords to provide relief employment whilst simultaneously ensuring lasting improvements on their estates. Although drainage accounted for only a fraction of the total of relief work in the county, it provided employment in the following areas: Eslin, Bunduff, Glencar, Lurganboy, Ballaghameelig, Shriff, Drumhierny and Drumcliff. Some four thousand acres along the rivers Rinn/ Blackwater on the Leitrim/Longford border were also drained.[30]

In rare examples of private initiatives, A. Pollen Esq., subscribed £100 to offer employment to the 'poor men and labourers' in the village of Carrigallen building a 'parochial school house'. Similar work was offered for carpenters, masons, sawyers and plasterers with the construction of a new cottage in Clooncoo by Viscount Clements.[31]

One of the main criticisms of the public works scheme was that it encouraged large gatherings of people, many of whom were suffering from disease and illness, and thereby facilitated the spread of disease and contagion. Consequently, many perished through contracting disease or from sheer fatigue and in February Captain Layard, writing from Mohill, related how the assistant engineer had reported the deaths of two men who had died from exhaustion having finished a day's work. However, the fatalities on the works were small in comparison to the government's favoured expedient for poverty – the recently-established workhouses.

## WORKHOUSES

### Manorhamilton

In Manorhamilton workhouse the effect of the second blight was highlighted by the admission of thirty applicants in the week ending 15 October 1846. However, in the coming weeks, and unlike in other unions, there was no huge influx and between 22 October and 31 December a total of 228 applicants were admitted and 143 rejected.[32] Consequently, the house did not come under the same level of stress as the other two workhouses in the county. Nevertheless, problems with the increased numbers had an impact on the running of the establishment. In November 1846 the master argued that the nursery was now too small for the expected number of admissions while with 'an appearance of the progression of fever' extra nurses had to be recruited to cope with those labouring under the malady.[33] Of course, the close proximity of so many people in the one building only acted as an incubator for various diseases. In reporting the deaths of three inmates in January, the medical officer stated that James Bradly had entered the house 'in the last stage of dysentery' while Ellen McNiff had been sent there 'speechless and in a dying state'.[34] Attempts to deal with the enhanced numbers were not aided by the fact that the pumps failed to function. On 19 November the master reported how they had been unable to procure water from them for three weeks necessitating the use of a horse to draw supplies from a local river. He insisted that, due to the increase of inmates, a regular supply of water was more important than ever.[35] However, more than one month later the situation had not been rectified with the consequence that children were unable to receive supper. The guardians reacted by immediately ordering the inclusion of an extra quarter of beef in the paupers' soup for dinner the following day.[346]

Perhaps aware of the consequences of allowing too many applicants to enter the house the guardians maintained a strict policy of relatively low admissions; while there were forty-two admissions recorded on 28 January, thirty on 18 March, forty-six on 6 May and forty on 27 May, the numbers were generally well below this. However, those rejected on 28 January (fifty-nine), 4 February (seventy-five) and 27 May (sixty) indicated a significant demand in the union for relief.[37]

The increase of distress in the latter part of 1846 was reflected in the relatively poor returns of the rate collectors. In October they remitted a total of £1/7/3; in November £18 and in December £40. Given that the average weekly expense was in excess of £41 (12 November, £41/7); (3 December £41/12/6); (24 December £41/2/3) such figures obviously created difficulties for the board.[38] Indeed, the clerk alleged that an effort was being made to prevent collection of the rate in the divisions of Drumkeerin and Inishmagrath 'by deterring persons from becoming sureties for the collector'. He pointed to the fact that the person recently appointed as a collector for Drumkeerin had not come forward with sureties.[39] Adding to the burden of expenses was the fact that an assistant matron and head nurse had to be appointed while, in an effort to create more space, galleries were erected at a cost of £147.[40]

The extent of contagious disease in the house was emphasised by the death of the medical officer, James Dundass, 'of fever contracted in the discharge of his duty'.[41] Dundass appears to have been a caring individual given that until his illness (which can be traced to the start of July) he named each individual who had died in the house. This was an extremely rare occurrence in workhouse minute books and it was not continued by his successor, Dr Davis.[42]

## Mohill

On 7 May 1846 the Mohill guardians received a communication from the poor law commissioners permitting them to store provisions belonging to relief committees.[43] On 14 May no board meeting was possible as the local committee held their meeting in the workhouse.[44] The minutes do not state whether or not any further meetings were held there but no board meetings occurred on 28 May and 4 June.[45] On both occasions only one guardian, John O'Brien, attended. This pattern became more marked in the weeks to follow with meetings adjourned on 25 June, 2 July, 9 July, 16 July, 23 July, 13 August, 3 September, 10 September and 24 September.[46] When they did take place they were attended by just enough members to ensure business was transacted; five on 18 June, four on 30 July, three on 6 August and five on 20 August. On 30 July four guardians had to deal with six weeks of business in time allocated for a standard weekly meeting.[47] So blatant was this disregard of the law that the poor law commissioners sent a letter to the board reminding members that they were legally obliged to hold meetings at least once in every week. In their defence they argued, with some justification, that their attendance at local relief committee meetings precluded their attendance at the workhouse. Less convincingly, they pointed to the necessity of their being at the local assizes and quarter sessions.[48]

By the end of August the first contract for supplying yellow Indian meal to the house was agreed with Alexander Dickson at £10/10 per ton.[49] In October the board received another bill from the Public Works Loan Commissioners for £65 due on a loan of £650.[50] With only £14 in their favour the rate collectors were issued with a threat to have all their monies paid to the union treasurer by 12 November.[51] However, the situation was so stark that the same treasurer was asked to advance a £500 loan over three months 'to meet the great liabilities of the union' until the rates were made available.[52] The guardians could not fail to have been aware of the increased expense consequent upon the inexorable rise in the number of inmates in the house. At the end of August there had been 226; by 17 October this had increased to 401 and at the end of November it had surpassed 500.[53] Thus, within three months, numbers in the house had doubled to a level not witnessed before.

With increased numbers came increased deaths. Prior to this period, workhouse fatalities had been confined to the old and very young and averaged a couple every month but on 22 October the master, in ordering various items, included, for the first time, 10½ yards of shrouding. By 3 December this had been increased to twenty-one yards with an additional order for eight coffins and in the succeeding weeks coffins were ordered on a regular basis.[54] The first week to witness significant mortality was that ending 5 December when ten deaths occurred with the same number dying three weeks later.[55] An indication of the condition of those entering the house can be inferred from the percentage of inmates in the hospital:

**Table 4.2: Numbers in Mohill Workhouse and Hospital**

| Week Ending | Admissions | Number in Workhouse | Number in Hospital | (%) |
|---|---|---|---|---|
| 5 December | 44 | 473 | 35 | 7.4 |
| 12 December | 26 | 452 | 41 | 9.0 |
| 19 December | 26 | 448 | 44 | 9.8 |

| 26 December | 25 | 465 | 48 | 10.3 |
| 2 January | 38 | 484 | 66 | 13.6 |
| 9 January | 26 | 486 | 63 | 12.7 |
| 16 January | 59 | 504 | 52 | 10.3 |
| 23 January | 128 | 590 | 61 | 10.3 |
| 30 January | 19 | 569 | 70 | 12.3 |
| 6 February | 7 | 529 | 199 | 37.6 |

Source: Leitrim County Library, Ballinamore, Mohill board of guardians' minute book, BG 122/A/4, pp.371, 377, 383, 389, 395, 396, 403, 408, 411, 415.

While significant numbers looked to the workhouse for succour others were disappointed. On 31 December just two applicants were rejected but on 21 January eighty-eight people were refused entry.[56] In the first week of January 1847 the master stated that there had been an 'unusual' number of sick 'in consequence of fever having set into the workhouse'.[57] January witnessed forty-five deaths but the level seems to have accelerated greatly in February and there were twenty-four deaths recorded in the first week of that month.[58] Unfortunately so all-consuming was the sickness in the house that no statistics were recorded so that the next available figures were for the week ending 6 March when twenty-nine deaths were recorded. On 11 March the master placed an order for seventy coffins and 150 yards of shrouding.[59] On that same day the guardians stated to the commissioners their anxiety to have a fever hospital erected adjacent to the workhouse. However, in the absence of sufficient union funds or public or private finance, they appealed 'for a government loan similar to that which had been agreed for the building of the workhouse.[60] In the week ending 13 March there were 104 admissions to the house and thirty-three deaths while the following week seventy-seven were admitted and twenty-seven died.[61] The enormous level of sickness can be gauged by the fact that out of a total of 626 workhouse inmates, 240 were in the hospital. Despite this, demand for entry remained unabated and on 25 March sixty-nine people were refused admission.[62] The huge numbers of sick placed renewed pressure on the administration and the commissioners instructed the barrack master at Longford to issue sheets, blankets, rugs, etc to the guardians on demand.[63]

Throughout the months of April, May and June fatalities remained at a consistently high level, as illustrated by the following table:

## Table 4.3: Deaths in Mohill Workhouse, April–June 1847

| Date | Number in Workhouse | Number in Hospital | Deaths | Deaths as % |
|------|---------------------|--------------------|--------|-------------|
| 3 April | 656 | – | 42 | 6.4 |
| 10 April | 648 | 241 | 30 | 4.6 |
| 17 April | 602 | 203 | 40 | 6.6 |
| 24 April | 557 | 175 | 44 | 7.9 |
| 1 May | 557 | 211 | 33 | 5.9 |
| 8 May | 576 | – | 39 | 6.8 |
| 15 May | 626 | – | 23 | 3.7 |
| 22 May | 667 | 200 | 31 | 4.6 |
| 29 May | 644 | 327 | 27 | 4.2 |
| 5 June | 614 | 280 | 26 | 4.2 |
| 12 June | 610 | 187 | 32 | 5.2 |
| 19 June | 618 | 144 | 34 | 5.5 |
| 26 June | 601 | 127 | 40 | 6.7 |
| **TOTAL** | | | **441** | |

*Source:* Leitrim County Library, Ballinamore, Mohill board of guardians' minute book, BG 22/A/5, pp.5, 6, 11, 15, 16, 21, 26, 31, 36, 41, 46, 51, 55.

Such were the level of deaths that, in mid April, the guardians resolved 'that the dead should for the present be interred without coffins'. They subsequently instructed Garret Beggs to make a bier for the interment of the dead, a move objected to by the commissioners. In reply the guardians bluntly stated that 'due to the awful state of the union it is more advisable to feed the living than to provide coffins for the dead'.[64]

The available figures strongly suggest that throughout these months the workhouse was little more than a hospital, with the staff attempting to deal with outbreaks of various diseases such as fever and dysentery. In fact, in the week ending 29 May more than half the total inmates of the establishment were situated in the hospital. Given such circumstances it is perhaps surprising that the level of deaths was not appreciably higher. Despite this such was the desperation of the local population that applications for admission were unrelenting. For example, on 3 April there were sixty admissions while the following week sixty-four applications were rejected.[65] In the first three weeks of May the number of admissions totalled 222.[66] At a board meeting on 27 May, attended by seven guardians, it was noted that 'the applicants for admission were so numerous they were not entered in the Application and Report Book but were upwards of 300 persons seeking for relief'. The following week the master and medical officer advised that any further admissions would result in 'considerable danger' to the present inmates and in that week only seven people gained admittance.[67] This policy of restricting entrants had the desired effect and although thirty-three deaths occurred in the first of July the number gradually declined so that by the end of August the figure was two. Significantly, the numbers hospitalised also fell and by the end of that same month there were forty-two inmates in that part of the institution, though this almost represented 10 per cent of the total of 465.[68] ·

The government departments responsible for erecting workhouses appeared oblivious to conditions in Ireland. Thus, on 26 March the guardians received a letter from the Public Works Loan Commissioners requiring payment of the fourth and fifth instalments – a total of £800 – of the original workhouse loan of £8,000.[69] In addition £775, originally demanded on 22 May 1845 was still outstanding. Given that the cost of 'necessaries and provisions' in the last week of March had been more than £240 there was absolutely no chance that this debt would be repaid.

Throughout the first seven months of 1847 the attendance of guardians remained consistently in the low single figures. Indeed, on most occasions the business of the union was conducted by a handful of men such as Lord Clements, John Lawder, John Reynolds, John Gannon, and Dominick and Francis Quinn. Evidently, this responsibility and workload took its toll and in the first week of August Gannon and Reynolds, together with Farrell Kernan, all resigned their positions.[70] As before, lack of attendance resulted in meetings being adjourned on 8 April, 29 April, 1 July and 22 July.[71] In such a scenario it is not surprising that much of the administration necessary for the effective maintenance of the workhouse was disregarded. For example, the medical officer's books were reported as being 'totally neglected' while the weekly relief list and provision check account were not made out.[72] Although such inattention may well have been the consequence of the workhouse being in the grip of a medical crisis, with staff concentrating more on their immediate duties than keeping records, disease amongst staff members undoubtedly exacerbated the situation. No hospital statistics were available for the week ending 8 May due to the fact that the doctor was unwell while the apothecary – Dr Soden – was ill with fever, a position compounded by the death of the latter the following week.[73] Throughout this period the clerk's books remained in an incomplete state and in the opinion of the board he had 'wilfully neglected' his duty. Hence on 13 May the guardians accepted the resignations both of the clerk and the medical officer, Dr Duke.[74]

## Carrick-on-Shannon

On 22 August a memorial from several contractors to the Carrick union was read to the board in which they stated their 'entire inability from want of funds' to continue supplying the union. The guardians subsequently used this as an opportunity to outline their 'critical position':

> That the present amount of uncollected rate (£2,000) appears to us to be generally due from persons quite unable to pay. Therefore little or no funds are to be expected from the collection of the residue of this rate. In relation to the rate now struck, the collection will be very partial – an amount totally inadequate to meet the exigencies under which we now labour both regarding debts to contractors, around £1,484, and arrears (large) of salaries to officers and debts due to former contractors, around £900.[75]

Thus, with at least £2,384 outstanding, and given the 'very distressed state of the union', the board asked the poor law commissioners to 'devise some means' to enable them to discharge their debts and avoid the 'lamentable alternative' of being forced to close the house. The reply of the commissioners was as predictable as it was disappointing. They urged the guardians to adopt measures which would 'effect the prompt collection of the outstanding arrears of rates' and, in spite of what the board had said, suggested the possibility of voting a larger rate than that determined upon. When they also enquired as to why a sum of £5/10 due to the Audit Fund had not been paid the guardians, stating their lack of resources, outlined the situation regarding rate collection in the district. They revealed that all efforts with collectors had 'proved ineffectual' and that there was 'no prospect' of a collection of the arrears by them. They therefore suggested that the commissioners dismiss them so that others 'more efficient' could be appointed. However, the reality of the situation was evident in their conclusion that 'in the present very distressed crisis we have reason to fear a very small portion of the arrears can possibly be now collected'.[76]

The mood of the board would not have been improved by a letter from the commissioners on 10 September in which they told members to anticipate 'a great increase in poverty and distress among the labouring population' due to the second successive failure of the potato crop.[77] Hence, at the next meeting Charles R. Peyton argued that 'as the calamity which has caused the destruction of the potato crop has in its ravages been uniform over the whole union', a standard increase of 7½ pence should be added to the rate struck earlier in the year. Despite an amendment supporting the notion of increasing the rate on each division in proportion to the number in the house Peyton's proposal was passed.[78] Nevertheless, the board unanimously agreed:

> That under the peculiar distressing circumstances which at present exist in this locality the great bulk of the population of which being now in a state bordering on utter destitution and consequently the almost certain prospect of our expenses being considerably increased, we have increased the rate by 7½ d in each electoral division but in the present state of this union we are firmly and decidedly of opinion it will be almost impracticable at present to collect and therefore our only alternative must be to close this workhouse. It is our most anxious desire to prevent the calamity of being obliged to resort to so very painful and disastrous an alternative at this so trying a period but we have every reason to believe it will be inevitable unless a loan of £5,000 can be obtained from the government as a charge on the present and future rates of the union.[79]

Members also revealed that on examining the tenders for the ensuing twelve months prices quoted 'exceed the present very exorbitant market prices by at least 50 per cent'. They claimed this was due to the fact that they already owed large amounts to their present contractors while new contractors did not expect to be paid in the immediate future.[80] As if to emphasise their predicament the board received a solicitor's letter demanding payment to R.W. Bournes of Summerhill who was owed almost £782 for the supply of potatoes.[81] Slight respite came with the news that the bread and coal contractors had agreed to provide supplies as long as they were paid on a weekly basis.[82] However, the situation was not helped by the fact that rate collectors were unable or unwilling to do their job. Thus two, James Reynolds and Mark McDermott, were dismissed while it emerged that another, Peter Conry, had left the country with £26 of rates he had collected.[83]

The real impact of the failure of the potato crop began to be felt in the workhouse from the last week of August when there were thirty-three people admitted. The following week this figure was twenty-eight while on 12 and 19 September it was thirty-three and thirty respectively. However, in the latter week a significant number – thirteen – was rejected and this reflected the fact that, for some, the workhouse was now the only place in which they thought they could survive. As the following table shows, numbers increased dramatically from the beginning of October:

**Table 4.4: Admissions to Carrick-on-Shannon Workhouse, September–October 1846**

| Date | Number Admitted | Number Rejected |
|------|----------------|----------------|
| 26 September | 51 | 3 |
| 3 October | 53 | 47 |
| 10 October | 63 | 26 |
| 17 October | 124 | 17 |
| 24 October | 70 | 37 |
| 31 October | 50 | 87 |
| **TOTAL** | **411** | **217** |

*Source:* Leitrim County Library, Ballinamore, Carrick-on-Shannon board of guardians' minute book, BG 52/A/3, pp.1521, 1529, 1535, 1543, 1551, 1558.

Probably in response to the concerns voiced earlier by the commissioners, the dietary of the house was altered so that the proportion of Indian meal was reduced. At the same time the use of potatoes in the diet was stopped. Hence, 'as soon as possible' adults were to receive 6 oz of Indian meal and 2 oz oatmeal for breakfast and 6 oz Indian meal and 3 oz oatmeal for dinner, four days each week. On the other days they received bread made from 6 oz Indian meal and 3 oz oatmeal while children received the same rations in smaller portions.[84] The determination of the board to further cut costs was reflected in their decision to discontinue supper to children above nine years, their breakfast and dinner instead being increased by a combined total of 1½ ounces. In addition, milk supplied to children below nine years was reduced from one half to one quarter for dinner and supper.[85]

On 24 October, the day on which seventy people were admitted to the house and thirty-seven rejected, the commissioners dealt the board a blow with the news that there was 'no prospect' of obtaining any financial assistance from the government. As usual, they repeated their mantra by urging the guardians to collect the arrears of rate and to make a new rate as soon as possible.[86] In the previous week the master of the house had informed the board that with only £7 available to purchase food there was barely enough Indian meal in the house for a further eight days.[87] Given the attitude both of the government and the commissioners the board sought desperate means to meet the emergency and they requested that the treasurer lend them £60 to purchase provisions for the following week. At the same time, they were very much aware of the difficult situation in which local businesses found themselves as a consequence of workhouse debts. Acknowledging this 'great hardship' they offered to pay contractors a rate of 6 per cent for the use of their money 'from the period at which they became entitled to payment under their contracts'. Significantly, this offer did not extend to those contractors who intended to 'put the union to any law costs'.[88] Nevertheless, in relation to the critical supply of Indian and oat meal, it was stipulated that contractors would not be paid for twelve months from the period of delivery. Not surprisingly, only one tender was received under such conditions and Lancelot Lawder agreed to supply thirty tons of oatmeal at £30 per ton.[89]

With the vastly increased numbers in the house in early November it was perhaps no surprise that disease should make its appearance. However, when the medical officer reported such as being 'prevalent' he blamed it on the diet then in use, especially that amongst the infants. The board was both surprised and angered by this statement given that the medical officer was 'responsible for giving all directions regarding diet'. They commented that 'he can't seek to throw blame on this board and his report is in very many respects unfounded, uncalled for and unjust'.[90] However the doctor's report concerning the spread of disease appeared to alert the guardians in relation to the overall condition of the house. In referring to 'the gross irregularity prevailing all through the establishment and the very filthy state in which several parts of the house are allowed to be in' they remarked on the 'absolute necessity' of an investigation by an assistant poor law commissioner.[91]

The immediate consequence of the medical report was yet another change to the dietary, but not for financial reasons. On 11 November adults were to receive from the following day, instead of 8 oz oatmeal stirabout, 6 oz rice boiled with one nagen of milk and 1 oz of molasses.[92] By 21 November the situation had obviously deteriorated and due to the 'frightful extent of disease and mortality' the board agreed to allow the medical officer a temporary assistant – Dr Sullivan. An assistant was also supplied to the Catholic chaplain, Fr Thomas Fitzgerald, due to the conditions in the house combined with his 'very arduous parochial duties'.[93] At the same time, the medical officer recommended an increase from 6 oz to 8 oz of rice in the adult diet.[94] In order to provide an extra twenty-four beds 'at small cost' the medical officer recommended the removal of brick walls in the male and female wards in the infirmary and the renovation of a shed in the west yard adjoining the hospital as an additional fever hospital.[95]

Having carried out his investigation, poor law inspector Caesar Otway commented on the 'none-efficiency' of the schoolmistress and porter, both of whom were asked to resign by the commissioners. While the porter did so the guardians expressed their support for the schoolmistress and requested that she be given another opportunity. However, she subsequently also resigned, along with the schoolmaster and matron.[96]

Given the condition of the house, the constant change to diet, the attempts to reduce costs with cheaper food and the influx of large numbers it was perhaps inevitable that deaths would soon follow. At a meeting on 12 December the guardians considered a letter from Rev. William Percy, a local Protestant clergyman, in which he referred to the 'improper interment of deceased paupers in the church yard of the local parish church'. However, the members took issue with him stating that:

> We have ascertained that in no instance were the coffins piled on each other as complained of but that in some instances as many as four coffins were put into one grave dug of a double size, but only two deep. Almost all the persons who died were small children.[97]

However, as a consequence of this communication the guardians directed the master to 'appropriate the north corner of the workhouse grounds for the burial of the dead'.[98] The situation deteriorated rapidly from the start of January and, as the following table illustrates, the workhouse authorities were overwhelmed with applications for relief:

**Table 4.5: Admissions to Carrick-on-Shannon Workhouse, January 1847**

| Date | Number Admitted | Number Rejected |
|---|---|---|
| 2 January | 26 | 254 |
| 9 January | 22 | 147 |
| 16 January | 36 | 216 |
| 23 January | 42 | 283 |
| 30 January | 1 | 214 |
| TOTAL | 127 | 1,114 |

*Source:* Leitrim County Library, Ballinamore, Carrick-on-Shannon board of guardians' minute book, BG 52/A/3, pp.1621, 1629, 1635, 1643, 1650.

At a board meeting on 2 January of the 254 rejected 227 were not even brought before the guardians due to lack of space in the house.[99] 'Want of accommodation' was also used to justify the rejection of hundreds of applicants in the weeks that followed as, by the beginning of February, (the date from which statistics are first available) the number in the workhouse reached 829.[100] Evidence that such action was not taken lightly by the guardians was reflected in their comments. For example on 30 January, when 254 applicants were rejected, they regretted how 'vast numbers of applicants labouring under destitution and disease in its most aggravated form are obliged to be rejected for want of room'. Similarly, on 13 February they expressed their 'deepest regret' at being 'obliged' to refuse admission to the numerous applicants.[101] As the following table reveals, numbers of sick had more than doubled within two months:

**Table 4.6: Numbers in Carrick-on-Shannon Workhouse, January–March 1847**

| Week Ending | Total Number in Workhouse | Number in Hospital/ in Fever | Total of Sick Number | % |
|---|---|---|---|---|
| 30 January | 829 | 170/53 | 223 | 26.9 |
| 6 February | 817 | 165/50 | 215 | 26.3 |
| 13 February | 805 | 171/69 | 240 | 29.8 |
| 20 February | 806 | 179/121 | 300 | 37.2 |
| 27 February | 798 | 179/169 | 348 | 43.6 |

| | | | | |
|---|---|---|---|---|
| 6 March | 811 | 220/164 | 384 | 47.3 |
| 13 March | 797 | 174/228 | 402 | 50.3 |
| 20 March | 771 | 180/235 | 415 | 53.8 |
| 27 March | 776 | 178/237 | 415 | 53.5 |

*Source:* Leitrim County Library, Ballinamore, Carrick-on-Shannon board of guardians' minute book, BG 52/A/3 and BG 52/A/4.

With the numbers of sick almost doubling within two months it was no surprise that mortality continued apace and, as the following table illustrates, there were more than 500 deaths in the four-month period:

**Table 4.7: Deaths in Carrick-on-Shannon Workhouse, 30 January–22 May 1847**

| Week Ending | Deaths |
|---|---|
| 30 January | 15 |
| 6 February | 25 |
| 13 February | 21 |
| 20 February | 22 |
| 27 February | 23 |
| 6 March | 27 |
| 13 March | – |
| 20 March | 38 |
| 27 March | 11 |
| 3 April | 50 |
| 10 April | 52 |
| 17 April | 53 |
| 24 April | 67 |
| 1 May | 56 |
| 15 May | 43 |
| 22 May | 25 |
| **TOTAL** | **528** |

*Source:* Leitrim County Library, Ballinamore, Carrick-on-Shannon board of guardians' minute book, BG 52/A/3 and BG 52/A/4.

The extent of the ravages caused by death and disease in the workhouse can, ironically, be traced through the gradual decrease in the number of books being maintained by various officers. On 27 February the porter, master and schoolmistress were all reported as being ill in fever with the latter dying the following week.[102] On 27 March the death of the master, Mr Bell, also occurred while the doctor had been labouring under a 'violent attack' of dysentery accompanied by fever.[103] At a meeting on 27 March the clerk noted that an increasing amount of work was falling to him due to the 'incompetency' of Mr Forde, the new temporary master who was unable or unwilling 'to make a single entry in any of the books'.[104] This impacted on the returns for the week ending 3 April when the clerk made the following note: 'I regret not being able to complete this return none of the books from which the particulars are extracted having been kept for some time back, the parties in charge being in fever.'[105]

Thus, for the weeks ending 10 April–12 June the number of paupers admitted and discharged was not kept while only occasional references were made to those who were in the hospital, suffering fever, or who had died. While of course this is frustrating for the historian of the period it reflects the extent to which the workhouse was decimated by disease. With many officers ill and unable to fulfil their duties it was almost inevitable that conditions within the establishment would deteriorate, thereby further endangering the lives of all concerned. For example, on 13 February the guardians received a report from the medical officer which stated that several departments of the house, but especially the dormitories, 'have been allowed to be in a very disgraceful and filthy state'. They called the attention of the poor law commissioners to 'this most unpardonable neglect on behalf of the workhouse officers'.[106] The following week it emerged that provisions belonging to the house had been sold by paupers for money and this caused outrage amongst the board members:

> For want of necessary discipline and attention of the officers of the house … that the house continues in a most disgraceful and unsatisfactory state and that we entertain little or no hope of an amendment with the present officers … and we therefore request that the commissioners will at once cause such necessary measures to be adopted as may ensure to us efficient officers for the establishment.[107]

The severe weather conditions exacerbated conditions for inmates. On 9 and 10 February the only food available was bread as frost and snow in the area had resulted in supplies of fuel being disrupted. Indeed, the board minutes of 13 February, made reference to the 'frozen state of the river'.[108] On 27 February, with the medical officer reporting fever 'rapidly increasing with dysentery', the guardians held their weekly meeting in the court house in Carrick, where they were to convene 'until notice to the contrary'.[109] At the same time the finance committee was forced to rent an apartment in town from 23 March to 22 June in order to conduct business in safety.[110] At their meeting the guardians appointed Biddy Gibbons, a pauper inmate and until now a hospital nurse, as the new workhouse matron. However, in early April, after an examination of the board's complaints, both Gibbons and the schoolmaster resigned, such action having been demanded by the poor law commissioners.[111]

On 10 April the guardians lamented the 'deplorable state of inmates' and pointed to the fact that there were not a sufficient number of paupers in the house 'in a fit state' to discharge various duties, such as ward women, laundry women, nurses, etc. Doctor Munns made the case for the employment of four women as temporary nurses and this was acceded to by the board at a wage of 1/3 per day with normal rations. The sense of desperation in this move was exemplified by the determination that 'any wards women who decline or neglect their duty will be dismissed from the house'.[112] From the middle of April a slow improvement in the management and conditions of the workhouse began to be achieved. A new master and matron – Mr and Mrs Daly – were appointed[113] while the guardians, having read the recommendations of the assistant commissioner and their own medical officer, decided to refuse all admissions until the house was in 'a fit state to admit without endangering human life'.[114] They also established a committee of five to ensure the weekly purchase of goods and provide 'proper persons to bury the dead and have cess pools cleared'.[115] All old clothes and bedding was burned while ten men were employed to clean and whitewash the house with lime. In addition, local parish priest, Rev. Dr Dawson, decided to suspend celebration of Mass in the house for a fortnight.[116]

With the workhouse filled to capacity by early 1847, the financial position of the union became increasingly precarious. As more than 50 per cent of inmates were recorded as being either in the hospital or in fever, the medical costs of the establishment witnessed a huge increase. This was reflected in the fact that between the end of October 1846 and the middle of January 1847 the average cost of a pauper more than doubled from 1/1 to 2/4.[117] Thus, at a board meeting on 30 January, the members decided to approach their treasurer once again in order to seek a loan of £1,000 and offered their personal security for the payment of interest until the loan was repaid.[118] This proposition was refused but on 27 March the board received a payment of £95 from the poor law commissioners and for the next three months they continued to receive this amount.[119] However, board members realised such short-term finance was not the solution to their problems and on 3 April they resolved to apply to the bank for a loan of £1,500 over five years.[120] This was deemed essential due to the 'lamentable and destructive consequences which our contractors have been subjected to as a result of large sums due by the board sometimes stretching back two years'.[121] They also informed the commissioners that they needed to obtain a loan from government which, if provided, would 'save contractors from immediate ruin'. In the event of the government agreeing they stated they would use 'all exertions' to recover arrears of rates.[122] As before, the commissioners' reply was swift and emphatic. Whilst expressing 'regret' at the 'difficult position' of local contractors, they advised the board that there was 'no prospect' of a government loan. In response, the guardians commented that in the absence of a loan, and the difficulty of collecting poor rates, 'we find all our efforts paralyzed to remedy this evil' and made reference to 'the impossibility of longer continuing to discharge our duties as guardians'.[123]

While weekly disbursements from the commissioners helped their cause this money was loaned on the express understanding that it would eventually be repaid from local rates, was for current expenditure only, and was not to be used to meet any former expenses. Indeed, as part of the agreement, the guardians had to furnish the commissioners with a detailed statement of their weekly expenditure.[124] The significance of such short-term advances was emphasised when the union treasurer once again refused to sanction a loan of £1,500.[125] However, in the week of 24 April it emerged that the weekly expenditure of the house had exceeded the £95 by almost £15 and the commissioners were asked to add this extra amount on to the following week's advance, a request that was ignored.[126] Nevertheless, the importance of the weekly payments was that they enabled the guardians to obtain provisions given that contractors were prepared to deliver goods provided they received payment each week.[127]

As before, the board attempted to make savings in the house, but unlike on previous occasions the cuts imposed impacted on the officers and not the inmates. Thus, when the clerk, M. Rutherford, resigned on 22 May his replacement, John Clarke, was paid an annual salary of £40 as opposed to his predecessor's wage of £60.[128] Further, the board stipulated that if any workhouse officers applied for an increase of salary 'it will be decreed by the board as a resignation of that situation'. The almost total reliance of the board on the commissioners' weekly loans was evident in the panic engendered as a consequence of such monies not being lodged in the weeks of 29 May and 5 June. On the latter date members resolved:

> That our clerk do immediately write to the Commissioners the awful state our workhouse is likely to be thrown into in consequence of not having received funds from them to enable them to enable us to pay the expenses incurred for the past week and there is every reason to believe that no provisions will be supplied us unless immediate payment be made for the supplies of the former week.[129]

However, from 12 June the commissioners recommenced their weekly disbursement of £95.[130]

Due to the lack of various workhouse administration books from 10 April to 19 June it is difficult to estimate the numbers applying and being accepted or rejected. The last complete figures, showing admissions, discharges and deaths, were for the week ending 27 March when 776 paupers were in the house. The next available complete figures were for the week ending 19 June when the total was then recorded as 536.[131] Given the huge demand for entrance to the house it seemed that the guardians, in the face of huge debts and struggling to meet even agreed weekly expenses, opted to essentially run the workhouse down. Thus, while there were forty-four admissions on 3 July, this was the last of such, and between 10 July and 25 September a total of twenty-two people were admitted.[132] In the week ending 3 July there were 570 in the house but by the last week of September this had fallen to 155, well below capacity. On 3 July the board had noted that no money had been received for that week and stated that unless it was forthcoming no provisions could be sent to the house.[133] However, the lack of money was not an oversight by the commissioners and on 10 July it was revealed that the government had ordered them to terminate their weekly advances to the union. The shocked board informed the commissioners that if this policy was maintained 'the instant results would be the instant discharge of all the pauper inmates and the closing up of the workhouse'. Given the 'utter impossibility' of collecting rates to the amount required merely to feed the inmates the guardians also claimed that another 'inevitable result' would be to leave the paupers without food.[134] They revealed that having advertised for tenders all but three had 'distinctly expressed' that their supplies would be predicated on weekly payment and, until now, this had been made possible by the weekly loan of £95. The action of the government totally deflated the board and they effectively gave up:

> That under all these circumstances the Guardians have to express their profound regret that it is no longer in their power to conduct the affairs of the union with any prospect of comfort to the paupers or satisfaction to the public and they would therefore respectfully submit for the consideration of the Commissioners the propriety of appointing paid guardians for the Carrick-on-Shannon Union.[135]

They added their hope that the commissioners would adopt 'immediate measures' to prevent the 'lamentable consequences of a want of food for paupers which three days will bring about'.[136] Thus, in a desperate move it was decided to stop all but a few admissions to the house. This was never actually stated as a policy but the figures outlined above support this contention. At the same time, they pursued any avenue which would lead to a reduction of the numbers already there. For example, when the master was ordered to select paupers to clear out the sewers and cess pools he was told that if any declined they were to be discharged from the house.[137]

In the meantime, the workhouse struggled on from week to week and with the matron ill, the schoolmistress was appointed to her position. However, due to 'an insufficient number of women to perform the duties of the house', the new matron was authorised to hire four females at wages of not more than 6*d* per day with paupers' rations.[138] Given the pressure on food supplies those apprehended in attempting to misappropriate stocks were severely dealt with. For example, Michael Cullen was found to have stolen rice and bread out of the store and his punishment was 'to be "whipt" twice by the schoolmaster in the presence of the clerk and to be afterwards distinguished from the rest of the paupers by putting on him a paper cap with the word "thief" written in ink'.[139]

Not only paupers were misbehaving and on 31 July it was reported that the books of the master 'still remain in a state of the greatest disarrangement' while the schoolmaster was 'very unsatisfactorily tendering an account of the provisions consumed in the house'.[140] It was also revealed that the latter gentleman had distributed passes to female paupers 'to go to town

… and shamefully return to the workhouse in a state of intoxication'.[141] Given such reports it came as no surprise when the guardians suspended the schoolmaster and asked the commissioners to immediately dismiss both the master and matron. The following week they left of their own volition to be replaced by Mr and Mrs Kelly.[142]

## GOVERNMENT-AIDED RELIEF COMMITTEES

In the aftermath of the latest crop failure those local relief committees which had been established in March and April 1846 were now forced to continue their endeavours. The Mohill committee, in estimating that over 6000 families were totally reliant on the potato, wrote to the Lord Lieutenant stating that unless assistance was afforded to the area without delay, the result would be 'disastrous in the extreme'. In the meantime, the independent Mohill Benevolent Relief Society had been established and was distributing soup at one penny per quart or gratuitously from a sixty-gallon boiler provided by government to between 200 and 300 people daily. A small-scale bakery had also been established to provide white and brown bread with the soup.

In Cloone, the local rector, Andrew Hogg, reported that thousands were on the point of starvation and surmised that the Mohill committee would be unable to meet the increasing demands of those in distress. Thus, together with his wife, he oversaw the work of the Cloone Soup Shop which by January 1847 was distributing 1,500 quarts of soup gratuitously to 400 people on a weekly basis. Nevertheless, he anticipated that at least 4,000 gallons would have to be distributed 'to prevent thousands perishing of starvation'. At the same time the Carrick soup kitchen provided rations to about 2,500 people while local man, Coote Mulloy, had established a rice shop in the town believing that this was the only way of preventing deaths from diarrhoea in the area.[143]

In Fenagh up to 400 were fed on a daily basis and similar efforts were evident in Glencar, Drumkeerin, Carrigallen, Manorhamilton, Ballinamore, Annaduff, Jamestown, Leitrim village, Dromod, Derrycarne, Lavagh and Drumsna.[144] Increasing hardship, rising prices and pressure on workhouses, meant that the work of such relief committees became even more important than before. However, much as they attempted to offer some respite, they were limited by the tight parameters enforced by the Relief Commissioners. Loftus Tottenham, writing from Glenfarne Hall, Manorhamilton, stated that north Leitrim was in a 'lamentable state' and the following extract, from one of many letters written by him, offers an insight into the feelings of someone genuinely concerned for the welfare of those around him, but constantly constricted by bureaucracy and dogmatic adherence to principle:

> I beg to bring again under your notice, the necessity of a depot of Indian meal and oatmeal at Manorhamilton. The state of the people here cannot be conceived – they will be absolutely starving before two weeks. Little or no corn is grown in these mountain districts and the potatoes are totally diseased. The Government stores at Sligo are too distant and the supply there dwindled to a mere nothing this week. With difficulty, two tons of Indian meal were given to our committee, but the moment it was sold, the shopkeepers in the town instantly raised oatmeal from 20s to 24s per cwt – hundreds had to go home without getting any. The whole district around Manorhamilton, for seven or eight miles, is dependent on imported food, and surely when plenty of storage room can be had in the town, the people will not be forced eighteen or twenty miles to Sligo to buy two or three stone of meal or left dependent on a few huxters who charge what they please and raise the price to an exorbitant height the moment the market is left dependent on them alone. Surely it is high time for Government to step in now.[145]

The Commissioners' reply, in which they stated that depots could only be established in areas 'where peculiar circumstances render them indispensable' gives an idea of the opinions which prevailed in the government at that time and the fact that laissez-faire doctrine was to prevail beyond the needs of a starving population:

> The certain consequence of depots is to check trading enterprise and the public welfare so that a permanent evil would be inflicted in relieving a temporary inconvenience which in such a town as Manorhamilton requires only that persons of local influence should unite in exerting to have additional supplies of food brought to the market. It is not intended to interfere with trade prices by Commissariat sales.[146]

Similar replies were received by other committees requesting the establishment of depots. In Annaduff and Kiltoghert it was reported that prices were so dear in the immediate vicinity that, even allowing for transport costs, provisions were cheaper in Longford. As the following letter from Father Henry O'Brien of Killegar illustrates, many businessmen realised that buyers were at their mercy:

> The supply from Belturbet for which I contracted is exhausted to less than fifteen tons and Mr Dixon has both broken his contract with me, and supplied me with a very bad quality on one or two occasions. In fact he feels that we are in his power and it would be most important to keep him in order by having the command of the stores at Longford. It is much more convenient, however, to get wheat and meal from him as he is within a day's journey from Carrigallen, so that the men can return at night whereas Longford is two or even three days' journey in the present state of the roads, and the carts have to pass through a very bad country.[147]

Local correspondents and government employees emphasised the fact that a local depot for Leitrim would greatly facilitate the purchase and distribution of food. Without such, areas such as Dromod, Drumsna and Killegar, which were all a great distance from any ports, were unable to buy large quantities of corn and meal. Indeed Arthur Birchill, writing from Blackrock House, Drumshanbo, stated that due to such difficulties 'it has sometimes occurred that many persons who have had money could not get food to buy'.[148] After much persuasion, with even their own inspecting officer, Captain Legard, imploring the need for a depot, the commissioners eventually opened a store in Carrick in March 1847, with oatmeal being sold at 3s per stone.

In addition, bureaucratic mishaps and delays caused panic in some quarters. For example, when John Dickson applied for a government contribution of £73 in aid of the Rossinver relief committee he was informed that this had been 'necessarily delayed until a certificate shall have been received'. This in spite of the fact that such had been 'already forwarded, signed by the chairman and secretary'. Similarly, George Beresford sought a reply to his previous communication enclosing a list of subscriptions made to the Fenagh relief committee. His irritation was heightened by the fact that committees in Ballinamore and elsewhere had received such replies.[149]

In the midst of such governmental procrastination some decided to develop alternative methods of supplying their needs. It is difficult to ascertain whether or not Drumsna was one of the earliest areas to be affected by blight or whether Rev. George Shaw was simply very much aware of the need for outside assistance. At any rate Shaw was one of the first clergymen in the county to demonstrate an awareness of the effects of the blight and his name recurs consistently in correspondence to a variety of agencies from 1846 onwards. For example, on 24 March he had informed F.R. Bertolacci of the Irish Reproductive Loan Fund of the 'very urgent distress' in the area and the likelihood of it increasing. Hence he enquired as to the possibility of obtaining money either as a grant or loan from the fund in order to supply cheaper food or employment.[150]

On 30 November Shaw was the first individual in the county to make an application to the Irish Relief Association. He informed them that the state of the district was 'most miserable' consequent upon the failure both of the potato and oats crop. Relief committees had been established in the nearby towns of Carrick and Mohill but they were too far from Drumsna and therefore a committee had been formed for that district. Although the government works had afforded employment to around 500 people, the floods on the Shannon had forced them to be halted, leaving all men idle. Up until this date Shaw had offered relief by selling Indian meal at a 'trifling loss' but he was anxious to extend his efforts by opening a soup kitchen at Annaduff Glebe 'which is a central location in the midst of a poor population'. This initial request proved more successful than that to Bertolacci and Shaw, along with his curate Francis Kane, was granted £10 together with a boiler.[151]

Meanwhile, another name which would become synonymous with the relief effort was Rev. Andrew Hogg of Cloone and a few days after Shaw's application he also informed the Irish Relief Association that the poverty in his locality was 'beyond all description' with sickness on the increase. However, he maintained that the poor could be relieved at a cost of one penny per day per person 'by judicious management of funds'.[152] Together with some of the local gentry, he had established the Cloone Relief Association, independent of the local relief committees which were under the auspices of the government. By October they had raised £228 and were endeavouring to supply the poor of Cloone and the surrounding district.[153] For their part, the Manorhamilton committee having raised £300 sent an agent to Liverpool to purchase 100 tons of Indian meal and contracted for further supplies from the Mediterranean.

Another method of raising money was that attempted by the Rev. Robert King of Kilmore. He addressed letters to his 'esteemed and respected brethren' in England through the columns of newspapers and related how he was attempting to combat the 'agonising pangs of hunger' of his 'fellow-creatures' which had been sharpened by the 'afflicting clamorous wails of their children'. To this end, he appealed for 'kind interference and assistance towards furnishing aid for the relief of such famishing fellow-creatures'.[154]

With levels of suffering increasing on a daily basis, relief committees themselves underwent important changes. Whereas, before, there were perhaps two or three in each barony, these were sub-divided in the hope that they would be able to refine their operations and devote more energy to the needs of particular areas or parishes. Thus, by the end of 1846 there were a total of eighteen committees in the following localities (see Map Six):

**Table 4.8: Government-Aided Relief Committees in County Leitrim, December 1846**

| Barony | Location |
|---|---|
| Carrigallen | Ballinamore |
| | Carrigallen |
| | Oughteragh |
| Dromahaire | Dromahaire |
| | Drumkeerin |
| | Glenfarne |
| | Killargue |
| | Manorhamilton |
| Leitrim | Carrick-on-Shannon |
| | Drumshanbo |
| | Fenagh |
| Mohill | Aughavas |
| | Cloone |
| | Kilmore |
| Rossclogher | Glenade |
| | Glencar |
| | Kinlough |
| | Lurganboy |

*Source*: National Archives, Dublin, Abstracted from Relief Commission Papers.

By this stage hunger had been joined by its natural concomitant – disease. Edward Richards reported how in the Drumkeerin area there were 'numerous cases' of English cholera and fever which had resulted in many deaths. Seven hundred heads of families were entirely dependent on the public works for their support but he described this as a 'precarious employment' which was 'quite insufficient to maintain a large family'.[155] Meanwhile, in Mohill dysentery was described as being 'very prevalent' whereas fever was 'not so great an extent as formerly'. Continuing his report Lord Clements made the observation that there were no private works going on due to the lack of resident landlords. He also echoed the sentiments of government engineers when maintaining that as 'no proper test' existed for the public works 'small farmers have too often obtained employment to the exclusion of their more needy neighbours'. In an effort to aid the latter he, together with Arthur Hyde and John Veevers, had decided to establish a fund to feed the poor and the aged. He stated that a house had been hired for establishing a soup kitchen but as yet no boiler had been set up. However, in a rare move the Irish Relief Association refused to aid Clements citing 'more urgent cases' and, significantly, the lack of 'sufficient local exertions'.[156]

As 1846 moved into 1847 the grim reports of hunger and disease throughout the county gave way to horrifying details of deaths by starvation. The following report from Pat Browne, a poor law guardian from Aughrim, in the Carrick union, on 22 February 1847, was to become all too familiar in the months ahead:

> The deaths from actual starvation during the last week were sixteen. The previous week nearly the same number and three unfortunate creatures were found in the fields dead, not having the strength to make their miserable dwellings. The corpses are in many instances uninterred for some days until they become putrid for want of means to purchase coffins. In some instances the unfortunate people actually tramp on the dead to create compassion from the charitable and humane. They go about collecting money to bury the dead but in fact the small sums they are able to procure are expended in purchasing food for the surviving starving family. The corpse is in many instances enclosed in straw, tied round with hay ropes, and in this manner interred.[157]

The reality of the situation appeared to cause unease even amongst some government employees. For example, on 7 February Mr Prendergast, Inspector of Drainage in Carrigallen, described conditions in the town as being 'such as no newspaper stories can exaggerate'. He gave some examples of distress therein:

> Famine actually prevails and the deaths are frightfully numerous from want and disease caused by insufficient food and clothing. Some poor women were in this town before daylight last market day to conceal their bedding and a few articles of furniture that were to be sold for a few days' food. A man was in the town carrying a dead child on his back, himself half stupefied by want, and wondering in and out of doorways without asking aid...Pale sickly faces surround me when I am in the fields; and I assure you the country presents a picture like the storied famines of old.[158]

One week later, inspecting officer, Godby, reported that thirty deaths had occurred during the previous week in the Mohill workhouse while there had been forty-three fatalities in the vicinity of Dromod within five weeks. However, his account included a description of a particularly heart-rending scene in which two carts of orphan children, 'whose parents died from starvation, I suppose' were sent to the workhouse but were refused entry due to the fever prevailing inside. Revealing that a man had been found dead in the snow outside Mohill, he argued that such occurrences 'prove the necessity for the establishment of a provision depot at this town'.[159]

An important journey through the county was undertaken by two members of the Society of Friends (Quakers), Joseph Crosfield and William Forster. On 6 December they visited Carrick-on-Shannon and witnessed the following 'most painful and heart-rending' scenes as people waited outside the workhouse in the hope of being admitted:

> ...poor wretches in the last stage of famine, imploring to be received into the house; women who had six or seven children begging that even two or three of them might be taken in, as their husbands were earning 8d per day; which, at the present high prices of provisions, was totally inadequate to feed them. Some of these children were worn to skeletons, their features sharpened with hunger and their limbs wasted almost to the bone. From a number of painful cases,

the following may be selected. A widow with two children who for a week had subsisted on one meal of cabbage each day; these were admitted into the poor-house, but in so reduced a state, that a guardian observed to the master of the house that the youngest child would trouble them but a very short time. Another woman with two children, and near her confinement again, whose husband had left her a month before to seek for work, stated that they had lived for the whole of this week upon two quarts of meal and two heads of cabbage.[160]

Forster further remarked that 'the children exhibit the effects of famine in a remarkable degree, their faces looking wan and haggard with hunger and seeming like old men and women'.[161] These first-hand accounts were sent to the recently-established London Relief Committee of the Society of Friends and no doubt played a significant part in ensuring that the lives of thousands in Leitrim were saved by the efforts of this organisation.

# Chapter 5

# NOTHING BUT WATERCRESSES AND CABBAGE

TO THE

# GENTRY,

## CLERGY, AND FREEHOLDERS

OF THE

### COUNTY OF

# LEITRIM.

GENTLEMEN,

I THANK you very much, for the confidence which you have hitherto reposed in me as your Representative in Parliament; and it is with the deepest regret that I now inform you, that I must decline to offer myself to you again as a Candidate for a repetition of that important trust.

As I still entertain the same lively interest for your welfare, and sincerely deplore the awful and disastrous calamity which we are suffering, let me hope that, though no longer your Representative in the Imperial Legislature, I shall still continue to enjoy that confidence and good will which I have ever experienced at your hands, and for which I feel truly grateful.

Let us, at the same time, unite in renewed efforts for the Salvation of our County; by earnest endeavours to restore Society to a state of confidence and kindly feeling, and, by the encouragement of habits of industry and regularity, endeavour, under the bounty of Divine Providence, to obtain those rewards, and that plenty and prosperity, which may reasonably be expected from fair dealing and honest industry.

*Believe me to be,*

*Gentlemen,*

*Your obedient, humble Servant,*

## CLEMENTS.

London, July 6th, 1847.

Poster on behalf of Lord Clements declining the opportunity to run as a candidate in the 1847 Election. Courtesy of Seamus Geraghty Collection, St George's Heritage Centre, Carrick-on-Shannon, County Leitrim.

I N FEBRUARY 1847 Lionel Gisborne, one of the government's conducting engineers for the county, remarked that, due to increased levels of destitution, 'the calls on private charity' were 'very great'. In his opinion:

> The establishment of a few soup kitchens, by private individuals, tends greatly to support the portion of the population unable to work, and having no means of support; but it is a system which cannot be made pay on a small scale, and must consequently be to a limited extent.[1]

While Gisborne acknowledged the role of private relief he certainly underestimated its extent (see Map Seven). Two organisations which facilitated the expansion of a network of private relief funds were the Irish Relief Association and the Society of Friends. The observations in letters and application forms from applicants illustrated the extent of the catastrophe at parish and townland level to a degree not available in other official correspondence. A constant theme in such was the lack of resident gentry and the subsequent difficulties in establishing funds large enough to meet the crisis. For example, George Shaw, the first applicant from the county to apply to the Quakers, informed them that there were 'very few' gentry or local proprietors to give assistance as the latter were 'encumbered' and most of them involved in law'. Consequently 'only about £10' had been received from absentee landlords. In noting the prevalence of 'much dropsy and dysentery', but little fever, he reiterated that 'any grant of money would be most acceptable as we almost fear to encounter the expense of the soup kitchen with our limited means'. In his district of Drumsna, as elsewhere, food prices had doubled and in an effort to mitigate the rising costs he had been selling wheatmeal at cost price and intended to sell soup at one penny per quart. However, given his estimate of 1,600 labourers without employment and a further 2,000 people incapable of labour and 'suffering want of food' the initial grant of £10 per month from the Quakers was more symbolic than utilitarian but indicative of the funding to be supplied to the county over the next four years.[2]

Significantly, the Lord Lieutenant, Lord Bessborough, was the largest absentee proprietor in the parish of Fenagh and, in the first week of 1847 he, along with other absentees, had still not made a contribution to local relief. Consequently, even though an investigation had been made into the circumstances of each family, relief efforts were on hold 'from a want of means'. Thus, in an application to the Quakers, John Lawder and parish priest Father Francis Reynolds, indicated their intention to immediately set up a boiler in the parish but lamented that lack of funds would not allow for free distribution of rations 'even were it thought advisable'. In support of their request they related the events at a recent coroner's inquest where a verdict was reached that a man had died of dysentery caused by 'bad and insufficient food'. It emerged that the deceased, together with his family of six, had lived for three days on two sixpenny loaves weighing 2½ pounds. Numerous similar cases abounded: another inquest revealed that a man had died after eating nothing but cabbage for three weeks; six persons had been found trying to survive on a total of two stones of meal for ten days, while some families were attempting to survive on 'nothing but watercresses and cabbage'.[3] In another case it transpired that a family had sold the door of their cabin in order to procure daily food.[4]

Unlike in Fenagh, it was reported that the absentee landlords of Cloone had made interest-free loans available to the Cloone Relief Association in order to permit the purchase of provisions to be sold at cost price to the poor. This initiative was timely given Rev. Andrew Hogg's estimate that relief totalling 250 gallons each day would soon be required. Until now the twice weekly distribution of 224 gallons had sufficed, being sold at 1d per quart and some given out free. Hogg's remarks gave an indication of the rapid deterioration of the district and the need for urgent and immediate aid.[5]

In such a scenario, concerned individuals were forced to focus on their own immediate neighbourhoods and from January 1847 small-scale private relief efforts proliferated throughout the county. For example, Rev. James LaTouche who applied to the Irish Relief Association for aid to the poor in the vicinity of the villages of Leitrim and Battlebridge revealed that a soup kitchen had been opened in Leitrim with soup sold at a penny a quart. However, the boiler only had a capacity of fourteen gallons and a new one was deemed essential to meet increased demand. He also added that any local farmers who owned corn were making meal and 'selling it in the market at high prices'.[6]

Penelope Johnston claimed that three-quarters of the population of Kinlough was in need of public relief and so she had established a soup shop by which means she was able to distribute ten gallons each day. Some of the food was given out freely and some at 1*d* per quart. The Quakers informed her that if she was able to raise more subscriptions and increase the daily distribution to between seventy and one-hundred gallons per day they would support her with a new boiler and £20 cash. The problem for Johnston, as with others attempting to stem the tide, was the fact that, as she put it herself, 'many persons of large property do not reside here'.[7]

While 2,300 able-bodied labourers in the Mohill union were engaged in public works, 'vast numbers' incapable of labour were in serious want of food. However, the fact that they possessed land, and were not destitute in the eyes of the law, meant they were not permitted to enter the workhouse. As with other areas, the proprietors in the union were absentees and although money had initially been subscribed in the months of August/September 1846, nothing had been forthcoming since then.[8] Thus, on 13 January 1847 Rev. Arthur Hyde established a privately-funded soup shop by which tickets were sold to individuals who then distributed them to those in need. By this means, forty gallons of soup, at a penny per quart, together with bread, were distributed on a daily basis. By the end of the month Lord Clements had initiated a similar project with a large boiler capable of holding one hundred gallons.[9]

The observations of Hyde and Clements highlighted specific problems in an area which had suffered regular food shortages in the past thirty years:

> This district is so poor, the holdings so small and the land so much impoverished by frequent croppings without manure and the pernicious practice of burning the land that there has not been a remunerative harvest for several years. It is difficult to draw a line between the farmers and the labourers – there are holdings of four to five acres who have improved their mode of cultivation, being beyond want, but there are other instances of less industrious men who hold thrice the quantity of land who are on the verge of starvation ... All will however sooner prevail than give up their land for the purpose of going into the Poor House.[10]

In Carrick-on-Shannon, where the public works employed only half those in need of such, absentee proprietors had contributed £40 in the summer of 1846 but had made no effort since then. Local private subscriptions totalled £104 in January and included £30 from the owner of the town,

Charles Manners St George. By these means oat meal had been purchased for sale at cost price while a soup kitchen was in the process of being established.[11]

In more rural areas the difficulty was one of being able to raise any sufficient funds. Thus, Archdeacon Strean of Elphin revealed that he had been frustrated in his attempts and had received no subscriptions except from 'a few friends in England'. Consequently, his area did not even boast the existence of a relief committee 'except for the purpose of recommending labourers for the public works'. In addition, he was unable to obtain a site for a boiler and was restricted to making 'about a few gallons in the day at home which is given gratis to orphans and widows'. Together with distributing Indian meal he was attempting to save thirty-nine families 'from death by starvation'. The reality of such was revealed in his examples of families surviving for days without food and resorting to 'eating the stumps of cabbage stalks pulled from the ground'. Others had taken the peelings of turnips and cabbage leaves which had been 'rejected by the soup kitchen cook as unfit for food'. The consequence was, as he described it, 'wide-spreading dysentery of the worst type which has carried off many and is extending its ravages'. He added that five, eight and even eleven funerals in one day were now not uncommon. Revealing that only one sheep had been stolen in the entire district so far he noted how 'the poor people are enduring slow death with the greatest patience'.[12]

A similar situation prevailed in Dromod where, despite three-quarters of the population being in 'a state of extreme poverty' there was no relief committee, no subscriptions and no soup kitchen. Indeed, the only relief measure in operation was the public works which employed 'about one-eighth of the peasantry' on 'unprofitable, useless roads'. The village appeared to suffer from its 'particularly unfortunate position' as it was in a remote part of the barony, was 'totally neglected thereby' and had 'derived no relief from any society or public fund whatsoever'. It was not helped by the fact that the property of the main owners was in the Court of Chancery, 'thereby depriving the owners of the means of affording relief to the poor'. At the same time, as in all other areas, most property belonged to absentee landlords and Francis Nesbitt and Reverend Francis Kane argued that unless immediate aid was forthcoming the number of deaths from hunger and destitution would increase to 'a fearful extent'. They stated that:

The few labourers who are now employed on the public works have been reduced to such a state of debility from long starvation that some of them have died and many have been obliged to relinquish their work, the only hope left them of themselves and their families from death.

Revealing how a recent inquest had discovered that a father of seven had died after frequently not eating for forty-eight hours at a time, probably to save his children, they stated how it would require a 'considerable fund' just to supply coffins for the dead 'who are frequently kept so long from burial that it is injurious to the health of the living, owing to the want of means to bury them'.[13] The experience of Dromod was replicated in Glenlough, 'a narrow valley between two ranges of mountain' in the Manorhamilton poor law union. Perpetual curate, John Hudson, revealed that his parish had received no assistance whatsoever from a relief committee established in Manorhamilton, as the committee 'could hardly supply their own locality'. Hudson's attempts at relief had been frustrated by his inability to solicit subscriptions due to 'no gentlemen residing in the parish'. Indeed, locally he had only received £5 from John Wynne of Hazlewood and £4/10 from the Manorhamilton committee which had been augmented by a total of £8 from two members of the clergy. He had applied these sums in distributing bread and meal free to the 'most destitute'. Interestingly, while observing that 'the amount of distress and want is exceedingly great' he noted that 'the Protestant population not being in want generally have not witnessed any cases of extreme suffering'.[14]

Evidently, both the longevity and intensity of distress proved crucial in terms of the amount of money raised. While initial appeals in the autumn of 1846 had generated significant amounts both from resident and absentee landowners the fact that increased sums were required six months later proved problematic. For example, in Ballinamore a soup kitchen had been distributing 100 gallons on a regular basis but by the beginning of February this operation had ceased due to want of funds. Rev. William Percy seemed to despair of obtaining any further subscriptions when informing the Quakers that 'it is extremely difficult to get up anything like a large subscription in this district – the resident gentry being very few, as nearly all the property in fee belongs to absentees'.[15]

With the British government pinning its relief efforts on public works local people were forced to rely on a variety of agencies in order to try to ameliorate the terrible consequences of the famine. Hence, Father Connolly, parish priest of Crieve, received £20 and a 100 gallon boiler from the Central Relief Committee, Sackville Street, Dublin. He also hoped to open a meal store and soup kitchen, if the Quakers agreed with his idea, which, if successful, would see at least 100 gallons distributed every day. The urgent necessity for such was evident in this excerpt from his application to the latter body:

> Believe me gentlemen, it is not a time for deliberation but for action for the poor are dying by degrees in this parish alone and that for want of food. Yesterday I visited a wretched abode where two females were lying on the same bed of dirty straw almost expiring from hunger (I should not wonder if they are since dead) and I found on enquiry that two members of the same family had fallen victims to famine within the last week and this is only a small portion of the horrors I could relate if I did not feel a reluctance to harrow up the souls of persons who come voluntarily forward in aid of suffering humanity.[16]

With prices of essential foodstuffs doubling in price individuals such as Gilbert King, Rector of Kilmore, acknowledged that 'numbers are perishing due to extreme destitution in consequence of the high prices of provisions in our markets'. Due to 'huxters selling at high prices' he added that: 'this district is most appalling. Fever is very prevalent and the poor are dying every day. The dead are buried by the dying. Some have no coffins – most have only a few rotten sticks put together and sometimes only straw'.[17] The continuing distress was such that:

> Words cannot convey an idea of the prevailing destitution of this parish, for thousands are starving, having nothing to eat except the doubtful nutriments of the wild herbage of the fields and in their appearances they present all the horrors of destitution. The strong peasant of a few months ago is now an emaciated wretch – tottering in his gait, worn … and sunk into the lowest dejection of the appalling contemplation of his position, his children crying around him – some dead and the others dying – his neighbours unable to assist him for the same fate has fallen on all and unless a new Providence will avert the Calamity a general pestilence will ensue – for every cabin will be a cemetery and every village a desolation.[18]

King's words were reflected in other parts of the county as the crisis deepened. In the Drumshanbo area, where out of a population of 14,000 it was estimated that 10,000 required public relief, two soup kitchens were supplying around forty gallons each day. In the rural district rations were distributed free of charge while in the town they were sold at one penny per quart.[19] However, for some this relief had come too late and parish priest Father Heslin related how 'a poor woman (herself a picture of famine and wretchedness) has been at my home carrying her dead child in her arms – it was a skeleton and must have died of hunger'. From the same source, related to him by John Gellmor, a labourer on the public works, came the following harrowing scene:

> A number of the men employed on a public road subscribed to get a coffin for a child which had died of starvation. But the mother of the child spent the money meant for the coffin on food. When the child was eventually buried by the same group of men they noticed that the eyes and parts of the legs and thighs had actually been eaten by rats.[20]

In areas where subscriptions were forthcoming relief was available. By early February the Mohill Benevolent Relief Committee, had established two soup kitchens selling soup at one penny per quart. They had also set up a bakery and were offering bread at a penny per pound. No food was given out free but tickets were sold to subscribers at half price and they were at liberty to issue these to individuals they believed were unable to purchase. By this means 'hundreds are daily relieved' with the committee suffering a weekly loss of between £3 and £4.[21] By the middle of that month due to the demands for aid the relief district of Dromod had been subdivided into Dromod and Derrycarne. James Thompson of Aughey informed the Quakers that a relief effort had just been started and forthcoming funds would be applied in the purchase of food and materials for a soup kitchen. All those requesting support would be visited to ascertain their circumstances and the soup sold at one penny a quart. The only food available locally was in the hands of two small retailers 'who retail at exorbitant prices and leave very little on hands'.[22]

In the town and vicinity of Drumsna a population of 17,800 lived on an area of 24,000 acres and Francis Kane estimated that 'seven-eighths' of this number required public aid. In order to address this need a relief committee had just been sanctioned for Drumsna. The area had previously been designated part of the Carrick-on-Shannon relief district but had 'derived no benefit whatever' from that source. The need for wholesome food was evident in his comment that although fever was not prevalent 'a severe bowel complaint is carrying off many'. Further financial support was required given that although a soup shop had been established in the village it was limited to a daily distribution of sixteen gallons.[23] J.M. Kirkwood lamented the fact that in her district on the outskirts of Carrick-on-Shannon 'there is not a single person able to afford the least relief but Mr Kirkwood'. She revealed there were only four families not in want and dismissed the utility of the public works where the average eight to ten pence daily wage 'will purchase a very scanty portion of food for six, eight and, in some cases, ten persons'. Since November 1846 the Kirkwoods had been making a daily distribution of soup to a dozen families while at the same time endeavouring to find as much work as possible for labourers, However, as Kirkwood herself admitted, such schemes could not employ 'one in ten' of those seeking it.[24]

However, isolated areas continued to suffer as distress deepened. In echoing the comments of John Hudson in nearby Glenlough, Cairncross Cullen of Glenade 'sixteen miles from the nearest meat market' informed the Quakers that his district had not obtained 'the slightest relief' from either the Kinlough or Manorhamilton relief committees, despite the fact that their combined resources totalled around £1,200. Nevertheless, in remarking on such, he stated:

> Besides, even were we to be supplied from their store it would not be worthwhile for those who can purchase to walk five miles there and back to save one penny in the store which is all they are selling below market price, besides loss of their day and the wages besides.[25]

Apart from his own private expenditure in the locality the only other money available was that sent by his sister-in-law and her friends in Cheltenham, England. His next comment simply reiterated the observation from every individual who sought aid on behalf of his or her district:

> The greater part of my district is property of absentees who have not I believe subscribed a shilling towards relief of destitution. But in justice to the landlord I must say most of the lands are held on a lease by middlemen who whatever they may drain from the tenants are not the persons to restore these times.[26]

Cullen also added that, in relation to the workers on the public works, 'the Barony Constables are actually watching the poor wretches receiving their scanty earnings to get from them the amount of their county cess'.[27] Similarly, in Lurganboy it was revealed by parish priest Father James McGauran that the only sum received in answer to an appeal was £5 from J.M. Clements Esq., who had specified that it be spent on feeding the poorest inhabitants of only two townlands (presumably owned by him). Significantly two of the main proprietors in the area, James Wynne of Hazlewood, Sligo and Cairncross Cullen had not made any subscription. With such meagre finances it is no surprise there was no soup shop in the district despite the fact that 'numbers are dying daily, some of starvation…'[28]

Writing from Dromahaire on 27 February 1847 William Whyte noted that the Drumlease parish relief committee had received £100 in subscriptions and this had been used to purchase meal which was then sold at half price to those most in need. His communication to the Quakers was to seek assistance to establish a private soup shop and he was successful in that the latter agreed to grant him £20 as soon as it was in operation.[29]

In a similar application Nicholas Tottenham revealed that out of a total of 'many absentees' only three had made subscriptions to the Manorhamilton relief fund and added that 'almost every proprietor is an absentee with very few exceptions'. Consequently:

> The population [of Glenfarne] have no-one to look after them but myself as all the other proprietors are absentees. Many of the people are on the verge of death from starvation as the pay on the public works is not near adequate to support their families. The prices of provisions are so high. Please send as much as you can recollecting *'bis dat qui cito dat'* [he gives twice who gives promptly].[30]

Tottenham's plea was successful and the Quakers sent him an eighty gallon boiler together with £15 to establish a soup kitchen.

George Mansfield of Kiltubrid, Cashcarrigan believed that the wages on the public works were so insufficient that it would require the wages of three men to maintain a family of ten or more. He revealed that even though a relief committee had been formed in his parish it had been found necessary, by the end of February, to appoint a sub-committee. Up to this period two small private soup kitchens had been attempting to deal with demand as best they could. One at the glebe house dispensed fifty gallons a week while another one was sited at Laheen under the superintendence of Mr Peyton. At both sites the food, which was distributed free of cost, had been made possible due to subscriptions from the National Club, London and St Jude's in Liverpool. However, demand now meant that two further kitchens were necessary – one in the village of Keshcarrigan and one at the cross-roads in Mohergregg on Lord Viscount Southwell's estate.[31]

A similar initiative was in operation in Cloone where the local soup kitchen was distributing 2,400 quarts of soup made from beef, meal, rice, vegetables and spices free each Wednesday, Thursday and Saturday to a total of 600 families.[32] In Dromahaire a small soup kitchen had been opened under the patronage of absentee landlord, George Lane-Fox, supported by some local subscriptions. It, together with another under the supervision of Fr Thomas McKeon and Mr Whyte at the Bonne, was distributing ten gallons per day but Rev. William Wynne appealed to the Irish Relief Association for another boiler to increase supply.[33]

In Eastersnow, just outside Carrick, a soup kitchen was in 'active operation and doing much effectual good'. However, Henry Irwin lamented that 'want and sickness is greatly increased in the locality with several deaths from dysentery and fever besides many from actual starvation'.[34] Meanwhile, at Corry, near Drumkeerin, Marianne Cullen, wife of Francis Cullen, secretary to the Drumkeerin Relief Committee, had established a small independent soup kitchen to daily feed thirty-six people and to aid her in this endeavour she received a half ton of rice from the Quakers.[35]

Such correspondence revealed the overwhelming level of distress in early 1847 and the urgent need for direct feeding of the people. Hence, in February the British government rushed through special legislation – the Temporary Relief Act, known locally as the Soup Kitchen Act – for the setting up of relief committees under the auspices of a new relief commission. Consequently the public works were to be run down as food was provided for those unable to enter workhouses. However, the sudden closure of most of these and the inevitable bureaucratic and administrative delays in establishing a system of national soup kitchens resulted in a hiatus in relief provision.

The importance of such works to thousands of people was crystallised in the words of T. Curly, a conducting engineer for the county, who commented that one week's suspension of wages 'would bring them to actual starvation'.[36] Thus, while there had been universal criticism of the wages paid to labourers on the public works, there was incredulity at the news that those works were to be phased out. The problem for private funds was that they would inevitably face much greater demand in the period between the works being closed and the new relief mechanism coming into operation. Also evident was a hesitation by already diffident subscribers to give further support to soup kitchens, and on 8 March John Hudson informed the Quakers that a proposed private soup shop had not yet been established in Glencar as people were 'waiting to see what the new Government measure will be'.[37] On being asked to comment on Hudson's application for aid, Nicholas Tottenham was somewhat euphemistic in stating there would be 'some little confusion on the discharge of the people from the works under the relief act before the new one comes into full operation'.[38] A more realistic assessment came from George Shaw who bluntly stated that 'we have a gloomy prospect, I fear, for many months to come'.[39] Fulfilling his own prediction, Shaw later wrote of 'the increased distress occasioned by the reduction of the number of men employed on the public works' and by the end of March was requesting further aid from the Quakers to meet the 'emergency'.[40] His letter was one of many which reflected the frustration and helplessness experienced by those who were daily witnesses to indescribable suffering.

In Drumkeerin, the majority of public works had focussed on land drainage on two estates but by early April this had ceased. With no work available from 'large farmers' distress in the district had markedly increased with many being 'obliged to dispose of every trifling article of furniture they possessed to prevent starvation'. While there were few cases of fever in the district 'dysentery and swelled limbs and general debility are the prevalent diseases'. Thus, a soup kitchen was employed to distribute almost 100 gallons free every day while bread and rice was sold at a reduced price.[41]

Having written to the Quakers on 2 March, George Mansfield wrote a month later to inform them of the changes in the district. He had discontinued his private soup kitchen as a larger enterprise had commenced nearby but at the same time noted that distress was 'much aggravated' by the withdrawal of people from the public works. While prices had declined somewhat in the past month 'means have declined also'. Being aware that it would be some weeks before the new relief act would come into operation he therefore requested aid to supply the people in the interim, by means of a fourteen-gallon boiler.[42] In early April the soup kitchen established two months previously by Nicholas Tottenham in Manorhamilton, 'the only one within twenty miles in County Leitrim', was running out of funds. He had been distributing sixty gallons of soup on a daily basis free of charge but believed that with extra funding this amount could be doubled and relief extended for a further two months.[43]

By mid-April most of the public works had been wound down and relief lists, to be made out in strict conformity with the law, were in the process of being drawn up. Given the tens of thousands demanding food it is no surprise that correspondents to the Quakers complained of widespread inefficiency and delays.

On 22 April William Noble of Prospect, Drumshanbo informed them that the relief lists had been made out but were 'not so full and accurate as they will be'. This had occurred because it had proved impossible to obtain an accurate return in time, 'so anxious were the committee to commence affording relief'. In the meantime, he had established his own soup kitchen and employed ninety-two women and sixteen weavers in order to provide work for those able to avail of the opportunity. However, despite this, and the imminent new relief act, he argued that 'further and great exertion on the part of societies and individuals will still be most necessary'.[44]

John Dickson, of Woodville, Bundoran, commented that more than half of all labourers had been turned off the works while the lists for the district of Tawly had been made out but were now being revised. He projected the cost at around twenty shillings but believed this would barely meet the required expenditure for three months. Together with Captain Johnston he had employed a 'few' able-bodied labourers and this had been the only labour available outside that of the public works. He revealed that they had applied to the government for a loan to drain and improve their property: Johnston had been refused while Dickson was still awaiting a reply. In the months prior to this he had been selling meal and rice at cost price and he now felt the need to maintain this effort 'to keep half the inhabitants from starving for the next three months in consequence of the number of small holdings of land'.[45]

Meanwhile, John Warren estimated that in Aughavas, where, by 30 April, the lists had not been made out, it would be 'fully three weeks' before a rate under the new measure would be struck. However, as in other areas, he maintained that 'much greater exertion' would be necessary as 'the electoral division is quite unable to pay one-quarter of the rate required to be levied on it for its poor'. He believed that without a 'few private subscriptions' having been raised in Eslin 'hundreds would, ere this, have perished'. Also, at least 1,000 individuals occupying holdings not more than three acres in extent were in 'a starving state' while others on larger plots were described as 'wretched'. He drew a graphic picture of the suffering in his area:

> The cries of upwards of 1,100 tongues for daily food can be more readily imagined than calmly borne, while every sunken eye is gazing intently on our relief committee whose delays (though essentially necessary) are yet unavoidably attended with sad results to the wretched poor of this locality. No pen is willing nor pencil able to attempt even a slight sketch of the misery which each day brings to light. To say that we are worse than any other districts would not be true – but to state that we are not in a very wretched state would be equally false.[46]

In nearby Killegar works had ceased at the beginning of April and in the three weeks since then the entire labouring population was 'in the extremity of want'. The situation was not helped by confusion over the mechanism of the new law. Relief lists had been completed but no rate had been struck by the finance committee as they had been under the mistaken apprehension that a rate could not be established for an individual electoral division. Thus, they had refused to forward the estimates until the returns of all the divisions had been made. Although the relief lists contained all those eligible for relief, it excluded 'many more who have been refused in consequence of their having more than three acres of land'.[47] In the Eslin electoral division most of the labourers had been discharged from public works and some had gone to Scotland and England 'and left their families in a poor state'.[48] Meanwhile, in Drumkeerin it was estimated that the lists would be completed by 3 May, two days after the cessation of the public road works. Nonetheless, Thomas Cullen had no doubt that the initial number of 1,500 names would be doubled within one month.[49]

Evidently, there was no uniform closure of the works and it appeared that dismissals impacted to a greater degree on some areas than others. For example, Letitia Veevers, who afforded relief to more than 100 labourers, explained that their 'abrupt dismissal' was particularly severe in the Mohill area due to the fact that in her locality spring work was always a few weeks later than in those parts of the country where the soil was of a better quality and less wet. Thus, the huge demand for work from labourers could not be met by local farmers 'who continue as much as possible to perform their farming operations with the aid of their own families or servant boys'. Despite her realism that 'some time must elapse' before the new measure came into operation she painted a stark picture of the impact the crisis had made on her community:

> The people are daily dropping off all around us. In the barony of Mohill – on 1 January 1847 – there were 35,714 people and I have heard those who ought to know and to be well informed on the subject state that there will not (if deaths continue at the same ratio) till the 1 July next, including those who are flying to America and elsewhere (as the means will carry them) there will not be 24,000 remaining.
>
> In the small townland near this containing only forty acres – and on which there were only thirty-six inhabitants – eighteen have died since the scarcity began to be felt. Everything was sold before death for sustenance and they did not leave as much as would procure coffins for their remains. It is remarkable that the great majority of those who have fallen were boys and men.
>
> There are instances not far from this where the survivors, not able to procure coffins, have buried their dead under the floor of their cabins in which the deceased had lived – others conveying them to bogs and gardens.
>
> Last week I heard of a young man having been met on the road carrying on his back the bodies of his little brother and sister who had died of fever. They were slung on by a hay rope and the bodies only covered with hay and the poor mother followed to the field holding up the limbs of the deceased to prevent them dragging on the ground.[50]

As in Mohill, George Peyton of Driney House, Keshcarrigan noted that distress was now so extensive people were forced to bury their dead 'even without coffins'. He was adamant about the shortcomings of the new measure maintaining that 'very few' of his tenants would receive relief and that even those entitled to such would have to wait at least three weeks to receive rations. Consequently, he established his own family relief effort in conjunction with his neighbours the Slackes of Annadale to supply food

to 120 industrially-inclined families 'in great distress'. His effort received
the support of the Quakers who granted him one ton of Indian meal for
those in most difficulty 'selected with strict impartiality'.[51]

Harrowing reports of death had become widespread by late April
and Denis Booth submitted the following account to the Irish Relief
Association:

> Ellen Beirne of Headford, in this part of the parish of Annaduff,
> died of starvation. She was not interred for fourteen days and on
> the fifteenth day part of the remains (the remainder having been
> torn and eaten by dogs) was buried and not in consecrated ground
> but in a hole in a bog. When she was some days dead her husband
> John Beirne died of the same dreadful cause. Also a child of John
> Maxwell's aged thirteen years died last night in the same townland
> and I am just after giving assistance to have the poor child's remains
> interred, who also died of starvation.[52]

Booth, together with Rev. George Shaw, sought the help of the Irish
Relief Association in establishing a soup kitchen independent of the
relief committee acting under the new law. Prior to this they had been
supervising a soup kitchen in the townland of Lavagh where forty gallons
of soup, together with biscuit and cooked rice were distributed to the
most destitute poor. To those deemed able to purchase it was sold at a
penny per quart but many people had received free rations.[53]

By the middle of May regular correspondent George Mansfield had
distributed half a ton of rice to almost two thousand people in Kiltubrid.
He commented that demand for it had been very great due to the fact
that 'distress in this quarter has greatly increased and both sickness and
death prevail here at present to a terrific extent'. On 20 April, the first day
of distribution, he had given half a stone to fifty people but by 3 May the
number seeking food had increased to 200, all of whom received a portion
of two stones of rice. Such was the overwhelming demand that he ran out
of supplies five days later.[54]

In addition to supplies of food the Society of Friends was particularly
keen to support those who endeavoured to establish small-scale local
industry, usually in some branch of the weaving industry. For example,
they sent funds to William Noble who was employing fifty-two women at
spinning and five men at weaving in Drumshanbo,[55] while in Derrycarne

Letitia Nisbett was aided in her employment of 'a few men' to weave linen, drugget and corduroy.[56] Elizabeth Peyton had engaged some people in 'fine knitting' and spinning wool and flax and hoped the Quakers would be able to initiate something on a larger scale:

> Your benevolent society might perhaps be able to get something established in these backward parts of the North which might give permanent employment to many of our poor women and children. We have numbers who can spin and knit but no market to be had for either stockings or linen save the purchase of a few individuals of that class who make the best bargain they can and consequently as our poor people put it 'they have only bought work, I might, Sir, as well have been idle'.[57]

Her husband maintained that this initiative had been 'the means of raising a spirit of industry in this neighbourhood hitherto unknown to them' with some children earning nearly £3 in six weeks. However, as his wife had alluded to, the problem was obtaining a market for the finished goods and he enquired if the Quakers could help in this. However, even the latter were not disposed to obtaining sales of clothes.[58] In Kinlough Penelope Johnston was managing a similar operation and with a grant of £10 from the Quakers she was able to employ spinners and weavers in making flannel and linen. This was then sold to the needy of the area who paid in weekly instalments.[59]

Always keen to acknowledge the humanity of those they were supporting, the Quakers diversified their relief effort from the spring of 1847. Hence, in addition to continuing their food distribution, and aware of the needs of the increasing numbers of distressed, they also invited applications for clothing.

By April, William Noble of Drumshanbo, who had received 'the making of thirty petticoats', estimated there were at least 200 heads of families, both men and women, in want of various items such as coats, trousers, gowns and petticoats. In addition 'a great many children and young persons of both sexes are in these respects wretchedly off'.[60] Similarly, in Fenagh it was reported that 'a great proportion' were in a 'miserable state for want of clothes' while George Mansfield noted that those in Cashcarrigan who would have previously been considered as 'wanting' were now 'nearly naked'.[61] When J.M. Kirkwood of Woodbrook Lodge received 100 articles of clothing from the Quakers, including calico and blankets, she assured them that there was no danger of such items being pawned by recipients due to their fear of subsequently 'never receiving other relief'. Such a grant was invaluable given that 'there is scarcely a single person who does not want clothing' while 'even those who have not hitherto a need for food are nearly naked, having spent their all'.[62] Anne Devenish, writing from nearby Rush Hill, estimated there were 'not less than 200 families' who were in a 'wretched condition for every description of clothing'. She had previously received some supplies from a ladies' society in London but by the middle of April this had all been distributed. She was sent two bundles of clothes – a total of 100 garments – by the Quakers.[63]

The need for multiple relief efforts in adjacent localities was reflected in the fact that Lady Louisa Tennison had received £2/10 worth of clothing from the Ladies Relief Association in Dublin; while Mary Johnston of Aughacashel estimated the number in need of clothing in her area was around 250 people.[64] In the same area Elizabeth and Hannah Peyton of Driney House were clothing thirty families while Annadelia Slack was supporting sixty families (a combined total of around 400 individuals) in the townlands of Corglass, Leitrim, Lisdrumacrone, Drumbuedey, Aughrim, Kiltubrid and Drumtubride.[65] Similar clothing funds were established in Mohill, Keadue, Carrigallen, Kinlough and Croghan.[66]

While many individuals either chose or were forced to labour in isolation some were willing to combine their efforts. Thus, in an attempt to supply clothing in the Carrick area, where there were 'instances of widows with young children in a most destitute state', J.M. Kirkwood of Woodbrook Lodge, informed the Quakers she would work with Margaret Kirkwood of Lakeview and Mary Peyton of Springfield.[67] Although Matilda Shanly of Riversdale 'would as soon act on my own responsibility' she stated her willingness to work with Rev. Clifford and Fr Cassidy to clothe the poor in Riversdale and Aghoo West where there were 'at least sixty persons in the most wretched state for want of clothing and at least twenty men who cannot work in the cold for want of garments'.[68]

In appealing for clothing for the area in the vicinity of Annaduff Glebe George Shaw noted that 'scarcely any clothes have been provided or purchased by the poor for the last two years' with the consequence 'that they are in rags and the absence of cleanliness has become most offensive and injurious to health'.[69] In her application Jane Banks of Rose Bank,

Dromahaire stated that at least several hundred people were in need of clothing, especially bed clothes and petticoats. However she informed the Quakers that she would only observe their rules on the condition that any clothes would be sent free of charge and that if she was unable to sell any she would be allowed to return the clothing, after deducting any money expending in their making. However, the society was not happy with her comments and did not send a grant explaining that 'the regulations were not likely to be complied with'.[70]

While the Irish Relief Association and the Society of Friends were the main sources of relief outside the government initiatives there was one group which stepped in at this time. The Irish Reproductive Loan Fund had developed from the London Committee for the Relief of the Distressed Irish (also known as the London Tavern Committee) which had been the main source of relief during the Famine of 1822. On 15 March 1847 George Shaw wrote to the secretary of the fund, R. Bertolacci, to enquire if money in the hands of the Leitrim trustees of the fund could be made available as loans to enable people to seed their land. However, Shaw's letter hinted at problems connected with the finance:

> Around £500 was in circulation a few years ago but was called in by the trustees – or at least the holding of it made so disagreeable that we were glad to pay it off since which time it has lain idle. If it could be now restored to us under a milder and kinder regime we would employ it most usefully to encourage the seeding of the land which otherwise I fear will be quite neglected by the small farmers from want of means for purchasing seed.[71]

Having been told by the fund to make a direct approach to the local trustees, Shaw revealed how he had been 'so often put off that I am doubtful of getting any speedy aid such as the emergency of the case demands'.[72] Indeed, in a subsequent letter Shaw alleged that the £500 previously referred to 'was withdrawn from us by the caprice of Lord Clements and the county Leitrim trustees', continuing: 'It was repaid without the loss of a farthing and we think ourselves entitled to your consideration but we wish to correspond with you and not with the Trustees who treated us so badly before.'[73]

Perhaps having been informed of Shaw's advances Lord Clements, in a letter to Lewis Jones, one of the administrators of the fund, asserted that it was 'quite out of our power to undertake anything of the kind', adding that even if such a plan were feasible it was now too late in the season for planting.[74] However, in a further letter written on the same day to the governors of the fund he was much more forthright in his opposition:

> I am sorry that I cannot recommend to give the application of any part of your funds to the giving out of seeds in the way of loan; as from all the enquiry that I have made on the subject I fear that very little if any part of such a loan would, in the present unfortunate state of Leitrim, ever be repaid. As far as my experience goes I have found it a very losing concern even in better times and I have consequently been obliged to limit the issue of seeds to my tenants, upon credit, very considerably.[75]

Clements was supported in his opposition both by John Duckworth, a member of the board of guardians in Boyle, County Roscommon and Carrick-on-Shannon and Guy Lloyd of Croghan, also in County Roscommon, who also maintained that it was too late in the season for planting. Indeed, Duckworth concurred in the opinion of Clements that at a time like the present the erection of a fever hospital in Mohill would represent the optimum use of such money. He pointed to the experience of Boyle 'where we have not a single case of fever in the [work] house and only two in our fever hospital'.[76]

Nevertheless, 'anxious to afford as much pecuniary assistance as lies within their power to poor and indigent landholders'[77] the Loan Fund sent a circular to Catholic and Protestant clergyman throughout the county which, among other things, outlined how each farmer had to be recommended by their landlord and another 'good and acceptable surety'. The following examples are typical of the agreements entered into by local farmers:

> 8 May 1847, Mary Nesbitt, Dromodbeg, Annaduff – 11 acres held – received £5 to plant three acres oats, payable 1 October 1847.
>
> 11 May 1847, David O'Brien, Derrywillow, Annaduff – 10 acres held – do declare that 1½ acres have been tilled and are ready to have seed sown in it but that I have not the means to buy the seed – received £3 to plant oats, payable 1 October 1847.

11 May 1847, John Donnelly, Dromodbeg, Annaduff – 4½ acres held – received £3/10 to plant oats.

17 May 1847, Hugh Maxwell, Furnance, Annaduff – 3 acres held – received £1/10 to plant 3 roods of oats.

22 May 1847, John Trice, Fearnaght, Annaduff – 1¼ acres held – received £1/11 to plant 3 roods of oats (to be repaid within eight months).[78]

However, not everyone was so fortunate and it was reported that in Dromod three cases (amounting to £10/10) were rejected as their securities were 'reported bad'.

At the same time, some areas declined such aid. From Drumkeerin, Rev. Wynne informed the fund that the two principal landlords and himself had already supplied their tenants with seed while William Macartney reported that assistance would be of no benefit to the farmers of the Manorhamilton area as sowing was too far advanced.[79] In Aughnasheelin Rev. Richard Clifford made known that he had distributed £80 worth of seed oats to the tenants of the glebe lands at his own expense,[80] while in Kinlough Penelope Johnston had bought 'a great deal' of seed oats, turnip and flax, and was delighted that 'thank God they have been blessed and the crops unusually speaking are good'.[81]

Another reason for refusal emerged in Cloone where it was revealed that as a very large part of the parish, the property of the heirs of Colonel Madden, was in chancery and the agent being absentee, people were therefore unable to receive the recommendation of their landlords.[82] In the policing sub-districts of Clooncaohear, Clooncumber, Dromod and Farnaght, constable Neon Tucker believed that due to the difficulty of obtaining rents there would be few landlords willing to enter into security for loans.[83] A similar fear was voiced in relation to the parishes of Carrigallen, Drumreilly, Fenagh and Kiltubrid.[84] However, individuals within these areas did eventually receive loans with £60 distributed to Dromahaire and Drumkeerin, £37 to Mohill and Dromod and £34 to Ballinamore, Carrigallen, Corduff, Fenagh and Rantogue.[85]

While increasing numbers of people were forced to rely on small private relief efforts the strain of those involved in maintaining such emerged in a number of letters to the Society of Friends. In particular, individuals were aggrieved when it appeared that those for whom they sought aid were being ignored or faced discrimination. For example,

Francis Kane maintained that the Derrycarne soup kitchen had been run solely for the benefit of those in its immediate vicinity while none of the money entrusted by the Quakers to Francis Nesbitt had found its way to his locality in Drumsna. In addition, he believed that the relief committee to which he had been treasurer had not taken the 'active measures' he thought necessary and maintained he could do nothing by himself 'as the gentleman in the immediate locality was jealous of interference and indisposed to much exertion'.[86] Similarly, George Beresford informed the Quakers that none of the grants made to Ellen Lawder in Fenagh were of any benefit to the poor of the parish, adding that the only food they received was through him. He continued:

> As our committee, or rather our chairman, John Lawder, refused entering the Government arrangements and on that account you refused to give our committee a grant you will now think that your money will be much better disposed of going into my relief fund which I do not hesitate to say ... is doing great good.[87]

In justifying his stance Beresford gave examples of cases where he had personally rescued people:

> There are many relieved by me that I have not put down on the list – an orphan and his mother died in fever in the locality of an old house. She had an infant at the breast and I hear it was sucking her breast when the mother was in the agonies of death. With great trouble I had her buried. The oldest child is on my list – the girl of 10 years still wandering around with the infant on her back.[88]

On 28 July local parish priest, Father Francis Reynolds, received a reply from the society to his request for aid. They informed him that several grants of money, meal and rice had already been made through John Lawder JP and George Beresford and that, if he would act in conjunction with them, further assistance would be considered. In his reply Reynolds was condemnatory both of Lawder and Beresford:

> Now, gentlemen, as a member of that relief committee composed of the above [Lawder and Beresford] and one or two more I truly state to you that I own nothing of the above grants save that I have been

informed that J. Lawder has distributed some meal and rice amongst his own tenantry who were not in distress, some of whom have five or six cows, but no portion of it has been added to our funds for the general benefit of the starving people. Nor am I aware of G.D. Beresford having received any assistance from your committee for when I moved on a certain day that he, as our secretary, should leave on the table before the committee a true and accurate account of all the subscriptions, the sums of money and meal, etc, he had received, he positively refused to do so although he was in duty bound to do it. How then am I to act in concert with the above gentlemen who have neither acted in concert with me nor with the rules of distributive justice. Some hundreds of our poor people are actually starving particularly those whom the Finance committee has struck off the relief list and as the Irish Relief Extension Act cannot be put into operation in this parish for some weeks to come because no steps have been yet taken by the Board of Guardians to that effect may I in the name of charity and humanity implore and beg that your committee will transmit to me some relief in meal or money to preserve the lives of those starving wretches until the above Act will come into operation.[89]

Meanwhile, in Mohill James Hoope estimated that due to delays in ascertaining numbers eligible for relief no distributions would take place for at least another month. Apparently, in early May, there were only 320 people deemed eligible for gratuitous relief and he regarded these numbers as 'not being one-quarter of those in absolute state of starvation'. More controversially, he believed that the board of guardians would delay 'as long as possible'. Thus, while the Mohill Benevolent Relief Society had a small balance it was 'not at all adequate to meet the present awful distress', adding that 'numbers are daily falling and dying in the streets of the town'. In the absence of gratuitous relief to those holding land he maintained that 'the small landholder will be left to starve'. Also, due to the prevalence of fever and dysentery, he had been witness to 'the dead and dying lying in the same room for days together'. Hoope explained that he had spent the last twelve months of his life entirely devoted to the work of the relief committee but that business was 'generally transacted' by those members who lived in the town. His frustration, occasioned by bureaucracy and local sectarian rivalries, was evident in the following comments:

I met with much arrogance and opposition from some parties of old committees and especially from the parish priest Mr Evers but had the unqualified support and approbation of every member who had really the interest of the poor at heart and continued to transact the business until the new committee was formed from which all the curates are excluded by an Act of Parliament ... As the business of the committee is chiefly done at adjourned meetings held almost daily therefore those out of town cannot consistently attend and thus the chairman [Fr Evers] can do generally as he pleases as to which I can make one fact. On Friday last the committee met to issue tickets for the gratuitous relief of a small quantity of meal I got from the British Relief Association which in dissolution of the old committee I handed over to the new. They issued 250 tickets for a half stone each and in the district where the average of members of the Established Church are at least one-quarter or one-fifth of the entire population – out of the 250 they liberally allowed meal to twenty-two out of my poor flock. They gave to some who to my own knowledge hold from five to eight and ten acres of land and rejected widows and applicants without a piece of land or any other means whatever. After much opposition I induced them to add twenty additional names the following day when they were issuing tickets to 150 more.[90]

Consequently, Hoope, in stating that at least 1,000 would need gratuitous relief, was adamant in his application to the Quakers that if he received food 'I would look neither to creed nor profession', and concentrate on supplying 'the most distressing and urgent cases'.[91] Three days later, on 7 May, Father Evers reported that the original lists had been returned by members of the finance committee who maintained that many people entitled to free rations were not included. He estimated that as a consequence it would be at least three weeks before a rate could be struck. In the meantime, 3,000 people survived on one ton of Indian meal which was still in the hands of the old relief committee alongside small-scale relief from various individuals. Given the earlier complaint of James Hoope the Quakers decided to grant Evers two tons of Indian meal. However, they placed the responsibility of the distribution in the hands of the government inspector, Lieutenant Primrose, 'to be presided over by him ... pending the start of the new arrangements'.[92]

Meanwhile, the Protestant vicar of Killargue, George Hindes, observed that in his area poverty and sickness was manifested to a greater degree among the Catholic population 'which is natural as they are more than ten to one'. However, he acknowledged that, although, unlike his Catholic counterpart, he had not witnessed any cases of 'heart-rending distress', still, 'even in my own flock there are a great number of persons in the utmost want' with many existing on 'watercresses and things of that kind'.[93]

In the Ballyshannon district Primitive Wesleyan Methodist preacher, R. Kerr, argued that as his paucity of funds made it impossible for him to 'pay attention to one-tenth' of the number in need he was forced to focus on 'Protestant small farmers' claiming that they were the 'most overlooked'. Hence, his resources would be concentrated on 200 families (around 1,000 individuals). In a rare reference to religious difference he alleged that many of those he intended to aid 'would rather waste away with want than apply for relief, and it is only by visiting them in their houses … that their real state can be ascertained,' adding:

> The Roman Catholics make much greater effort to obtain relief and have succeeded pretty generally in getting themselves put in the way of relief but after all that has been done and is still doing the amount of misery among all sects is, I fear, largely increasing. Several deaths have occurred in this neighbourhood thro[ugh] want of food.[94]

While Kerr may have been subtle in his comments the same could not be said of Rev. John Strean who, in a letter seeking aid on behalf of the poor of Toomna, urged the Quakers 'Please do not ask the Priests on any account to have anything to do with this grant.'[95]

## THE TEMPORARY RELIEF ACT

On 1 May the Temporary Relief Act came into operation in the county with the opening of soup kitchens in the Carrick-on-Shannon electoral division. Five days later they opened in Glenade and Kinlough, in the Ballyshannon union and by 17 May all divisions in the Carrick union were in operation. However, in the parish of Kiltoghert Fr Peter Dawson stated that 'not half' those in need were included with only 'the helpless' – a total of 1,280 – eligible out of a population of 13,000. He also asserted that 'in most cases' people would surrender their land if allowed to remain in their houses, 'which would not be permitted'. Evidence of inertia in the Carrick area emerged with his claim that 'those who should be most active seem paralysed by the extent of the calamity'. It transpired that the town soup kitchen had closed on 21 April yet in spite of having a total balance of £207, which was transferred to the new finance committee, no relief had since been forthcoming.[96]

On 18 May, over a fortnight after the electoral division had been operating the act, Jane Isabel Banks informed the Quakers that the clerk of the Carrick-on-Shannon relief committee had not received enough of the official sheets from Dublin, thereby ensuring a delay of another fortnight. She was working in conjunction with Martha Brown in the only relief effort then in existence in the town. They had received food from the society and had distributed this as wages to 130 people whom they had employed at knitting. To try to ensure the success of their enterprise they were seeking orders for clothes from friends 'in England and elsewhere'. In the past three months she had sold more than £100 worth for the benefit of her school and this had placed those in receipt of aid 'above want'. She asked the Quakers to help her obtain orders for 'plain and fancy knitting, shawls of the most beautiful finish, stockings, collars, [and] cuffs'.[97]

The following day Jane Corbett also wrote to the Quakers from the town. Her letter received the endorsement of Elizabeth Forster, a member of one of the prominent Quaker families, who stated that her brother had been witness to the efforts of the Corbetts and 'felt great confidence in them'. Corbett painted a grim picture of the town, where there had been 'such a change these last few days' due to further increases in the price of provisions and 'greater numbers falling ill'. She spoke of 'children dying in the streets and older persons on the roadsides and in fields' and alluded to the fact that the new relief had proved disappointing in that only two pounds of meal a day was allowed to families of five or six. She regarded this as 'a mere morsel' and stated that people 'appear exasperated'. Previous days had seen a 'significant ingress of country people' who had warned the magistrates 'they would not starve while they had cattle to stay ... or shops to rob'. Consequently there was 'great excitement in the area'. On 21 May Forster described the previous two days as being 'so full of trouble and anxiety' but things appeared to have subsided in consequence of the rations of meal being increased and the fact that 'Miss P.' had distributed food. She added, with some relief, that Peyton's initiative had moved people away from her locality, noting how 'they flock where there is a morsel to eat'.[98]

A couple of weeks after soup kitchens had opened in Keshcarrigan and Drumshanbo the ineffective nature of the relief operation had become apparent to Mary Johnston and Annadelia Slacke, whose house overlooked Kiltubrid graveyard. After witnessing the supplies distributed they were adamant that alternative measures would have to be pursued in order to feed those not placed on the lists due to possession of a couple of acres of land. For example, in the 'very mountainous district' of Aghacashill the people were in the 'greatest possible distress', particularly the 'poor females who are most anxious to get employment of any kind'. To aid them in their endeavours Johnston received half a ton of rice and a similar quantity of Indian meal, which could be utilised as payment to females, while Slack obtained a half ton of the latter.[99]

The relief effort in Annaduff was helped by the fact that Rev. George Shaw had an 'excellent steel mill' which meant he was able to grind any Indian meal he received. By the beginning of May he was daily feeding 132 children, forty widows and destitute families – all free of charge. He also sold food to 'as many more' at a penny a quart. In total this operation required about one hundredweight of rice each day. Remarking that distress was 'truly awful' and the mortality 'unprecedented', he therefore intended to continue both feeding schoolchildren and selling food at a cheap rate to farmers 'who will be shut out from public aid', many of whose families 'are in a starving condition equally with the poorest of their neighbours'.[100]

On 20 May every electoral division in the Mohill union started to operate the new measure and on that date William Lawder of Carrigallen informed the Quakers of his belief that many would be left unaided by the new measure. Up to the middle of that month he had been supporting only disabled persons but with the closure of public works he now had to cater for labourers and their families which was proving 'overwhelming'. Therefore, he intended to supply these greater numbers with the assistance of the Quakers. However, in a rare example, they refused to do so as they had been made aware that a rate had been struck and money distributed, thereby enabling relief to commence. Hence, they expressed the hope that 'a necessity does not exist for funds for this committee'.[101] However, Lawder was swift to reply and informed the Quakers that the new system did 'little or nothing' to relieve fever sufferers in that the only food distributed – meal – was 'useless to the sick'. As a consequence, he succeeded in obtaining a grant of a half ton of rice which was to be distributed in a cooked state to those not receiving assistance under the government system.[102]

In the Manorhamilton union the first electoral division to operate the soup kitchens was that of Dromahaire which opened on 31 May, one month after that of Carrick-on-Shannon. A week later (on 7 June) kitchens commenced distributing rations in Manorhamilton and Killenummery and it was not until 25 June that all divisions in the union were operating the act. By this stage complaints about various aspects of the system were commonplace. Certainly the evidence from those who had been previously running their own private relief schemes was that the government initiative was extremely limited. Rev. Hamilton, the vicar of Eastersnow, expressed disappointment that the measure 'does not afford that full measure that has been supposed it would or that is required':

> It makes no provision that is practically of any use for insufficient employment and wages as may be seen by looking at the fourth class of persons to be relieved. The lowest food of a cheap description it is intended to be sold to such persons and yet in another part of the act nothing can be sold under market price. But the truth is no measure can at all meet all want in a calamity like the present.[103]

However, Hamilton's next comments articulated what many people had been thinking:

> The impression on all persons is that the destitution is rather greater under the new measure than under the works. If there were works along with the measure there would be something like adequate provision then.[104]

For example, Jane Ellis of Brooklawn, Ballinamore, had been distributing meal and cooked rice and she intended to pursue this in light of the fact that people holding land or in employment were officially excluded. In this area, she noted that almost all the able-bodied men were still employed in early June on public works. However, she maintained that 'many' of these were in a 'most destitute state'. Her efforts were boosted by a grant of a half ton of Indian meal.[105] Similarly, Alicia Crofton of Lakefield, Mohill was determined to feed all those excluded from public relief by means of her private fund which she intended to operate with her children, Duke and Alicia Maria. The effects of fever and dysentery in the area were evident in that people were 'afflicted with swollen limbs' and were unable to move about 'except with difficulty'. The Quakers sent her one ton of Indian meal and five hundredweight of biscuit.[106]

A familial approach was also in evidence in Drumshanbo where the Nobles, Rev. William and his sister Mary Ann, were engaged both in feeding those in need and continuing, and indeed, expanding, their employment scheme with 170 women at spinning and twenty-eight men weaving. Their food supply was largely dependent on the Quaker fund and on 7 June they received a further half ton of Indian meal and rice. With the aid of the relief committee's boilers they were thus able to feed those in need three days a week.[107]

At the beginning of June, George Shaw was distributing eighty gallons of 'rice porridge' every day, and double on Saturday in Drumsna. This was given free to 140 children attending his infant and female school, while whatever remained was sold at one penny per quart to around fifty families 'of the industrious labouring class'. He informed the Quakers that due to their assistance 'multitudes in this neighbourhood have been preserved from perishing by famine'. On 10 June he received an order for a further ton of rice.[108] Similar sentiments were expressed by Ellen Lawder who commented that if it had not been for the Quaker charity those in receipt would 'inevitably follow hundreds of their poor countrymen to the grave'. She was supplying 120 people independent of the relief committee.[109]

Despite the new relief measures Fr Edward Keogh, parish priest of Kilmore and Cloonaff, commented that 'the people are reduced to skeletons and are daily dying in large numbers of starvation'. Many were in receipt of only one pound of meal daily while very few families were receiving full rations 'on account of the dread of taxation with which mostly all relief committees are very naturally impressed'.[110]

Writing from Glenfarne Hall, Loftus Tottenham complained of the many cases, such as those recovering from disease, fever, dysentery, etc, which the act did not cater for. In order to aid these he received a grant of one half ton each of Indian meal and rice, which was to be distributed 'without religious distinction'.[111]

The Vicar of Oughteragh, Richard Clifford, complained that in order to both 'clothe the naked and feed the poor' daily demands were made upon his own 'scanty resources'. He added that 'I need scarcely observe that all that is done under the government sanction leaves much still to be done in individual cases.' Thanks to the Quakers he, together with his wife, had been able to relieve 500 individuals and in the process preserve them from 'utter destitution'. However, such was the level of demand, he now requested a boiler of 100 gallons.[112] In Newtowngore, Rev. Henry O'Brien maintained a soup kitchen distributing rice and oatmeal but Catherine Godley of nearby Killigar wished to establish her own relief effort to feed those holding land and hence barred from receiving government support. She wished to support them until the next harvest because if they were 'forced to sell their last cow or give up their land now to enable them to apply for relief they will be kept in perpetual poverty'. Indeed, she believed that many who were unable to support themselves until that time 'still have good prospects … if we are to be blessed with a plentiful harvest'.[113]

In a letter to the Quakers, dated 25 June, Francis Kane of Drumsna stated his embarrassment at having to once again apply for a grant. He had resisted doing so in the belief that it would have been 'unreasonable' but due to the fact that there was 'much suffering which the government measures do not alleviate', he was once again forced to seek their help. On 2 July he was granted one ton of Indian meal.[114] In the same way Jane Isabella Banks received a half ton of Indian meal and rice to aid those recovering from sickness in the Carrick-on-Shannon area.[115]

Due to 'small subscriptions obtained from various sources' George Hindes had been able to support some people in the Killargue area until the new act commenced. However, when it became obvious that many were excluded from official relief he combined forces with Fr Felix MacHugh to feed those in Killargue and Cloonlougher holding more than four acres. To support them in their efforts the Quakers sent them one ton of Indian meal.[116] By the end of June the situation faced by those attempting to do the best they could in difficult circumstances was encapsulated in the following comments from Anne Percy of Garradice, Ballinamore:

> In the district of Lower Drumreilly, which contains thirty-eight townlands, there is much poverty and destitution, especially amongst small farmers holding from one to five acres of ground. The public works were a great source of relief and means of subsistence but for some time back an entire stop having been put to them the poor have been entirely thrown on the relief committee which for some unaccountable circumstance are now without funds or in a position to afford relief. Hence, there is the greatest possible distress in the locality.[117]

To aid her in her relief efforts with the vicar of Drumreilly, Rev. Thomas Pentland, she received a grant of one ton of Indian meal from the Quakers.[118]

Alicia Crofton and Loftus Tottenham had made reference to the effects of disease in their localities and in June J. Peyton of Springfield and Thomas Kirkwood revealed the extent to which disease was now ravaging the area around Carrick-on-Shannon. In remarking that there was increasing sickness of every kind, with fever in particular spreading to a great extent, Peyton revealed that 'between this [Springfield] and Carrick-on-Shannon are six fever huts in which none of those a tall man stand upright and yet in some a family of six or seven struggle for existence'.[119] Similar reports emerged from Margarita Kirkwood in nearby Lakeview who sought support for parts of the parishes of Toomna and Killukin. She reported that fever and dysentery prevailed to 'a frightening extent', the former increased considerably since the hot weather at the start of July. She remarked that there were now 'fever huts in every direction' with the fear of the contagion so great that 'mothers move their own children into the huts and leave drink outside for them'. She also noted that several churches had been 'deserted' due to the small numbers able to attend while bodies were being buried without coffins in ground 'so shallow as to shock human nature'.[120]

Although the Manorhamilton divisions had been the last to start operating the public soup kitchens they were the first to close them, on 15 August while those of Mohill, closed two weeks later. However, such was the extent of distress in the divisions of Glenade and Kinlough in the Ballyshannon union and the entire Carrick-on-Shannon union that kitchens there remained open until 12 September. The following table illustrates the government's figures for those in receipt of rations in the county during the period the act was in place:

**Table 5.1: Numbers in Receipt of Food in County Leitrim under the Temporary Relief Act**

| Electoral Division | Pop In 1841 | Max Number | Number when Ceased | Period of Relief |
|---|---|---|---|---|
| Ballyshannon Union | | | | |
| Glenade | 4,234 | 685 | 205 | 6 May–12 September |
| Kinlough | 4,646 | 1,097 | 274 | 6 May–12 September |
| **TOTAL** | **8,880** | **1,782** | **479** | |

| Carrick-on-Shannon Union | | | |
|---|---|---|---|
| Carrick-on-Shannon | 5,695 | 1,604 | 457 | 1 May–12 September |
| Aughrim | 4,469 | 2,628 | 1,143 | 15 May–12 September |
| Creeve | 2,872 | 1,257 | 686 | 15 May–12 September |
| Drumshanbo | 6,000 | 1,682 | 1,143 | 10 May–12 September |
| Drumreilly | 3,735 | 1,402 | 1,143 | 15 May–12 September |
| Drumsna | 3,028 | 649 | 182 | 9 May–12 September |
| Elphin | 5,363 | 3,544 | 990 | 10 May–12 September |
| Gilstown | 4,600 | 3,244 | 1,108 | 13 May–12 September |
| Keshcarrigan | 4,932 | 1,829 | 775 | 17 May–12 September |
| Kilglass | 5,759 | 3,147 | 571 | 29 May–12 September |
| Killukin | 3,863 | 2,015 | 890 | 6 May–12 September |
| Kilmore | 5,164 | 2,692 | 457 | 28 May–12 September |
| Kiltubrid | 3,949 | 1,151 | 709 | 18 May–12 September |
| Leitrim | 4,244 | 2,669 | 743 | 17 May–12 September |
| Tumna | 3,449 | 2,541 | 745 | 18 May–12 September |
| **TOTAL** | **67,077** | **32,090** | **11,742** | |

| Mohill Union | | | |
|---|---|---|---|
| Mohill | 7,990 | 1,705 | 1,073 | 20 May–26 August |
| Aughavas | 4,779 | 1,463 | 928 | 20 May–29 August |
| Annaduff | 6,469 | 1,563 | 888 | 20 May–29 August |
| Annaveagh | 5,627 | 1,106 | 672 | 20 May–29 August |
| Ballinamore | 6,970 | 1,606 | 857 | 20 May–29 August |
| Carrigallen | 4,763 | 2,032 | 1,428 | 20 May–29 August |
| Cloone | 7,038 | 1,287 | 903 | 20 May–29 August |
| Drumreilly | 3,700 | 1,231 | 953 | 20 May–29 August |
| Eslin | 3.095 | 388 | 118 | 20 May–29 August |
| Fenagh | 4,374 | 429 | 423 | 20 May–29 August |
| Newtowngore | 3,337 | 976 | 685 | 20 May–29 August |
| Oughteragh | 4,714 | 1,051 | 914 | 20 May–29 August |
| Rinn | 6.003 | 1,322 | 994 | 20 May–29 August |
| **TOTAL** | **68,859** | **16,159** | **10,836** | |

| Manorhamilton Union | | | |
|---|---|---|---|
| Manorhamilton | 8,074 | 1,600 | 1,246 | 7 June–15 August |
| Cloonlogher | 2,451 | 255 | 252 | 17 June–15 August |
| Dromahaire | 4,182 | 471 | 459 | 31 May–15 August |
| Drumkeerin | 5,923 | 1,275 | 1,275 | 25 June–15 August |
| Inishmagrath | 3,712 | 954 | 945 | 11 June–15 August |
| Killenummery | 4.605 | 711 | 571 | 7 June–15 August |
| Killargue | 3,616 | 508 | 506 | 17 June–15 August |
| Kiltyclogher | 4,728 | 637 | 626 | 16 June–15 August |
| Lurganboy | 4,011 | 480 | 171 | 17 May–15 August |
| Rossinver | 4,686 | 534 | 526 | 15 June–15 August |
| **TOTAL** | **45,988** | **7,425** | **6,577** | |

*Source*: Reprinted British Parliamentary Papers, volume 8, Distress (Ireland), Supplementary appendix to the seventh, and last, report of the Relief Commissioners, pp.28, 33, 67 and 68.

The figures illustrate that, at its height, the relief act was supporting 36,388 people in the county. In Manorhamilton there was a maximum dependency figure of 16 per cent; in the two divisions in Ballyshannon, 20 per cent; in Mohill 23 per cent and in Carrick-on-Shannon 48 per cent. However, statistics within the unions varied widely. For example, in Manorhamilton they ranged from 10 per cent in Cloonlogher to 22 per cent in Drumkeerin, while within the Mohill union the disparity was even greater with a figure of 10 per cent in Fenagh contrasted with 43 per cent in Carrigallen. Other areas with substantial dependency in the union were Newtowngore (29 per cent), Aughavas (31 per cent) and Drumreilly (33 per cent). In Carrick the lowest figure was the 21 per cent recorded in Drumsna followed by Carrick and Drumshanbo on 28 per cent, Drumreilly and Keshcarrigan on 37 per cent and Leitrim, where almost two-thirds of the population (62 per cent) were in receipt of rations.

However, this cannot be taken as an accurate estimate of the numbers in distress. In fact, analysis of the various electoral divisions reveals the extent to which the government measure failed to deal with thousands deemed ineligible. For example, Drumsna was evidently one of the worst-affected areas and yet the official figures record a maximum of 649 people receiving relief, with only 182 on the lists at the termination of the measure. As well as demonstrating the restrictive nature of the new legislation these figures simply serve to illustrate the dependence on private relief efforts in the area. Similarly in Fenagh, the local relief committee had been distributing bread and soup three times each week, supplementing this with the sale of meal twice a week. On 17 April members had declared their intention to 'avoid as long as possible the necessity of striking a rate' and with £276 in money and provisions it appears that this committee was therefore able to support 'a numerous class of persons whose names can not be placed on the relief lists'.[121]

The table below is a synopsis of the material gleaned by the relief commissioners but as the following illustrates many thousands availed of this aid throughout the period in question.

**Table 5.2: Monthly Rations Issued under Temporary Relief Act**

| | Number of Rations | | | | | |
|---|---|---|---|---|---|---|
| Union | 8 May | 5 June | 3 July | 31 July | 28 August | 11 September |
| Carrick-on-Shannon | 786 | 16,772 | 23,582 | 24,120 | 20,396 | 10,275 |
| Manorhamilton | 0 | 164 | 3,337 | 6,096 | 0 | – |
| Mohill | 0 | 10,410 | 11,823 | 13,460 | 8,544 | – |

*Source*: British Parliamentary Papers volume 8, second report of the Relief Commissioners, pp.24–5; third report of the Relief Commissioners, pp.30–1; fourth report of the Relief Commissioners, pp.6–7; fifth report of the Relief Commissioners, pp.7–8; sixth Report of the Relief Commissioners, pp.8–9; seventh report of the Relief Commissioners, pp.8–9.

The Mohill figures demonstrate numbers consistently in excess of 10,000 in receipt of relief. Emphasising the extreme deprivation in the Carrick union was the fact that relief commenced there in early May and the numbers had reached almost 17,000 by the first week of June. From then until the end of August they remained above 20,000. In consequence, relief was only terminated in the union on 12 September.

As the soup kitchens began to wind down their operations, those involved in private relief continued to appeal for aid. For example, on 14 August, a fortnight before the official soup kitchens closed, Richard Conolly applied for help for his private kitchen in Clooncumber. From this he had been supplying Indian meal and rice to those not on the lists and was sent twelve hundredweight of rice by the Quakers.[122] For his part, George Mansfield stated that the 'public relief measure necessarily mitigated the general distress considerably' in Cashcarrigan. In spite of this however, levels of sickness prevailed and the grants of rice sent by the society proved 'of incalculable service'.[123] However, Matilda Shanly of Riversdale was scathing in her criticism of the relief effort in the Ballinamore area. As in other areas no share of the 'scanty allowance' was given to those with land or in employment. Nevertheless, she alleged that 'no attempt' had been made to obtain aid under the Temporary Relief Act 'due to the want of exertion on the part of the landed proprietors'. She had been feeding between a dozen and fourteen families (c. 100 individuals) in the townlands of Riversdale and Aghoo and noted that, as in the Carrick area, 'between this house and the town, a distance of one mile, at least thirty persons are lying in fever at the back of ditches and at the roadside'. She also remarked that on the land of her neighbour, Dr Collins of Murrin, 'I have known many of his tenantry to die from want and he sent, I believe, nearly 100 of them free to America.'[124]

On 16 August George Beresford requested a grant of food to assist him in his continuing endeavours in Fenagh. However, he was disappointed to hear that the society had no source of food in that part of the country while 'distribution has very much ceased for the present'.[125] When E. Lawder of Mough House, also in Fenagh, informed the society that many people 'have not a morsel to put into their mouths but what they receive from you at my hands' she was told that Beresford had already received a grant of rice which, they hoped would 'suffice for the district at present'.[126] However, a more definite response was given in reply to a request for food from John Strean who sought aid on behalf of the poor of Toomna. The society replied that it had discontinued grants of food and money for general relief purposes adding that 'it appears indispens[a]ble that some means be taken to leave the people to rely more on their own resources'.[127] They may have been influenced in their thinking by correspondence from individuals such as Denis Booth in Drumsna who, in acknowledging receipt of four sacks of wheaten meal on 16 August, stated that 'this is the last time I intend to solicit your help'.[128]

However, Booth's apparent optimism was counterbalanced by a report from Emily Auchmuty in the same locality, who, by the end of August, had distributed 10 cwt of rice to 250 families 'of the most destitute', encompassing '720 souls' – more than the total maximum number recorded for the electoral division under the government measure. Their existence depended on either the unlikely possibility of work or 'public charity' due to the fact that the destitution suffered by them some months earlier had precluded cultivation of their land. In order to help her cope with the fever which was 'now raging very much in the locality' the society sent her a half ton of rice.[129]

With such numbers still reliant on private charity there was a mixture of uneasiness and foreboding as to what the future held. This was epitomised in comments made to Mr Bertolacci of the Irish Reproductive Loan Fund by John Duckworth who suggested that money accumulated by the Carrick-on-Shannon and Drumshanbo funds could be 'well applied in the way of loans to poor people who will, when the relief works stop on 15th August, be sadly off'. Revealing that he had employed night 'watchmen' to ensure the safety of his cattle he lamented that 'I do really think that when the works and relief cease … we will have some awful scenes of plunder by persons who are destitute and starving.'[130]

Duckworth's apprehension was consequent upon the lack of a long-term strategy being adopted by the British government which now embarked upon yet another initiative. Thus, with the closure of the public soup kitchens, relief for the thousands in the county still in need of aid now devolved solely upon the poor law.

# Chapter 6

# NO POOR LAW CAN MEET IT

Statistics for indoor and outdoor relief in Carrick-on-Shannon Poor Law Union, February 1848. Courtesy of Leitrim County Library, Ballinamore, County Leitrim.

I N THE SPRING of 1847 the British government, in light of a good grain harvest and a successful, if tiny potato harvest, made the decision to place future responsibility for the poor entirely under the auspices of the poor law authorities. Hence, the Poor Law Extension Act enabled boards of guardians to offer indoor and outdoor relief, the latter for the first time while, as historian Peter Gray has acknowledged, there was to be 'only very modest transitional assistance from state and charitable funds'.[1]

By the middle of September, even allowing for the inaccuracy of the government's own statistics, there were, according to the official figures, more than 23,0000 people still in need of relief in the county. By this time the poor were facing difficulties on two fronts: the government soup kitchens had been closed down and, as pointed out by J.M. Kirkwood of Woodbrook Lodge, near Carrick, 'the funds of the societies who have so kindly given relief are exhausted' leaving 'hundreds of poor creatures on the verge of starvation'.[2]

At the same time, in the inevitable hiatus between establishing the new law and bringing it into operation, there was a certain amount of uncertainty, not to say confusion, about the immediate future. This was epitomised in the response of the Society of Friends in this period. In a letter from Ballinamore, Jane Ellis outlined how she had fed around 120 people with meal sent by them. However, with no public works, these remained in danger 'having neither food nor clothes' and hence she requested another donation. However, the society replied that they had 'at present discontinued food issues', stating their 'hope that in the present state of the country the local resources will be found generally sufficient to meet the existing distress'.[3] However, in refusing a further request from Francis Kane of Drumsna their position appeared to change in that they claimed they had stopped giving out any grants 'on grounds of greater need in the future'.[4] Denis Booth of Drumsna, who reported that the price of potatoes was 'beyond the reach of the poor', was similarly informed that 'grants may be more called for' in the winter.[5]

Nevertheless, the fact was that food grants, albeit small ones, were being made by the Quakers. On 3 October Emma Lawder sent her thanks for three bags of rice received by her in Drumsna on 9 September, although she regretted that it represented 'a drop of water in the ocean'. With 'distress getting greater every day' on account of the closure of the government scheme she requested further food but was told that the Quakers found it 'necessary to economise' and assured her that if she could purchase a quarter ton of Indian meal they would send her the same amount in rice.[6]

Throughout the months of September to December constant references were made by correspondents to the fact that the closure of government soup kitchens and introduction of the poor law extension act had resulted in large numbers being left in want. For example, Emily Auchmuty stated that the hundreds 'who had before lived on the rations issued out under the operation of the Relief act are now in the greatest destitution'. With the 'poor house the only asylum available' she was now 'for want of means' unable to give any more aid. Between 15 September and 5 October, in her efforts 'to rescue members of the human family from starvation and fever', she had distributed three bags of rice to 109 families 'of the most distressed' comprising 565 individuals.[7] The termination of government relief meant that in the Killukin area '700 of our poor people are by the order of the Relief Commissioners deprived of all means of support'.[8]

By November the poor of Drumsna were 'in the most deplorable state of destitution' and Jane Ireland, in seeking aid for 'the starving population of this locality' revealed that distress was becoming more widespread. This was consequent on the 'country being overburdened with taxes' which meant that, significantly, 'the hitherto comfortable farmers are almost reduced to beggary, unable to meet many demands thereby leaving a vast number totally unprovided for'.[9]

Rather than simply distribute food, the society appeared to prefer supporting private work initiatives. For example, when Penelope Johnston reported increasing distress in the Bundoran area she also revealed that she was attempting to maintain employment of 'a great number of women' who were paid both in food and clothing. She was sent an order for one ton of Indian meal from Sligo.[10] However, despite reporting that 'many poor creatures' in Drumsna had been eking out a 'miserable existence on no other nutriment but the wild herbage of the fields' and their position was 'more distressing than ever', John B. Hogg was refused a grant and told that Emily Auchmuty had already been sent half a ton of rice and some rice.[11] Similarly, G.H.C. Peyton, of Carrick, was informed that the committee 'for some time past have not distributed food'.[12]

When Emma Lawder requested some aid her appeal was directed to the temporary inspector of the Mohill union, Major Haliday, for his observations. This was done for two reasons: first Lawder, 'although having received a small grant is a stranger to us'; second, and of more relevance issues of food had been 'very much discontinued' especially in those districts where the British Relief Association were giving assistance through the various inspecting officers 'as we find to be the case in the Carrick-on-Shannon union'.[13]

## WORKHOUSES

### Carrick-on-Shannon

On 7 August twenty of the Carrick-on-Shannon guardians, together with, assistant poor law commissioner Ganly, met to consider both the organisation of the union into relief districts and the salaries of relieving officers.[14] The following week they elected the relieving officers but a dispute arose between the commissioners and themselves. The commissioners wished to see nine relief districts whereas the board sought one for each of the fifteen electoral divisions of the union.[15] In early September the commissioners granted permission for the board to grant outdoor relief to able-bodied men during the autumn but the latter protested that the appointment of relieving officers was 'premature' as there were 645 vacancies in the building. In addition, their appointment would necessitate unnecessary expense, with the board stating that 'we can scarcely maintain the inmates now in the house'.[16] Indeed it was not until 23 September that the guardians actually agreed to organise the union into relief districts, eventually acquiescing in the commissioners' wishes for nine as follows:

**Table 6.1: Relief Districts in the Carrick-on-Shannon Union, September 1847**

| Number | Electoral Division |
|--------|-------------------|
| 1 | Drumreilly |
| 2 | Kiltubrid/Drumshanbo |
| 3 | Keshcarrigan |
| 4 | Leitrim/Toomna |
| 5 | Elphin |
| 6 | Drumsna/Kilmore |
| 7 | Creeve/Aughrim |
| 8 | Kilglass/Kiltoom |
| 9 | Carrick-on-Shannon/Killukin |

*Source*: Leitrim County Library, Ballinamore, Carrick-on-Shannon board of guardians' minute book, BG 52/A/4, 23 September, p.333.

By the beginning of November 1847 there were still only 304 paupers in the Carrick workhouse[17] and the guardians, aware of the destitution in

Government-Aided Relief Committees in County Leitrim, December 1846. Drawn by Sean Gill.

all parts of the union, once again asked the poor law commissioners for a loan, this time of £300, until the new rate would be 'put in collection'.[18] The need for such, and their awareness of the implications of not receiving it, were laid out in a statement of the condition of the union:

> The immense amount of the most utter destitution that exists requires absolutely that immediate assistance be given to many not at present in the house and as the rate is a large one and that so large a portion of it is payable by the proprietors the funds must be very soon available but we know not where to obtain even small funds to enable us to receive into the house the very worst cases of destitution until then.[19]

The obvious inability of the Carrick workhouse to deal with the level of applications, and to sanction outdoor relief, had repercussions. On 16 November George Shaw claimed that the poor of Drumsna received 'no relief whatsoever, either indoor or out of door' due to the fact that the local guardians 'plead utter inability to collect rates'. He continued:

> A few who were formerly inmates of the Poor House have been retained but no new applicants are received – at least I have applied in vain for relief for many starving objects. At this moment there are immediately around my own residence ten families of orphans left deserted by the deaths of parents (in several instances of both) and were it not for the food Mrs Shaw and I endeavour to supply them with, they would actually perish. We also continue to feed the children of our infant and work school who receive a comfortable meal daily.[20]

Parish Priest of Kilmore and Cloonaff, Father Edward Keogh, wished to acquaint the Quakers with his observation that 'without the least exaggeration' distress and destitution in the area was 'much more appalling than any which the people have as yet witnessed'. The consequences of such were as follows:

> The population of this parish and a half in the last census was more than 7,000 and this is now reduced by famine and other diseases consequent, together with emigration, to around 5,000 and of this number 1,500 at least are without any present means of support save

the very little which they are casually able to procure by begging from persons placed only a degree or two above themselves.[21]

In similar fashion to George Shaw he criticised the guardians of the Carrick union claiming that 'at the termination of the Temporary Relief Act they were told that the new poor law would amply provide for every case of destitution but no effort is being made in this union to put the law into operation or even fill the poor house'.[22]

One man who sought to intercede on behalf of the guardians was local parish priest, Fr Peter Dawson, who wrote to the commissioners to ask them to 'assist in saving human life which is periled to a fearful extent at present'. Noting that the guardians 'seem determined to turn over a new leaf and act with energy' he remarked that while the books of the institution were being arranged 'numbers will die of starvation'. In the absence of their requested loan 'this town especially must suffer' due to the fact that the destitute who came in from remote districts seeking admission to the workhouse 'are unable to return and crawl through the town begging, or die by the way-sides'.[23] However, Dawson's appeal was rejected by the commissioners who alleged that the difficulties in the union had been 'produced by the negligence and unfitness in the collectors employed by the … guardians'. They stated their belief that the situation would improve once 'proper exertions' were made to collect the rate.[24] In his reply, Dawson remarked that although he had been 'grieved and disappointed' their stance 'did not much surprise me':

> The commissioners coolly reply that the present difficulty arises from past misconduct and that they cannot recommend a loan, where the distress arises from want of exertion. Did the men who directed that answer believe that even a British House of Commons would sanction such conduct? Are the innocent, whose distress arose not from want of exertion on their part, to perish, because the Guardians were remiss last year and because the Commissioners, their Inspectors, and their Auditors, neglected to apply a remedy, which they alone could apply? The Temporary Relief Act last year might palliate the management of the Poor Law; but this season it is the only hope of starving thousands. I therefore ask again what I solicited in my letter of the 14th and beg to add that the Commissioners are accountable to God for the lives sacrificed by negligence, at which they connived.[25]

In response, the commissioners stated that none of the surrounding unions had requested such temporary aid and felt sure that once rate-payers were made aware of the 'true state of the union and the necessities of the poor' they would no longer 'permit the latter to suffer' by continuing to hold rates.[26]

Turning instead to the under-secretary of state, Thomas Redington, Dawson expressed his surprise that Carrick had not been included amongst a group of twenty-two unions designated as distressed remarking that 'the Commissioners reported it third amongst the five worst in the kingdom. Captain Wynne says it is the very worst'.[27] Indeed, the guardians expressed how they were 'astonished' at this decision 'in consequence of the extreme state of destitution' therein. Not surprisingly, Redington reflected the ethos of the commissioners and emphasised that it was on 'local exertions and sources the main reliance must be placed for the future support of such destitute persons as cannot obtain employment'. He was confident that once the collection of rates commenced 'the immediate difficulty arising from want of funds will be overcome', adding that 'there appears no reason to apprehend that the actual destitution at present in the Union cannot be relieved by the rate payers'.[28]

Having received this letter Fr Dawson replied that 'further correspondence is useless':

> Since I came here last March, 1,000 of my poor parishioners have died of famine and disease the effect (immediate effect) of famine. The Poor Law Commission, the Relief Commissioners and the Government were appealed to in vain. The mortality in the poor house – 89 deaths in February, 189 in March, 295 in April, etc., was allowed to increase until the house literally emptied itself into the graveyard.[29]

Referring to the commissioners' charge that distress was due to 'local neglect, local responsibility, the guardians in fault', he asked if the government was satisfied to have 'the lives of one class at the disposal of another' adding, 'if so, further interference is utterly useless'.[30] Captain Edmund Wynne, who had been appointed as temporary poor inspector, was aware of the correspondence and stated that there was 'too much truth in the picture Mr Dawson has drawn of the past and present condition of the poor of this union'. He added that 'the great pressure on him may, in some degree, excuse his unreasonableness and importunity'.[31] However, the commissioners had obviously been examining the condition of the Carrick union and on 20 November 1847 Wynne made his first appearance at a board meeting.[32] His initial experience of the union would have been all too familiar to the other five guardians who attended: a demand from the Public Works Loan Office for the second and third instalments (£180 total) on the £1,200 loan foisted on the board; the news that four rate collectors had used almost £54 of rate for their own purposes; a subpoena on behalf of William O'Donnell of Dublin for debts of almost £240; a contract for Mr Dowd to supply water to the workhouse at 5*d* per puncheon. Indeed, the financial state of the house was epitomised by the fact that only five shillings was lodged for this week with the treasurer, and this from the sale of old rags.[33]

On 27 November Wynne informed the commissioners that he had spent the day meeting local people of influence and explaining to them that the rates were the 'sole source' for dealing with the current situation. At the same time he made reference to the 'multitudes of destitute at present crowding the roads in every direction'.[34] Wynne's impact was dramatic and he informed the commissioners that any suggestion made by him 'was readily and promptly adopted' by the guardians; at the following meeting on 27 November 387 persons (rising to 415) were admitted to the house while none were rejected.[35] It is difficult to ascertain if Wynne was responsible for another initiative but it was something which had never previously been contemplated by the guardians. With just over £3,000 remaining uncollected, the board (and Wynne) stated that if any principal rate payer remitted their rates within one week they would be allowed the collectors' fees of 2/6 in the pound on the amount paid.[36] This resulted in almost £300 being received in that week and as this 'inducement for rates was considered too short' it was extended for another week.[37] The next week saw a payment of over £437 and thus the policy was extended for a further fortnight.[38]

By the end of December the house was filled with 869 inmates but unlike earlier in the year the number in hospital and fever (sixty-three) was significantly smaller.[39] Nevertheless, with the house now having reached capacity Wynne suggested that the guardians should approach the Shannon Commissioners to ask on what terms they would rent the Jamestown Mill to the union. He had ascertained that this building, just a couple of miles from Carrick and situated on the Shannon, would be able to hold a further five hundred inmates.[40] This initiative was necessary as, in Wynne's words, the Carrick union presented 'peculiar difficulties' in that 'vast numbers of families have been unhoused and their houses destroyed'. Consequently:

> You cannot admit them to the workhouse, there is no room; you cannot give them outdoor relief, they have no houses, nor does the union afford any building or buildings that might be purchased or hired for the purpose.[41]

On 22 December he highlighted the fact that of 916 in the workhouse, 207 still retained houses, 709 were 'houseless' while a further 337, without homes, had been denied entry. Further, there were 'at least 1,200 wandering about the union' meaning there were well in excess of 2,200 'without homes or houses where they could receive out-door maintenance'. Those who refused were forced to wander the streets of Carrick and Wynne reported how 'their cries may be heard all night in the streets of this town'. He added that he had often been forced to find shelter in stables for those 'found perishing in the streets at night' before gaining provisional admittance to the workhouse the following morning. In addition, 'a considerable number of temporary huts may be seen erected against the backs of ditches on the road-side; and even these, I find, are rarely inhabited two consecutive weeks by the same family'.[42] He also suggested that where numbers in a family were small such would be encouraged to take in another family as lodgers which could, he estimated, account for between 300 and 400 individuals.[43]

Prior to his appointment to Carrick, Wynne had spent time working in County Clare and his following reflections on the condition of the people in the union in late 1847 highlight the extremity of their situation:

> I have met a greater amount of urgent and pressing destitution in this union than in any part of Ireland I have visited, as in addition to want of food, which exists to as great an extent as in any other part of Ireland, want of shelter from the inclemency of the season exists to a far greater extent than in any other part with which I am acquainted.[44]

On 31 December, Wynne reiterated this point claiming that 'I fear the extent of destitution in this union has never been fairly represented.' In his opinion, it was 'perfectly frightful', adding that even though he was 'accustomed to scenes of misery in the western counties' he had 'never met with so extensive and almost hopeless destitution'.[45] Nevertheless, he believed in adherence to the philosophy of strict economy and when the parish priest of Drumshanbo, Father Heslin, pleaded for the distribution of food to the poor from government depots Wynne maintained that he had actually 'retarded the relief' of the people by leading them to believe that, by such a measure 'other means than those provided by the Poor Law' were available.[46] He rejected the demand to, as he put it, 'throw a quantity of provisions now in government store, into his locality, the distribution of which should be placed under local control and supervision' simply dismissing this as representing 'the universal demand'.[47]

Referring to the operation of the tenth section of the Irish Poor Relief Extension Act, he alluded to the people as being 'impracticable' and appearing to 'run contrary to every effort made for the purpose of mitigating their sufferings', noting:

> They will not apply to the workhouse till too late for human aid, as will clearly appear from the hundreds of absolute spectres who are this moment inmates and who, in my opinion and that of the medical attendant, cannot recover.
>
> Nor is it possible to persuade even these wretched persons to remain in. They are constantly demanding their discharge and leaving the house in such a state of exhaustion as causes them to sink under a degree of cold that would not affect persons in a state of ordinary health and strength.
>
> This case applies also to those persons who, still clinging to their cabins, leave them occasionally to buy or beg their bread and returning home, sit down to rest themselves and overcome by exhaustion and cold rise no more. This is the immediate cause of (I believe) every case of death in which an inquest has been held in this country where the verdict has been 'death from starvation'; and it is very difficult, if possible, to prevent it whilst there is the slightest prospect of any relief in their own cabins where they have that combination of diet, smoke and warmth which they love. They will cling to them, in many cases, to the death, and more especially when they are certain that immediately on their leaving them those cabins will be destroyed.

> It is a sad state of things difficult to remedy and especially so on
> account of the impracticability of the poor creatures themselves.[48]

Having seen an improved rate collection and subsequent balance in
the bank of more than £762, one of the final acts of the board was to
investigate the debts due to contractors and staff up to 25 March 1847.
On receiving these it was decided to make an effort to pay and in this
way contractors received one-quarter of the total amount owed while
workhouse staff received one-half.[49]

In his first report to the poor law commissioners Wynne focussed
on the problems surrounding collection of rates. He revealed that he had
held an interview with two new collectors and informed them that the
rates must be collected 'on any terms, at any risk and notwithstanding any
difficulties or obstacles that may be thrown in the way'.[50]

However, the reality of the threats to rate collectors was made clear
within three days as both men had resigned as a result of the assassination of
Rev. John Lloyd near Aughrim 'and the general alarm which the event has
produced'.[51] Consequently, £100 which they had advanced was withdrawn
leaving the guardians in a serious financial difficulty. This money had facilitated
the admission of a large number of paupers and payment of outstanding bills.
Its sudden removal meant that there was 'scarcely provision for three days'
consumption in the house', leaving the guardians in a worse position than
before.

For paupers, such occurrences exacerbated an already dire situation.
Wynne estimated there were at least 1,600 persons, 'most of whom have
given up their houses and land', waiting for admittance. This was in spite of
the condition of the house and grounds which he stated would be 'highly
discreditable to the master and other officers' except that everything
required to ensure its running was 'wanting' having been applied for to
the guardians 'in vain'.[52] As examples of such, he cited how:

> It is necessary to have three breakfasts and as many dinners, per day,
> in consequence of there being only one-third of the tins required,
> even for the comparatively small number at present in the house.
>
> The urine-tubs are out of order and fast going to pieces and
> cause great inconvenience.
>
> The rain comes in, in various directions; and the pipes and
> cocks are so much out of order that the boilers overflow on a wet
> day, producing great inconvenience and disorders.[53]

Wynne also highlighted the urgent necessity for the graves 'which were never sufficiently covered' to be properly maintained as the ground had started to crack consequent upon holes made by rats.[54]

At a meeting of the board attended by Wynne on 1 January 1848, the guardians 'resolved forthwith on tendering their resignations'. Citing their incapability to cope with the huge levels of distress in the union, the lack of funds for outdoor relief and their inability, or unwillingness, to dedicate the time required, they called on the commissioners to appoint paid guardians in their place. However, Wynne suggested that they meet on a daily basis to deal with the various matters and informed the commissioners that he was 'anxious to work on with the present board rather than be driven to the alternative of paid guardians, although aware that the latter would considerably lighten my labours and responsibility'.[55] But, while daily meetings took place until 9 January, there were none for another week. Given his confinement to bed with illness at this time Wynne considered such meetings to have been 'peculiarly necessary' in that the measures for outdoor relief required 'prompt execution' as the 'lives of hundreds' depended on them. He was forced to admit that 'I never expected active assistance and zealous co-operation from the guardians' and given their attitude he informed the commissioners that 'in the present state of the union the exertions now made by the guardians will not be found at all adequate to meet the difficulties of the case'.[56] Thus, on 19 January, he informed the commissioners that:

> I can no longer hope to get on with the present Board of Guardians, who appear to have completely deserted their post, and at a time when increased exertions and energy are required to meet the increasing difficulties consequent on the commencement and daily extension of out-door relief, and the execution of movements which become necessary almost daily, to enable us to test the applicants.[57]

He continued:

> I have been obliged to take upon myself much responsibility and many arduous duties that belong entirely to the Guardians, and which I do not conceive myself empowered by law to perform without at least the sanction of the Guardians; but I have taken this course to save the lives of the starving multitude, and under the

promise of that assistance which I now feel assured I shall not receive from the present Board.[58]

On 21 January the clerk of the union received notification from the commissioners of the dissolution of the board of guardians. Referring to Wynne's comments they stated that:

> At an important juncture, the Guardians not only permitted the execution of their functions to depend upon the personal exertions of the Inspector of the Union, and of persons officially unconnected with the administration of the Poor Laws but they did not even make an effort to discharge their duties by their presence and advice. Due to the serious failure of the Board of Guardians in the execution of their duties, the Commissioners are deprived of all reliance upon the Guardians for an effectual administration of relief of the poor of the Union.[59]

On 26 January 1848 the vice-guardians assumed control of the union and one of their first acts was to instruct the visiting committee to carry out an in-depth inspection of the house. Many defects were found: for example, the supply of bedding was described as being 'so meagre' that many of the inmates were found huddled together in the dormitories 'and with the animal heat generated by close contact, tried to make up for the absence of covering'.[60] The description of the temporary fever sheds illustrated the filthy conditions in which those who were in serious ill-health faced:

> Eleven wooden huts, formed of thin boards, rags and mud, capable of containing three patients each, resting on a bog, surrounded by manure heaps which reach the interior, in danger of destruction by fire or storm, under no management, without proper nurses, no fixed dietary or adequate accounts kept, out of the way of any supervision, seems to us a very imperfect description of fever hospital, and its use we think should be only the last resource ... and we think that persons would be more likely to acquire diseases therein caused by cold and wet than be cured of fever.[61]

In requesting a meeting with the old relief committee, which had been responsible for the fever sheds, the vice guardians found that a number of them were ex-officio members of the late board of guardians 'and certainly did not seem actuated by very benevolent or philanthropic motives'.[62]

As a result of this report the vice-guardians resolved to bring about an improvement in the condition of the house. Therefore, they ordered that whitewashing be carried out vigorously, yards cleaned, food cooked earlier and manure gathered into heaps. New clothing was to be utilised 'with the least delay', the inmates being 'previously washed' and their old clothing fumigated. In addition, able-bodied men were to be employed in making 'proper sewers'. Lastly, they decreed that 'classification, discipline and cleanliness throughout the establishment be better observed'.[63]

However, despite their best efforts the vice guardians, just like their predecessors in the old elected board, were to find that the maintenance of the workhouse was dependent on a variety of factors, not least of which was the susceptibility of staff to contracting disease. On 12 February the clerk reported that the master, matron and schoolmaster were all suffering from fever and this had caused 'great difficulties for the management of the workhouse'.[64] When a new temporary master, Mr Horan, was appointed the guardians were 'much gratified' to perceive an improvement throughout the establishment under his management.[65] However, by 11 March he, together with the new schoolmaster, William Ness, were both suffering from fever, while the matron was recovering from dysentery. As with the illness of their predecessors just one month before, these afflictions had created 'much confusion' in the house 'causing a great want of cleanliness'.[66]

Although the Poor Law Extension Act allowed for distribution of food outside the workhouse it did so within strict parameters. Hence relief was restricted to three categories: the permanently disabled; those disabled by temporary sickness; and widows with two or more legitimate children. However, under section, outdoor relief in food only was permitted to other classes if the workhouse was full or if contagious disease prevailed.[67] The rations in the Carrick union consisted of 16 oz bread for adults; 12 oz for children aged 12–15; 10 oz for those from 9–12; 8 oz for 2–9 year olds and 6 oz for those under two.[68]

As with the workhouse, the necessary returns for all aspects of outdoor relief relied on the ability and conscientious nature of each relieving officer. This was to prove somewhat problematic in the months ahead. Thus, for the week ending 22 January it was noted that 'from the defective state of the relieving officers' books this return cannot be made up'.[69] However, these were soon in order and the figures illustrated the dramatic rise in numbers in receipt of relief, despite the fact that Captain Wynne assured the commissioners that 'we are rigidly enforcing the quarter acre clause'.[70] This had been included as part of the new act and stipulated that anybody holding land of greater extent than one-quarter of an acre was ineligible for relief:

**Table 6.2: Numbers in Receipt of Outdoor Relief in Carrick-on-Shannon Union**

| Week Ending | Number in Receipt of Relief | Amount | Cost |
| --- | --- | --- | --- |
| 29 January | 2,268 | 245 qts | £112 |
| 5 February | 3,396 | – | £177 |
| 12 February | 5,905 | 23½ tons | – |
| 19 February | 11,207 | – | £322 |
| 26 February | 13,654 | 24 tons | £340 |
| 4 March | 14,821 | 29 tons | £353 |
| 11 March | 12,716 | – | £328 |
| 18 March | 11,857 | – | £259 |
| 25 March | 12,063 | – | £248 |
| 1 April | 10,788 | 29½ tons | £300 |

*Source*: Leitrim County Library, Ballinamore, Carrick-on-Shannon board of guardians minute book, BG 52A/5, 29 January to 1 April 1848.

As is evident from this table the relieving officers' books were not properly completed on a regular basis and this led to gaps in the statistics presented to the board each week. The vice-guardians regularly commented on the defective nature of relieving officers' returns and in one case the clerk noted that two of them had neither sent in returns nor attended the board. His frustration at their inaction can be gauged from his unusually candid comment that 'from the apparent stupidity of those two relieving officers he believes there is little hope of them performing their duties in a zealous, efficient, manner'.[71] However, the one constant in the returns was the numbers applying for outdoor relief, which were said to be 'increasing with alarming rapidity',[72] as evidenced by the table below:

**Table 6.3: Numbers in Receipt of Outdoor Relief by Electoral Division**

| Electoral Division | Date | | | | |
|---|---|---|---|---|---|
| | 5 February | 12 February | 19 February | 26 February | 4 March |
| Drumreilly | 139 | 271 | 319 | 351 | 326 |
| Kiltubrid / Drumshanbo | 203 | 315 | 1,249 | 1,284 | 1,001 |
| Keshcarrigan | 71 | 143 | 551 | 552 | 1,780 |
| Leitrim / Toomna | 373 | 284 | 963 | 1,421 | 1,449 |
| Elphin | 400 | 240 | 1,382 | 1,438 | 1,525 |
| Drumsna / Kilmore | 368 | 1,071 | 1,857 | 2,266 | 2,167 |
| Creeve / Aughrim | 336 | 1,006 | 1,373 | 1,750 | 1,796 |
| Kilglass / Kiltoom | 618 | 1,390 | 1,707 | 2,169 | 2,272 |
| Carrick-on-Shannon / Killukin | 888 | 1,186 | 1,806 | 2,443 | 2,505 |
| **TOTAL** | **3,396** | **5,905** | **11,207** | **13,654** | **14,821** |

*Source*: Leitrim County Library, Ballinamore, Carrick-on-Shannon board of guardians minute book, BG 52A/5, pp.515, 529, 539, 549 and 559.

In the fortnight from 29 January to 12 February this figure more than doubled but in the following week there was a surge in applications to 11,207 with the numbers eventually peaking at almost 15,000 at the beginning of March.

Doubtless this was due to various initiatives agreed by Wynne, the guardians and, later, the vice-guardians. For example, on 3 January it was decided to discharge those who, although not able-bodied, could provide lodgings for themselves and avail of outdoor relief.[73] In similar fashion, on 12 February the guardians instructed that a list be drawn up of all the aged and infirm women, together with those women who were able-bodied with one or more children (but not deserted), who had been in the house for three months, so as to be able to encourage them to voluntarily seek outdoor relief.[74] The intention was to ensure that any man who was able-bodied would have to face the workhouse test and in March relieving officers were instructed to offer the workhouse option alone to those men not having more than two children. On 26 February each relieving officer was informed that he was to transfer ten able-bodied men from his relief lists to the workhouse.[75] However, the long-term intention was clear in that they were also told to offer this option to 'any further classes of able-bodied men' should the necessary space be found.[76] Nonetheless, the rise in the figure for 25 March was due to the fact that, despite there being 230 able-bodied being struck off by application of the workhouse test, many new applicants 'who have given up their ground who have hitherto clung to it' had now been added to the number.[77]

Indicative of the all-prevailing distress was the fact that in the week ending 12 February 1,444 people were refused while for that ending 4 March, 299 cases were rejected. Two weeks later the figure was 264 and the following week 177.[78] On 13 March the vice guardians reported that 'numerous fresh applications for relief have been made during the past week, many of whom have recently surrendered their land'.[79] On 6 May Wynne reported that numbers on outdoor relief had increased due to the fact that 'numbers of women' had been deserted by their husbands, while 'parties who have been lately evicted from lands have fallen on the poor laws now that the disability is removed'.[80]

Those rejected, referred to by Wynne as 'a mass of undefinable diseases'[81] had only one alternative under the law – resort to the workhouse. The purchase of stone hammers and sledges for those able-bodied receiving outdoor relief epitomised the attitude of the authorities who required that each able-bodied male 'shall perform a task of work during eight hours at least of every day for which relief is received'.[82] In the words of Wynne, 'stone-breaking and the sweeping of the streets of towns will, we trust, drive to independent exertion all who can possibly do so'.[83] In a telling reference to able-bodied men receiving outdoor relief, the vice-guardians stated that:

> Their only resource from starvation is the relief we extend to them, and its paucity, compared to the work they perform, is, we conceive, unerring evidence of their destitution and the total absence of any means of independent exertion.[84]

With the house full and the board involved in negotiations about Jamestown Mill they also enquired about renting Smithill stores near Elphin to provide extra accommodation.[85] Wynne reported that destitution in the union had increased to a 'fearful extent' and claimed that in some localities it had 'reached the entire population' with Drumshanbo, Kilglass and Coothall amongst the most destitute parts of the union.[86] He commented how 'I could discern a palpable change in many of the persons whose appearance I recollected in December, and who were then comparatively in health and vigour.'[87] The difficulties faced by such individuals were outlined by him:

> In most cases these poor persons are landholders, who though apparently willing to surrender their land, still clung to their cabins and were, therefore, unable to prevail on the landlord to take the land and give them a certificate to that effect, which the relieving officers require. In some cases the multiplicity of applications to the relieving officers rendered it impossible for them to visit all the parties, place their names on the list, and issue rations, with that dispatch which would be desirable; but the preliminary steps are found to be indispensable as all cases are represented as most destitute and urgent, and every species of fraud and imposition practised by the applicants.[88]

The dreadful situation had been compounded by the implementation of the crass and punitive 'Gregory Clause' or 'Quarter acre Clause'. As well as ensuring that thousands were left homeless this clause created practical difficulties for those wishing to comply but, through no fault of their own, being refused. For example, on 15 February 1848 the vice guardians informed the commissioners that property owned by the late Mr Waldron, was in the Court of Chancery has residing on it a great number of pauper tenants 'who are every day applying to the relieving officer but he finding them in occupation of more than a quarter acre refuses relief'. It was ascertained that the occupiers were 'anxious to give up possession of land' but they did not know 'to whom they should surrender'. The bailiff had refused to take the land off them and the vice-guardians commented that 'the people may die of starvation as we cannot take them into the workhouse'. The commissioners replied that occupation of land, not title, was the issue and if tenants were prepared to give up their holding they became eligible for relief.[89]

Similarly, what was termed a 'deputation' from Elphin visited the vice-guardians to enquire of the procedure to be adopted in relation to those holding more than a quarter acre of ground who were 'in a state of destitution'. They were told that if the relieving officers who were familiar with them 'would swear that such families would perish if relief were not afforded' then their wives and dependents would be relieved in the workhouse.[90] Despite such reassurances, Wynne admitted that some of the relieving officers had used the quarter acre clause 'with too much vigour'.[91]

George Shaw of Drumsna had no doubt that 'such is the mass of destitution that no poor law can meet it' and reported that by 14 January the outdoor relief system had not yet been established in the district. Revealing that, in consequence, 'the distress of the poor people here with regard to food is extreme', he outlined how he had been dealing with the situation:

> We feed 130 children every day at our schools adjoining my gate for only part of which number we receive aid from the British Association as they exclude children under six and above fourteen, thereby shutting out many of the poor children of our Infant school who are most in need and for whom we are most interested. Also the hard, dry rye bread given by the Association, however fit for elder children, does not suit the young.

Shaw made reference to the British Relief Association and on 1 October 1847 that organisation, under Count Strzelecki, began feeding and clothing children in twenty-seven poor law unions. Between then and the end of April 1848 they advanced £118,000 and distributed more than twenty-one million rations (typically one half-pound of meal). Each of the three Leitrim unions benefitted, with a total of 4,830 relieved in Carrick-on-Shannon; 1,946 in Manorhamilton; and 526 in Mohill.[92]

Thus, in early February, with 2,268 on the outdoor relief list, 830 in the workhouse and 4,300 children in receipt of daily rations, Wynne admitted that a 'very large amount of relief' was being given in the Carrick union but lamented that such was the demand, and the amount of suffering 'that in some localities our efforts are scarcely perceptible', adding how destitution was assuming a 'more formidable character than during any period of the past year'.[93] As an example he offered a graphic description of scenes he had witnessed in the electoral division of Kilmore:

> We found a fearful amount of suffering from want of shelter and from fever amongst the adults, and dysentery among the children ... The sufferers were all, without exception, in receipt of outdoor relief; but they were in the ditches, with a few sticks and a little straw thrown over them, forming their sole shelter from the severe weather that has just passed. In one of these abodes of misery we found the mother dead, with five children around her. She had been dead some time, and no doubt, would have remained unburied, but that Captain Routh and I gave money to procure a coffin. She had died of fever.
>
> The state of things on the townland on which we found this wretched family is not to be wondered at. 22 families or 132 individuals, were unhoused on the 25th of October, the houses or cabins destroyed, and the wretched inhabitants sent wondering through the Union, half-naked, without any means of subsistence, not even a day's employment.
>
> I give no opinion on the propriety or expedience of this step; but I do not hesitate to say, that it has given rise to a state of things that neither I nor any other person in my situation can cope with, under the circumstances of the Union, and the local difficulties they present.[94]

He described the area as 'the scene of more misery than any other in the union' and estimated that its population had fallen by around 700 people to 4,500 out of which 2,136 (47 per cent) were in receipt of relief.[95]

In the midst of the protracted negotiations over Jamestown Mill further accommodation for 100 children was found with an agreement to rent a three-storey building close to the bridge in Carrick owned by Mrs Dockary, at £18 per annum. This was first occupied in the week ending 22 April.[96] Such was essential given the vulnerability of children at this time. Wynne remarked that those who had suffered the loss of parents had been placed on the outdoor list and refused lodgings with their relatives 'on any terms'. Consequently, he believed they were sent to the workhouse 'past all hope of recovery from previous neglect' and the administration was forced to admit them.[97]

Given that the vice-guardians were paid officials appointed by the state they did not have to concern themselves with opposition to rate collections. All that mattered was that the house, and indeed union, was run in an efficient manner and those deemed to be in need of relief catered for. After the initial benefits of the initiative of December 1847 the amount of rate being remitted slowed to its usual pace. Thus, on 12 February, when it was reported that no rates had been lodged for that week, there was £9,245 outstanding and the efforts to attain some semblance of organisation in the house were all proving costly. For example, an assistant to the clerk was employed at a cost of £1 per week in order to prepare the books for audit. Due to the prevalence of disease, an apothecary was appointed at an annual wage of £25.[98] As food supplies had to be stored in various divisions this required the rent of stores and on 26 February Alexander Douglas was paid £1/4 for the use of a house as a store.[99] Further, it was agreed that long-term debts left by the old board should be dealt with by 'some sort of arrangement'.[100] Hence, on 6 May it was decided to pay Robert Bournes, owed more than £1,800, £250 as part of the debt incurred by the old board.[101] On 29 January the vice guardians had stated that it was 'their fixed course of action that the claims of those who persist in compulsory measures shall be the very last which shall receive the benefit of any future resources that may be available'.[102] In addition they believed that such creditors would be 'content with receiving 5s in the pound out of the amount of their claim'.[103] However, Bournes was not satisfied with such ad-hoc payments and he instructed the sheriff to make a seizure of workhouse property to the value of £1,006 This was only prevented when the vice guardians agreed to pay him £50 each week until all the debt was paid.[104]

With such enhanced costs and little or no rate coming in the vice guardians sought alternative means of finance. On 11 March, with expenditure approaching almost £400 per week,[105] they applied to the poor law commissioners for a loan of £500 worth of commissariat provisions to 'meet the immediate pressure and collection of the rates'.[106] The minutes do not state the outcome of this request but the commissioners appeared to intercede on behalf of the vice guardians with the British Relief Association and on 15 April they revealed that the latter had agreed to loan them £270.[107] This was followed by regular weekly disbursements of around £300, which, given the relatively small totals returned by rate collectors, proved vital in maintaining both the outdoor relief lists and the workhouse. In spite of this, the guardians attempted to obtain as much rate as possible, even though Captain Wynne informed the commissioners that 'every gentleman's door was shut against them and they received no rates except from the poorest class'.[108] On 24 June they issued a list of immediate lessors owing rates and instructed that they be served with fifteen days' notice:

### Table 6.4: Poor-Rate Debtors in Carrick-on-Shannon Union

| Immediate Lessor | Amount of Rate Owed |
| --- | --- |
| Richard Henry King | £15/5 |
| Charles J. Peyton, Esq. | £32/17 |
| Ferdinand Keon, Esq. | £44/19 |
| William Slack | £10/18 |
| William Lloyd & Co. | £21/7 |
| Pierce Simpson | £87/12 |
| Peter De La Touche | £24/1 |
| Francis O'Beirne | £10/3 |
| Captain Moreton | £10 |
| Mrs Slack | £2 |
| Colonel Anderson | £7/5 |
| James McTernan, Esq. | £7/15 |
| Hon. Major Ripple | £28/3 |
| Reynolds Irwin, Esq. | £10/5 |
| **TOTAL** | **£312/10** |

*Source*: Leitrim County Library, Ballinamore, Carrick-on-Shannon board of guardians' minute book, BG 52/A/5, 24 June 1848, p.A 231.

These names included some of the most prominent individuals in the county and reflected the financial difficulties then being encountered by men such as Ferdinand Keon and Pierce Simpson, who were struggling with non-payment of rents.

On 22 July the last loan from the British Association was received bringing the total to £3,064, all of which had to be repaid out of local rates.[109] Due to the receipt of such monies the vice guardians were enabled to carry on a widespread and liberal distribution of outdoor relief. The figures on the scheme had been continually around 11,000 each week since 22 April and they gradually increased to a peak of 13,927 (at a cost of over £383) in the week ending 17 June.[110] Whether or not this figure would have increased further is difficult to ascertain but a couple of factors ensured that it did not. The last loan from the British Relief Association was received a couple of weeks later and this was followed by a communication from the poor law commissioners that all aid advanced by government in aid of rates would 'cease absolutely at harvest'.[111] At the same time the commissioners also instructed the vice guardians to discontinue outdoor relief to those categorised under section two, while able-bodied men were henceforth to be relieved 'solely by workhouse admission'.[112] Thus, by the beginning of August the number had fallen to 10,873 and four weeks later it was 6,520. The decrease continued until it reached 2,513 in the first week of October where it remained until the middle of November.[113] However, demand remained at a high level as evidenced by the fact that from 10 June to 8 July 2,403 applications for relief were refused.[114]

Life in the workhouse continued to prove a miserable experience. As has been noted earlier, a graveyard had been opened in early 1847 in the north corner of the grounds.[115] Given that none had been necessary before, with the small numbers of paupers who died either been returned to their families or interred in the local Church of Ireland graveyard in Carrick, it was probably expected that this plot would suffice for years. However, as the following table illustrates, the highest level of mortality occurred in the first half of 1847:

**Table 6.5: Mortality in Carrick-on-Shannon Workhouse, January 1847–February 1848**

| Month | Deaths |
| --- | --- |
| January 1847 | 15 |
| February 1847 | 91 |
| March 1847 | 76 |
| April 1847 | 222 |
| May 1847 | 124 |
| June 1847 | 21 |

| | |
|---|---|
| July 1847 | 55 |
| August 1847 | 21 |
| September 1847 | 6 |
| October 1847 | 2 |
| November 1847 | 5 |
| December 1847 | 20 |
| January 1848 | 51 |
| February 1848 | 108 |
| **TOTAL** | **817** |

Source: Leitrim County Library, Ballinamore, Carrick-on-Shannon board of guardians' minute book, BG 52/A/3, BG 52/A/4 and BG 52/A/5.

This table does not include a further ten weeks when deaths were not recorded so the total figure for this period would be substantially higher. On 18 March 1848 the guardians ordered that 'the portion of land at present in possession of Lancelot Lawder adjoining the left flank of the workhouse be solicited as the site for the proposed fever ward and new burying ground'.[116] In early June, by which stage a further 198 deaths had occurred, the new burying ground was opened. A gate was placed between it and the workhouse grounds and an order given 'that a deep trench be opened to divide the burying ground from adjacent land and drain it'.[117]

In April the vice guardians remarked that 'the management of the house gives cause of dissatisfaction from the attention bestowed by the temporary officers'.[118] The perennial difficulties with water supply continued as the guardians had to advertise for a horse and cart to carry supplies from the Shannon to the house. At the same time they made 'further efforts' to procure a 'proper person' to deepen the well. Such 'further efforts' included the suggestion of the construction of 'a small canal out from the Shannon ending in a basin to the bottom of the hill on which the poor house is situated'. In the middle of December they were negotiating with Captain Cox, the agent of Charles Manners St George, the owner of the land through which the proposed canal would run.[119] However, within a couple of weeks the visiting committee described the house as being 'clean and orderly' while the inmates were noted as continuing to 'improve as to health' and were 'looking robust'.[120] In early June the schoolmaster was suspended for being repeatedly intoxicated and he eventually left of his own volition.[121] In that same month a reduction in the diet provoked a reaction from the inmates, some of whom refused to carry out any work. Subsequently, four were convicted and sent to prison for a month each while the others were punished with a loss of food and confinement. These punishments 'had the effect of subduing the refractory spirit that was manifested'.[122]

## Mohill

On 12 August 1847 one of the largest gatherings of guardians took place to consider the election of relieving officers to serve under the board in the execution of the poor law extension act.[123] On 11 September almost the entire board assembled when twenty-one guardians once again met to discuss the issue.[124] Large attendances invariably occurred when elections of staff or large-scale financial issues were at stake and throughout 1847 the finances of the board remained in a perilous condition. Such a huge proportion of the inmates being in the hospital necessitated expenditure on various medicines which could often double the expense of a standard inmate. Thus, in the first week of May the rate collectors were urged to use their 'best exertion' to collect the rates as several of the contractors required immediate payment.[125] By the beginning of June the clerk had written to the commissioners requesting that they pay the costs of the recent guardians' elections and a bill for clothing supplied to the house.[126] In that same month more that £2,304 remained uncollected and in the first week of August the union went into debt for the first time.[127]

From 3 June to 16 September (a total of seventeen weeks) slightly more than £604 was collected making an average of £35 per week. However, in six of those weeks no money was remitted.[128] At a board meeting on 23 September it was revealed that George Church of Carrick-on-Shannon had issued a civil bill against the clerk and three weeks later the master was instructed to buy meal from the local market as the board could not obtain a contractor for such.[129] This was due to the fact that each one of the preferred contractors refused to accept contracts unless they received payment on delivery.[130] Desperate to obtain funds the board, in similar fashion to that in Carrick, took the decision to proceed against rate defaulters, particularly immediate lessors amongst whom was Lord Clements and its own attorney, Robert O'Brien. The latter was advised that, unless he paid the rates for which he was personally liable, together with those landlords for whom he acted as agent, within one week, he would be removed from his position.[131]

Temporary Poor Law Inspector, Major Haliday, made his first visit to the workhouse in early November and his subsequent report made for grim reading:

> The house is in a very dilapidated condition. In the kitchen only one boiler is serviceable, and all the dormitories, day-rooms, school-rooms and wards are open to the weather, through a number of large square holes broken through the walls during the time that the house was ravaged by fever. No provision has been made for repairing these or inserting windows and much of the glass is broken.[132]

In addition, all the pumps of the establishment were 'choked or useless', resulting in paupers spending several hours every day carrying water from a well in the street close to the house.[133] His conclusion was that 'the house may justly be designated as little better than a large shed and it is liable to be absolutely closed any week upon a trifling diminution in the amount of rates now obtained weekly by the collector and paid into the treasurer'.[134]

Haliday revealed that such was the financial state of the union that many applicants for relief were turned away. On one occasion, with a crowd of forty to fifty gathered at the gate, the master was ordered to admit those who appeared most in need, without enquiring into the other cases. On another, with fifty applicants congregated at the gates, only three orphans, who had been sent in from the fringes of the union, were admitted on the basis that they would otherwise starve.[135]

This policy impacted on individuals such as Matilda Shanly who was engaged in distributing rice to sixty-nine people in Ballinamore. She stated that the workhouse was filled to capacity and hence 'numbers of creatures are turned out homeless on the world'.[136] By mid November the situation was deteriorating and Haliday reported on how the 'pressure of extreme want' was making itself more visible in the 'emaciated appearance of the women and children who may be seen in the country roads'. He also noted that:

> Fever is extremely prevalent in many districts of the union and so disheartened or reckless are the people that I have been informed of a case where, within the last fortnight, the body of a woman who died of that disease was left in a ditch with merely some straw thrown over it, where the effluvia from the progress of decay attracted

attention and the collector of poor rate, near whose residence it was found, was obliged to hire men to dig a hole to cover it.[137]

Throughout his reports Haliday focused on what he considered the major difficulties in running the workhouse: the apathy of the guardians and problems with collecting rates. Referring to the latter as 'the prime cause of all the evils and difficulties here' he ascertained that the 'large portion' of arrears was held by 'immediate lessors' – the owners of land. Much of it was due from estates over which receivers had been appointed by the Court of Chancery and 'a very large amount' by non-resident proprietors.[138] Having been made aware of such difficulties and Haliday's believing that 'in the present crisis starvation to a lamentable extent may ensue', the commissioners applied to the Lord Lieutenant for a loan of £150 to the union to remedy 'some of the most serious defects and evils'. However, they remained dogmatic in their belief that poor rates should fund the union:

> With respect to the general state of the union funds, the Commissioners have to state that, lamentable as the condition of the destitute poor in the union is, the commissioners are determined not to make any application for pecuniary assistance to the guardians to meet their current expenses for relief. The commissioners are sensible that their determination on this point will add materially to the difficulties of your [Haliday's] position; but still they are desirous that it should be generally understood in the union that the responsibility, the disgrace, and the guilt of any deaths from starvation, if any should unfortunately occur, rest with the guardians and the rate-payers; and that the poor-rates are the funds to which the poor must look for relief. If the Mohill Union were now to receive aid from government, the Commissioners are apprehensive that the reluctance to pay rates would still be greater than at present, and that the spirit of depending upon Government for loans would become habitual and incurable amongst the rate-payers.[139]

Given such an attitude it is perhaps no surprise that the guardians were described as being both 'indifferent' and 'despondent' and thus Haliday believed there was no prospect of achieving anything more than simply keeping the workhouse open 'as a bare protection from starvation to 700 ill-sheltered paupers'. He therefore advised the commissioners to either prepare for the closure of the building or 'to have in view some competent persons who can act as guardians and devote the necessary time and attention to the business of the union'.[140]

On 23 November an 'extraordinary' meeting of the board was called to discuss the lack of supplies in the workhouse but only three guardians – Clements, John Gannon and William Smith – attended. They heard the master declare that he had barely enough food to furnish the inmates with dinner that day. It was subsequently decided that a cheque be made out for £12 for purchasing such, supporting the inmates and ensuring that the house remain open until the next board day.[141] However, it appears that such action came too late for the commissioners. With the board in debt and unable to effect an efficient collection of the rates the commissioners acted decisively. In the weeks of the 4th and 11th of November the numbers of guardians attending had been five and three respectively. Haliday revealed that the meeting on 11 November only took place due to 'the exertions of the master seeking for and inducing three of the guardians to attend' adding that, but for this, 'the ordinary machinery of the house must have stopped, as the master would not have had the means of procuring food for the inmates during the ensuing week'.[142]

At a meeting on 18 November, attended by four guardians, a letter was read from the commissioners in which they noted and criticised the 'small attendance of guardians of this union at their weekly meetings' and on 8 December a sealed order was received from the central body dissolving the board.[143] In justifying this step the commissioners pointed to the 'disastrous and disorganised' state of the union's finances and of the 'deplorable state of destitution of the labouring classes in the union'.[144] They also argued that it was improbable that a number of guardians sufficient to transact business would be procured in the temporary absence of 'the hitherto indefatigable and assiduous chairman of the board', Lord Clements.[145] This was followed two days later by the announcement of James M. O'Reilly and Robert A. Duncan as vice-guardians of the union.[146] It can be argued that the issue of poor guardian attendance was merely a pretext used by the commissioners to replace a board which was becoming increasingly indebted and appearing unequal to the task of running a workhouse in the most trying conditions. Poor attendance had been a feature of the Mohill board for years and if that had been a valid and pressing reason for removal it could have been carried out at any time during the year. Replacing the board with two professionals, with no ties to the area, seemed the obvious method by which the workhouse and union could be returned to something resembling efficiency.

Perhaps due to the fact that the new regime was closely connected to the central commissioners and had their ear, alternative funding became available to them almost immediately upon their assuming their positions. Thus, by 16 December they had attained a loan of £200 from the British Association, to eventually be repaid out of the rates. They also declared that while the claims of contractors could not presently be met, they hoped to satisfy some of these as 'vigorous efforts' would be made to enforce payment of the rates.[147] Two weeks later the commissioners announced that they had advanced a loan of £300, also to be paid out of the rates 'when collected'. In their statement they expressed the hope that 'every effort will be made to place the union in funds before the temporary advance becomes exhausted'.[148] However, while the financial problems of the union were being alleviated, albeit in a very short-term manner, the vice guardians, even though 'guided by the most rigid economy'[149] faced difficulties in attempting to effect proper management of the workhouse. On 30 December they stated:

> The unceasing attention of the vice guardians is directed towards the removal of the numerous defects which exist in every part of the establishment. The officers were informed to use increased zeal and vigilance in their duties which the Vice Guardians from their experience of them regret being obliged to despair of seeing.[150]

They later, in their first report to the commissioners on 20 December 1847, revealed that members of the former board had visited them. They remarked that Mr Godly, a former ex-officio guardian, had offered them 'every assistance' while 'it appeared to be his feelings, in common with others, that the administration of the Poor Law here being placed under control which would ensure its receiving more time and attention, was a step absolute necessary'.[151]

On 24 December Haliday informed the commissioners that the most trustworthy information available to him suggested that distress among the poor was extreme, their food consisting 'very much of the tops and refuse of turnips'.[152] He also noted that the vice guardians had not been able so far to procure houses for additional accommodation 'in this miserable town'.[153] Due to this situation the commissioners permitted outdoor relief to be issued to those classes beyond those specified in section one of the Irish Poor Relief Extension Act.[154] This was essential due to the fact that the vice guardians had decided to stop any further admissions in an attempt to sort out the various problems in the house. However, by the end of the year it had been agreed to rent a property in Mohill, in the ownership of Terry Tierney, to be converted into an additional workhouse at an annual rent of £18.[155]

Another aspect which received their immediate attention was burials of workhouse dead. Referring to the policy of burial by means of a re-usable bier they maintained that 'the mode of interment in operation here must have a degrading and brutalizing effect on the minds of the people' and ordered that all future burials should be accompanied by a coffin and shroud.[156]

However, the new regime faced problems in attempting to effect change and on 3 January 1848 complained that:

> Interminable difficulties arise to us in the prosecution of our duties. The workmen of this place are the most worthless set possible, and can be got to do almost nothing; so that the execution of the repairs, etc., is proceeding but slowly. The illness of our clerk, the resignation of three other officers, and uselessness of all the rest, are sources of great discouragement.[157]

Haliday also remarked that 'it is scarcely possible for me to convey an adequate idea of the difficulty attending every project for improvement in this Union, which affords so few of the conveniences of civilised life'.[158] Indeed, he voiced his opinion that the only means to avert 'the miseries of unassisted destitution' would be a 'large extension' of outdoor relief.[159] Consequently the vice-guardians were forced to offer this option to classes not included in the commissioners' order of 29 December 1847, thereby making it available to the able-bodied.[160] They justified this decision on the basis that, although it was 'the last resource', yet 'their famishing state on the one hand, and the absence of workhouse accommodation on the other, leave but the one line of conduct'.[161]

With almost 1,000 people in receipt of relief the vice guardians were gratified to report that there had been hardly any in possession of more than one quarter acre of land who had applied. Instead, 'the great mass ... are widows and orphans, who, on the removal of their protectors, principally by death, during the past year, relinquished their holdings'.[162] They noted how a 'great change' had taken place amongst the people 'who have no hesitation in giving up their little farms', as:

> When they are inclined to relinquish their land, impelled by no strong motive, they cannot be expected to linger much on the decision, when they understand it to be a barrier to the need of the relieving officers – their only hope of life.[163]

Just as the elected board had found, so the vice guardians discovered that collection of rates was a serious problem. They put this down to 'the extreme poverty of the district, in which we regret to say it is retrograding still further each day' with 'every description of chattel property fast disappearing'. Difficulty in engaging rate collectors was due to 'its lawless state, the unusually high rates, and the previous irregular habits formed in meeting this species of demand'. Even with the offer of 'extravagant rates' of fees (2s in the pound) nobody was willing to undertake the position.[164] The Cloone division was regarded as 'the worst in the union as regards poverty and lawlessness' and it was noted that the rate had '*never* been properly collected there', large arrears having accumulated 'in consequence'.[165]

However, while those who held more than a quarter acre of ground were forced to relinquish it in order to obtain relief, the owners of land were being pursued for non-payment of poor rate. By November 1847 legal proceedings had been instituted against a number of prominent landowners, including Dr Robert Collins of Dublin, who owed £12/10; Henry John Clemants of Cavan (£2/6); William Acheson O'Brien, Fermanagh (£1/5); John B. West, Esq (£4) and William West, Esq, (£1/18).[166] As in Carrick, reference was made to the fact that extreme difficulty was being experienced by rate collectors in recovering dues from immediate lessors on estates over which receivers had been appointed by the Court of Chancery. Estates proving particularly troublesome were those of Francis Nisbett, Westby Percival and the late Colonel Madden.[167] In fact, the collector for the division of Annaduff reported how he had been unable to recover £42 from Nisbett's demesne and grounds at Derrycarne 'in consequence of the gates being always kept locked and admittance refused to him'. He also stated that Nisbett, a deputy-lieutenant and magistrate of the county, employed men to keep a look out and prevent him gaining admittance in order to distrain goods in lieu of rates.[168]

By 10 January, with 'the pressure for relief … increasing beyond our immediate expectation', the vice-guardians had once again to apply to the commissioners for an extension of the earlier permission to relieve the able-bodied.[169] Four days later there were almost 2,000 on the outdoor lists and Haliday informed the commissioners that when the relief offered by private charities came to an end due to exhaustion of their funds 'a very considerable increase' to the lists could be expected.[170] With outdoor numbers edging up towards 3,000 the vice guardians determined to restrict workhouse admissions to able-bodied men and in an attempt to prevent imposition on the outdoor lists they circularised the chairmen of the former relief committees to request their aid in ascertaining evidence of fraud. They suggested that two or three members could form themselves into an 'auxiliary body' to inspect the books of relieving officers. However, this proposal was swiftly rejected by the poor law commissioners who pointed out that such committees would 'have no authority whatever over the relieving officers'.[171]

By the end of January a house had been obtained in Carrigallen to act as a temporary fever hospital[172] while the vice guardians proposed to raise another floor over the idiot wards and remove all the subdividing walls in the lower story of the workhouse. They also wished to build additional sheds at the back of the children's yards – such alterations affording extra accommodation for 250 paupers.[173]

On 24 January the vice-guardians reported how they had occupied a house in Mohill to relieve 'the sick labouring under infectious diseases'. However, having removed thirty such cases to the building a deputation of the townspeople remonstrated against the introduction of a fever hospital in the centre of town and instead suggested the site of the temporary fever hospital which had been utilised in the early months of 1847. This offer was accepted and after fumigating the house in Mohill, it was instead used to accommodate mothers and infants.[174] Of course, by this means they were able to extend the space in the main house for able-bodied men and with upwards of 4,000 on the outdoor list on 31 January they reported that there were none of that description on the lists. Indeed, they were determined to 'exert ourselves to the utmost by taking more houses in the town, if necessary, rather than be obliged, by want of space in the workhouse, to relieve one man who could be considered as coming under that objectionable class for outdoor relief'.[175]

Such was the demand for outdoor relief that in February it was decided to divide the electoral divisions of Newtowngore, Drumreilly and Carrigallen, all under one relieving officer, into two – one for Carrigallen and another for the latter districts. Haliday reported that some people had been struck off relief lists when it was ascertained they had misrepresented their position and maintained that 'many in this position are using every artifice to obtain outdoor relief and others preparing to make bargains for giving up their land'.[176] However, he also emphasised that such cases were 'of little importance as compared with the opposite danger, that any should be left unrelieved who are in extreme want, and legally entitled to assistance'.[177]

An indication of the increasing desperation of people was evidenced by the discovery of three bodies which had lain in the workhouse burying ground for two or three nights. They were subsequently interred without coffins:

> And as the law does not admit of providing coffins for the destitute who have not been relieved within the workhouse, it will be necessary to discourage in every possible way, the tendency manifested to throw upon its officers the task of interring those whose relatives are unable or unwilling to provide a decent burial.[178]

By early February a further 1,000 individuals had been added to the outdoor list while Haliday believed that amongst able-bodied men there had been 'numerous cases' in which they had deserted wives and families 'rather than submit to entry to the workhouse'.[179] That same month witnessed the death of the clerk, William Simpson, while the master also resigned.[180] Haliday decried the fact that there was not 'a single effective officer in the house', the consequence of which was complete chaos while '[odour] and filth defile the premises even in front of the main building'.[181] In his opinion, 'were it even possible to procure at once a complete and effective staff of experienced officers from the best Union workhouses in Ireland, I do not believe they could establish the order, discipline, and cleanliness that is essential to the conduct of these institutions in a month'.[182]

By the end of that month there were 6,000 on the outdoor lists and in the opinion of Haliday this was partly due to 'so manifest a disposition among the labouring able-bodied men, who will not submit to the workhouse, to desert their families and thus get them taken on the relieving officers' books'.[183] With the fever hospital in Carrigallen opened for admission of patients it, together with the Mohill hospital, meant that the vice guardians were able to keep the workhouse 'perfectly free' of infectious disease.[184]

By the end of February the circumstances of the union appeared to be improving. With the appointment of an acting master the sanitary state of the house was reported to be 'no longer the source of uneasiness it was for some time for us'. Similarly, numbers on outdoor relief diminished 'slightly' due to increased public and private employment in the area.[185] Indeed in Ballinamore it was reported that, due to the demand for labourers in works of general drainage and land improvement, 'farmers complain of want of sufficient hands for field work'.[186]

However, by 24 March the numbers had risen again and Haliday put this down to two factors: first, there was a 'prolonged delay' in works intended to commence under the Land Improvement Act; second, farmers were reluctant to pay labourers any more than 3*d* to 4*d* per day with diet. They cited the heavy burden of rates but in Haliday's opinion their actions only 'aggravate the general distress'.[187] Despite witnessing and acknowledging the distress around him Haliday argued that the quarter-acre clause had to be rigidly adhered to:

> It will be of the utmost importance for the future self-supporting condition of this union that the disqualification for relief attached to the occupancy of more than a garden plot of land should be felt as effective and permanent. The deeply-rooted habit of idleness for many months of the year, and of preferring to lie all day on straw, fed on a weekly dole of relief-meal, rather than subsist in comfort by their own industry, and the infatuated attachment to the possession of a small bit of land which is lying absolutely waste in large tracts all over the country, are the very worst and most discouraging symptoms of the low social state of this country, which exceeds in wretchedness any part of Ireland I have yet seen.[188]

Notwithstanding their best efforts, out of a total of 7,849 persons on the outdoor relief register, 2,754 were being relieved under Section 2 of the Act and although this total gradually declined, numbers remained well above three thousand until the end of the year.[189]

## Manorhamilton

As in the other unions, the largest meeting of the Manorhamilton board of guardians took place on 9 September 1847 to elect relieving officers to the following districts:

**Table 6.6: Relief Districts in the Manorhamilton Union, September 1847**

| Number | Electoral Division |
|--------|-------------------|
| 1 | Manorhamilton and Kiltyclogher |
| 2 | Rossinver and Lurganboy |
| 3 | Dromahaire and Cloonlogher |
| 4 | Killenummery and Killargue |
| 5 | Drumkeerin and Inishmagrath |

*Source*: Leitrim County Library, Ballinamore, Manorhamilton board of guardians' minute book, BG 117/AA/3, 29 July 1847.

With the onset of another winter the medical officer recommended the erection of stoves in the school rooms as he believed that 'dysentery will set in with double force … if the boys are not kept warm'.[190] Until October the workhouse appeared to cope with the consequences of hunger and disease and at the start of that month the master was given £15 to buy materials 'to set the female paupers to work'.[191] One of the major concerns was the fact that some of those same female paupers were reported to be 'in the habit of scaling the walls of the yards for the purpose of stealing turnips'. Hence, the master suggested the propriety of raising the walls.[192] However, unlike twelve months previously, huge numbers applied, and were accepted, to the workhouse:

**Table 6.7: Admissions to Manorhamilton Workhouse, October–December 1847**

| Weekend Ending | Number Admitted | Number Rejected |
|----------------|-----------------|-----------------|
| 7 October | 47 | 0 |
| 14 October | 51 | 1 |
| 21 October | 65 | 13 |
| 28 October | 55 | 4 |
| 11 November | 88 | 6 |

| 7 December | 123 | 9 |
| 30 December | 150 | 0 |

*Source*: Leitrim County Library, Ballinamore, Manorhamilton Board of Guardians Minute Book, BG 117/AA/3, 7 October to 30 December 1847.

These figures support the contention that the Manorhamilton guardians had settled on a policy of admitting as many paupers as possible in an attempt to keep expenditure on outdoor relief to a minimum. Every inch of available space was to be utilised in furtherance of this policy as exemplified by the conversion of half of the straw house into a nursery.[193] At the same time, while outdoor relief costs were £14/14 per week at the beginning of January 1848 and gradually increased to £39/19 in mid-March they did not exceed this and indeed by May 1848 were just over £25.[194]

The eagerness of the guardians to restrict outdoor relief was no doubt influenced by the fact that the new rate bill for the union totalled £5,359 by the middle of November 1847.[195] Not surprisingly rate collectors were urged to issue summonses 'without distinction, whether they be rich or poor' and were informed that they needed to bring 300 defaulters before the magistrates each week until the entire rate was collected.[196] The determination to enforce penalties for late payment of rates was reflected in a resolution to 'proceed for the recovery of rates due on the Glebe lands of the Rev. C.S. Montgomery in the division of Inishmagrath now under sequestration'. However, an interesting intervention was evidently made by Nicholas Tottenham who noted in the minute book, 'confirmed, except the last resolution'.[197] Nevertheless, as the following table illustrates, this policy paid immediate dividends:

**Table 6.8: Poor-Rate Collected in Manorhamilton Union, January–March 1848**

| Week Ending | Rate Collected |
| --- | --- |
| 6 January | £302 0s 9d |
| 13 January | £156 |
| 20 January | £314 13s |
| 28 January | £280 |

| | |
|---|---|
| 3 February | £260 |
| 10 February | £508 3s 6d |
| 17 February | £158 6s 6d |
| 24 February | £263 15s 9d |
| 2 March | £87 10s |
| 9 March | £65 |
| 14 March | £219 14s 10d |
| 21 March | £446 0s 9d |
| 25 March | £185 |

*Source*: Leitrim County Library, Ballinamore, Manorhamilton board of guardians' rough minute book, BG 117/AA/3, January to March 1848.

Despite such sums, and having a balance in their favour of £932, the board refused to pay a debt to a meal contractor of £130/12/6, though this appears to have had as much to do with the contractor apparently failing to fulfil the terms of his contract as much as anything else.[198]

In March the clerk was instructed to 'post lists of persons relieved in and out of the workhouse on the chapel doors within each division on the [first] Sunday in every month'.[199] At the end of April 1848 the clerk was instructed to print 500 copies of lists of those receiving relief while at the same meeting it was announced that the infirmary building was now completed.[200] In the meantime, John Maley was employed as a watchman from 6 am to 8 pm 'to prevent paupers from scaling the walls and carrying away property'.[201] The minutes do not mention it but his tenure was presumably short as in May a tender from William Rutledge to increase the height of the walls by 105cm was accepted.[202]

Throughout 1847 the Society of Friends had supported dozens of local private initiatives by supplying food and, to a lesser extent, clothing. However, in 1848, aware of the chronic condition of the people after almost three years of distress, they attempted to clothe as many as possible. Once again, concerned individuals sought to obtain as much of this relief as possible. Two of the most important questions on the society's clothing application forms concerned the cost of clothing as the Society sent the materials which were then made into trousers, shirts, coats etc., by those in receipt. However, they hoped that people would be encouraged to purchase these rather than receive them free. In addition, they were concerned to ensure that clothes received would not be pawned for money, food or alcohol. Certainly, with regard to Leitrim they were left in no doubt that clothes could be neither purchased nor pawned.

For example, Emily Lawder, writing from Fenagh informed them that at least 100 people were without clothing but that it would be very difficult to sell any amount received. She also emphasised there was 'no danger' of clothes being pawned as 'such a thing as a pawn office is not more than ten miles'.[203]

Clara Dickson, writing from Woodville, Bundoran, sought clothing for the people of the townland of Tawley in the parish of Rossinver. She claimed that two-thirds of them were now in a 'suffering condition' through want of clothing as 'everything has been expended on provisions since the potato blight'.[204] On 1 May she began distributing clothing to people from a number of townlands and the following list is typical of those aided:

**Table 6.9: Clothes Distributed by Clara Dickson in the Parish of Rossinver, May–June 1848**

| Date | Name | Residence | Number in Family |
|------|------|-----------|------------------|
| 1 May | John Conolly | Tawley | 2 |
| 8 May | Biddy Gilmartin | Gortawly | 8 |
| | Neddy Gallagher | | 9 |
| 10 May | Mary O'Beirne | Tawley | 9 |
| 15 May | Mary Murray | | 6 |
| 18 May | Pat Sheils | | 14 |
| 20 May | J. Conolly | Cloonty | 9 |
| 29 May | Biddy McGowan | Tawley | 4 |
| | Mary Reilly | | 14 |
| 8 June | Mary Sweeney | Tullaghan | 6 |

*Source*: National Archives, Dublin, Society of Friends Relief of Distress Papers, box 2/506/37.

William Noble of Drumshanbo stated that his wife and sisters would help in the distribution of clothes to 'at least 700 in need'. He asked for shirts, coats and trousers for men and shifts, petticoats and gowns for women. As in Fenagh, nobody could afford to purchase and hence he also requested a supply of second-hand clothes if they were available.[205] A similar family effort was evident in Drumsna where Jane King proposed to work in conjunction with her husband, the Rev. Robert King. She estimated that out of a population of 5,000 at least two-thirds 'are in a state of the utmost destitution and have not means to procure food, much less clothing'. Her demands centred around blankets, 'warm clothes', and shoes.[206]

Two days later two requests from the same area indicated a desire to focus on small groups in need. Rev. Francis Kane had decided 'for many reasons' to restrict his effort to sixty children aged six to fourteen years and one of these appears to have been his experience that 'the system of selling clothes made up by benevolent persons has been tried and failed signally'.[207] Meanwhile, another small-scale effort was evident in a scheme managed by Emily Auchmuty of Kilmore House in Drumsna who wished to clothe 180 women and children in Kilmore and Skea.[208]

The preponderance of females in this particular aid effort was emphasised by the application of Elizabeth Peyton of Driney House, Cashcarrigan, who, in attempting to clothe twenty-nine families (110 individuals) in Gubnaveigh and Derigvon, revealed 'there is none to join in the management, it being a large mountainous district'.[209]

However, while some were forced by circumstances to labour by themselves others chose to do so. Writing from Drumdarton, Ballinamore, Richard Clifford asserted there were 1,000 persons in need of clothing. However, with nobody of 'substance' living within three miles of him he preferred to work alone in 'selecting those for relief from my own personal knowledge'.[210]

Often ailments peculiar to a particular district necessitated specific aid. For example, Margarita Kirkwood made reference to the fact that in part of the electoral division of Killukin there had been an outbreak of fever accompanied by 'sore eyes'. The latter was 'prevalent to a great degree' with the pain continuing for six weeks.[211] Letitia Veevers of Mohill revealed that the situation in Mohill was worse than it had been twelve months previously: 'the want of clothing is much more apparent this year than it was last as destitution has increased ... and all want clothing – they are in wretched tatters'. In an attempt to alleviate the situation she had tried to encourage others to manage and distribute clothing 'but did not succeed in getting any to join her'. Thus she had spent much time working single-handedly on 'teaching and taking in and giving out needle-work'.[212] Remarking how 'nakedness abounds to such an extent that I could not possibly get money here for any article', she pleaded for supplies of leather and flannel clothes of all kinds 'as poor men are out in the wet lands here draining'. She also stated that bed coverings such as sheets and blankets would be 'most valuable and wanted here' as 'fever, dysentery, influenza and smallpox are raging here at present'. Although the Quakers had officially ended food grants she also asked for a supply of rice as 'dysentery prevails so much and the poor are constantly coming to me for it but I have to give them a denial, which goes to my heart'. She received a grant of 5 cwt of rice and a supply of clothing with the society 'leaving it to her own discretion whether to sell it at a reduced price or [have it] given gratuitously'.[213]

Evidence of distress amongst all creeds was provided by an application from Thomas Hayes of Mohill. Hayes was connected to the Primitive Wesleyan Methodist Society which ran a free school about two miles from the town. Here the pupils were supplied with books, slates and pencils whilst being 'daily instructed in the Scriptures of Truth'. He wished to obtain clothing for the parents of such children, all of whom were 'in a wretched state for want of clothing' and 'have hardly as much Indian meal at present to eat per diem as will support their half-naked and starved frames'.[214]

While Letitia Veevers maintained that the situation in Mohill was as bad if not worse than that twelve months earlier the local clergyman in Dromod gave thanks that 'we are not in such a lamentable state as regards famine as we were last year'. However, the reason was not an improvement in the condition of the people but rather the fact that 'our population is so much reduced accounts in some measure for it'. Thus he estimated that the population had been reduced from 10,500 at the beginning of 1847 to around 6,000 a year later. At the same time, provisions were now cheaper 'but there is no money' while the situation was exacerbated by the fact that 'the income of the clergy is so much reduced that we are not able to afford the relief we were usually enabled to give'.[215]

Another long-term strategy implemented by the Society of Friends sought to reduce dependency on the potato. To this end they made available grants of seeds of alternative foods such as cabbage, turnip, peas, etc. These grants were taken up with alacrity by individuals throughout the county who continued, in the face of huge destitution, to do all they could to aid their local populations.

Nicholas Tottenham of Glenfarne Hall, Manorhanilton, welcomed the renewal of this initiative as 'nothing in my mind was so useful as your doing so last year'. He informed the society that:

> Large breadths of it were sown in my part of the country and a great deal of food made of the crop arising from it. I would advise your committee, however, to restrict their issue, if any, to turnip seed

alone as the cultivation of it is easy and simple and it is pretty sure of succeeding which neither mangle or carrot are.[216]

Andrew Hogg of Cloone concurred in this opinion and as evidence of the 'incalculable amount of good done in the locality by last year's distribution of turnip seed' pointed to the fact that more than 1,700 people had been 'kept from actual starvation by the produce of the seed'. By the end of January, Hogg had distributed 1,300 lbs of turnip seed, 50 lbs of white stone, 50 lbs of early green and 120 lbs of carrot seed.[217]

While welcoming a grant of cabbage, onion and parsnip seeds, G. Peyton of Driney House, Cashcarrigan hoped that the lack of turnip was 'an oversight' as 'the principal grain crops sown by the poor in this locality is turnips'.[218] As with clothing, local circumstances dictated aid requirements. Hence, on 22 February John Lawder of Lowfield, Drumsna requested a grant to purchase potatoes and rye to be sold at a reduced price.[219] Similarly, William Parke of Clogher House, Drumsna, distributed ten barrels (200 stones) of rye seed in his locality.[220] By the end of March Nicholas Tottenham had distributed all the rye seed but there remained 'many still looking for it among the mountains here'. However, his belief in the efficacy of turnip was evident in his comment that 'the sooner the turnip seed could be forwarded the better'.[221]

In Annaduff the 'chief and urgent demand at present' was for help in planting the oat crop in consequence of the fact that this was the only crop 'for which much of our land is suited'.[222] George Shaw revealed that a loan fund had been established in the locality to provide small loans to 'industrious persons' repayable by instalments after the next harvest. However, 'the applications are so numerous that we cannot attend to one half of them' and the reason for such was evident in his following comments:

> I need scarcely tell you that this parish is in a most deplorably distressed condition and that we have scarcely any local aid. Were it not for the feeding of so many at our boiler here which we still continue and which has been going on for 15 months, principally through your liberality, the deaths from starvation around me would have been frightful. As it is, fever and dysentery are fatally present.[223]

In Kinlough there was huge demand for pea seeds, given that they required little manure. The importance of such grants was reflected in the following comments of Penelope Johnston:

I never saw such excitement as the peas have caused. I have already been obliged from the demand to reduce the quantity. I intended giving four stones but now only two to each person unless extreme cases. I really think if I had 500 stone I could dispose of them at one shilling a stone. In Ballyshannon where peas are sold they pay two shillings a stone and even at that price quantities sold. I am getting lists for turnip seed made by persons I can rely on being exact.[224]

Such was the demand in Drumsna that John Lawder complained that his grant was 'quite insufficient for the applications making'.[225] As far as Mary Johnston of Aghacashill, Keshcarrigan was concerned the distribution would give the people 'habits of industry and honesty' and at the same time 'prevent the country shopkeepers from charging so exorbitantly as they do'. Such a supply would, she believed, 'be the means of keeping many in their houses which will otherwise be obliged to go to the workhouse'.[226]

By April 1848 grants of seeds were making their way to various parts of Leitrim as follows:

**Table 6.10: Grants of Seeds Made by the Society of Friends in County Leitrim, 1848**

| Item | Amount Distributed | Acres Sown | Number Supplied |
| --- | --- | --- | --- |
| Turnip | 5,247 lbs | 1,143¾ | 6,406 |
| Carrot | 197 lbs | 34 | 731 |
| Parsnip | 204 lbs | 45½ | 608 |
| Cabbage | 379 lbs | 61¼ | 2,193 |

*Source*: National Archives, Dublin, Society of Friends Relief of Distress Papers, box 2/506/38.

Amounts distributed varied from area to area. For example, in Annaduff 725 people received 392 lbs of turnip, 32 lbs of brown onions, 15 lbs of carrots and 15 lbs of parsnip. Meanwhile James Kirkwood of Woodbrook Lodge obtained 220 lbs of turnip and 15 lbs of cabbage.[227]

In an attempt to facilitate allocation of various seeds locals were aided by James Cody, a Practical Instructor, who had been sent to the county by the Royal Agricultural Society. As well as distributing seeds he also gave advice to local farmers as to how to sow them.[228] However, Cody's appearance in the area was important in that he offered an independent assessment of the condition of the people. In reading descriptions of the various localities described in great detail to the Society of Friends and the Irish Relief Association it seems that perhaps at times correspondents were maybe tempted to exaggerate somewhat in order to obtain as much relief as possible. For example, Emma Lawder, in requesting another grant from the Society of Friends, stated that distress was 'beyond her pen to describe', relating how 'they come here by tens and twentys looking for relief and sit from morning until night as remonstrance with them is useless'.[229] Cody had no such vested interest. And significantly, in relating how 'the poor are both naked and starving', he echoed the descriptions of those who had been corresponding with the Society of Friends since the autumn of 1846:

> There are a large portion of the poor of this district who live principally on cabbages for three months or four in the year for the last three years and as those poor creatures here with smallholdings of land are not able to procure one pennyworth of it–beside it is not to be got in this backward district and the lands admirable adapted to grow cabbages.[230]

While the distribution of seeds helped to some degree to alleviate the situation, it was very much a tiny percentage of what was required.

There were a number of circumstances which ensured that the destitution continued. Firstly, sickness continued in all localities necessitating further aid from the Society of Friends. On 2 May J. Feld wrote that 'sickness prevails very much again' in Kiltubrid, and requested 'even a small quantity' of food. He received 5 cwt of rice.[231] In addition, Emma Lawder of Lowfield, Drumsna requested a grant of rice, Indian meal, biscuit, sugar, soup and pea meal due to the fact of 'all the poor Irish that were in England and elsewhere having been sent home naked'. She described how 'they were beyond lament all that called yesterday for relief who were sent away in a most distressing state when they found they had none to get as my distributions were on Mondays and Thursdays'.[232] As in other areas dysentery and fever were rife in Drumsna and Lawder revealed that 'a great number' of those given aid were supplied in their own homes 'being sick and weak and unable to come for food'.[233] Mary Johnston of Aghacashill reported six families in one townland ill with fever and she was attempting to aid them by supplying rice water seasoned with sugar.[234]

Given the continued pressure on resources various individuals had to be more selective in their supply of food. Hence, Emily Auchmuty of Kilmore

House, Drumsna selected eleven families 'of the poorest and most distressed' and gave them food twice weekly. She also supplied sixty 'diseased and sickly persons' on a daily basis.[235] In the same way, J.M. Kirkwood of Woodbrook Lodge daily cooked two stones each of meal and rice and distributed a quart of the resultant stirabout to a variety of individuals. Those in fever received a further two pounds of rice each day as a drink. She complained that 'even those receiving the outdoor relief are dying of starvation' in part due to the fact that 'the bread is so bad invalids cannot eat it'.[236]

Perhaps of even greater significance was the fact that those who had previously just been able to survive were now coming into the circle of desperation. At the beginning of April Letitia Veevers noted how:

> The small landholders are heavily pressed with the rents, county cess and poor rates and with the support necessary for their families and renders it almost certain the bringing them on the list of paupers in the course of a very short time.[237]

The final sting in the tail emerged in a letter from James Cody who was distributing seeds in Mohill in late July:

> The seeds arrived and I am giving them out today in Mohill Courthouse to persons holding from only ½ rood to 5 acres. I have been travelling through the different districts taking down the names of the distressed only and giving them from 1 oz to 2 oz according to their circumstance and number in family. I have the poor of the greater part of six parishes to divide it with which I fear may well be short as this class is very numerous it is the greatest relief to them and doubly so as the potato is I fear destroyed here again. There is not one field of potatoes that I have seen in my district that is not diseased. They have a decided appearance for the worse since the 27th of July.[238]

Thus, by the end of July 1848 it was being reported that a serious failure of the potato crop, the third in four years, had occurred. Despite the deaths of thousands and the emigration of thousands more, this development would place further demands on the fast-diminishing resources of those who had been labouring for two years to feed and clothe their neighbours.

# Chapter 7

# THE HAGGARDS ARE EMPTY

List of those in receipt of outdoor relief in the electoral division of Rynn in Mohill Poor Law Union, 1848-1849. Courtesy of Seamus Geraghty Collection, St George's Heritage Centre, Carrick-on-Shannon, County Leitrim.

**B**Y MID-AUGUST the potato crop in the Mohill area was 'destroyed', much to the anguish of small farmers who were already 'on the eve of ruin'.[1] In the wider union area Major Haliday reported the 'extensive and now rapidly spreading appearance of disease in the potato crop' which, in many cases, had occurred 'with a suddenness equal to that of the blight of 1845 and 1846'. The contents of a detailed return revealed a mixed pattern throughout. For example, in Annaduff almost every field was discoloured while in Annaveagh there was 'great and general discolouration'. The two worst affected areas appeared to be Rynn, where every field was 'blackened', and Eslin, where fields were 'generally blackened'. In Fenagh the potato gardens were 'all black' while the fields were beginning 'suddenly to be discoloured'. However, in Ballinamore, while potato gardens were 'showing discolouration' there was very little appearance of the blight. The same situation applied in Oughteragh division but Haliday added the coda that as these two areas contained much mountain land the crop was always later than the other divisions and hence he described the non-appearance of disease as 'probably fallacious'.[2]

Captain Edmund Wynne stated that in the Carrick union the extent of potatoes planted was 'not more than one-fifth' of that in 1845 and 1846, compared to one-third in the neighbouring union of Boyle. However, the disease 'though as general as that of 1846, is by no means as malignant'.[3] A few days later John Lawder reported how, due to the rot of the crop, the people in Drumsna were now removing potatoes 'as fast as they can' and replacing them with turnip, onion and cabbage seeds[4] although he subsequently noted 'great destruction of the turnip crop by the "fly"'.[5]

So desperate were the people around Carrick to obtain potato ground that ninety-seven of them were forced to lease a 'small piece' from their neighbours. To facilitate this several of the girls attending a school run by the Kirkwoods paid for a rood, half a rood 'and in some instances a few yards of ground' by making shirts or socks for the person who intended to grow it.[6] The locals were helped in a great degree by the fact that Kirkwood had distributed portions of between two and three acres to individuals in order to facilitate the sowing of turnip seed. He also employed men and boys to till this land while paying them with meal and rice received from the Society of Friends.[7]

Kirkwood was only one of a number of individuals who had established schools and was now attempting to feed children while their relatives received outdoor relief. For example, in Eastersnow Ursula Hamilton was feeding her girls in the industrial school with Indian meal.[8] Meanwhile, the indomitable

George Shaw maintained a boiler at his gate-house by which means he daily supplied eighty children from the infant school and thirty pupils of the female work school together with 'several other poor persons' who received whatever was left. He regarded this as the best means of support 'as it secures the education of the poor in habits of cleanliness, industry and order at the same time that it secures food to those who would otherwise be in a state of starvation'.[9] At the same time, a 'great number' in and around Carrick had been struck off the outdoor relief lists 'and are without any work'.[10] Hence, 'though almost ashamed to apply … again' in late November 1848 George Shaw requested some 'fragments of relief left' to feed the children of his schools, emphasising that this request would be 'the last'. He subsequently received half a ton of rice and ten bags of peas.[11]

## WORKHOUSES

### Manorhamilton

Amongst the worst divisions in the Ballyshannon union were Glenade and Kinlough while in Manorhamilton there was disease in every division but it varied as to its extent.[12] However, for much of 1848 the Manorhamilton union minute book reads very much like one from the pre-Famine era. While outdoor relief was being dispensed this was at a significantly lower level than either of the other unions in the county and the maximum cost of such was slightly under £27 per week.[13] On 5 August there were 1,429 on the lists but within one month this had fallen to 474 and from 9 September to 30 December numbers were negligible, never rising above sixty-two.[14] Correspondingly, expenditure from 14 September until the end of January 1849 was significantly below £2 and in the week of 19 October 1848 there were no costs.[15] On 7 September the board dispensed with the services of wardsman John Maley whose role was deemed to be 'unnecessary in the present state of the workhouse'.[16] Even the combined resignations of the master, matron and schoolmistress did not appear to upset the running of the institution,[17] although the two chief officers, unhappy with their remuneration, eventually agreed to continue on the basis of accepting an extra £5 each per annum in lieu of rations.[18]

When the central board of health sanctioned the continuation of temporary fever hospitals at Manorhamilton and Grouse Lodge, Drumkeerin, the guardians argued that the latter was 'totally unnecessary' given the 'present sanitary state of the district'. In addition, the fever hospital at Skreeny, with potential accommodation for 130 patients, was

BUNDORAN (Woodville)

KINLOUGH

**County Leitrim.**

PRIVATE RELIEF FUNDS
IN COUNTY LEITRIM, 1846 - 1850.

● Represents a Fund.

GLENADE
GLENLOUGH

MANORHAMILTON

DROMAHAIRE

KILLARGUE

DROMAHAIRE
(Rose Bank)

CORRY

DRUMKEERIN

Lough
Allen.

MOHER (Gregg)

DRUMDARTAN

AUGHACASHEL

BROOKLAWN

KEADUE

ANNADALE

DRUMSHANBO

BALLINAMORE

GARADICE

KILTUBRID

RIVERSDALE

KESHCARRIGAN

FENAGH

KILLEGAR

CARRIGALLEN

WOODBROOK

CARRICK
on
SHANNON

AUGHAVAS

CLOONE

SPRINGFIELD

DRUMSNA

MOHILL

EASTERSNOW

KILMORE

ANNADUFF

RUSH HILL

AUGHRY

CLOONAFF

DROMOD

LAKEVIEW

NEWTOWNFORBES

Private Relief Funds in County Leitrim, 1846–1850. Drawn by Sean Gill.

only half-filled. The union supplied a horse and covered spring car for conveying patients to Skreeny and it was therefore felt that the cost of between £500 and £600 for the Drumkeerin hospital was not justified. To reinforce their argument they pointed to the fact that in each of the unions of Sligo and Carrick-on-Shannon there was only one fever hospital while Ballyshannon had none. All of these unions, as they pointed out, contained 'much larger populations'.[19] The board of health eventually acceded to the guardians wishes and the Drumkeerin hospital was closed on 31 October, the patients there being removed to Skreeny.[20] A further indication of the lack of pressure on the union at this time was the notification to James Geren that his house at Donaghmore, used as an additional workhouse for the aged and infirm, would not be required after 1 November 1848.[21]

From 11 May to 14 September more than £1,179 of rates was lodged with the union treasurer; however, in the same period over £1,027 was paid out so that the union was just about maintaining a position of solvency.[22] In September the board asked the bank for a loan of £500 to meet current expenses until the new rate became available. The treasurer agreed to a three-month loan at an interest rate of 6 per cent and on the personal security of some of the guardians.[23] However, with £5,201 of rates being collected in just over three months, the board was able to repay the loan in the first week of January 1849.[24]

The obvious intention of the guardians to severely restrict outdoor relief in preference to the workhouse test was noted by the poor law commissioners who instructed them to keep the numbers to a maximum of 900 inclusive of those in the main workhouse and the Commons auxiliary.[25] However, the guardians replied that with the recent re-hiring of Geren's house at Donaghmore, capable of holding fifty inmates, the total additional accommodation now amounted to 200 spaces.[26]

By the beginning of February 1849 the guardians appeared to be in a strong financial position. Much of the new rate had been paid and they enjoyed a balance in their favour of almost £3,000.[27] but there were signs that distress was not yet terminated. In the first two months of the year there were 322 admissions to the house.[28] At the same time outdoor relief costs increased from a nominal £1/8 on 4 January to almost £14 in the first week of March.[29] At the end of that month the board paid £1,451 to meet various expenses thereby reducing its balance to £514.[30] While temporary inspector, Captain Gilbert, paid tribute to the guardians for their 'economy and good management' which gave the appearance of the union being 'favourably circumstanced', he painted a grim picture of the prospects for the future:

The means of the proprietors and occupiers are exhausted. Rents are not to be had except in part in some electoral divisions. The stock of cattle is decreasing amongst tenants; the haggards are empty; and many townlands waste and deserted. The causes of destitution are – the failure of the potato crop, absenteeism, and the consequent lack of employment. There are no potatoes in this union except some retained for seed. The food in general use amongst the peasantry is Indian and oat meal; turnips as an article of food was much in use up to the present time, but the store is now exhausted.[31]

Gilbert's observations were corroborated by a series of letters from Penelope St George during these months. In late December 1848 she had received a bale of clothing from the Society of Friends and by January was endeavouring to sell them but she informed the central committee that such sales would 'take some time' as 'the distress has lately increased'.[32] By March 1849 she was enquiring as to the possibility of receiving food for 'some very poor families whose wages are not sufficient to support their families' around Kinlough. Assuring the Friends that she had 'assisted all classes and denominations' she lamented that she was unable to do more as 'clergymen now are not only badly paid but highly taxed'.[33] In a further letter she requested some cabbage and parsnip seeds to assist 'the small struggling industrious farmers' who would be unable to crop their land without it. Although acknowledging that there was 'less sickness and distress than in the two former years' she added that 'still, there is a great deal'.[34] Having failed to secure a favourable reply she revealed that the poor were now suffering and 'vast struggles' had been made by them to get a crop down, despite being 'half-starved and getting worse every day'.[35] Upon eventually receiving a grant of £7 from the Society she utilised it in the employment of a dozen women each week working at flax, the latter supplied free by her brother. In this way she was able to produce cheap clothing which she then sold to the poor. The women, being 'industrious heads of families', received one stone of meal per week along with a dinner provided by herself. In addition, St George supplied seven sick people with barley sugar and cocoa.[36]

By 11 April 1849, the first time that official statistics for the Manorhamilton workhouse are available, the numbers on outdoor relief totalled 999 at a cost of more than £41/6 with the areas most in need being Killenummery and Killargue.[37] At the same time there was a huge increase in numbers being admitted to the workhouse, though, as the following table illustrates, equally large numbers were discharged:

**Table 7.1: Admissions and Discharges, Manorhamilton Workhouse, April–June 1849**

| Week Ending | Number Admitted | Number Discharged |
| --- | :---: | :---: |
| 11 April | 47 | 35 |
| 14 April | 107 | 123 |
| 21 April | 177 | 152 |
| 28 April | 196 | 188 |
| 5 May | 140 | 132 |
| 12 May | 263 | 68 |
| 19 May | 211 | 82 |
| 26 May | 142 | 110 |
| 2 June | 96 | 79 |
| 9 June | 83 | 69 |
| 16 June | 98 | 86 |
| 23 June | 101 | 96 |
| 30 June | 90 | 87 |
| **TOTAL** | **1,751** | **1,307** |

*Source*: Leitrim County Library, Ballinamore, Manorhamilton board of guardians' minute book, BG 117/A/3, pp.11, 22, 32, 42, 52, 62, 72, 82, 92, 102, 112, 122, 132.

As is evident from these figures, in spite of the large number of discharges there was a net influx of more than 400 people to the house (capacity 1,100) and this, coupled with the rise in outdoor relief costs, placed renewed financial strain on the union's finances. When the poor law commissioners gave their sanction to the board to borrow money to construct a permanent fever hospital they replied that, with less than £300 in the bank, 'it would be a fruitless effort on their part to attempt to borrow money on the credit of the union under present circumstances'.[38] However, money spent earlier on an extension above the female school meant that by the first week of May the workhouse capacity had increased by 320 to 1,420.[39] Thus, by the first week in July there were 1,376 people in the workhouse and a further 1,455 in receipt of outdoor relief.[40] Given the huge numbers being relieved indoors it is no surprise that a significant number of deaths occurred in April (twenty-nine) and May (forty-four). However, these were dwarfed by the huge level of fatalities in June (ninety-five) and July (ninety-seven) which then declined to sixty-four in August and twenty-seven in September.[41]

It appeared that Manorhamilton was experiencing in the summer of 1849 what the workhouses in Carrick-on-Shannon and Mohill had experienced two years earlier. The gradual decline in deaths was mirrored in the numbers on outdoor relief which fell dramatically at the start of August. Between the end of May and the final week of July numbers had remained at a consistent average of between 1,300 to 1,500 individuals.[42] However from 1,417 on 28 July they declined to 904 within one week and rapidly fell to stand at 119 in the first week of September.[43] At the same time, numbers in the workhouse declined from 1,420 in the final week of May to 1,376 a month later and 931 at the start of September.[44] With this number falling further, to 809 on 15 September, the guardians ordered that the auxiliary houses in Donaghmore owned by James Geren and Christopher Wilson, be returned to them on 1 November.[45] On that same date, the clerk received an order which reflected the fact that the worst of the Famine years were over when he was instructed to advertise for, amongst other items, potatoes.[46] By mid-October the steam boilers previously used by local relief committees were being advertised for sale while the rent of the Skreeny fever hospital was terminated.[47] In the first week of December, with the news that the relieving officer of Manorhamilton/Kiltyclogher had emigrated to America[48] the board decided to amalgamate relief districts one and two (Manorhamilton/ Kiltyclogher and Rossinver and Lurganboy) and reduce the wages of the other two relieving officers by £5 per annum[49] although this latter decision was subsequently rescinded.[50] By the end of the year the number in the workhouse – 885 – was still substantial but was significantly lower than six months previous, while there remained only fifty-six cases of outdoor relief.[51] The financial position of the union remained just about solvent, with a balance in the bank of £220[52] but the reality of long-term debt, occasioned by the years of famine, were noted in the minutes of 27 September. The board owed seven instalments on a loan of £6,400 (£2,240); five on borrowing of £500 (£125) and two payments on a loan of £800 (£80). Thus, in total, the Loan Commissioners were owed £2,445.[53]

## Mohill

By 16 November 1848 the total amount of food being distributed throughout the five relief districts of the Mohill union was 3,402 lb of bread together with three tons and 18 cwt of meal. This had been given to 1,379 people who represented a total of 3,293 individuals[54]. Of these, 2,689 were relieved under section one and 604 under section two of the Poor Law Extension Act.

As the winter progressed and the numbers seeking indoor relief invariably increased, being almost 1,300 in early December,[55] the vice guardians were unsuccessful in trying to rent a house in Mohill previously occupied as a military barracks. In addition, it was ascertained that the roofs of new sheds had not been water-proofed leaving them almost unfit for occupation. It was also reported that diarrhoea and inflammation amongst children were on the increase due to the fact that the schoolrooms and nurseries were overcrowded.[56] Thus, even though it had not been finished, the new fever hospital was commandeered in the first week of December and all patients suffering from scarlatina were removed to there from the infirmary.[57] In an obviously desperate effort to alleviate pressure on the house a number of paupers 'just recovered from sickness and suffering from chronic diseases' were discharged and placed on the outdoor relief register.[58] In December 1848 the school master – Mr Brown – died of fever,[59] while one week later it was reported that the matron, assistant school mistress and porter had all succumbed to illness.[60] The last week of the year witnessed eighty new cases of various diseases and the hospital wards were almost filled to capacity.[61] In an attempt to 'check the tendency to dysentery at present in the country' the vice guardians resolved that outdoor relief supplies should in future be given in half measures of Indian meal and rye, instead of solely in Indian meal.[62] As the following table illustrates, in less than five months the numbers in need of outdoor relief more than doubled from just over 3,000 to more than 7,000:

**Table 7.2: Numbers in Receipt of Outdoor Relief in Mohill Union**

| Date | Number | Cost |
| --- | --- | --- |
| 18/11/48 | 3,293 | £75 16d |
| 30/12/48 | 4,000 | £94 12d |
| 10/2/49 | 5,747 | £137 10d |
| 22/2/49 | 6,110 | £145 |
| 8/3/49 | 6,699 | £212 |
| 31/3/49 | 7,251 | £199 |

*Source*: Leitrim County Library, Ballinamore , Mohill board of guardians' minute book, BG 22/A/6, pp.9, 13, 71, 73, 131, 135, 143, 163, 165, 193 and 195.

In small part, this was due to a determination of the vice guardians, under pressure from the poor law commissioners, to reduce numbers in the workhouse to their limit of 1,130. On 11 January 1849 they had directed that any numbers in excess of that figure should immediately be placed on outdoor relief.[63] However, this would only have accounted for a few dozen at most, from the workhouse. The huge increase was a reflection of the widespread distress which still pertained in the Mohill union well into 1849. Offering an explanation of the situation to the commissioners, which read almost exactly like those from Manorhamilton, the vice guardians maintained that:

> The heavy demands for rent, county cess, and poor rate since last harvest, have well nigh exhausted the occupiers, and their stock reduced piece-meal to a state beneath the requirements of proper farming, to meet successive demands of this kind; and the fact that members of the family perform the work formerly done by hired servants attest the conclusion.[64]

In an attempt to estimate the 'precise causes' of the destitution they calculated that the majority in need – 40 per cent – were those classed as old, infirm and sick. Widows and children of labourers accounted for 10 per cent; a further 15 per cent were widows and children of farmers evicted or forced to give up their land; those deserted by husbands or parents totalled 15 per cent. The final 20 per cent arose from the lack of work for labourers alluded to in the statement above which was a consequence of the reduced state of farmers. This group also consisted of 'mendicants, travelling dealers and tradespeople being no longer able to live by their calling' and therefore more vulnerable due to the 'almost complete cessation of private charity'.[65] The following list of those in receipt of outdoor relief in the Rynn electoral division reflects this assessment:

**Table 7.3: Outdoor Relief in Rynn Electoral Division, 1848/9**

| Name | Age | Townland | No. of Lbs of Meal Weekly |
|------|-----|----------|---------------------------|
| Mary McCanna | 36 | | |
| Peter McCanna | 9 | | |
| Hugh McCanna | 7 | Cattan | 24½ |
| John McCanna | 5 | | |
| John McCanna | 3 | | |

| | | | |
|---|---|---|---|
| Mary Duignan | 70 | | |
| Jane McCormick | 70 | | 7 |
| Biddy Duignan | 70 | Clooncoo | |
| Margaret Heslin | 46 | | |
| Biddy Heslin | 14 | | 21 |
| Mary Heslin | 11 | | |
| | | | |
| Christopher Donnelly | 76 | | 14 |
| Catherine Donnelly | 65 | | |
| Mary Kerr | 5 | Errew | 7 |
| Anne Kerr | 4 | | |
| Margaret Kane | 40 | | 14 |
| Anne Kane | 12 | | |

*Source*: St. George's Heritage Centre, Carrick-on-Shannon, County Leitrim, Geraghty Collection, Mohill Union, Electoral Division of Rynn, List of destitute persons relieved out of the workhouse during the Half-year ended 25 March 1849.

Such destitution, with adults being forced to subsist on 7 lbs of meal each week, was all too obvious to Letitia Veevers. Her efforts to sell clothes in the Mohill area had proved fruitless due to 'the recipients being all too poor a class to admit of their contributing any portion'. In some cases, the families were in fever while others consisted of 'poor, reduced mothers of families' of 'poor tradespeoples' children'. The latter were amongst the 'numerous struggling families whose earnings are not sufficient to sustain nature' but were deemed ineligible for entry to the workhouse or to receive outdoor relief.[66]

Despite their best efforts, the vice-guardians were unable to adhere to the commissioners' stipulations and on 15 February 120 people were admitted to the workhouse although in the previous week it had contained 1,164 inmates.[67] Similarly on 12 April a further 144 people were admitted.[68] While the numbers in the house and on outdoor lists continued to rise the inevitable corollary was a huge increase in weekly costs and by the middle of April the vice guardians sought the aid of the commissioners in obtaining an advance of £500 to pay debts and purchase food for outdoor relief 'which will be stopped unless cash payments be made'.[69] In the midst of these difficulties the poor law commissioners, hardly anticipating a favourable reply, advised the guardians that £1,600 due on the loan of £8,000 would be due for payment on 14 April.[70]

Indeed, an indication that the former communication was simply a circular sent to unions throughout the country was the fact that the commissioners contributed £104 towards the cost of provisions for the first week of May.[71] Such aid was essential given that in the same month a total of only £10 in rates was collected[72] and despite the obvious inability of rate payers to contribute the guardians struck a new rate of 2/6 on all divisions except Newtowngore (where it was 6*d*). The smaller levy on the latter area would suggest that things were not as bad there as in other areas but in January a correspondent to the Society of Friends had spoken of the 'prevailing distress' necessitating supplies of clothes and food in the district.[73]

By the end of May the Cloone division owed £706/5/7 in rates and the insistence on attempting to squeeze more money out of the rate payers meant that with the new rate added this debt amounted to £1,202/19/9.[74] In that same month, Rev. Andrew Hogg, in requesting seeds and clothing, assured the Society of Friends that 'nothing but the present distress' of Cloone could induce him 'again this year to apply to you for aid'.[75]

In the first week of June the union received a further £450 from the commissioners[76] which was a welcome boost given the significant increase that had occurred in those receiving outdoor relief in the summer months. At the end of April this figure stood at 7,726; by the beginning of June it was 9,734 and in the week ending 30 June it peaked at 11,357.[77] As a consequence, expenses had risen from £236/5 per week in April to £308/10 by the end of June.[78] Throughout these months numbers in the workhouse remained between 1,100 and 1,300 and the huge increase in outdoor relief recipients reflected a policy of limiting indoor relief, in spite of the fact that both George West in Cloone and Francis Nesbitt of Derrycarne offered to lease properties to the union as auxiliary workhouses.[79] However, a decision was taken in August to make a significant reduction in outdoor relief numbers and by the end of that month they had fallen to 6,550. A few days later the guardians noted that although 724 individuals had been struck off the register and told to apply to the workhouse only forty-six had done so. By the end of September there were 1,575 people registered for outdoor relief and 1,088 in the workhouse.[80]

The elected board of guardians made their return on 2 November 1849 when sixteen of them, alongside Captain Haymes, attended at the workhouse.[81] Two weeks later, the decision was taken to close the relieving officers' store and discontinue outdoor relief from 24 November.[82] Given the anticipated influx of those presently on the list it was also decided to rent a house in Mohill belonging to Mr Norris as an auxiliary workhouse, which was subsequently used as the female schoolroom.[83] As the following figures illustrate the guardians were correct in assuming a large number of admissions to the house:

**Table 7.4: Admissions to Mohill Workhouse, November–December 1849**

| Week Ending | Number Admitted |
| --- | --- |
| 24 November | 171 |
| 1 December | 180 |
| 8 December | 39 |
| 15 December | 101 |

*Source*: Leitrim County Library, Ballinamore, Mohill Board of Guardians' Minute, BG 22/A/7, 23 November, 1 December, 8 December, 15 December 1849.

The extent of residual distress may be gauged by the fact that Ellen Lawder of Mough, Fenagh was still seeking clothes for men, women and children in November of that year.[84]

### Carrick-on-Shannon

On 25 July 1848 the Carrick union finally obtained a lease of the Jamestown Mill and the newly-appointed master began employment there on 7 August.[85] In September, the guardians applied to the commissioners (who later consented) for permission to rent a small garden and store adjoining the mill at £4 per annum. They deemed this essential in that it was needed to increase the size of the plot to create a drying yard.[86] By October the capacity of workhouse accommodation was 1,500 – 800 in the main workhouse, 600 in additional buildings, sixty in temporary buildings and forty in fever sheds.[87] Nevertheless, the persistence of disease meant that fever wards were 'becoming so thronged' that the vice-guardians emphasised the importance of the completion of the new fever hospital as soon as possible.[88] By the end of the first week of November the total capacity had been exceeded (1,544) and the master was ordered to furnish a list of paupers who could be discharged to make way for able-bodied paupers 'whose applications have become so numerous'. In the meantime, the vice-guardians asked the commissioners to sanction the leasing of three houses in town which they believed would accommodate boys and create further space in the workhouse for adult males. The commissioners agreed but stipulated that the houses should be 'contiguous to each other'. The vice guardians had originally intended to pay a maximum rent of £45 for these but the owner demanded £60 and so they asked the commissioners to sanction the transaction at the latter fee 'as there is no possibility of procuring more suitable houses for the purpose intended'. The commissioners complied and on 24 February 1849 an agreement to rent the three houses had been signed.[89]

On 11 November 1848 the vice-guardians were instructed by the commissioners to discharge from the workhouse to the outdoor relief lists all widows having two or more children dependent on them. By this stage, the number in workhouse accommodation was 1,612 while those on outdoor relief numbered 2,631.[90] Within a week, and probably due to the recent discharges, the latter figure increased to 2,944 even though 321 were refused such relief which was now restricted to widows with children and orphans. However, workhouse numbers also increased to 1,699.[91] By the middle of December those on outdoor relief reached 4,555 while the total in workhouse accommodation was 1,910, well in excess of the new limit of 1,700. This development prompted a letter from the commissioners in which they voiced their 'concern' about such trends. However, the guardians replied that they were actively engaged in taking steps to reduce numbers but this had proven more difficult than anticipated 'owing to the want of clothing of the paupers and the inability of the vice guardians from low funds to buy the necessaries for those leaving'.[92] Of course, the commissioners had believed that with the discharge of women and their children to the outdoor relief lists the latter would see an increase, while able-bodied males, when offered the sole choice of workhouse accommodation, would refuse such and numbers therein would decline. Indeed, the vice-guardians remarked that so great was the abhorrence of able-bodied men to enter the workhouse 'that they will submit to deprivation that none who have not witnessed it can believe'.[93]

However, this supposition severely underestimated the extent of poverty in the union and consequent demand for poor law relief. Thus by the last week in December 1848 the number on outdoor relief was 5,495 while there were 1,670 in the workhouse.[94] As the following table illustrates, these numbers persisted in spite of the strenuous efforts of the vice guardians to restrict relief:

**Table 7.5: Numbers in receipt of Poor Law Relief in Carrick-on-Shannon Union, 4 November–30 December 1848**

| Week Ending | Number Admitted to Workhouse | Number Discharged from Workhouse | Number Refused Outdoor Relief |
|---|---|---|---|
| 4 November | 114 | 40 | 169 |
| 11 November | 185 | 97 | 321 |
| 18 November | 138 | 81 | 100 |
| 25 November | 200 | 111 | 360 |
| 2 December | 194 | 42 | 97 |
| 9 December | 192 | 222 | 222 |
| 16 December | 114 | 87 | 176 |
| 23 December | 42 | 193 | 163 |
| 30 December | 137 | 88 | 276 |
| **TOTAL** | **1,316** | **961** | **1,884** |

*Source*: Leitrim County Library, Ballinamore, Carrick-on-Shannon board of guardians' minute book, BG 52/A/6, pp.A 420, A 426, A 430, A 434, A 438, A 444, A 447, A, 453, C 2, C 8, C 12, C 18, C 22, C 28, C 32, C 38, C 42, C 48.

Thus, it was no surprise when, on 23 December, the vice-guardians applied for an extension of outdoor relief which had been due to expire on 6 January 1849. This request was made 'in consequence of the very great destitution prevailing throughout the union and the house being at present as full as the medical officer deems advisable'.[95] The latter comment referred to a plethora of diseases of all types throughout the various establishments under the union's auspices. In January, the schoolmaster was reported 'dangerously ill of typhus fever' while the assistant master had contracted fever.[96] The medical officer reported an increase in cases of fever, dysentery and measles while bronchitis was 'very general' in the house.[97] In the first week of March, both fever and dysentery were continuing to ravage the buildings and children were suffering greatly.[98] Some entered in 'the last stages of fever' while five children died in the Jamestown auxiliary of marasmus 'without any particular or marked affliction'. Indeed, the latter ailment was said to be 'very general' amongst children there and the doctor ascribed this to 'previous want and exposure'.[99] After an examination by the vice guardians into the 'declining condition of female children' in the auxiliary it was decided to supply those aged nine to twelve years with a bread supper.[100] The impact of such diseases was evident in that from the start of January to the end of April 1849 there were 258 deaths in union buildings.[101]

Of course the huge numbers receiving relief placed further strain on finances. In January, a rate of £6,828 remained uncollected and, as in Manorhamilton and Mohill, this was attributed to the 'poverty of the ratepayers of every class, even the gentry to a great extent'. Significantly, however, the vice-guardians argued that the flight from the land was having a detrimental effect:

> We are of opinion a great deal of this poverty is attributable to the emigration of that class of farmers holding from ten to twenty acres of land who, on their leaving, have disposed of their farms to a class who were desirous of obtaining possession; such have given their entire capital, leaving themselves unable to stock the land or to pay either rates or rent ... also the loss of the potato which has affected men of every degree, for we may say the rent was chiefly paid by means of feeding pigs on the refuse of that esculent.[102]

In the meantime, numbers on outdoor relief continued to increase from almost 5,500 in the first week of January to 6,582 one month later, peaking at 7,307 in March.[103] It must be remembered that by this time such relief was restricted to widows, single women with children and orphans.[104] Over the same period, from 1 January to 17 March, 2,430 applications for outdoor relief were rejected, although 940 of these coincided with a comment by the vice-guardians that they were 'making arrangements to remove widows with one child from the outdoor relief register and offer them the workhouse'.[105]

The effect on those attempting to provide relief from their own means was reflected in the comments of J. Kirkwood to the Society of Friends. On 12 March she informed them that outdoor relief had been 'taken from my poor school girls' and maintained that if they were able to continue at school until September more than fifty would earn a 'decent livelihood'. The girls had been given tickets for entry to the Carrick workhouse but Kirkwood refused to allow their admission. Referring to it as 'a den of iniquity', she maintained that 'the poor house of the district is not a fit place for young females and I am most grateful for everything that will enable those I have been teaching to exist out of it'.[106] Justification for Kirkwood's allegation was to be found in a charge of sexual molestation against the apothecary, Alan Rutherford. He was accused of 'having taken liberties with some of the female inmates and of frequently being intoxicated'. His conduct was the subject of an enquiry conducted by Captain Wynne and the vice-guardians but he resigned before it was completed, fuelling suspicions that he was guilty.[107]

Despite their best efforts, the vice-guardians were unable to reduce the numbers as anticipated, a sure sign of the prevailing misery and poverty amongst the population – while those on outdoor relief initially declined from 6,458 in the week ending 17 March to stand at 5,271 on 14 April. They began to rise again so that by the beginning of July they peaked at 8,560.[108] In the week that the number had fallen to 5,271 the number of applicants rejected was 389 and from then until the July peak a further 2,384 people were refused.[109] Such rejections were probably the consequence of a resolution by the vice guardians on 30 May to restrict outdoor relief to widows with one or more children. This order was then extended until 24 July then to 7 August and finally to 21 August.[110]

The initial decline in outdoor relief numbers in March and April saw a consequent increase in workhouse numbers. On 7 April they stood at 1,551 but the following week 182 admissions were made and the total increased to 1,701. Further huge admissions of 221 in the week ending 21 April and 200 the following week brought the overall figure to 2,020, seventy more than the new capacity (due to additional fever sheds) of 1,950.[111] However, as has been pointed out, this number was not a result of people being forced off outdoor relief and when the latter figure stood at 8,117 in mid-July the inmates of the workhouse and its auxiliaries totalled 1,739.[112] For most of August the figure remained at an average just under 1,600 but by the third week of September it had fallen significantly to 1,066.[113] Thus, the summer of 1849 witnessed a huge strain on the union in relation both to indoor and outdoor relief. For example, in June, due to the 'great number of children in the female school at Jamestown', in excess of 230, it was necessary to appoint an assistant schoolmistress.[114] With so many people confined it was inevitable that death and disease would be a regular accompaniment to dry statistics. In that same month, the medical officer noted that fever and dysentery were continuing to increase, the former being 'of a much more malignant type than for some time past'.[115] While fever had declined by the beginning of July measles were said to prevail 'to a great extent' and 'rapidly extending' among the children. In the week ending 21 July the medical officer reported fifteen deaths, 'many of whom were infants admitted in a hopeless state of marasmus'.[116]

During this period correspondents to the Society of Friends revealed what conditions were like for those outside the realm of poor law relief. Having been made aware that the Friends still had supplies of food William Parke of Clogher House, Drumsna asked for a grant of this and guaranteed that it would be 'given exclusively to those engaged in planting seeds and who are excluded from outdoor relief on account of holding a small patch of land which their spirit of industry and enterprise compels them to cling to'.[117]

George Shaw's comments reflected the grim reality for those who had survived the worst of the Famine. In relating how he had fed sixty to seventy children each week day from the start of January, as well as giving assistance to widows and sick persons, he added:

> The relief thus afforded has been very considerable, especially to many of the struggling small landholders around us who are endeavouring to keep themselves and their families out of the poorhouse and yet are but one degree removed from pauperism.[118]

By the middle of June any food in the hands of J. Kirkwood was gone while distress was 'every day increasing'. Just as in other areas, those who had endeavoured to put down a small crop were unable to avail of poor law relief and were 'literally in many cases starving and without a hope for the next few months'.[119] After his earlier letter George Shaw felt 'compelled reluctantly to trouble you again and ask whether any fragments of relief remain which you could give to our wretched neighbourhood'. In his opinion, formed out of many years observation at close quarters, the 'class of small farmers' were still in 'dire destitution' which would continue at least until the new harvest. In answer to his plea he received £5 from a fund established by Joseph Bewley for private distribution. By this means, Shaw was able to afford a 'comfortable cooked dinner' to an average of eighty to eighty-five children for two months.[120] Seeking meal and rice on behalf of the half parish of Toomna Margaretta Kirkwood remarked on the 'extreme poverty, starvation and want of clothes'. There was no means of relief, little or no work and the pay for one day's labour was 'so trifling' that it would 'only afford enough to feed one in a family' while the rest were left with a stark choice – to 'beg, or steal or starve'.[121]

In spite of such prevailing distress, the commissioners recommended an 'immediate and considerable reduction in the number of persons requiring outdoor relief' from the beginning of August.[122] As the following table illustrates, this order resulted in a huge decline in those on the lists:

**Table 7.6: Outdoor Relief in Carrick-on-Shannon Union, 21 July–22 September 1849**

| Week Ending | Number on Outdoor Relief | Number Rejected |
| --- | --- | --- |
| 21 July | 8.002 | 383 |
| 28 July | 7.639 | 610 |
| 4 August | 6,479 | 1,359 |
| 11 August | 5,914 | 1,706 |
| 18 August | 5,914 | 706 |
| 25 August | 3,425 | 1,630 |
| 1 September | 2,956 | 666 |
| 8 September | 2,460 | 677 |
| 15 September | 956 | 200 |
| 22 September | 880 | 200 |

*Source*: Leitrim County Library, Ballinamore, Carrick-on-Shannon board of guardians' minute book, BG 52/A/6, pp.1296, 1302, 1306, 1312, 1316, 1322, 1326, 1332, 1336, 1342, 1346, 1352, 1356, 1362, 1366, 1372, 1376, 1382, 1386, 1392.

Within two months outdoor relief had been reduced by almost 90 per cent and on 26 September the only orders received from relieving officers were for Leitrim/Toomna and Kilglass/Gillstown.[123]

As the autumn approached and numbers in the workhouse fell, sickness also began to decline both in terms of numbers and severity. By mid-September the new fever hospital had been opened and patients moved there from the workhouse fever wards.[124] The poor law commissioners also gave the vice guardians permission to obtain the house and additional plot of land in front of the Jamestown auxiliary. This was deemed important as a means of affording additional accommodation along with offering further space for yards 'and more effectually to enclose the premises from trespass'.[125]

However, the promise of an improved future was evident in the following letter written by Matthew O'Connor from Lough Allen Island, Drumshanbo on 16 November:

I am glad to inform you that the crop in this part of the country has been good both for quality and return and not more than one-third of the potato crop has been lost. There is consequently abundance of food here but all are complaining of low prices at which they must dispose of everything. If the harvest next year is good and that the poor rates are not extravagantly high we may hope for very much better times here.[126]

The fact that a loss of one-third was still regarded as a good crop simply reflected the extent of devastation suffered throughout the county in the years since 1844. When the blight first struck in 1845 eleven of the county's thirty-eight electoral divisions suffered a decline of a third or less and this was regarded as a catastrophe. Yet, four years later, a similar loss was seen, by some, as a relatively successful harvest and the importance of such for the population was evident in the statistics from the county's workhouses throughout 1849. Although a cholera outbreak caused havoc in other parts of the country there were few cases in Leitrim. Yet, this year witnessed the worst level of mortality in the Manorhamilton establishment since the famine commenced while large numbers continued to perish in the Carrick-on-Shannon and Mohill workhouses. These two unions also had to cope with huge demand both in terms of pressure on workhouse accommodation and requests for outdoor relief. The many thousands already in need had been augmented in this year by those now unable to cope with huge levels of poor rates, cess and rental demands. Consequently, the increasing impoverishment of the people left them almost entirely dependent on the machinery of the poor law. In the face of such demand, the private relief offered by a few hardy souls who had been doing their best for more than three years was merely a drop in the ocean. Nonetheless, the relatively successful crop and the re-introduction of potatoes into the diet in the Manorhamilton workhouse hinted at a brighter future for the people of Leitrim.

# Chapter 8

# THE TIMES ARE BETTER NOW

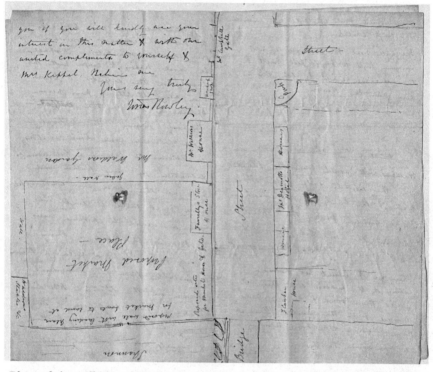

Plan of the village of Drumsna drawn by Josias Rowley in May 1849. Public Record Office, Belfast, D 4123/5/5/37. Courtesy of Deputy Keeper of Records, PRONI.

O N LEAVING HIS position as vice guardian to the Mohill union, Robert Duncan sent a rather self-serving report to the commissioners on the improvement effected by his colleagues and himself. He stated that on entering his post 'every regulation for the management of a workhouse had become inoperative and it must have soon ceased to exist as a means of relief'. He maintained that the officers were 'unfit for their duties' and 'perfectly careless as to their performance'. All this had occurred at a period of 'unexampled destitution in a peculiarly impoverished locality'. By contrast, the workhouse, in January 1849, was, with regard to cleanliness, order and discipline 'now almost perfect'. Finally, he maintained that, despite the expense of extensive outdoor relief the vice-guardians had been able to 'avoid an extravagant expenditure'.[1]

However, this perspective was somewhat at odds with that of the returning elected boards of guardians in Mohill and Carrick-on-Shannon, both of which launched vitriolic attacks on the regime of vice-guardians in their respective unions. Amongst numerous complaints was the fact that huge amounts of money had been spent leaving the unions with massive debts. Thus, the Carrick board estimated that the total costs accumulated under the regime, exclusive of rates arrears, amounted to £45,271 which resulted from £17,351 in government advances and three rates of £8,918 (November 1847), £9,537 (September 1848) and £9,465 (May 1849). They compared these figures to the fact that the liabilities of the union on their being replaced were £4,615. In a petition to the British parliament they remarked that they had recently been 'compelled to go through the ceremony of imposing a new rate' amounting to £15,000 and despite asking the commissioners to permit a levy in two instalments, which was refused, they had 'more than once informed the commissioners that it could not be collected'. As well as uncovering alleged fraud in the supplies of coal and milk to the workhouse they maintained that 'contracts of a most extravagant description' were entered into by the vice guardians. As a consequence, the union now faced a debt of £6,500 to be paid by the 'oppressed rate payers'. In addition, the books of the workhouse were found to be 'in utter confusion' with two hundred people included on the workhouse register who were not actually in the house. A similar situation pertained in relation to the outdoor relief register where hundreds were named as recipients but were not obtaining supplies. Their petition ended with an attack on the Poor Law which they declared to be 'unsuited to Ireland'. In addition, they asked to be 'emancipated from the tyranny of the Poor Law inquisition which has been permitted to coil itself, as it were, around their existence' while the law itself had been 'forced upon us by the ravings of English theorists or the schemes of needy speculators anxious to fasten themselves upon the public purse'.[2]

At a subsequent meeting on 6 April 1850 the Carrick board of guardians expressed approval of the Marquis of Westmeath's 'unwearied zeal and great exertions ... to rescue the union from the ruinous condition in which it had been plunged by those who, for a time, had been appointed to preside over it'.[3]

Nevertheless, for their part the re-instated Mohill board alleged that the last rate struck by the vice guardians, with rates ranging from 4s to 8s 2d, was illegal in that the books had not been open for inspection by rate payers for fourteen days. They claimed that the striking of a new rate, just days before the vice guardians left office, was 'carried out in haste' with the rates books made out in an 'imperfect and irregular manner'. They also noted that the new rate had not been included in the union minute book.[4] The board members felt so strongly about the matter that they determined not to collect the rate and sent their case to legal counsel to ascertain the viability of their proposed action. However, they were advised against any such move and therefore, in the words of their chairman Lord Clements, the law was unable to offer 'adequate means of redress against the injustices and misconduct of the officers of the Poor Law Commissioners'. As a result, the rate payers 'must submit to extortion and to the confiscation of their property'. His strength of feeling on the matter can be gauged by subsequent comments:

> That, while we have been given the semblance of free institutions we live, in point of fact, under a despotism, which neither respects the rights of industry or of property engaged in the cultivation of the land. With an unjust law so administered it is vain and hopeless to expect prosperity or happiness.[5]

Thus, the Mohill guardians, like their counterparts in Carrick, were reduced to sending a petition to parliament outlining their grievances. In brief these were the fact that the vice guardians were 'strangers' who had been invited in, did not contribute to the rates and were paid £250 per annum from the funds of the union. They alleged that blank cheques had been signed and money was 'squandered and misapplied under the

County Leitrim, Population Decline by Parish, 1841–51. Drawn by Sean Gill.

pretence of relieving the destitute'. Indicative of such alleged waste was the fact that a temporary dispensary had been established while a perfectly adequate one already existed in Mohill. This expense meant that in the early months of 1850 the Mohill union was in debt to the amount of £5,881. The petition ended by demanding that the powers of the poor law commissioners be 'considerably circumscribed'.[6]

Both boards received support from English newspaper the *Morning Chronicle* which, in relation to what it termed the 'ill-fated union' of Carrick-on-Shannon argued that the poor law commissioners should have monitored events much more closely. They also maintained that the vice-guardian system was 'intrinsically and fatally unsound' and described it as 'one of the worst features of a law which in its very nature is prolific of social evil'.[7]

In July 1850 the local press informed the public that, despite recent bad weather, the potato crop was 'unusually abundant' while the quality was 'never surpassed'. However, within a couple of weeks blight was again reported as affecting it but nevertheless it was felt there would be an 'average' harvest.[8] Indeed, in his first report from the Carrick union poor law inspector Captain Haymes had stated that 'should the season prove propitious there will be abundance of food about the end of July'. Haymes had earlier noted that there had been a 'very limited number of applications for relief' in the district and with 'plenty of work in the country' numbers in the workhouse were 'rapidly diminishing'. He also remarked that local farmers were struggling to obtain labourers while the latter were earning 1s 3d a day – 'a rate never known in this country before'.[9]

Haymes made similar comments in relation to the Mohill union where, due to the lack of sufficient labourers, 'many able-bodied' had been 'taken from the workhouse'.[10] His optimism appears to have been well-founded as Matthew O'Connor wrote to the Society of Friends from Lough Allen Island, Drumshanbo, informing them that the harvest of 1850 had been a good one and 'the poor people are recovering very fast from the effects of the terrible ordeal they had to pass through'.[11] Nevertheless, an indication of continued distress was the robbery of 'a large quantity of potatoes' from the infirmary in Carrick.[12]

The hopes raised by the successful crop of 1850 appeared to have been built on with the first reports of the 1851 crop. The *Leitrim Journal* noted that 'in every part of the country and even in the immediate vicinity of this town [Carrick] large numbers of our able-bodied and hardy population are busily employed putting down potatoes'. The paper argued that if the blight 'continues to abate as it has for the last two years' an 'abundant supply could be expected'.[13] However, this optimism was tempered by reports in August of the rapid progression of potato disease in Ballinamore while in Fenagh there had occurred the 'entire destruction of a crop of stalks … and the partial destruction of the potato itself which appears to be fearfully infected'.[14] Later that month the same source noted that:

> Throughout Leitrim there is a prevalent blight in the potato crop but we are happy to state not in the aggravated form of past years … Throughout Counties Leitrim, Sligo, Roscommon and Cavan … the foetid air arising from the fields told the fearful tale but the disease is to a great extent confined to stalks and the greater part of the bulbs are safe.[15]

Thus, the paper was happy to report that, from the 'immense quantities' of potatoes planted, there would still be a better than average crop, a fact alluded to by Haymes who earlier lamented that 'the experience of four years famine [is] thrown away on the people who consider potatoes and prosperity synonymous'.[16]

In 1853 there appeared instances of localised blight and although it was commented that only some tubers were tainted Joseph Dunwoody reported 'signs of disease to a fearful extent' in the neighbourhood of Keonbrook.[17] However, in early September the *Leitrim Journal* reported that the crop would be 'well above average'.[18]

## WORKHOUSES

### Carrick-on-Shannon

The impact of these partial crop failures was evident in the numbers still repairing to the county's workhouses. On 1 June 1850 there were 1,476 inmates in the various buildings of the Carrick-on-Shannon union[19] and only six cases of outdoor relief (in Drumreilly and Leitrim/Toomna). Despite the prevalence of dysentery the sanitary condition of the house was said to be 'improving' and the visiting committee noted that females were engaged in sewing, mending and spinning while the boys and men were busy at shoemaking and tailoring.[20] However, in early July, with a total of 1,617 inmates, the medical officer reported that fever had 'augmented considerably this week and opthalmia is epidemic amongst the children'.[21] The newly-installed board initiated an investigation into the numbers and established there were 996 inmates in the workhouse, infirmary and fever hospital; 196 in the town auxiliary and 378 in Jamestown. They also discovered that 'a number of these have entered without undergoing the required rules of admission and registry' which they blamed on 'the negligence of the vice-guardians and the undue influence of the late inspector [Wynne]'.[22] In an attempt to reduce numbers they resolved that all paupers 'having parents and relations liable and able to support them be discharged forthwith … and forced to apply again if they wish'.[23] They also signalled their intention to return the buildings in Carrick currently used as auxiliary workhouses.[24] By 3 August the number in the house totalled 1,294 and the guardians ordered that paupers currently in the town auxiliary be removed immediately to the main workhouse and by 31 August the town auxiliary was closed. They also agreed to lease the Quarry Field from Charles Manners St George for the erection of water works.[25] By 12 October the numbers in the workhouse had been reduced to 780 and although they increased again as winter set in the guardians were able to concentrate on matters with which they had been very familiar in their previous tenure.[26] With uncollected rates standing at £5,773 they established that a number of immediate lessors were liable for over £169 between them and requested the poor law commissioners to sanction proceedings against them.[27] Included in this group were some high-profile local personalities such as John Duckworth, Rev. Thomas Larange and Josias Rowley.[28] After gaining the affirmation of the commissioners the guardians instructed their solicitor to 'take immediate proceedings by civil bill' against all such defaulters. Similarly, rate collectors were threatened in late September with legal action if they did not have their rates collected within three weeks.[29] Given the uncollected debt, and the fact that much, if not most of it, would not be remitted, the guardians proposed that the government extend the payment for workhouse loans to a period of forty years.[30]

Although potatoes were being used in the house in May oatmeal and Indian meal still remained an important part of the dietary throughout the rest of the year.[31] However, on 18 December the guardians resolved that the inmates of the main house and auxiliary should receive beef for their Christmas dinner.[32] However, both the persistent nature of residual poverty and perhaps continued aversion to workhouse relief was evident in the minutes of 20 and 27 November when it was noted that 'there were many applicants on the relieving officers' books ordered to the workhouse'.[33]

Despite such aversion, by the beginning of February 1851 the number in the Carrick workhouse stood at 983 and despite falling to 735 in May it reached 973 in the first week of July. In that week there were ninety-seven admissions but this was offset by 103 discharges while a month later there were 116 discharged so that by the beginning of August the number stood at 730. Further discharges that month resulted in a huge decline so that by early September the number had fallen to 488.[34] From then until February 1852 the figure remained below 500 and although it climbed to 546 in March there was a gradual decline thereafter and with forty-two discharged in the week of 7 August the number fell to 399.[35] Although there remained 379 at the end of January 1853 this number continued to gradually fall throughout the rest of that year so that by the middle of November there were 226 inmates in the workhouse and one in the fever hospital.[36]

## Mohill

On 15 August 1850, the *Impartial Reporter* remarked:

> During the past week we had an opportunity of visiting this workhouse [Mohill] and never were better pleased at the general management of a house than in this instance – especially in that part under the charge of the matron. In the school- room the children have every facility for a thorough English education, nothing being neglected on the part of the schoolmaster to ensure it.[37]

One year later there still remained 845 inmates in the workhouse although in that same week seventy-five were discharged and over the following five weeks 159 more left while only twenty-eight were admitted. Thus, by the beginning of October the figure stood at 707[38] and remained just above 700 until mid-November when it started to gradually climb to a peak of 818 in the week ending 21 February 1852.[39] Between then and July the total fluctuated but by the end of the latter month it had fallen to 601 and in early September it had been reduced to 430.[40] Numbers remained above 400 and fell to 398 in the week ending 23 April 1853 before eventually declining to 244 at the end of September.[41]

## Manorhamilton

In May 1851 a local paper noted that the Manorhamilton workhouse was 'remarkable at present for nothing but the absence of disease' adding that it was 'very clean and under very correct discipline'.[42] However, evidence of continued distress in the area was indicated by the fact that between October 1850 and February 1851 numbers in the house increased from

478 to 633.[43] This represented the peak and although the total remained above 500 until July 1851 there was a gradual decline throughout the succeeding months until October when it stood at 291.[44]

Numbers started to increase again in the winter of 1851–2 so that by the end of February 1852 they had reached 394.[45] They persisted above 300 until September when they fell to 271.[46] Although they reached 301 at the end of January 1853 they slowly declined to 237 at the beginning of July.[47] Thus, it was not until mid- and late 1853 that the workhouses in the county were able to return figures that matched their pre-Famine averages. However, a number of developments suggested that the county had been, to a certain degree, recovering from the Famine from 1850 onwards.

In November 1850 the Leitrim Fair was reported as having been 'one of the best held in that county for some time past',[48] while the following month the Leitrim Races 'came off with greater éclat than could be expected' over a course consisting of 1½ heats, intersected with twelve stone walls.[49] On 1 September 1851 the Lough Allen Regatta, 'the first for many years', took place. Sailing matches were open to all with a prize of a silver challenge cup being awarded to the winners. It was reported how 'a numerous and highly respectable attendance comprising many of the elite of this and neighbouring counties' spectated at the event.[50]

On 31 July the *Leitrim Journal* reported that Charles Manners St George, together with his family, had arrived from the Continent after an absence of two years. One of his first actions was to instruct his agent, Charles Cox, to have the town clock, which had 'lain silent' for many years 'repaired and put in order'.[51]

St George's return was marked by a ball which was attended by all the local gentry including the Lawders, Kirkwoods, La Touches, Coxs, Rowleys and Peytons. Also in attendance was the local parish priest Fr Dawson who shared a supper 'when every delicacy the country and season could afford was provided by the hospitable host and hostess in great profusion'. The group were entertained by 'an excellent band' which completed 'a delightful evening of unalloyed happiness and amusement'.[52]

Such entertainment was by no means uncommon in the early 1850s in Carrick and a series of concerts and variety acts took place in the local court house. In May 1852 a 'Grand Orchestral Concert' included the 'following extraordinary and unrivalled combination of musical novelties' such as a steel band and Swiss bells.[53] The same month saw a Classical Walhalla Entertainment starring Monsieur Gerhard.[54] On 21 July 1854 a circus, with 'a troupe of American artistes and a magnificent stud of highly

trained horses and ponies' entered Carrick in procession 'led by the Grand
Chariot Car of Hindostan'. Prices for the circus ranged from 6*d* for the
promenade to 2*s* for first–class seats.[55]

On 17 August the *Leitrim Journal* reported on the first Carrick Regatta:

> On Tuesday the 15th of August the monotony of Carrick life was a
> little broken into by an enlivening scene on the Shannon. Crowds
> of respectably dressed people thronged into town and took up their
> positions on the banks of the river, thronging the quays, the stand-
> house and every available spot, where a glimpse of the race might
> be had. The river swarmed with all manner of small craft. On board
> the Midland Great Western Railway's steamer were congregated the
> elite of this and the neighbouring counties.[56]

The following year the court house played host to a 'grand vocal and
musical entertainment' accompanied by a lecture on 'music and the vocal
art' followed in October by an evening of 'ventriloqueal and polyphonic
novelties'.[57] After its initial success the Carrick regatta, now under the
patronage of Charles Manners St George, was repeated in 1855 on a larger
scale. With the races completed a 'grand display of fireworks' took place
in the evening followed by a concert given by the brass band of the Sligo
Rifles. That evening's dinner included 'everything in season' and 'all were
happy and jolly in good champagne, toasts and speeches'. However, due to
the 'ungentlemanly conduct of some would–be gentlemen' the climax of
the festivities, the evening ball, was a failure, 'as all respectable people left
in disgust'.[58]

Clothing and provisions for such events were provided by a variety
of new shops which appeared in the county. In November 1850 Thomas
Feely opened his 'New Grocery Establishment' opposite the Shambles in
Carrick. In his adverts he claimed to stock malt whiskey and tea 'of the
richest and most delicious flavour at unusually low prices'.[59] In similar vein,
Henry Buttler's 'Scotch House' in Mohill offered the latest fashions while
in March 1851 Miss E. King commenced business at her new 'Grocery and
Bakery Establishment' in Carrick.[60] In May James Redington announced his
return from Dublin 'with all the new and fashionable designs in millinery'
while his Woollen Hall, in Carrick, offered 'gentlemens' silk handerchiefs,
scarves and opera ties'.[61] Another clothing shop in the town, belonging to
N.J. Tunney, reported that the establishment was 'replete with the choisest

novelties and latest fashions of the season'.[62] On 23 February 1854 James Pigott's 'New Drapery Warehouse' opened close to Church's Hotel in Main Street, Carrick and offered a 'large, useful, elegant and fashionable stock'.[63]

Such commercial ventures were aided by a number of developments. In October 1850 boat owners, Bernard and Patrick Beirne, offered the traders and merchants of Leitrim and the surrounding counties the prospect of leaving Dublin each Monday and arriving in Carrick the following Saturday by means of the Royal Canal and River Shannon Navigation.[64] In December it was announced that Leitrim village was to have a post office while the government had contracted for the mails, by car, between Carrick, Leitrim, Drumshanbo, Drumkeerin and Dromahaire.[65] At the same time the canal being constructed in 1851 from Leitrim village to Belturbet, where it would join the Ulster Canal, was expected to be ready in a year. In this way the county would be connected to the seaport towns of Belfast and Newry and the Northern Railway. Meanwhile, from September 1855 a new butter market was held in Drumshanbo on each Friday.[66] Indicative of the growing middle-class in Carrick was the establishment of the town's Literary and Scientific Society which held its first meeting in Lucy's Hotel on 10 May 1854.[67]

Despite these developments the local paper bemoaned the commercial, physical and social condition of Carrick. Declaring that 'this is a bustling time in which we live … an age of go-ahead activeness', it lamented how 'we are so far behind that its spirit scarce breathes upon us'. Claiming the town was 'in many respects' trailing Ballinamore and Manorhamilton 'with regard to improvements' it demanded that a meeting of local landlords and traders was necessary 'to shove the town out of the social stagnation in which nature's blessings are suffered to rot'.[68] The same paper later referred to 'the wheel of progress which has seldom, if ever, been moved in the county Leitrim'.[69] As a start it urged that the land lying between the Court House and river should be transformed into a public promenade. When 'laid out in walks, bordered by flowers or aromatic shrubs' it would, it maintained 'make a delightful addition to the town'.[70]

Apparently, such 'social stagnation' was not confined to Carrick, as evidenced by the following unflattering description of the neighbouring town of Drumshanbo:

The entrance from the north is not amiss; but when the upper portion of it is viewed, as we viewed it, at an early hour, with houses closed and chimneys smokeless, a more dreary picture – one so racy of desolation, is scarce conceivable. The street is sunk, and looks as if the trampling of cattle and rooting of swine had wrought it to its present state of delectable ruggedness. The street grins up at the houses; the houses look down in lugubrious desolateness on the street, and both form a sadly ludicrous picture of Irish neglect. The word *Drumshanbo* signifies the back of the old cow. There is a disease, called by the country people warbles, to which the backs of old cows are liable, and the town in question does honour to its name as the back of a warbled old cow.[71]

Meanwhile, an enterprising suggestion for the rejuvenation of the village of Drumsna was made by retired naval officer, Josias Rowley in May 1849. Rowley, not known for his letters to relief organisations from an area immersed in poverty and a poor rate debtor, wrote to the landlord of the village, Colonel George Keppel. He believed that adverts should be placed in 'the Naval and Military papers' aimed at 'half-pay officers and invalids' in the British Navy. He wished for them to avail of several houses to let in 'the beautiful town of Drumsna' with 'the following advantages': 'a good spa; cheap living; communication with Dublin twice a day; a pretty situation on the River Shannon; good fishing and shooting; fresh fish and oysters from the sea coast'.[72]

He continued:

> I well know by experience that in my profession several officers who, when they retire from service exist on half pay, which is generally from £90 to £200 per annum [and] have not the most minute idea where they are to pass the remainder of their days. Their principal object is to live cheaply, in retirement and quiet. Therefore, I think this town would be admirably suited for the purpose.[73]

Enclosing a plan of the village, with a suggested market place, Rowley informed Keppel that 'there are at present two houses or cabins on the proposed site. These I would throw down and their gardens would form the market place'.[74] Fortunately for the families living in these houses, Rowley's plan came to nothing.

In 1853 the interest of Leitrim's landed classes was soon consumed by news of the Crimean War involving Britain and a number of allies on one side and Russia on the other. Meetings were held in Manorhamilton and Mohill and committees established in various baronies to raise subscriptions in support of the Patriotic Fund. The Manorhamilton gathering raised £79/6 (which included £50 from the Earl of Leitrim) and pledged itself to 'use our utmost endeavours to carry into effect Her Most Gracious Majesty's benevolent intentions by collecting subscriptions in aid of the Patriotic Fund for the relief of the widows and orphans of our brave fellow countrymen'.[75] In Mohill, where £97 was raised, Lord Clements remarked that as 'the times are better now than they were a few years since ... I trust we will make such a subscription as will be creditable to Leitrim'.[76] At the final meeting of the Leitrim baronial committee, it was announced that £203 had been raised.[77] Doubtless the contributors would have shared in the 'rejoicing in Carrick' with the news of the British victory at Sebastopol, as reported in the local press:

> The inhabitants of this usually quiet town testified their joy on the fall of Sebastopol by erecting a bonfire containing 150 boxes of turf, six tar barrels and everything in the shape of fuel that would add flame to the heap. The police and militia fired several rounds in several parts of the town; lighted torches, preceded by a band, passed through town shouting for the Queen, Napoleon and the Allied Armies and 'Down with the Russians'.
>
> The Gaol, Military barracks and a few houses in town were illuminated and ... W.P. Clarke, Governor Leitrim Gaol, had erected on the piers of the entrance gates the national flags of England and France with a transparency in the centre bearing the word 'Sebastopol' surrounded by the ensigns of France, England, Turkey and Sardinia.[78]

One of the most significant events in the county in these years was the election of 1852. In May two men announced their candidature: William Johnston of Kinlough House and Hugh Lyons Montgomery of Belhavel, north of Drumkeerin. The former declared his intention to 'stem the torrent of misfortune and Whig misrule' and stated he would 'strenuously support the improving tenant'. For his part, Montgomery promised to support the present government while maintaining his belief that the 'improving tenant' was 'entitled to receive remuneration for his outlay'.[79] Both men were later joined in the contest by Charles Clements, Edward

King Tenison and an unknown – Dr John Brady, originally from Cavan town but now living in London. In his election literature Brady announced that he was a 'thorough and hearty supporter of Sharman Crawford's bill' and declared how he would 'put a stop to landlord injustice and oppression and thereby destroy the sole origin of tenant, of secret, assassination, of peasant crime and outrage'.[80]

Brady's campaign was ridiculed in the local press which referred to his supporters as 'illiterate country people'.[81] However, he, along with Montgomery, was elected as MP for the county – a highly significant result in that for the first time the farmers of the county had a voice to represent them. For the first time, also, Leitrim had elected a Catholic and the sectarian undercurrent which had always been present in the county manifested itself after the election. The chief supporters of Brady had been the local Catholic clergy. For example, in reporting Brady's arrival in Carrick to canvass voters the *Leitrim Journal* sneered at how he had been 'welcomed by Rev. Dr Dawson and Rev. Thomas Fitzgerald *only*'.[82] Nevertheless, these men and their colleagues carried great weight amongst the population. This had been evident during the election of 1847 when Fr Thomas Maguire who, in urging support for Edward King Tenison, had publicly vilified John Robert Godley as labouring under 'a great disadvantage with regard to hereditary associations for his father was not only the political and religious foe, but he was also the personal enemy of the people'. By comparison:

> During the time that famine and fever had been committing amongst the people, Mr and Lady Louisa Tenison did not shun contact with the poor, but rather leading in the works of heavenly charity and compassion, they entered their miserable dwellings, and like servants they ministered to their relief and supplied their necessities (loud cheers). They could not work harder, if the objects whom they served were some of themselves, and were those people to be kicked out for Mr Godley, of whom they knew nothing? Would bribery buy the voters of Leitrim (loud cries of 'no').[83]

Maguire's speech evidently succeeded as Tension, together with Viscount Clements, was subsequently elected.[84]

Further, in February 1851 a meeting of the parishioners of Kiltoghert was called as a consequence of the controversy over the British government's reaction to the decision by the Pope to appoint bishops in England for the first time since the Reformation. With parish priest Father Dawson in the chair, a resolution, moved by his curate, Father Fitzgerald, was carried to the effect that 'the attempt of the Minister to return to penal enactments fills us with disgust equalled only by our indignation'. Calling on parliament to reject any such measure they warned:

> That the injustice to the Irish Catholics in obliging them to support a Church Establishment from which they receive but abuse as well as in the distribution of patronage, and even in the administration of justice, has taxed their patience and loyalty quite enough.
> That we humbly submit it is unwise as unjust to draw further on their forbearance.[85]

In that same month it was noted that Father Dawson had subscribed five shillings to the funds of the Tenant League while Father P. Byrne contributed £1.[86] On 12 July 1854 the County Leitrim Liberal Club held a meeting in Carrick-on-Shannon and voted to establish sub-committees in Ballinamore, Carrick, Manorhamilton and Mohill. Significantly, those present included thirteen members of the Catholic clergy, comprising eight parish priests and five curates.[87]

Of course, such overt support of what was regarded by the establishment as radical politics left the clergy open to various accusations. For example, in March 1853 elections were held for the Mohill board of guardians. The *Leitrim Journal*, in stating that 'a new method has lately been adapted by the Ribbonmen' reported that houses of farmers in the neighbourhood of Rantogue had been entered and voting papers in favour of Mr Creamer – who had opposed John Brady – were carried off. Similarly, in Manorhamilton, signed papers in favour of Mr Ruinan, were stolen. Of course, as noted earlier, this was not a new method and had occurred in the very first election to the boards of guardians in 1839. However, the paper was more than happy to place the blame for such events at the feet of the Catholic clergy when surmising that 'probably if the truth were known "stations" were held in those townlands a short time previously in order to secure the return of Bradyites'.[88]

Alongside such political matters there occurred two financial transactions which epitomised the change taking place in post-Famine Leitrim. In April 1852 the Catholic parishioners of Carrick, Gowel,

Jamestown and Leitrim combined to buy the Carrick-on-Shannon Commercial Hotel in the Encumbered Estates Court. At a cost of £400 the building was to be converted into a new parochial house.[89] A few months later, the new MP, Dr Brady, purchased, through the same court, thirteen townlands which comprised the Drumbibe estate close to Ballinamore. In spending £12,650 Brady hoped 'by his treatment of his tenantry to show an example which would have beneficial effects on the tenantry of the entire county'.[90] Within a couple of months he had established an agricultural society on his estate.[91]

However, in the months that followed Brady's success, religious divisions became marked. An immediate consequence for those who had supported him was evident in the dismissal of twenty labourers employed on the Ulster Canal. They had spent the week of the election 'procuring and securing votes for Brady under the particular directions and instructions of our clergy'. Consequently, they were 'in great distress' and stated that they expected to be 'liberally rewarded for our faithful services'.[92] In the same way, Father Peter Curran, parish priest of Ballinamore, alleged that tenants who had voted for Brady had been turned off their land.[93]

In November 1852, the *Leitrim Journal* noted the appearance of what it referred to as 'incendiary placards' advocating 'exclusive dealing'.[94] It revealed how these called on Catholics not to conduct business with any of those who had signed a letter of thanks to Viscount Clements for the manner in which he had maintained peace during the election.[95] A similar notice posted on the gates of the Catholic church in Drumcong advised people not to send grazing cattle to a local farm held by William Draper as he had voted for Hugh Lyons Montgomery. The local press declared that 'those Protestants who exercised their brains contrary to the views of the Fathers, of Holy Mother Church, are to be immolated on the altar of blind subservience, hypocrisy and exclusive dealing'.[96]

In the same month, the windows of the Church of Ireland in Cloone were smashed with stones. Such attacks on churches were by no means uncommon. For example in December 1851 the Church of Ireland in Kiltubrid was entered by raising the windows and once inside the culprits 'stole there from every portable article they could find within its walls'.[97] A month later, the Catholic church at Corglass, near Drumkeerin, was entered by thieves who stole brass candlesticks.[98] Similarly, in March 1853 the Church of Ireland in Mohill was broken into and 'twenty pew candlesticks, a communion table cover and a surplice' were stolen.[99]

However, the attack on Cloone church occurred at a time of heightened tension and appears to have been sectarian. Such tensions were not helped by a number of factors.

In 1850 the Irish Society, a proselytising body, reported great success in its branches at Dromahaire and Drumshanbo. It described Dromahaire as 'a most interesting district' where 'the thirst for Scriptural instruction is increasing' and revealed how, when one of its clergymen preached in the area, he was 'surprised and delighted to see at least twenty of our Irish pupils (men) open their Irish Bibles and read with him the 10th chapter of Romans'. The report noted how:

> The greatest opposition prevails on the part of the priests through this entire district, notwithstanding which we have 1,445 Roman Catholics under instruction and of the 709 pupils who passed inspection this period, 612 of them were of that religion.[100]

In light of such figures they claimed that it was 'no wonder that the priests should tremble, for their craft is in danger; the fear of man is evidently vanishing and large numbers attend every fortnight in a school-house to hear a sermon preached by some of the local clergy' (see Appendix 3).[101]

A variety of incidents reflected the continuing sectarian nature of life in the county. For example, in December 1851 William Lawder and Henry Huson received threatening notices 'for presuming to stock the country [around Mohill] with County Cavan Protestants'. It transpired that a number of people from that county had taken land from which locals had been evicted.[102] In February 1853 Fr Tom Fitzgerald was rebuked by Michael Cox for officiating at an interment in Killukin graveyard without the 'expressed consent' of the parish (Protestant) clergyman. Twenty-four years after the repeal of the Penal Laws such an action by the priest was deemed to be 'at variance with the law'.[103] That same month saw the first in a series of what were termed Controversial Sermons by Protestant clergyman Rev. G.W. Dalton, the vicar of Kilbryan, County Roscommon, and one of the missionaries to local Catholics. Held in the Church of Ireland in Carrick, Dalton's lectures focussed on various aspects of Catholic dogma and featured titles such as: 'Is the Church of Rome the true Church?'; 'Purgatory'; 'Has the Church of Rome the truth?' and 'Does the Bible teach us to put our trust in the Blessed Virgin Mary?'[104]

For the vast majority of those who had not succumbed to death during the Famine, life continued along very similar lines. Reading the newspapers of the early 1850s is akin to perusing those of the 1830s. The Molly Maguires remained a constant thorn in the side of the authorities and anyone who would cross them. For example, in January 1851 they entered several houses in the townland of Gunan near Mohill and swore the tenants not to pay rent. At the same time, the house of a process-server, together with a number of processes, was destroyed near Keshcarrigan.[105] On 25 September the *Leitrim Journal* reported an attack on Edward and Robert Duke who were employed to watch crops seized for county cess in Cloonboney, near Dromod. Around ten men, dressed as women, and armed with pitchforks, beat them. They then attacked William Moran of Dromhaney, near Mohill who had taken possession of land from someone who had been evicted.[106] Meanwhile, in January 1852 poor rate collector Christopher Kenedy was 'dreadfully beaten' by two men near Farnaght.[107] Such occurrences prompted the press to refer to an armed and well-trained 'organised banditti'.[108]

As in the pre-Famine era, Cloone was the centre of much activity. For example, in June 1851 five Molly Maguires, dressed again in women's attire, burgled Cloone House and attempted to kill the caretaker. The *Leitrim Journal* declared this to be 'only one outrage of the many which have within the last fortnight disgraced the parish of Cloone and its neighbourhood' and reported that:

> Illegal nightly meetings under the denomination of 'a dance' are held at least once a week (generally Sunday evenings) at which resolutions are entered into and instructions given for the carrying of such into effect.[109]

At the presentment sessions of 3 June 1852 Viscount Clements 'adverted to the lawless state of Cloone' labelling the local population as 'regular *Kaffirs*', adding that he would 'take good care that the Cloone, otherwise Ribbon Laws, should be put an end to'.[110] It was therefore with undisguised pleasure that the same paper announced a successful application (at a cost of £540) by the county surveyor:

> For a new line of road to open up that wild and lawless part of the country, the townland of Cattan, in which more numerous murders

and outrages have been committed than in the most feared part of Tipperary.[111]

The importance of such an initiative can be gauged from the following description of the problems faced by the constabulary in entering the townland of Drumshanbo in the parish of Cloone, 'as lawless a spot as in either Longford, which it borders, or Leitrim': 'This townland is almost insulated by lakes, rivers (rapid ones) and bogs so that it is a matter of great difficulty to get into this place even in daylight except in frosty weather or summer.'[112]

In commenting on these events the *Impartial Reporter* had no doubts as to the catalyst for such occurrences:

These things are to be deplored; they will be quoted as evidence of Irish barbarism and of Leitrim ruffianism. But they teach another lesson; and that lesson is supplied by the answer to the question 'why does such a state of things exist?' Such things do not exist when the people are prosperous and contented. Open rebellion may spring from the ambition of one or more persons where the people in general have not much to complain of; but midnight outrages of the kind in question always originate in *the misery of the people*. When heavy burdens are laid upon them; when hunger stares them in the face or tugs at their hearts – they become desperate. And when their social superiors neglect, and the law ignores, a people, is it a mater of wonder that they become desperate…The extreme of misery causes some characters to sit down in heart-sick stupor; but it renders others recklessly active. In the greater part of Ireland, it has had the former effect; in Leitrim it has produced the latter.

Leitrim is a proverbially miserable and neglected county. We have repeatedly seen the misery with our own eyes, and heard it with our own ears. The land is neglected; the people are permitted to grow and wither and rot – a field of breathing weeds; and those to whom providence (or law) has given the prosperity of the county seem to have no sense of responsibility.

People cannot be expected to cultivate a good behaviour when they are baptised in wretchedness. They ought certainly to obey the law; but they will ask, 'what has the law done for us?' and that no man can answer. Let them have the means of life – let them get out of pig-stys and rags – let them have food fit for human beings – give them encouragement to toil – bestow hope upon them (a thing they know nothing of) and we will answer for the good conduct of the Leitrim people

Let it be borne in mind, as an axiom in Social Economy – that social outrages are committed only by miserable people; and that a miserable people are made by neglect and bad laws.[113]

Aside agrarian violence, alcohol-fuelled aggression also featured in these years. On 6 February 1851 a riot involving around fifty people took place in Kinlough, while Christmas Day 1853 witnessed a disturbance in Mohill involving a crowd of 300, 'the greater part of them having got the worse of drink'.[114] The police were attacked as they attempted to arrest the ringleaders and Viscount Clements read the riot act before clearing the streets.[115] In the aftermath, six men were indicted for riot and affray and assaulting the police and were each sentenced to two months in prison with hard labour.[116] In January 1854 twelve people were prosecuted for a riot at a fair in Kiltyclogher while in June 1855 a pre-arranged faction fight between the Murrys and Glanceys resulted in a serious disturbance in Carrick-on-Shannon. The local paper reported how 'from 7 pm to 8.30 pm the town was one continued scene of riot, bloodshed and confusion. The shops were all closed up at once and every sort of market business suspended for the day'. The violence included around twenty members of the Leitrim Militia and it was only when other members of that body intervened that it was brought to an end.[117]

There was no doubt in the mind of a correspondent to the *Leitrim Journal* that such trouble could be laid at the door of what he termed 'dance houses' by which the area around Carrick was said to be 'awfully infested'. These were centres of 'wickedness and immorality' and 'there it is from whence may be traced a very large portion of the moral degradation of an increasing mass of our people who are evidently sinking lower and lower into the deep abyss of utter destitution'. In addition, the Sabbath was 'openly, disgracefully and egregiously broken by the frequenters of these houses'.[118] In a subsequent article the *Journal*, referring to them as 'those dens of vice, those ways to hell', estimated there were at least six shebeen houses in Carrick, 'where the lowest and the very meanest people – the mere dregs of society – resort to satisfy their thirsty longings with the "fire water" sold under the name of whiskey'.[119]

While, life, in all its various guises – political, social and economic – continued, the reality was that the county had been devastated by the events of 1845 onwards. A population loss of around 50,000 within five years cannot but have made an impact, both physical and psychological. On 29 July 1851 the Friends of Leitrim Protestant Orphan Society met in the court house in Carrick-on-Shannon. In this, their twelfth report, they revealed that they had 104 children under their care while their finances had improved compared to previous years as a consequence of enhanced subscriptions and better contributions at charity sermons. Nevertheless, the committee felt compelled to comment that 'your county has not as yet emerged from the deep distress felt by all classes arising from heavy taxation and the general depressions of trade – the result of years of famine'.[120]

Such results were evident in a letter written by a correspondent to the *Leitrim Journal* who recorded his impressions of a recent visit to a town in the county in December 1850:

> I passed through a little town in the lower part of this county where I saw a few people collected in the street – it was a 'fair day' – but when I remember and look back some eight or nine years the comparison of what I witnessed then could not but bring to my mind the idea that our once happy and peaceful peasantry were banished from their native land. Oh, what a wretched condition the fragments of this miserable people are in – every house nearly roofless – uncultivated fields – deserted villages – poor houses filled with the offspring of parents who have long since paid the debt of nature! – these, and other pictures as much appalling to the sight of a civilised being, meet the eye and attract the attention of the traveller, but they are become so familiar to the people that a passing thought is seldom spent on them.[121]

# Chapter 9

# — GRAPPLING WITH — SHADOWS

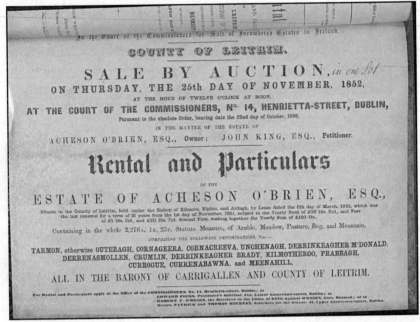

Advertisement of a sale in the Encumbered Estates Court, 1852. Public Record Office, Belfast, D 1201/45/4, Encumbered Estates, County Leitrim. Courtesy of Deputy Keeper of Records, PRONI.

CORRESPONDENCE FROM INDIVIDUALS throughout the county was permeated with complaints about the lack of resident gentry in the county. However, attempting to assess the role of both absentees and resident gentry is determined to a great extent by the availability of relevant estate material. Occasional references in the press gave a glimpse of their role during the crisis. For example, in 1850, as he had done for May 1849, George Manners St George offered an abatement of four shillings in the pound for the half year's rent due in November 1849.[1] The following year the *Leitrim Journal* reported that Mrs St George had distributed warm clothing to the poor while her husband was employing up to sixty labourers each day in the construction of the new town promenade.[2]

In September 1850 it was announced that Edward King Tenison had made an abatement of 20 per cent to tenants on his Leitrim and Roscommon estates, while the following year George Lane-Fox offered an allowance of 15 per cent on payment of the year's rent due by 1 May 1851 on his Dromahaire estate. He had adopted a similar measure in 1850 together with remitting around £7,000 arrears due.[3] Similarly, in April 1851 Alexander Faris reduced his rents and the local press reported how he had forgiven tenants three and in some cases, six, year's rent and let land at a new valuation that was considerably lower than the previous one. In the same month Reverend William A. Percy reduced rents on his property and Glebe lands by one-quarter.[4]

Hence, some local landlords were at least making some effort to alleviate the prevailing distress. However, for much of Leitrim little remains in terms of detailed estate papers which can be analysed but three estates did leave some rather eclectic documentation which reveals that the question of landlord–tenant relations in the county was both nuanced and complex.

While references were made in various letters about landlords employing tenants on local works schemes details of such were rarely available. One exception was the work carried out on the estate of Lord Leitrim at Lough Rynn in 1846–7. There, the landlord maintained a detailed ledger of all the work carried out on a daily basis on his estate together with payments made to those employed. For example, in November 1846 a number of men were engaged in spreading stones as part of the construction of a new farm yard road. When two of them, Con Flynn and John Deacon, were unwell and unable to work in the first week of December they were not paid. However, when Deacon was again unwell a few weeks later he was allowed his wages 'by order of Lord Leitrim'. Similarly, Pat Carter, who attended cattle on the estate, was sick between 14–19 December and once again, on the direct orders of Lord Leitrim, he received his wages. However, such relative generosity was tempered by the attitude to those who were deemed to have carried out substandard work. Hence, in the first week of January 1847, Anne Duke, Hugh Reynolds and John Duke were each fined 6*d*. For the week 15–20 February Pat Flynn, James Conlon and Pat Conboy were employed in 'spreading manure and digging ground at the old castle for parsnips' but due to their 'bad work' they were fined 2/6.[5]

In the last week of February Pat Reynolds was fined two shillings 'for acting contrary to orders and neglecting his duty by going to Mohill on the fair night instead of attending the horses, etc at 8 o'clock'. Given that Reynolds was paid at the rate of 8*d* per day this fine constituted more than one-half a week's wages. Such fines continued throughout 1847 and ranged from 4*d* to 2/6. Reynolds was fined twice in June: once 'for being so long in drilling the long field' (two shillings) and the following week 'for neglecting his work and keeping horses' (6*d*) In July, twelve fines were issued 'for not finishing an ordinary task of holing in the lawn' while August saw fifteen fines ranging from 6*d* to two shillings.[6]

During the nineteenth century William Lawder, resident at Mount Campbell House in Drumsna, acted as agent for the County Leitrim estate of the Earl of Albemarle (the title of the Keppel family). The latter owned 2,500 acres consisting of the townlands of Keelogue, Listermagiville, Gorthenury, Drumoula, Bonymore and Bonnybeg in the parish of Mohill and Annaghasna in the parish of Kiltoghert. An interesting collection of letters pertaining to late 1846 reveals that, although absentees, the Keppels appeared to take an active interest in the estate and by January 1846 Mrs Susan Keppel had patronised the establishment of a 'penny clothing club' amongst the tenants of Bonnybeg.[7] However, by the beginning of September such small-scale enterprises had given way to a realisation that a much larger-scale effort would be required with Keppel giving Lawder 'carte blanche to act as you think proper in the forthcoming emergency'. However, at the same time, he outlined the strategy he preferred to be taken by his agent:

> You know the principle on which I act and I believe it to be your own – give nothing but take everything out in work and let that

work be as remunerable as circumstances will allow. I would however, do all in my power to discourage the growth of potato planting. The land is, I am convinced, what chemists call potato sick and it will be much better for the tenants to grow something that will help to produce food than to sow that which will not grow. The present will, as you observe, be favourable to emigration. It will, I hope, also be a good opportunity for trying a better system of culture, but I know full well the difficulties you have to encounter and the disposition you have to overcome these difficulties.[8]

On 6 October Susan Keppel wrote to Lawder stating how 'we are very anxious to know the present state of the poor tenantry and whether they are in a great state of destitution'.[9] Emphasising this concern was the fact that a few days later she informed him that 'Colonel Keppel is so much engaged in Downing Street and will continue to be so much for some while to come that he has sent me your letter desiring me to say that the gathering in of the rents must for the present be quite a secondary consideration and the providing for the poor and destitute the primary object.'[10] However, in this letter she remarked that 'all the middlemen ... without exception who shall fail in their duty towards their poor under tenants in this hour of scarcity and shall be in arrears to him [Colonel Keppel] he will sue them at the law for the last farthing'.[11]

This stringent policy towards the estate's middlemen was immediately evident. In September Keppel informed Lawder how 'Mrs Mary Ann Walsh asks for "time" but I can not see what "time" it can take her to pay in rents which have been already collected. See what you can do with her.'[12] One of the most prominent middlemen on the estate was Denis Booth, who, as has been noted, played an active part in relief efforts. Feeling the pressure of Keppel's demands he felt the need to outline his difficulties:

We hold two farms from you – Lavagh and Lisdrumcar – and the tenants of the latter farm have become very refractory. They owe us two year's rent up to November last and they are well able to pay with the exception of one. Those persons have lately sold all their cattle or conveyed them away and they have sold their oats and put the money in their pockets. In order to obtain your rent I offered to forgive them a year's rent and abate their land 5 shillings an acre.

Mr Lawder admitted that was a very great sacrifice, still they will not pay though well able to do so. Your agent will take legal proceedings against us. We want him to wait until after the next January quarter sessions to be held at Carrick as we are going to process those very refractory tenants and if money cannot be obtained from them by that time other means will be resorted to for the purpose of raising money to pay your rent for I can assure you, Sir, that we never intend to benefit by that farm and very little out of this.[13]

Booth's protestation did not meet with an understanding landlord and Keppel left his agent in no doubt as to the course of action to be adopted:

I have not written to Booth nor do I intend to do so. These middlemen have been so often threatened and never actually proceeded against that an example is necessary and I know no better one than our friend Booth. Let therefore the law take its course. If land cannot pay two rents the middleman is clearly the one to go.[14]

However, Booth was not the only middlemen to encounter such a response. Referring to a holding in the possession of Mrs Simpson in Drumgowla, Keppel remarked 'I am of course most anxious to get rid of middlemen or women and should be happy to purchase the Simpson's interest in their townland. Will you tell me what I ought to pay for it?'[15] Similarly, in relation to Mrs Walsh he told Lawder:

I think the collection of rents you have made considering the circumstances a very creditable one to you saving that the middlemen figure so largely amongst the defaulters. I fear that I shall be under the painful necessity of proceeding to extremities with Mrs Walsh and I think it would be advisable to give her warning of what course I intend to take if she does not pay up her arrears.[16]

Significantly, Keppel remarked that 'I consider this an act of justice for if I leave the wealthy alone I should not feel warranted in endeavouring to recover from the poorer tenants.'[17] This attitude was reflected in his stipulation that under no circumstances were distressed tenants to be pressed for rent.[18] For her part Mrs Walsh informed Lawder that she had been unable to obtain her own rents and believed that such would not be available until October or November 1847.[19] However, Keppel remained unrepentant and revealed to Lawder that 'if my sole object is to rid the estate from the middlemen and if I am not interfering with your interests I shall gladly avail myself of the opening that presents itself'.[20]

The statements made by Keppel during 1846 certainly do not fit the stereotype of the absentee, evicting landlord. Indeed, if anything, it is very evident that he despised middlemen, who, on this estate anyway, faced vitriol from their head landlord and their undertenants. However, on the nearby Madden estate the stereotype was very much in evidence.

The Madden estate consisted of 3,500 acres, most of it contained within the parish of Cloone. The Maddens were absentees and lived in Hilton Park, Clones, County Monaghan. The correspondence between various bailiffs and agents shows little empathy with the tenants and demonstrates a resolve to obtain rents regardless of the cost to the people living there. Long-term problems with the estate had arisen due to the death of Colonel Madden in 1844 since when no rents had been paid by tenants. The average holding ranged between three and seven acres while there was also 'a great number' holding one to two acres. In July 1848 Richard O'Brien, bailiff on the estate, noted that 'the poor rates and county cess are so enormous that we are left in precarious way with the tenants here…'[21] However, as far as O'Brien was concerned, any difficulties faced by the latter had been self-inflicted as, in his opinion, 'they drank and revelled and idled; married their sons and daughters and sent more to America'.[22] Therefore, he was determined to collect any outstanding rent and commented how 'those incorrigible scoundrels on the … estate are still holding out, closed their doors and sought by intimidation to prevent the order to pay being served upon them…'[23] Nevertheless, he revealed that he had managed to have 'every man of them' (about 200) served with notices to quit 'and only for the combination that is still lurking amongst them the principal part of them would come in and settle but they are intimidated by the rest'.[24] However, O'Brien disclosed that the quit notices, in conjunction with Mrs Madden's resolve 'to submit to another nine months loss and [then] clear the estate of such a set of robbers at the next June sessions' had 'struck more terror in them than I ever expected'. It appears that, far from being intimidated himself, O'Brien was determined to take the fight to the tenants:

> I have sore work on the Madden property. The tenants are giving every possible resistance. I had the sheriff out with a force of police

but they were able from the sentinels they keep out to have their cattle taken off and locked up before we could reach them...[25]

Indeed, he admitted that 'although the campaign is severe on me I yet enjoy it from the prospect I have of subduing them for I have them in constant alarm and their cattle housed'.[26] As the following letter revealed, his job was not without its hazards:

> Since I wrote to you last I made a great trial of strength with them and being so often defeated in making seizures I got a small party of five chosen men to get in with a ringleader by going in different directions and the force that came against us was terrific. But I was determined to fight it out with the few I had and sent two of them driving the cattle at the top of their speed before us and our prisoners and I remained behind with the rest and gave them battle until with thus flying and fighting we got our seizure near the town of Cloon and had to go a mile beyond it to the pound when we got completely surrounded and the men and myself in every peril and struck with all kind of weapons and stones and I feel proud to say that at this crisis several of the inhabitants of the town of Cloon and some of the Madden tenantry that adjoin it came to my assistance with pitchforks and said they did not come to help me to drive but they would not let me or my men be further abused and among the rest the priests' servant assisted me and we secured our seizure...[27]

Despite such bravado, O'Brien was very alive to the realities of life for the tenants. He noted how their land was 'not more than sufficient to give them food even if well cultivated' adding that to expect to collect rent arrears from such people was 'utterly hopeless and ruinous for this reason that it will keep them still at a distance from us and be adding the future to the past and ultimately grappling with shadows...'[28]

Another correspondent, William Cochrane, argued that, given the failure of the potato crop in 1848 'which they greatly depended on in Leitrim', it would be an achievement to obtain anything more than one year's rent. He therefore added that 'it would be a great matter if they could by any reasonable compromise be brought into a regular system of acting for the future'.[29] Cochrane's desire for agreement was due to his previous experience dealing with the tenants. He related how he had faced 'great difficulty in proving payment or rents and occupancy' both of which were necessary to obtain court decrees:

> The first thing the tenantry did was to bribe the bailiff to go to America and he went there. I went to Leitrim to prove payment of rents but in the majority of cases I could not do so, the occupants in my time not being the occupants now: a great number of the old tenants have since that period died, others have gone to America and left new men in their holdings – in all such cases my evidence is not of any use.[30]

Aware of such opinions, O'Brien subsequently stated that 'on the whole if the property was mine and so circumstanced I would take half a year's rent gladly'.[31] His proposition, which allowed for the arrears to be cleared, was accepted by Robert Burrowes who said, that despite the fact he could not 'calculate on any integrity amongst them', he would recommend Mrs Madden to adopt this course of action.[32]

However the following year he was sorry to have to inform the landlord that he was unable to obtain much money from the tenants. Having collected just over £422 in June 1849 he commented that he was 'tied up from getting more until the harvest comes in'.[33] Obviously, as revealed in the following, even the harvest did not save some tenants:

> I proceeded by ejectment against seven holdings that were covered with squatters and paupers and obtained decrees and executed them and threw down all the cabins keeping up an odd good house that I built up the doors of with lime and stone … As you are aware I had a most desperate determined combination to contend with.[34]

O'Brien's attitude to the tenants on the estate was epitomised by the following to William Cochrane, shortly after these evictions had taken place:

> I felt and viewed it from the commencement … that it should be a desperate effort and struggle. But if firmly maintained that it would not last long and with that feeling I neither spared myself or my pocket … to defeat their combinations … and required the aid of both moral and physical force. It would not have done to bring hired bailiffs merely to drive cattle when they would be flying at the first

blow. I had to bring men who were zealous in my interest and who had to accompany me at night and remain concealed in corn fields and wastehouses until we made the seizures when the cattle were let out next day.[35]

However, as he admitted, ejection of a tenant did not necessarily mean the problem was solved as new tenants were unable to pay high rents, due to 'the heavy taxation, fall in prices of produce and failure of the crops'. Thus, it was 'utterly impossible' to ask new tenants to pay more than fourteen shillings per acre, although at one stage land on the estate had been let at £1/6/6 an acre. This was especially so as on other estates the rents varied between ten and fifteen shillings.[36] Even so, O'Brien believed that by May 1851 there was not 'an estate in this county more improved in industrious habits and tranquillity':

> There is no scheming but every tenant doing his best to pay his way. If not out he goes. I gave them a fair chance for their living and they feel it and I make them understand that I will not continue a bad tenant as an example to others.[37]

The following year he again referred to the superior condition of the estate:

> I am happy to inform you that your tenantry here are visibly improved in every respect which they openly acknowledge themselves and observed by every person who has any intercourse in the neighbourhood and they have so much candour as to admit that they are better off and more independent than when they were not paying.
>
> The survey has been a more difficult undertaking than I can well describe to you here from the confused state the property has been in – all the tenants generally being matted into each other in co-partnership holdings, seven or eight and ten together – and the great difficulty has been to get them to agree to divisions. Their opposition to each other on this change baffles description and in every case arbitrations by three disinterested persons until I have at length brought the most of them into compliance without leaving it in the power of any of them to say that they have been wronged of a perch

in any of those divisions either in quantity or quality which has been my object to effect. But there is yet the townlands of Aughnakiltubrit, Gubbs, Sunnamore, Bundarragh, Montda and Tully that some of the occupiers cannot yet be brought to fair partitions and I have been obliged to serve ejectments upon some of them to compel them to do what is right and with these exceptions I have the work done.[38]

O'Brien's propensity for evicting was not unique and reference has already been made to the devastating consequences of the Gregory Clause for thousands of tenants throughout the county. Indeed, poor law inspector Major Haliday, writing in 1848, remarked on the 'great extent of waste land from ejectments and surrendered holdings' in the electoral divisions of Annaduff, Cloone, Eslin and Mohill.[39]

By the early 1850s such evictions were commonplace in the county. For example, in January 1851 Mrs Mary Anne McNamara of Letterfine, parish of Kiltubrid, ejected 'a few tenants' who owed two and three years rent. Subsequently, 'an armed banditti' threatened the lives of those who were granted tenancies in their place.[40] In August, it was reported in the local press that 'a large number of persons' had been summonsed 'for taking forcible possession of the lands of Kiltoghert from which they were a few weeks ago dispossessed by the sheriff under an order from the superior courts'.[41]

Attempting to assess numbers of national evictions is a complicated procedure and estimates have ranged from one-quarter to one-half a million persons over the period 1846–54. The difficulty in seeking to make accurate assessments is compounded by the fact that reliable constabulary statistics only became available from 1849 onwards. The following table outlines the number of evictions in Leitrim from that year until 1860:

**Table 9.1: Evictions in County Leitrim, 1849–1860**

| Year | Number Evicted | | Number Re-Admitted | |
|------|------|------|------|------|
| | Families | Persons | Families | Persons |
| 1849 | 835 | 4,839 | 253 | 1,305 |
| 1850 | 678 | 3,453 | 191 | 1,046 |
| 1851 | 309 | 1,646 | 108 | 619 |
| 1852 | 213 | 1,122 | 77 | 406 |
| 1853 | 1017 | 5,369 | 232 | 1,310 |

| | | | |
|---|---|---|---|
| 1854 | 48 | 250 | 3 | 10 |
| 1855 | 44 | 213 | 13 | 69 |
| 1856 | 27 | 95 | 1 | 4 |
| 1857 | 59 | 264 | 10 | 62 |
| 1858 | 66 | 337 | 35 | 176 |
| 1859 | 36 | 153 | 10 | 23 |
| 1860 | 49 | 205 | 1 | 5 |
| 1861 | 42 | 195 | 7 | 23 |
| 1862 | 121 | 582 | 58 | 284 |
| 1863 | 109 | 584 | 8 | 42 |
| 1864 | 180 | 853 | 9 | 35 |

*Source*: H.C., 1881, Volume lxxvii, Return 'by the Provinces and Counties (compiled from Returns made to the Inspector General, Royal Irish Constabulary), of Cases of Evictions which have come to the knowledge of the Constabulary in each of the years from 1849 to 1880, inclusive', pp.8–15.

While 4,839 persons were evicted in 1849, 1,305 of these were subsequently re-admitted leaving a total number of 3,534 evictions. Similarly, allowing for re-admissions in 1850, the figure for that year was 2,407. Nationally, the figures peaked in 1850 when 19,949 families (104,163 persons) were evicted, although 5,403 of those families (30,292 persons) were later re-admitted. This number declined gradually until by 1855 there were less than 2,000 families evicted (1,849 evicted and 525 of those re-admitted).[42] While Leitrim's figures declined in 1851 and 1852 they increased substantially in the following year. Indeed, even allowing for re-admissions, the number evicted for that year was 4,059, the largest number recorded for the county. As can be seen from the following table, the level of evictions in Leitrim (not including re-admissions) was substantially greater than those in any of the neighbouring counties, apart from Roscommon. Further, the 1853 peak of just over 4,000 was more than twice the combined number of evictions in these six counties:

**Table 9.2: Number of Persons Evicted in Counties Bordering Leitrim**

| Year | Cavan | Donegal | Fermanagh | Longford | Roscommon | Sligo |
|---|---|---|---|---|---|---|
| 1849 | 2,184 | 1,364 | 209 | 1,537 | 3,643 | 1,527 |
| 1850 | 2,306 | 1,090 | 602 | 1,239 | 3,336 | 2,232 |

| 1851 | 792 | 1,155 | 337 | 1,101 | 3,406 | 565 |
| 1852 | 396 | 638 | 192 | 1,018 | 1,888 | 380 |
| 1853 | 180 | 265 | 197 | 145 | 602 | 386 |
| 1854 | 110 | 122 | 22 | 28 | 368 | 8 |
| 1855 | 143 | 123 | 20 | 193 | 245 | 93 |

Source: H.C., 1881,Volume lxxvii, Return 'by the Provinces and Counties (compiled from Returns made to the Inspector General, Royal Irish Constabulary), of Cases of Evictions which have come to the knowledge of the Constabulary in each of the years from 1849 to 1880, inclusive', pp.8–11.

An interesting addendum to the issue of evictions, and one that illustrates it was not confined to absentees in England or elsewhere, is to be found in memorials to Cardinal Cullen in the mid-1850s.

In 1845 the lands of George Lane-Fox in Greenane, near Dromahaire, were granted to William Kernaghan for 99 years with the current tenants to continue in possession. In 1849 Kernaghan was declared bankrupt and the land was sold to Dominick Henry who himself became 'embarrassed'. The tenants themselves also lost possession but this was soon restored by Fox's agent, Joshua Kell and shortly afterwards the friars of the Order of St Dominick, based in the Convent of Sligo, redeemed Dominick Henry's interest in the land. Two of the friars, Thomas D. Hibbett and Michael McEvoy, immediately obtained a re-valuation of the estate. Despite Hugh McGolrick paying two years rent he was served with an ejectment order and evicted. They also obtained a decree against Thomas Lynch and on 20 April 1854 'when he was attending the funeral of his late parish priest, Revd. Thomas McKeon, they caused the sheriff's bailiff to turn out his five motherless children from his house which they pulled down'. Subsequently, the friars issued notices to quit on Bartholomew McSharry, Owen Feeny and Edward McHugh.[43]

In one case, Michael Byrne had his rent increased by them from £5 to £6/7/2 and despite the fact that he had reclaimed land and improved his holding 'at great expense', they took four acres from him and eventually served him with an ejectment.[44] In another, the friars purchased the interest of Owen Feeny's land for £65 even though it had cost him £500 and he had spent more than £100 in improvements. Bartholomew McSharry stated that once the friars had become established as landlords they immediately began evictions, adding 'they ejected me out of the lands in October 1854 without mercy having 8 in my family'. Thus, McSharry, on behalf of the others, wrote to Cullen to 'beg and implore … that my sad condition may be justified at this time'.[45] Unfortunately, the fate of these individuals is not recorded and the same can be said for the vast majority of those ejected at the hands of evicting landlords. However, the records of the Encumbered Estates Court reveal the impact of the famine on some of the county's landlords.

On 29 November 1847, John B. Hogg, writing from Drumsna, alluded to the difficulties being experienced by landlords in that locality:

> I dare not tell you how the gentry of this neighbourhood are circumstanced − the eighth of their property withheld. They are unable to administer its duties and if they dare to ask for a half year's rent out of five years they are doomed to death as was Major Mahon.[46]

The pressure on head landlords was also evident in the instruction from George Keppel to William Lawder on 26 June 1850 to 'take proceedings' against Pierce Simpson Esq and Dr Dunn, for rents due by them.[47] The plight of such was reflected in a letter from Ferdinand Keon of Newbrook, to Francis O'Beirne of Jamestown. On 19 October 1850 he wrote to the latter asking for 'the lend of a small trifle until November' when he would make an application to the court. He outlined his position:

> I suppose you must have heard of my unfortunate circumstances. Until now I was by my creditors always left Newbrook and demesne for support but now I have met with two harsh creditors that hasn [sic] not left me for my support and nine in family one shilling. I have now no friend I could ask as the only one that would look to me in my present state poor Mr Walsh is no more, but yourself.[48]

It appears from this correspondence that Keon was preparing to make an application to the Encumbered Estates Court which had been established under the Encumbered Estates Acts of 1848–9. These allowed the court to sell estates on the application of the owner or encumbrancer (who had a claim on an estate). After the sale, the court distributed the money among the creditors and granted clear title to the new owners. Between 1849 and 1857 there were 3,000 estates totalling 5,000,000 acres disposed of under the acts and by 1850 the *Impartial Reporter* suggested the court was 'becoming quite a favourite with all parties'. It appeared to the writer that 'the creditors like it – as it "polishes off" quickly the non-paying debtors, and obtains them their money, if that be possible – the insolvent landlord, too, seems to like it, as it puts him speedily out of pain.'[49]

Amongst those who either willing availed of, or were forced into, the court were such prominent individuals as Cairncross Cullen, Acheson O'Brien, Mary Anne Walsh, Westby Percival and Francis Nesbit. Of course, it has already been noted how Walsh had been under pressure from Colonel Keppel in 1846 while the latter two were included in a list of poor rate defaulters. Their debts eventually forced them, together with dozens of others, into the court (see Appendix Four).

## EMIGRATION

While landlords and middlemen faced the indignity of losing their land many of those evicted ended up many thousands of miles away from their native home. One of the earliest references to a Leitrim emigrant is that of Miles McIldrew of 'Kiltocher' (Kiltoghert). In October 1729 he was accused of 'fire-raising' in Argyle, Scotland and despite the fact that no trial took place he admitted 'throwing a firey coal on the thatch of a house'.[50]

A century later a scheme established by the British government to grant 'free passage' for those wishing to emigrate to North America received enquiries from a variety of places in the county including Ballinamore, Carrick-on-Shannon and Mohill.[51] The apparent willingness of people to emigrate, together with the enthusiasm of landlords to encourage such, was evident in an 'emigrant account' maintained by Viscount Clements on his estate at Lough Rynn. On 25 March 1832 it was noted that £568/2/6 had been spent on assisting twenty-nine families and five individuals to emigrate to America.[52]

Indeed, in its edition of 28 March 1840 the *Roscommon and Leitrim Gazette* remarked that for some time past 'large numbers' had been emigrating to America. This year appears to have witnessed an increase in such as 'not merely families but the inhabitants of whole districts have, with one accord, abandoned their native country for ever'. In the opinion of the paper, those emigrating were 'not the idle' but instead were 'the most industrious, intelligent and moral of the Protestant yeomanry'. This, the writer argued, was a 'most distressing prospect for all the lovers of peace and the British connexion'. He placed this phenomenon in the context of 'an imperfect protection in a partisan magistracy, and what is now gradually becoming a partisan police'. He further alleged that 'they cannot go out to a fair or market without the apprehension of being waylaid and beaten on their return'.[53] Some months later the same journal carried an advertisement for emigration to Australia. The needs of the new colony were many and jobs were offered in a variety of positions. Thus, young males aged 18–30, 'well acquainted with agricultural work', especially shepherds, were required, the passage fee being £5. However, if they travelled with a sister she could accompany her brother free of charge. In Sydney, carpenters, masons and sawyers were able to obtain wages of £2/2 – £2/10 per week. Amongst females the need was for those acquainted with 'dairy and farm-house occupations', alongside good house servants, which were said to be 'greatly wanted'. Those aged 15–30 presenting a 'good testimonial' were offered free passage.[54] However, what had appeared at this time to have been a considerable level of migration was, in hindsight, merely a trickle. In the years during and after the Famine thousands of people left their homeland in the search for a better life abroad.

In April 1851 it was remarked that 'never before in the recollection of the oldest inhabitants have so many left this neighbourhood [Carrick] for the land of the Stars and Stripes'. A local paper noted:

> Travel on any road through the county and crowds of Ireland's stalwart sons are to be met, wending their way (accompanied by their families) to the seaports and with few exceptions they are comfortable farmers leaving behind the home of their birth and the lands which they tilled, to be turned into *grazing lands*, thus saving the landlords' pockets in the payment of poor rates![55]

Such was the demand in the Carrick area that Bianconi's coach had been replaced by a larger long car 'in consequence of the influx of emigrant passengers'.[56] On 18 September 1851 the *Leitrim Journal* editorialised as follows on the subject of emigration:

> The people of this land seem to have but one wish, one hope – to leave Ireland! to escape the misery which they behold around them, which they feel within them, which they see before them. To any

land on earth ... they are willing to fly: to America, where they will be railed at as ignorant, awkward Irish Greeks; to Scotland or England, where they will be damned as Paddies, or to the very ends of the earth, they are anxious to escape from home.[57]

Surmising that a spate of petty crimes was induced by a desire to be sentenced to transportation, the paper continued:

It is not that the love of home has departed, that the people are so eager to depart. But they see no hope here. Industry is fettered, discouraged, destroyed as Professor [William Nielsen] Handcock allows, by the laws as they stand; and people must go, if they can, to where they will not 'spend their strength for nought'.

They are flying thick and fast, and unless some encouragement be given them to stay, the world will see again the exile of a nation.

Is it not time that emigration were stayed? The most cold-blooded thing that calls itself a political economist will grant that the Irish have been sufficiently thinned – that those who are left may be suffered to remain. If our rulers are of the same opinion – if those who make our laws do not sweep our race from the land of our fathers, they will hold out some inducement to the people to stay.[58]

A month later the same paper commented once again on the phenomenon and the effect it would have on those forced to leave:

Those who were compelled to wait for want of means until now are selling off their crops and fleeing to the American shores with engendered hate in their bosoms against those who ought to have cherished and preserved their tenantry as Irishmen. The country is becoming one vast waste – Ireland emigrating – a whole people are passing from the land sad and silent and their hearts turn back full of grief for the land they leave and hatred for the system that has banished them.[59]

By April 1852 emigration from the county had commenced 'with redoubled vigour'. The local press reported how 'crowds of respectable farmers and farm labourers are every day leaving for the Far West'.[60] It was stated how in one district where thirty or forty families had resided a few weeks previous 'there is not now a trace of them to be found'.[61] This determination to emigrate is illustrated by the numbers (10,154) leaving from the following ports between 1851 and 1855, some of which were at least one hundred miles from Leitrim:

**Table 9.3: Numbers Emigrating from County Leitrim, 1851–5**

| | Year | | | | |
|---|---|---|---|---|---|
| Port | 1851 | 1852 | 1853 | 1854 | 1855 |
| Belfast | 66 | 165 | 227 | 121 | 217 |
| Derry/Moville | 207 | 441 | 301 | 297 | 315 |
| Drogheda | 710 | 922 | 641 | 483 | 202 |
| Dublin | 722 | 998 | 529 | 622 | 272 |
| Dundalk | 26 | 9 | 40 | 4 | 1 |
| Killala / Ballina | 266 | 516 | 380 | 262 | 183 |
| Sligo | – | 2 | – | – | – |
| Warrenpoint / Newry | – | 1 | 4 | 2 | – |
| TOTAL | 1,997 | 3,054 | 2,122 | 1,791 | 1,190 |

*Source*: H.C. 1856, volume xxxi, 1851 Census of Ireland, General report, pp.lxxvii–lxxxvii.

By this stage the process of 'sibling emigration' appeared to be well under away. It was reported that 'each American mail brings remittances to a large amount of persons in this neighbourhood to bear the expense of emigrants to the port of embarkation, the passage money being paid in America. The people are flying as if before a whirlwind'.[62] Ironically, due to increased levels of literacy it can be argued that papers such as the *Leitrim Journal*, while lamenting the exodus, were actually contributing to it by publishing letters from those who had made successful lives for themselves in America. For example, in an excerpt from a letter from California, the writer informed his audience that 'a good workman (operative mechanic) can get £2 per day and can live for 10s'.[63]

Despite the apparent number of letters arriving from America few have survived. The following, sent from John and Bridgett Flood in Philadelphia on 20 October 1850, to their father Edward in the townland of Lugganummer in the parish of Cloone, is, therefore, a rare Famine-period emigrant document that graphically reveals the importance of siblings in facilitating emigration. Ellen Flood had been unfortunate in being summonsed as a witness in a trial just before she was due to embark for America. The letter, written by her brother, reflects his frustration at the fact she had still not arrived. It is also instructive in that the attraction of the new country, and particularly the high wages compared to those at home, is discussed. Finally, the letter demonstrates that, despite the terrible events they had all witnessed, and the distance between them, the tensions of family life remained:

… we were very much surprised at Ellen not coming to this country after us sending the money to her last May and never sint one line to me to let us know if you got it or not. You said in youre letter that you sent one immedatley after you got my letter but if you did it did not come to me or ant person for my sake so I maid up my mind not to write one letter till I would get one you. Bridget was very uneasy to hear from you but I still told her that you were not very uneasy about her or if you were you would shurely write before you did. Catherine Naylor is in good health and her and Bridget is liveing very near each other. Bridgett is not liveing with the family that shee was with when I wrote last to you. Shee is with another Quaker family where shee has but one child to mind. Shee is better content in it than shee was in the other place. Shee has 4 s of youre money per week and no hard work and is well kept. So shee thinks shee is doing well when she shee can get more wages than a working man at home.

Catherine Naylor's brother Thomas did not come to this country after her sending for him twice. I was the man that brought the bill of exchange for her cash twice and sent the letter but he has not got this far yet and indeed she is not uneasy whether he comes or not. After he got the money last April he wrote her a letter letting know that he would start for America the first opportunity but he has not met with it as yet. My opinion is that you and him and Ellen and every one of you are well met for telling lies. Thomas Naylor said in a letter to his sister that he would be off the next day after he would get the money but when he got the money in his pocket he forgot the promise. In a letter I got in Ellen's own name shee maid the same promise if shee got the money shee would be off but shee forgot in like manner so we have maid up our mind not to give ourselves much more trouble with the same party. However, Ellen lost a nough both on me and herself when shee forfeited the five pounds that I paid for her passage, together with me going to the trouble of getting a boarding house for her and her wages would be from 15 to 20 pounds a year and it is nearly 2 years since I first sent for her so you may estimate the loss yourself. But it is my opinion that it was not the delicate state of her mother's health that was the caws of her staying at home I think shee has not got forwarder the case of the constabulary forse yet – you will let me know in your next letter.

The times here is very good at present. The general wages for labouring men is 1 dolar per day. Men that is hired by the month some has more and some less. My wages is 26 dolars per month and my business is packing hardware in a wholesale store. It is very hard work in the spring and fall as them is the two seasons the merchants comes from the South to buy there goods. Then we have to work till 12 oclock at night for 2 months each time. The rest of the year is not as hard.

I received a letter from my aunt Shusana Moor in August requesting me to pay for her daughters passage. You will please to give her my love and tell her that it is not in my power to do anything for her at present and also let her know that I will not forget her as soon as opportunity serves…

Catherine Naylor sends her love to her daughter Mary but shee thinks shee must be a very bad girl when shee did not learn to read her book as shee said shee left money to pay for her schooling when shee was coming to this country. You would not get one person out of every thousand either male or female that is brought up in this country but can read and write with the exsecption of the Negro population and a good many of them itself. Bridget and Catherine Naylor joins me in sending our love to you all. I have nothing more to say but remains your affectionate son and daughter Bridgett and John Flood.[64]

Between 1848 and 1850 the Colonial Land and Emigration Commissioners, capitalising on the demand for females in Australia, facilitated the shipment of 4,000 female orphans from workhouses in Ireland. The Carrick and

Mohill establishments both participated – the former sending sixty girls and the latter forty-five. Amongst those who left Carrick was seventeen-year old Anne Burke and she arrived in Sydney aboard the *Lady Peel* on 3 July 1849. Four years later, in March 1853, she wrote back home and the letter was published in the *Leitrim Journal*. She revealed that on the way to Australia two girls, Anne Faughnon and Anne Dunn, had died on the voyage. In the meantime she had been married to an Irishman and given birth to a son. She was keen to have her brother and sister – the latter still in Carrick workhouse – join her and therefore had paid £12 to cover their fares to Sydney. The attractions of emigrating were obvious when she pointed out that tradesmen were paid between nine and twelve shillings per day while labourers received from five to eight shillings. Female domestic servants earned on average from £18 to £26 a year and all were capable of purchasing 'plenty of provisions of the best such as bread, beef, mutton, tea and sugar, bacon, butter, milk and a plentiful supply of vegetables, etc'. Consequently, she urged her siblings to 'not lose such an opportunity as this is, or anyone else in poor Ireland, who is able to leave it by any means at all, for there is plenty of work'.[65]

In February 1849 the Society of Friends received a communication from Francis Gibbons of Mohill. The letter was not unusual in that it outlined how families were sleeping on bundles of straw and highlighted his endeavours to relieve 'a few extreme cases' that had proven 'too numerous' for his efforts to prove 'of any benefit'.[66] It is difficult to ascertain whether Gibbons was attempting to familiarise himself with the process of grants made by the Society but his communication was not a standard one given that he was the poor law inspector for the Mohill union. Between May and August he penned a further six letters to the Society outlining a scheme to send female paupers from the workhouse to America. What is most interesting is the fact that he sought its support in funding these efforts. Gibbons hoped to enable twenty women to emigrate but having spoken to 'various rate payers' he 'could not induce any person to subscribe'.[67] This problem was further compounded by the fact that because they were not emigrating to British America, they could not obtain assistance from the poor law authorities.[68]

While their passage to America had been secured by family and friends the difficulty had arisen with regards to paying travel costs to Liverpool. On 13 June his plea was successful when he received £20 from the Quakers.[69] By the beginning of August he had obtained passage tickets for fifteen 'poor destitute' individuals but informed the society that these were due to expire within a fortnight. Seven of them were children under the age of fourteen and he reckoned that a further £8 would secure their fare to Liverpool and buy them clothes and provisions. He also outlined how, in such circumstances, 'the more comfortable classes, instead of assisting … endeavour to obtain the tickets from the destitute persons under the original cost and proceed to America, leaving the destitute pauper a lasting charge on the union'. Given the likelihood of such a scenario the Friends remitted a further £10 and in this way thirty-two women were enabled to emigrate.[70]

While much emigration took place to America there were those who opted to travel to areas closer to home. Migration to Britain was common both in terms of people leaving permanently to better themselves or travelling to obtain temporary labour during harvest periods. For example, in the summer of 1841 the police were ordered to assist in an enumeration of all deck passengers who embarked on various packet ships travelling to Britain. Of the total number of 57,651, there were 2,860 who stated Leitrim as the place of departure. This figure represented 1 in 54 of the population of the county, a percentage which was third behind Mayo (1 in 37) and Roscommon (1 in 47).[71]

According to the 1851 Census of Scotland there were 319 people from Leitrim living in Scotland – 156 males and 163 females. Analysis reveals the following age and gender break-down:

**Table 9.4: County Leitrim Migrants to Scotland by Age and Gender**

| Age | Gender (%) | |
|---|---|---|
| | Male | Female |
| 0–10 | 13 | 11 |
| 10–20 | 31 | 38 |
| 20–30 | 29 | 28 |
| 30–40 | 16 | 13 |
| 40–50 | 6.4 | 6 |
| 50–60 | 2.6 | 1.8 |
| 60–70 | – | 1.2 |
| 70–80 | 1.3 | 0.6 |

*Source*: 1851 Census of Scotland.

The figures reveal that in both groups the vast majority of those emigrating were aged under thirty (73 per cent for men and 77 per cent for women) and consisted largely of married couples with children alongside young men and women. The following table illustrates where they were residing:

**Table 9.5: Destination of County Leitrim Migrants to Scotland**

| Destination | Gender (%) | |
|---|---|---|
| | Male | Female |
| Aberdeenshire | 1.3 | – |
| Angus | 29.5 | 47.3 |
| Ayrshire | 3 | 3 |
| Berwickshire | 0.6 | – |
| Clackmannanshire | 0.6 | – |
| Dumbartonshire | 5 | 9 |
| Dunfriesshire | 3 | 1.8 |
| East Lothian | 15 | 6 |
| Fife | 2 | 2.5 |
| Kirkcudbrightshire | 2 | 0.6 |
| Lanarkshire | 11 | 8 |
| Midlothian | 22 | 16 |
| Perthshire | 2.6 | 0.6 |
| Renfrewshire | – | 1 |
| Roxburghshire | 2 | 3 |
| Selkirkshire | – | 0.6 |
| Stirlingshire | 0.6 | – |

*Source*: 1851 Census of Scotland.

Almost one-third of males and one-half of females were resident in the county of Angus while substantial numbers of both sexes lived in Midlothian. Angus contained the town of Dundee and it was here that the vast majority of females obtained work in the local mills. While the bulk of their male counterparts were also employed as millworkers, many obtained work as weavers and agricultural and dock labourers.[72]

In 1851 in England there were 315 people of Leitrim origin (194 males and 121 females) as follows:

**Table 9.6: County Leitrim Migrants to England by Age and Gender**

| Age | Gender (%) | |
|---|---|---|
| | Male | Female |
| 0–10 | 6 | 9 |
| 10–20 | 30 | 21 |
| 20–30 | 34 | 25 |
| 30–40 | 11 | 28 |
| 40–50 | 10 | 7 |
| 50–60 | 5 | 7 |
| 60–70 | 2 | 2 |
| 70–80 | 1 | – |
| 80–90 | – | – |
| 90–100 | – | 0.8 |

*Source*: 1851 Census of England.

As in Scotland the majority of both sexes were aged under thirty (72 per cent of men and 55 per cent of women). However, a significant proportion of women were in the 30–40 age group while the oldest individual was 93-year-old Mary Kelly, probably a long-time resident in England. Again, as happened in Scotland, the overwhelming majority (50 per cent of females and 38 per cent of males) were attracted to industrial heartlands, in this case the Lancashire mills of Liverpool, Manchester and Preston[73]:

**Table 9.7: Destination of County Leitrim Migrants to England**

| Destination | Gender (%) | |
|---|---|---|
| | Male | Female |
| Berkshire | 0.5 | – |
| Cheshire | 9 | 7 |
| Derbyshire | 0.5 | – |

| | | |
|---|---|---|
| Devon | 2.6 | – |
| Dorset | 1 | – |
| Durham | 4 | 11 |
| Essex | 2 | 1 |
| Gloucestershire | – | 1 |
| Hampshire | 4 | – |
| Kent | 16 | 3 |
| Lancashire | 38 | 50 |
| Lincolnshire | 0.5 | 3 |
| Middlesex | 3 | 4 |
| Northamptonshire | 1.6 | 1 |
| Northumberland | 2 | 6 |
| Nottinghamshire | 0.5 | – |
| Staffordshire | 3 | 1 |
| Surrey | 1 | 1 |
| Sussex | 2 | – |
| Warwickshire | 1 | – |
| Wiltshire | – | 2 |
| Yorkshire | 10 | 12 |

*Source*: 1851 Census of England.

Nine Leitrim natives were recorded as living in Wales in 1851; however, five of these were British soldiers based at Brecon Barracks in Breconshire.[74] At the same time, two Leitrim families were living in St Helier on the island of Jersey in the Channel Islands. They were William and Catherine McNutley and their sons and Thomas and Frances Barker and their five children.[75]

However, for some the move from their native land was not successful. Thirteen men and one woman were imprisoned during the time of the Scottish census including 17-year-old John Logan from Kiltoghert and Rosina Mulloy, also aged 17 and from the same parish. Inmates of the Night Asylum of the Houseless in Glasgow included 12-year-old Patrick Gallagher, described as a general labourer, and 15-year-old Patrick Corlaw, 'a beggar'. Occupying similarly grim surroundings was 46-year-old Michael Gilfeather, who was an inmate of the Govan Poor House.[76]

There were seven Leitrim men in prison in England during 1851 including 14-year-old James McGuire who was incarcerated in the Westminster House of Correction.[77] Three men and a woman were inmates of workhouses as follows:

**Table 9.8: County Leitrim Natives in English Workhouses, 1851**

| Name | Age | Place of Birth | Workhouse |
|------|-----|----------------|-----------|
| Bernard Callighan | 63 | Drumshanbo | Sculcoates (Hull) |
| John Ferguson | 49 | Ballinamore | Tynemouth |
| John Heslin | 25 | Mohill | Chorlton (Hulme) |
| Rebecca Adams | 35 | County Leitrim | Liverpool |

*Source:* 1851 Census of England.

While such sad statistics represent less than 5 per cent of those who migrated to Britain the fact is that the bulk of material pertaining to Leitrim natives is to be found either in the poor law or criminal records of Scotland and England. The following examples reflect the contents of such documentation.

In 1847 James McCabe (native of Rossawn, County Leitrim), John McGrath (Doogora, Cloon) and Hugh McGovern, alias McParlane (Balnamore) were all accused of theft from stores in Begbie, Haddington, East Lothian. They were living in Hawick in Roxburghshire and had been employed on the Hawick railway although McGrath and McGovern had since become shearers while McCabe was a harvester.[78] In 1850 John Gallochar, a labourer and native of County Leitrim, but now of no fixed abode, was charged along with two others, one of whom was from County Sligo, of 'tendering and uttering base coin'.[79] Three years later 14-year-old Myles McFarlane, 'a native of County Leitrim', but now living in Edinburgh, was charged with 'theft, habit and repute' at Boyd's Close, Canongate in that city, the victims being Isabella Campbell and Walter March of the same address.[80] In 1855 Hugh Roden, a native of the county but living in Market Street, Edinburgh was tried for the crime of 'assault to the effusion of blood and serious and permanent injury of the person'. It emerged that Roden had previously been convicted of assault.[81] Finally, Bernard Gillooly a foreman labourer from Leitrim living in Canal Row, Coatbridge, Old Monkland, Lanarkshire, was one of ten men, the majority Irish, charged with 'mobbing and rioting' causing 'serious injury of the person'.[82]

The Scottish poor law records also offer an insight into the lives of those who were either forced, or chose, to leave their native county. In 1814 Charles and Elizabeth Murray had been married in Leitrim but by 1833 they were recorded as living in the village of Abbey in Dumfries and Galloway. Charles, a father of five, worked as a customs receiver and in 1841 moved to the booming town of Paisley. However, in April 1847, now aged sixty-three and reportedly in 'want of means' he was forced to apply to the local poor law authorities for parochial aid. Three of his children lived with him while one son was working in Glasgow and another had emigrated to the West Indies where he was employed as a baker.[83] Of course the 'pull factor' alluded to in letters from America and Australia was aided greatly by various 'push factors', such as continued poverty and punitive retribution for those poor who transgressed the law in Leitrim.

Gaol records for the county are extant from 1849 and they outline how those in dire need were dealt with by the judicial system. For example, in August 1849 Anne (aged 15) and Michael Reynolds (12) were tried for the offence of 'rooting potatoes'. Most likely brother and sister, they were each sentenced to be imprisoned for one calendar month. For the same offence Michael Parsons (13) was given the option of either imprisonment for one month or the payment of a fine of £1/1 in costs. Sixteen-year-old Darby Lenaghan also received a choice for the same offence: to pay 10 per cent of the value of the potatoes stolen or face two months in prison with hard labour. The most severe penalty was administered to John Runian (14) who, also for 'rooting potatoes', received a sentence of one month in prison 'and to be once whipped and then to receive twenty lashes'. Absconding from a workhouse was particularly frowned upon. When sixteen-year-old James Carney left the Manorhamilton establishment, taking with him a suit of union clothes, he was imprisoned for three months and received twenty lashes.[84]

In January 1851 a writer to a local paper in Carrick complained of the level of street begging claiming that despite being 'so heavily taxed for its maintenance' the town was 'really persecuted by beggars'.[85] Thus, it appears, there was little sympathy for those arrested for begging. In August 1849 Honor Gilhooly (40) together with her children – Mary (19), Catherine (17), John (14) and Michael (11) – were all sent to prison for one month with hard labour for this offence. In that same month Ellen

Doherty (34) and her young family – Mary (7), Catherine (6) and Ellen jnr (five months) – were similarly dealt with. Ellen received a sentence of one month with hard labour while the children were each sentenced to one month. Likewise, Mary Moran (20), Anne Gannon (21), Alice Maguire (24), Betty Early (20 and 'infirm') and Bridget Meehan (22) were all charged with 'being found on the public street of Drumshanbo as vagabond strollers on the night of 16th of August'. Each of these women was imprisoned for twenty-four hours.[86]

Meanwhile, the poor of towns like Carrick continued to live in squalor. In October 1853 the rears of Standing Barracks, Priest's Lane and Leitrim Street were, with few exceptions, described as 'a mass of filth and rags in which sickness and death is almost every day to be found'.[87] Despite their best efforts the authorities faced an uphill battle in attempting to improve the health of the locality. This was illustrated by the fine of 2s being imposed on Michael Connor for 'having his house in a filthy state – it being occupied by a horse, cow and litter of pigs in common with the family'.[88]

Obviously, indigenous poverty persisted long after the worst excesses of the Famine had abated but although these people lived a grim existence they had still managed to survive the crisis. Their ability, or luck, in being able to do so can only be appreciated in the context of an examination of the extent of population decline in the county during these years.

# Chapter 10

# — THE QUESTIONABLE — CENSUS

13

SUPPLEMENT TO THE VOTES AND PROCEEDINGS.

26° *die Januarii*, 1847.

EMIGRATION (IRELAND).

PETITION FROM MOHILL.

The humble Petition of the Farmers, Labourers, and Inhabitants of the barony of Mohill, in the county of Leitrim,

Humbly showeth,

That your Petitioners observe with great alarm and anxiety the present distress and destitution in which they are involved, in common with their countrymen, from the loss of the potato crop, which in the barony of Mohill has been deficient for several years.

Poverty and want of manure having induced the burning of the land to so great an extent, that it is at present in a state incapable of producing a remunerating crop.

That the mill power within the reach of your Petitioners is quite insufficient to grind corn for the subsistence of the inhabitants of this district, if they possessed the grain.

That the barony of Mohill contains 64,034 statute acres, including bog and water, and 35,714 inhabitants, or 1⅚ statute acres, exclusive of bog and water, to each individual, the total number of inhabited houses being 6,053, at the annual value of £997. 10*s.* deducting one-third for repairs, while the number of families is 6,380.

That your Petitioners have no other means of support than that which they derive from the soil, there being no manufactures or other industrial employment whatsoever.

That your Petitioners believe it to be utterly impossible for so large a population to exist under their present circumstances, and are apprehensive of the fatal consequences of such numbers remaining in an exhausted country without the means of providing for their subsistence.

And your Petitioners therefore humbly pray, that your honourable House will provide means for enabling the poor to emigrate to some other country, where they may be able to support themselves and their families, while they may yet be able to do so.

And your Petitioners, as in duty bound, will ever pray.

ALEXANDER BALLAM,
BERNARD ROGAN,
JAMES KENNY,
&c. &c. &c.

Petition from inhabitants in Mohill seeking help to emigrate, 26 January 1847. Courtesy of Seamus Geraghty Collection, St George's Heritage Centre, Carrick-on-Shannon, County Leitrim.

IN ANALYSING THE 1851 census the *Impartial Reporter* noted that the population of County Leitrim had fallen by just over 43,000 while 6,862 houses in the county had been 'thrown down'. However, in a lengthy article, the paper questioned the validity of the figures contained in the census:

> A decrease of 1,600,000 in ten years, when in the ordinary course of things, there ought to have been an *increase* of nearly two millions, is serious enough. But it is to be borne in mind that the decrease has taken place within about 4 years. At the ordinary rate of increase, the population, when the people began to die away, was about 10 millions; so that in four years there has been a decrease of about 3½ millions – being more than *one-half* our present population! … The government papers, terrified at the responsibility thrown on them by the census, labour to show that much of the decrease is owing to emigration. They would have it that about 1,700,000 have left Ireland alive in the last ten years. And how many of those who left the country to save their lives – lashed into exile by misrule and despair – how many perished on the way? Is there any return of the crowds that perished when the emigrant ships were floating graveyards, and the mortality on the sea was more terrible than on the land? But, granting that so many emigrated – though there is no living voices from our home burying grounds, or from the poor house Golgothas, to reproach our rulers; though the depths of the ocean and the maws of sharks smother the curses of the slaughtered who have gone down in the sea – there are, according to the *Times* itself, 1,700,000 hearts to hate, and living tongues to curse, the misrule that has left them without a country.[1]

The claims of the paper regarding the continual rise in the population are interesting. When historians calculate the population loss they subtract the 1851 figure from that for 1841. However, this ignores the fact that the population was still rising up until the first blight in 1845. Of course, the question is, to what degree was the population increasing and can one calculate an estimate for the population in 1845? In relation to Leitrim the quality of surviving church registers is very poor, particularly those for the majority Catholic population. However, as the following table shows, there is almost a complete set of ledgers for the Catholic parishes of Cloonclare, Kinlough, Mohill, Killenummery and Kiltoghert.[2]

**Table 10.1: Catholic Baptisms in County Leitrim, 1840–50**

| Parish | Year | | | | |
|---|---|---|---|---|---|
|  | 1840 | 1841 | 1842 | 1843 | 1844 |
| Cloonclare | – | 193 | 280 | 266 | 314 |
| Kinlough | 165 | 174 | 143 | 181 | 196 |
| Mohill | 228 | 185 | 362 | 210 | 213 |
| K'nummery | 192 | 205 | 165 | 117 | 225 |
| Aughavas | – | – | – | – | – |
| Kiltubrid | – | – | – | – | – |
| Fenagh | – | – | – | 74 | 63 |
| Kiltoghert | 169 | 178 | 185 | 181 | 186 |

| Parish | Year | | | | | |
|---|---|---|---|---|---|---|
|  | 1845 | 1846 | 1847 | 1848 | 1849 | 1850 |
| Cloonclare | 315 | 313 | 235 | 120 | 128 | 184 |
| Kinlough | 175 | 198 | 140 | 104 | 58 | 93 |
| Mohill | 289 | 221 | 143 | 122 | 145 | 139 |
| K'nummery | 195 | 120 | – | – | 42 | 69 |
| Aughavas | 27 | 116 | 89 | 70 | 73 | 68 |
| Kiltubrid | – | – | 118 | 76 | 31 | 56 |
| Fenagh | 30 | – | 47 | 49 | 48 | 57 |
| Kiltoghert | 172 | 183 | 109 | 72 | 86 | 70 |

*Source*: National Library of Ireland, parochial baptism registers for Cloonclare (p.7505), Kinlough (p.5344), Mohill (p.4239), Killenummery (p.4241), Aughavas (p.4240), Kiltubrid (p.4234), Fenagh (p.4239); Kiltoghert Parish Office, Carrick-on-Shannon, County Leitrim, Kiltoghert baptism register.

What these figures illustrate is that, although there were some fluctuations, there was no slowing down in the number of baptisms in the pre-famine era. Indeed, in the cases of Cloonclare, Kinlough and Kiltoghert the number of baptisms recorded in 1846 was on a par with the highest number in any year since the decade started.

Similarly, in the only two Church of Ireland parish registers available Kiltoghert and Mohill reveal figures that suggest the population was certainly not falling. The 1845 figure for Kiltoghert was the highest annual return in the decade while in Mohill the figure for the same year was similar to that of 1840 and 1841 and greater than that for 1843:

**Table 10.2: Church of Ireland Baptisms in County Leitrim, 1840–50**

| | Year | | | | | |
|---|---|---|---|---|---|---|
| Parish | 1840 | 1841 | 1842 | 1843 | 1844 | |
| Kiltoghert | 15 | 15 | 18 | 19 | 14 | |
| Mohill | 31 | 32 | 37 | 26 | 38 | |

| | Year | | | | | |
|---|---|---|---|---|---|---|
| Parish | 1845 | 1846 | 1847 | 1848 | 1849 | 1850 |
| Kiltoghert | 25 | 15 | 10 | 12 | 3 | 6 |
| Mohill | 31 | 27 | 22 | 24 | 24 | 22 |

*Source*: Church of Ireland Glebe, Mohill, County Leitrim.

Unfortunately, the marriage registers both for Catholic and Protestant parishes are of little use. Those for the Church of Ireland (below) only commence in 1845[3]:

**Table 10.3: Church of Ireland Marriages in County Leitrim, 1845–50**

| | Year | | | | | |
|---|---|---|---|---|---|---|
| Parish | 1845 | 1846 | 1847 | 1848 | 1849 | 1850 |
| Kiltoghert | 5 | 7 | 1 | 6 | 3 | 5 |
| Mohill | 1 | 11 | 4 | 11 | 2 | 2 |
| Kiltubrid | 3 | 4 | 2 | 5 | 4 | 0 |
| Cloone | 2 | 0 | 2 | 1 | 2 | 5 |
| Drumreilly | – | 2 | 1 | 4 | 2 | 1 |

*Source*: Church of Ireland Glebe, Mohill, County Leitrim.

The Catholic registers, while slightly better, still contain many gaps[4]:

**Table 10.4: Catholic Marriages in County Leitrim, 1840–50**

| Parish | Year | | | | |
|---|---|---|---|---|---|
| | 1840 | 1841 | 1842 | 1843 | 1844 |
| K'nummery | – | 47 | 42 | 24 | 56 |
| Cloone | – | – | – | 37 | 18 |
| Kiltubrid | – | – | – | – | – |
| Aughavas | – | – | – | – | – |
| Fenagh | 20 | – | – | – | – |
| Kinlough | 3 | 37 | 47 | 35 | 38 |
| Kiltoghert | 25 | 42 | 34 | 29 | 40 |

| Parish | Year | | | | | |
|---|---|---|---|---|---|---|
| | 1845 | 1846 | 1847 | 1848 | 1849 | 1850 |
| K'nummery | 48 | 50 | – | 3 | 29 | 21 |
| Cloone | 18 | 1 | 3 | 6 | 10 | 17 |
| Kiltubrid | – | – | 18 | 25 | 14 | 11 |
| Aughavas | 2 | 13 | 5 | 3 | 10 | 11 |
| Fenagh | 21 | 9 | – | 13 | 9 | 8 |
| Kinlough | 32 | 41 | 19 | 15 | 14 | 11 |
| Kiltoghert | 34 | 26 | 8 | 29 | 19 | 19 |

*Source*: National Library of Ireland, parochial marriage registers for Killenummery (p.4241), Cloone (p.4241), Kiltubrid (p.4234), Aughavas (p.4240), Fenagh (p.4239), Kinlough (p.5344); Kiltoghert Parish Office, Carrick-on-Shannon, County Leitrim, Kiltoghert marriage register.

However, it is interesting to note that the number of marriages in Killenummery in 1846 was more than double those of 1843. Similarly, the number in Kiltoghert in 1845 was greater than those for either 1840 or 1843 and the same as that for 1842. In Kinlough, the 1846 figure was the second highest of the decade, being six fewer than that recorded for 1842.

Although the surviving records are patchy it is important to note that they are geographically disparate; hence, their figures cannot be dismissed as representative of some local phenomenon. Of course, in the absence of a complete set of records it is difficult to generalise but the surviving registers strongly suggest that the population of the county was still rising right up to the Famine. Between 1831 and 1841 the population rose by 9.9 per cent from 141,303 to 155,297. If a conservative approach is adopted and the subsequent increase calculated at 5% over the following ten years we end up with a total in 1851 of 163,061. Thus, the baptism and marriage statistics up to 1845/6 suggest a population of at least 160,000 on the eve of the Famine.

Of course, such calculations require a certain amount of guesswork but what is not in doubt is the catastrophic effect the Famine had both on baptisms and marriages.

### Table 10.5: Decline in Baptisms in County Leitrim, 1840–50

| Parish | 1840–1846 | 1847 | 1848 | 1849 | 1850 |
|---|---|---|---|---|---|
| Cloonclare | 298 | 235 | 120 | 128 | 184 |
| Kiltoghert | 179 | 109 | 72 | 86 | 70 |
| Kinlough | 176 | 140 | 104 | 58 | 93 |
| Kiltoghert (COI) | 17 | 10 | 12 | 3 | 6 |
| Mohill (COI) | 32 | 22 | 24 | 24 | 22 |

*Source*: Church of Ireland Glebe, Mohill, County Leitrim and National Library of Ireland, parochial baptism registers for Cloonclare (p.7505), Kinlough (p.5344); Kiltoghert Parish Office, Carrick-on-Shannon, County Leitrim, Kiltoghert baptism register.

In the Catholic parishes the impact was particularly evident in 1848 when, with fewer people deciding to have children in the previous year, the numbers were less than 50 per cent of the pre-Famine average. While Kiltoghert showed an increase in 1849 it fell again the following year but in the other two parishes the numbers showed an appreciable increase in 1850, suggesting that they were making a recovery from the effects of the previous years.

In Kiltoghert Church of Ireland, there was a huge drop in 1847, a slight recovery the following year and then numbers fell dramatically in 1849 and 1850. Although the Mohill Church of Ireland figures were less than the average, they remained steady throughout the period 1847–50.

Similarly, the figures for marriages demonstrate how the famine impacted on all aspects of life:

**Table 10.6: Decline in Marriages in County Leitrim, 1840–50**

| Parish | 1840–1846 | 1847 | 1848 | 1849 | 1850 |
|---|---|---|---|---|---|
| Killenummery | 46 | – | 3 | 29 | 21 |
| Kinlough | 38 | 19 | 15 | 14 | 11 |
| Kiltoghert | 33 | 8 | 29 | 19 | 19 |

Source: National Library of Ireland, parochial marriage registers for Killenummery (p.4241),Kinlough (p.5344); Kiltoghert Parish Office, Carrick-on-Shannon, County Leitrim, Kiltoghert marriage register.

In Kiltoghert the number of marriages in 1847 was a quarter of the average for the previous seven years and although it increased in 1848 to almost attain the average it fell again in 1849. In Kinlough the 1847 figure was exactly half that of the average for the previous years and numbers declined significantly in the years thereafter. Unfortunately, the figures for Killenummery in 1847 are not available but in 1848 there were just three marriages in the parish and although the numbers were much greater in 1849 and 1850 they still represented less than 50 per cent of the pre-Famine average.

## PAROCHIAL MORTALITY

If the baptism and marriage statistics suggested that the Protestant population of the county were affected by the Famine the figures for deaths, although limited, confirm this:

**Table 10.7: Church of Ireland Burials in County Leitrim, 1840–50**

| Year | Oughteragh (Ballinamore) | Mohill |
|---|---|---|
| 1840 | 10 | 13 |
| 1841 | 12 | 13 |
| 1842 | 8 | 18 |
| 1843 | 2 | 13 |
| 1844 | 5 | 16 |

| | | |
|---|---|---|
| 1845 | 11 | 17 |
| 1846 | 8 | 24 |
| 1847 | 17 | 70 |
| 1848 | 4 | 24 |
| 1849 | 4 | 8 |
| 1850 | 11 | 19 |

*Source*: Church of Ireland Glebe, Mohill, County Leitrim.

The number of burials in Oughteragh was more than twice the average (eight) for the pre-Famine period while in Mohill the figures suggest that the impact was felt there in 1846 with a figure of twenty-four deaths as opposed to the average of sixteen. While the number remained high in 1849 the table reflects the devastation to the local Church of Ireland community in 1847. Although thirteen of the seventy deaths recorded were of workhouse inmates, the figure of fifty-seven parochial deaths was more than three times the pre-famine average.

The Catholic registers present a major problem in that there is no reliable data for the decade commencing 1840. The burial registers in Killenummery parish ends in March 1846 and those for Cloone and Fenagh in September 1845 and 1841 respectively. On the other hand, deaths in Kiltubrid are only recorded from 15 January 1847 so while we have detailed figures for that year and 1848, there are no earlier figures with which to compare them. Similarly, records of Aghavas deaths only commence in May 1845.

Thus, quite a lot of guesswork is involved in attempting to obtain constructive data from such material. However, the following table of deaths in Kiltubrid and Aghavas, although incomplete, appears to replicate the pattern set by the Church of Ireland parishes in Ballinamore and Mohill:

### Table 10.8: Catholic Burials in County Leitrim, 1845–50

| | Year | | | | | |
|---|---|---|---|---|---|---|
| Parish | 1845 | 1846 | 1847 | 1848 | 1849 | 1850 |
| Aughavas | 7 | 43 | 85 | 47 | 29 | 20 |
| Kiltubrid | – | – | 91 | 32 | 23 | – |

*Source*: National Library of Ireland, parochial burial registers for Aughavas (p.4240) and Kiltubrid (p.4234).

Evidence of deaths for this period emerges from two other sources. In the spring of 1847 the *Freeman's Journal* solicited information on deaths from various priests throughout the country. Those who replied from County Leitrim produced numbers which demonstrated the huge loss of life by April 1847 and are very much in keeping with the contemporary statements from a variety of observers. For the eight months from October 1845 to 1 April 1846 there were twenty-seven deaths in Cloone but for the corresponding period from October 1846 the figure was 260. In Killenummery the number jumped from twenty six to 172 and in Kiltoghert from ninety-eight to 320.

Similarly, the General Central Relief Committee for All Ireland circulated a 'statistical return' to parishes in all parts of Ireland. In Leitrim, six out of the seventeen parishes filled out the form by which it emerged that up to 25 September 1847 there had been 987 deaths from 'actual starvation' and 2,665 deaths from 'disease produced by want of food'.[5] Significantly, Father Peter Dawson, parish priest of Kiltoghert, remarked in May 1847, such was the number of deaths that 'many adults are allowed to die and are buried without the priest ever hearing of it'.[6]

## WORKHOUSE MORTALITY

The total number of workhouse deaths in Leitrim was 5,701 and this compared with 2,879 in Sligo; 7,001 in Roscommon; 9,624 in Mayo and 21,705 in Galway.[7] In Carrick workhouse there occurred 2,234 deaths (1,170 males and 1,064 females) and the following table illustrates the major causes[8]:

**Table 10.9: Selected Deaths in Carrick-on-Shannon Workhouse, 21 July 1842–30 March 1851**

| | Number of Deaths | |
|---|---|---|
| Disease | Male | Female |
| Smallpox | 24 | 23 |
| Measles | 45 | 59 |
| Whooping Cough | 2 | 1 |

| Croup | 2 | 1 |
|---|---|---|
| Dysentry | 668 | 636 |
| Diarrhoea | 15 | 12 |
| Influenza | 11 | 2 |
| Fever | 64 | 96 |
| Hydrocephalus | 1 | 2 |
| Paralysis | 3 | – |
| Consumption | 10 | 9 |
| Dropsy | 16 | 10 |
| Marasmus | 127 | 81 |
| Disease of Stomach | 5 | 1 |

*Source*: H.C. 1856, vol. xxx, 1851 Census of Ireland [workhouses, Auxiliary workhouses and Workhouse Hospitals], pp.106–7.

Of the deaths officially recorded in the workhouse there were 1,316 between the week ending 30 January 1847 and 28 December 1850. However, this record contains significant gaps and there are no statistics from October 1849 to May 1850. The breakdown is as follows:

**Table 10.10: Deaths in Carrick-on-Shannon Workhouse by Gender**

| | < 15 Years | | > 15 Years | |
|---|---|---|---|---|
| < 2 Years | Male | Female | Male | Female |
| 105 | 404 | 365 | 103 | 239 |

*Source*: Leitrim County Library, Ballinamore, Carrick-on-Shannon board of guardians' minute book, 30 January 1847 to 25 December 1847; 29 January 1848 to 30 December 1848; 6 January 1849 to 22 September 1849; 25 May 1850 to 28 December 1850.

Thus, adults (those aged above 15) accounted for 33.5 per cent of deaths and of this number 15.4 per cent were males and 18.1 per cent females. The majority of fatalities occurred amongst those aged between two and fifteen (58.4 per cent) with 30.6 per cent being boys and 27.7 per cent girls. Children under two years made up 8 per cent of the total.

In the Manorhamilton workhouse the most significant causes of mortality were as follows:

**Table 10.11: Selected Deaths in Manorhamilton Workhouse, 8 December 1842–30 March 1851**

| | Number of Deaths | |
|---|---|---|
| **Disease** | **Male** | **Female** |
| Smallpox | 5 | 1 |
| Measles | 3 | 2 |
| Dysentery | 349 | 270 |
| Diarrhoea | 75 | 81 |
| Influenza | 11 | 2 |
| Fever | 111 | 140 |
| Consumption | 25 | 23 |
| Dropsy | 36 | 30 |
| Marasmus | 24 | 23 |
| Teething | 21 | 16 |

*Source*: H.C. 1856, vol. xxx, 1851 Census of Ireland [workhouses, Auxiliary workhouses and Workhouse Hospitals], pp.106–7.

The total number in Manorhamilton was 1,481 (786 males and 695 females). Unfortunately, a similar age analysis to that of the Carrick house is not possible as such statistics are only available from May 1849.

But it is interesting to compare the main causes of death in the Carrick-on-Shannon and Manorhamilton workhouses. In the former, dysentery, the consequence of eating poor food, was the major killer, followed by marasmus (prevalent in the Jamestown auxiliary) and fever. At the same time, more than 100 people died of measles while in Manorhamilton this only accounted for five deaths. As in Carrick-on-Shannon, the main source of death in Manorhamilton was dysentery and fever. Emphasising the regional experience was the fact that in Manorhamilton there were over 150 deaths as a result of diarrhoea while in Carrick-on-Shannon this ailment resulted in twenty-seven deaths.

While a total number is available for the workhouse in Mohill – 1,986 – (1,019 males and 967 females) unlike Carrick and

Manorhamilton cause of death is not specified. The census enumerators noted how 'the clerk of the union states that "no further information can now be supplied" as in certain years between 1841 and 1851 it became impossible to keep a regular record of the number of deaths and causes'. A similar return was received from Loughrea Union in County Galway and Boyle in County Roscommon. In the latter no records had been kept from the winter of 1846 to August 1847 'in consequence of the extraordinary pressure on the time of the medical officers of that house'.[9] However, the minute books from Mohill do contain a breakdown of ages between 27 March 1847 and 1 January 1848 followed by a gap and further information from 1 November 1848 to 1 December 1849. The figures were as follows:

**Table 10.12: Deaths in Mohill Workhouse by Gender**

|            | < 15 Years |        | > 15 Years |        |
|------------|------------|--------|------------|--------|
| < 2 Years  | Male       | Female | Male       | Female |
| 66         | 245        | 226    | 119        | 143    |

*Source*: Leitrim County Library, Ballinamore, Mohill board of guardians' minute book, 27 March 1847 to 1 January 1848 and 1 November 1848 to 1 December 1849.

From 799 deaths recorded in these periods, adults represented 32.8 per cent of deaths, 14.9 per cent being male and 17.9 per cent female. Those aged between two and fifteen accounted for 58.9 per cent with boys being 30.7 per cent and girls 28.3 per cent. Finally, children younger than two made up the remainder, 8.3 per cent. These figures are almost identical to those for Carrick.

In terms of gender the deaths returned figures which illustrated a split of almost equal proportions:

**Table 10.13: Deaths by Gender in Connacht Workhouses, 1841–51**

| County  | Male   | %  | Female | %  |
|---------|--------|----|--------|----|
| Galway  | 11,387 | 52 | 10,318 | 48 |
| Leitrim | 2,975  | 52 | 2,726  | 48 |

| | | | | |
|---|---|---|---|---|
| Mayo | 4,993 | 52 | 4,331 | 48 |
| Roscommon | 2,570 | 51 | 2,488 | 49 |
| Sligo | 1,550 | 54 | 1,329 | 46 |

*Source*: H.C. 1856, vol. xxx, 1851 Census of Ireland [workhouses, Auxiliary workhouses and Workhouse Hospitals], pp.108–9.

## DEATHS IN COUNTY INFIRMARY, GAOL AND FEVER HOSPITALS

The figures for the county infirmary, based in Carrick, appear to reflect an institution that was strictly maintained. Although deaths increased from 1846 they did not come anywhere near the levels of those in the nearby workhouse.

**Table 10.14: Receptions and Deaths in Leitrim County Infirmary, 1841–51**

| Year | Receptions | Deaths |
|---|---|---|
| 1841 (208 Days) | 275 | 5 |
| 1842 | 502 | 14 |
| 1843 | 513 | 6 |
| 1844 | 501 | 9 |
| 1845 | 461 | 8 |
| 1846 | 532 | 16 |
| 1847 | 492 | 23 |
| 1848 | 509 | 16 |
| 1849 | 504 | 10 |
| 1850 | 487 | 8 |
| 1851 (89 Days) | 118 | 2 |

*Source*: H.C. 1856, volume xxix, report of tables of deaths. Table showing receptions and deaths in infirmaries from 1831 to the 30 March 1851, pp.370–1.

Therefore, from a total of 4,892 receptions (3,469 male and 1,423 female) over the period there were 117 deaths (82 male and 35 female). In the pre-Famine period the highest figure was fourteen deaths in 1842 as a consequence of the fever epidemic of that year.[10] Similarly, while the numbers entering the Mohill fever hospital showed huge increases in 1846–7 and 1850, there was no concomitant rise in deaths:

**Table 10.15: Receptions and Deaths in Mohill Fever Hospital, 1844–1851**

| Year | Receptions | Deaths |
|------|:----------:|:------:|
| 1844 | 3 | – |
| 1845 | 58 | 4 |
| 1846 | 75 | 5 |
| 1847 | 125 | 4 |
| 1848 | 4 | – |
| 1849 | 31 | – |
| 1850 | 132 | 7 |
| 1850 (89 Days) | 26 | – |

*Source*: H.C. 1856, volume xxix, report of tables of deaths. Table showing receptions and deaths in infirmaries from 1831 to the 30 March 1851, pp.378–9.

However, returns from the temporary fever hospitals reveal the huge demands placed on such institutions and the level of mortality consequent on the various diseases prevalent during the worst of the Famine:

**Table 10.16: Receptions and Deaths in Temporary Fever Hospitals, 1847–1850**

| Year | Receptions | Deaths |
|------|:----------:|:------:|
| 1847 | 674 | 37 |
| 1848 | 1,796 | 214 |
| 1849 | 1,210 | 135 |
| 1850 | 48 | 4 |

*Source*: H.C. 1856, volume xxix, report of tables of deaths. Table showing receptions and deaths in infirmaries from 1831 to the 30 March 1851, pp.378–9.

In all there were 3,728 (1,695 males and 2,033 females) admissions to the five temporary fever hospitals over this period. The number of deaths totalled 393 (204 males and 189 females), peaking at 214 in 1848.[11]

It has already been noted that a local paper surmised that a spate of petty crimes in the county was induced by a desire to be sentenced to transportation. In February 1848, poor law inspector, Major Haliday, remarked to the poor law commissioners that 'the gaol has rather attractions than terror for the wretched and degraded individuals who form the majority of the inmates and to whom the food and warmth of the gaol are actual comforts'.[12] He gave an example of how 'an able-bodied male pauper had deliberately broken several panes of glass in order to be sent to gaol'.[13] Certainly, as the following table illustrates, numbers entering the county gaol in Carrick increased substantially from 1848:

**Table 10.17: Committals and Deaths in Carrick-on-Shannon Gaol, 1841–51**

| Year | Committals | Deaths |
|---|---|---|
| 1841 (208 Days) | 231 | – |
| 1842 | 450 | – |
| 1843 | 397 | 1 |
| 1844 | 363 | 4 |
| 1845 | 431 | – |
| 1846 | 438 | 5 |
| 1847 | 476 | 100 |
| 1848 | 585 | 29 |
| 1849 | 607 | 2 |
| 1850 | 733 | 7 |
| 1851 (80 Days) | 41 | 2 |

*Source*: H.C. 1856, vol. 29, 1851 Census of Ireland. Table showing the committals, receptions into hospitals and deaths in the several prisons, 1831 to 1851, p.394.

In this period there were 4,752 committals (3,623 males and 1,129 females) while of the total of 150 deaths, 122 were amongst males and 22 amongst women. The figure which stands out is that for 1847 when, from 476 committals, there were 100 deaths. It is interesting to compare the mortality figures with those from other prisons in the province:

**Table 10.18: Deaths in Connacht Gaols, 1847**

| Gaol | Committals | Deaths |
|------|-----------|--------|
| Galway Town | 1,003 | 7 |
| Galway County | 2,948 | 97 |
| Castlebar | 1,982 | 83 |
| Roscommon | 1,443 | 67 |
| Sligo | 1,229 | 12 |

*Source*: H.C. 1856, vol. 29, 1851 Census of Ireland. Table showing the committals, receptions into hospitals and deaths in the several prisons, 1831 to 1851, p.394.

In terms of actual numbers the mortality level of the Carrick gaol was only surpassed by that of the Cork County Gaol where out of 6,948 committals there were 379 deaths (5 per cent). In the Kerry County Gaol the number of deaths was 101 out of 1,880 committals (5 per cent). Thus, the percentage of deaths in Carrick Gaol in 1847 – 21 per cent – made it the highest in the country and justified the statement made by the census enumerators that such establishments had 'in fact become hospitals'.[14] The latter also maintained that the huge increase in committals in the late 1840s was directly caused either by the pressure of want or the purpose of obtaining food and shelter at the public expense.[15] Hence, as the following table illustrates, the trend in Carrick was reflected throughout the country:

**Table 10.19: Committals to Gaols in Ireland, 1847–50**

| Year | Number of Committals |
|------|---------------------|
| 1847 | 70,166 |
| 1848 | 90,431 |
| 1849 | 107,210 |
| 1850 | 115,222 |

*Source*: H.C. 1856, vol. 29, 1851 Census of Ireland. Table showing the committals, receptions into hospitals and deaths in the several prisons, 1831 to 1851, p.396–7.

These figures compare with an average over the period 1842–6 of a committal rate of 45,170.[16]

# POPULATION DECLINE

Between 1841 and 1851 the population of County Leitrim fell from the official figure of 155,297 to 111,915, a decline of 43,382 (27.9 per cent). However, this figure masked a number of regional variations, as evidenced by figures for the same period calculated by barony:

**Table 10.20: Population Change by Barony in County Leitrim, 1841–51**

| Barony | Population in 1841 | Population in 1851 | Decline | % |
|---|---|---|---|---|
| Carrigallen | 28,293 | 20,469 | 7,824 | 28 |
| Dromahaire | 25,836 | 28,557 | 6,279 | 20 |
| Leitrim | 32,658 | 22,515 | 10,143 | 31 |
| Mohill | 35,714 | 22,164 | 13,550 | 38 |
| Rossclogher | 22,796 | 18,210 | 4,586 | 20 |

*Source*: H.C. 1852–53, volume xcii, 1851 Census of Ireland, County of Leitrim, p.112.

The level of disparity within each barony becomes apparent in an examination of the townland statistics:

**Table 10.21: Townland Population Change by Barony in County Leitrim, 1841–51**

| Barony | Number of Townlands | | |
|---|---|---|---|
| | Increase in Townland Population | Decrease in Townland Population | No Change |
| Carrigallen | 32 | 218 | 2 |
| Dromahaire | 71 | 317 | 7 |
| Leitrim | 27 | 315 | 4 |
| Mohill | 7 | 251 | 3 |
| Rossclogher | 34 | 182 | 5 |

*Source*: H.C. 1852–53, volume xcii, 1851 Census of Ireland, County of Leitrim, pp.89–112.

The seventeen parishes in the county demonstrated a varied range of figures (see Map Eight):

**Table 10.22: Population Decline by Parish in County Leitrim, 1841-51**

| Parish | Population in 1841 | Population in 1851 | Decline | % |
|---|---|---|---|---|
| Annaduff | 6,162 | 3,167 | 2,995 | 48.6 |
| Carrigallen | 8,100 | 5,940 | 2,060 | 25.4 |
| Cloone | 21,225 | 12,872 | 8,353 | 29.4 |
| Cloonclare | 10,524 | 9,303 | 1,221 | 11.6 |
| Cloonlogher | 1,248 | 910 | 338 | 27 |
| Drumlease | 4,182 | 3,655 | 527 | 12.6 |
| Drumreilly | 9,852 | 7,628 | 2,224 | 22.6 |
| Fenagh | 4,426 | 2,931 | 1,495 | 33.8 |
| Inishmagrath | 9,603 | 6,632 | 2,971 | 30.9 |
| Killenummery | 4,605 | 3,719 | 886 | 19.2 |
| Killargue | 4,873 | 3,673 | 1,200 | 24.6 |
| Kiltoghert | 17,581 | 12,779 | 4,802 | 27.3 |
| Kiltubrid | 7,228 | 5,287 | 1,941 | 26.9 |
| Killasnet | 6,286 | 4,708 | 1,578 | 25 |
| Mohill | 16,581 | 10,669 | 5,882 | 35.5 |
| Oughteragh | 9,255 | 7,023 | 2,232 | 24 |
| Rossinver | 13,566 | 10,989 | 2,577 | 19 |

*Source*: H.C. 1852-53, volume xcii, 1851 Census of Ireland, County of Leitrim, pp.89–112.

As the accompanying map illustrates, by far the worst affected parishes were those of Annaduff (48.6 per cent loss), Cloone (39.4 per cent), Mohill (35.5 per cent), Fenagh (33.8 per cent) and Inishmagrath (30.9 per cent), all of which, except the latter, were in the south of the county.

These parishes contained 1,475 townlands of which 172 (11.7 per cent) saw their population increase; twenty-two (1.5 per cent) recorded no change while the vast majority, 1,281 (86.5 per cent) witnessed a decline (see Appendices Five–Ten).

According to the stipulations of the census enumerators an urban area was classified as a town if it contained twenty or more houses. Thus, in 1851 the town of Kiltoghert, which contained 484 people in 1841, was included in the townland of the same name. However, in 1841 this townland was deemed to have no population while with the inclusion of the town it now had, in

1851, a population of 242.[17] Similarly, the town of Lurganboy, which had a population of 184 in 1841, was no longer deemed a town ten years later. Its population was therefore included in the townlands of Mountainthird and Poundhill in which it was situated. However, the level of population loss in Lurganboy was reflected in the fact that the population of Mountainthird only increased from 19 in 1841 to 35 ten years later.[18]

**Table 10.23: Population Change in County Leitrim Towns, 1841-51**

| Parish | Town | Population in 1841 | Population in 1851 |
|---|---|---|---|
| Carrigallen | Carrigallen | 473 | 387 |
| | Newtowngore | 187 | 193 |
| Oughteragh | Ballinamore | 946 | 704 |
| Cloonclare / Killasnet | Manorhamilton | 1,507 | 1,227 |
| Drumlease | Dromahaire | 348 | 346 |
| Inishmagrath | Drumkeerin | 469 | 400 |
| Annaduff | Drumsna | 516 | 384 |
| Kiltoghert | Carrick-on-Shannon | 1,716 | 1,100 |
| | Drumshanbo | 517 | 522 |
| | Jamestown | 315 | 212 |
| | Leitrim | 406 | 256 |
| Kiltubrid | Keshcarrigan | 132 | 117 |
| Annaduff | Drumod | 185 | 213 |
| Cloone | Cloone | 171 | 123 |
| Mohill | Mohill | 1,626 | 1,217 |
| Cloonclare | Kiltyclogher | 244 | 321 |
| Rossinver | Kinlough | 277 | 217 |

*Source*: H.C. 1852-53, volume xcii, 1851 Census of Ireland, County of Leitrim, pp.89–112.

Some interesting variations emerge from an analysis of the census statistics. In the parish of Carrigallen, a number of townlands such as Annagh (36 to 47), Cornafest (132 to 145), and Newtowngore (29 to 44) witnessed an increase in population between 1841 and 1851. Meanwhile, in Cloone parish, Kilmakenny (86 to 130) also increased.[19] In Drumreilly Corduff saw its population explode from 8 (4 males and 4 females) to 24 (12 of each gender) while Whiterock increased from 9 to 15.[20] Meanwhile in

Oughteragh, Aghatawny, Lower more than doubled its population from 9 to 21 while Cannaboe saw a huge increase in numbers from 93 in 1841 to 178 ten years later. Increases in the parish were also evident in Cornabroher (54 to 66) and Drumcromman (123 to 148).[21] Cloonclare saw increases in Annagh (57 to 71), Meenagh (89 to 112) Sranagross (168 to 205) and Tuckmillpark (7 to 17).[22] In Cloonlogher Lisgorman increased from 186 to 272 while in Drumlease, the townland of Aghameelta Barr saw its population rise more than five-fold from 4 to 23. In the same parish Doonmorgan increased from 15 to 41, Gleneige from 81 to 117 persons, while Rubbal increased from 22 to 42.[23] In Drumreilly both Drumristin (125 to 147) and Cleighranmore (138 to 157) saw significant increases while in Inishmagrath parish the townland of Drumkeerin increased from 18 to 50, Kilnagarns Lower from 53 to 86 and Lisnanorrus from 30 to 43.[24] In Killenummery significant increases were witnessed in Ardakipmore (63 to 82), Corglancey (122 to 152), Killananima (9 to 24) and Tullynascreen (90 to 159) while in Killarge Gubaderry rose from 51 to 68.[25]

In Fenagh, Commons increased from 13 to 24 while in Kiltoghert Carricknabrack rose from 14 to 24, Crey from 24 to 47, Drumduff South from 11 to 27, Drumnadober 125 to 166, Drumshanbo 58 to 75, Townparks (on the outskirts of Carrick-on-Shannon) 195 to 345 and Tullylannan 82 to 207.[26] In Kiltubrid there were increases in Drumaleague (from 73 to 91) and Scrabbagh (from 33 to 51).[27] In the parish of Cloone, Gortnalougher increased from 74 to 93 while Lear also rose from 67 to 108.[28] The townland of Kilmacsherwell in the parish of Fenagh increased from 82 to 109 while in the parish of Mohill Drumoghtybeg increased from 37 to 54.[29] In Cloonclare Aghavanny advanced from 62 to 78 persons and Corracloona from 175 to 193.[30] In Killasnet Barrackpark increased from 34 to 42, Dromore from 28 to 36, Largantemple from 3 to 12 and Mountainthird (due to the inclusion of the town of Lurganboy) from 19 to 35.[31] In Rossinver there were increases in Agharroo (from 156 to 178), Cloonawillin (37 to 71), Drumgane (18 to 32), Drummans (94 to 103), Fertagh (102 to 112) and Lissiniska (80 to 96) while Inishkeen doubled its population from 4 to 8.[32] In Annaduff, the townland of Drumsna increased from 19 to 46.[33]

There were twenty-two townlands in which the population did not change between the two censuses but this number was dwarfed by those which saw decreases in population. Indeed, sixty-five townlands witnessed a decline of 75 per cent with eight – Cornacreeve, Drummangarvagh, Moneynure, Cartron, Corduffhill, Mohill, Tawnylust Barr, Upper and Shancurragh - losing their entire population. In the case of Drumparsons, in the parish of Kiltubrid, the population declined from 46 persons (23 female and 23 male) to one female.

In relation to the flight from the land the number of people in the county per square mile of arable land fell from 398 in 1841 to 266 in 1851 – a decline of 132. This was greater than that of the neighbouring counties of Roscommon (77), Sligo (116), Cavan (131), Fermanagh (125) and Longford (108) but less than the 241 recorded for Donegal. Indeed, while the Leitrim figure was below the national average of 145, it was one of the highest in the country, surpassed only by Donegal, Mayo (220), Kerry (200), Clare (148), Galway (144), Monaghan (140) and Tyrone (136).[34] In terms of population loss per square mile of the total area, Leitrim suffered a decline of 70, from 253 to 183, above the national average of 60. Once again this figure proved to be one of the highest in the country, only being surpassed by Monaghan (125), Cavan (91), Roscommon (86), Longford (74) and Cork (72) and on a par with Armagh (70). Statistics for those remaining counties which bordered Leitrim were Donegal (22), Fermanagh (57) and Sligo (69).[35]

In terms of gender decline the percentages of male and female in the county were 77,501 (49.9 per cent) males and 77,796 (50.1 per cent) females in 1841 which fell to 56,111 (50.1 per cent) males and 55,786 (49.9 per cent) females ten years later. This represented a very slight increase in the number of males in the county and a corresponding decline in the number of females.[36]

As alluded to by the *Impartial Reporter* the number of fourth-class houses in the county fell dramatically in the years 1841–51. In 1841 there were 11,199 in Leitrim but ten years later this had declined by 8,188 to 3,011. However this figure, which represented a fall of 73 per cent, was some way behind the worst fall, that of County Antrim, which witnessed a decline of 89 per cent. Indeed, the Ulster counties of Derry (87 per cent), Down (85 per cent), Tyrone (85 per cent), Monaghan (80 per cent), Donegal (79 per cent), Fermanagh (77 per cent) and Cavan (75 per cent) all sustained a greater reduction than Leitrim while Armagh's decrease also stood at 73 per cent. For other neighbouring counties – Sligo (74 per cent), Roscommon (73 per cent) and Longford (70 per cent) – the a decline were similar to those for Leitrim. All of these counties, except Longford, sustained a decline greater than the national average of 71.5 per cent.[37] As the following table illustrates, the decline in population also had an impact on proportions employed throughout the county:

**Table 10.24: Employment of Population in County Leitrim, 1841–51**

| Occupation | Percentage | |
| --- | --- | --- |
| | 1841 | 1851 |
| Agriculture | 79.7 | 72.7 |
| Manufacturers / Trades, etc. | 14.9 | 13.4 |
| Other | 5.4 | 13.9 |

*Source*: H.C. 1856, volume xxxi, 1851 Census of Ireland, general report, p.xxxiv.

This was particularly evident when examining the means on which families depended for their livelihood:

**Table 10.25: Means on Which Families in County Leitrim Were Dependent, 1841–51**

| Means | Percentage | |
| --- | --- | --- |
| | 1841 | 1851 |
| Vested Means / Professions, etc. | 1.9 | 4.4 |
| Direction of Labour | 21.3 | 55.8 |
| Own Manual Labour | 75.3 | 35.0 |
| Not Specified | 1.5 | 4.8 |

*Source*: H.C. 1856, volume xxxi, 1851 Census of Ireland, general report, p.xxxiv.

## EDUCATION

Other changes consequent on population loss were to be found in the field of education, with slight improvements in the numbers of those above the age of five years able to read and write in English:

**Table 10.26: Literacy Levels (%) in County Leitrim, 1841–51**

|                        | Males | | Females | |
| --- | --- | --- | --- | --- |
|                        | 1841 | 1851 | 1841 | 1851 |
| Read and Write         | 35 | 37 | 12 | 18 |
| Read Only              | 18 | 18 | 21 | 23 |
| Neither Read nor Write | 47 | 45 | 67 | 59 |

*Source*: H.C. 1856, volume xxxi, 1851 Census of Ireland, general report, p.xlii.

As the table below shows, such figures were in line with the national averages:

**Table 10.27: Literacy Levels (%) in Ireland, 1841–51**

|                        | Males | | Females | |
| --- | --- | --- | --- | --- |
|                        | 1841 | 1851 | 1841 | 1851 |
| Read and Write         | 37 | 41 | 18 | 25 |
| Read Only              | 17 | 17 | 23 | 24 |
| Neither Read nor Write | 46 | 42 | 59 | 51 |

*Source*: H.C. 1856, volume xxxi, 1851 Census of Ireland, general report, p.xlii.

However, literacy levels in the county were the highest in Connacht, as indicated by the percentages of those who could neither read nor write:

**Table 10.28: Literacy Levels (%) in Connacht, 1841–51 (as distinguished by those who could not read or write)**

| County | Males | | Females | |
| --- | --- | --- | --- | --- |
|        | 1841 | 1851 | 1841 | 1851 |
| Galway | 71 | 65 | 84 | 77 |
| Leitrim | 47 | 45 | 67 | 59 |
| Mayo | 72 | 67 | 86 | 80 |
| Roscommon | 56 | 52 | 73 | 66 |
| Sligo | 61 | 58 | 76 | 68 |

*Source*: H.C. 1856, volume xxxi, 1851 Census of Ireland, general report, p.xlii.

The Leitrim figure is all the more remarkable given the statistics for school attendance in the various counties:

**Table 10.29: Numbers (%) aged 5–16 Attending School in Connacht, 1841–51**

| County | 1841 | 1851 |
| --- | --- | --- |
| Galway | 12 | 22 |
| Leitrim | 13 | 20 |
| Mayo | 8 | 18 |
| Roscommon | 14 | 21 |
| Sligo | 14 | 19 |

*Source*: H.C. 1856, volume xxxi, 1851 Census of Ireland, general report, p.xlii.

Hence, by 1851, all the counties in the province demonstrated similar levels of school attendance yet Leitrim enjoyed a literacy level significantly better than that of the other Connacht counties. A possible reason for this is revealed in an analysis of the 1855 report of the commissioners of national education. By the end of September in that year there were 130 schools being attended by 13,986 students (7,277 males and 6,709 females) in the county.[38] In Roscommon there were 119 schools with 12,313 students while the figures for Sligo revealed 96 schools and 11,408 students. Despite the number of schools in Leitrim being much less than that for either Cavan (178) or Donegal (240) the numbers attending in these counties at 14,537 in Cavan and 16, 499 in Donegal were not significantly greater than the Leitrim figures. The number of schools in the county was similar to the Fermanagh figure of 132, but the latter had an attendance of 9,055 while only 6,604 students attended sixty-six schools in County Longford.[39]

In terms of schools located in particular parishes, the statistics are as follows:

**Table 10.30: Number of Schools in County Leitrim, 1855**

| Parish | Number of Schools |
| --- | --- |
| Kiltoghert | 16 |
| Kiltubrid | 7 |

| | |
|---|---|
| Carrigallen | 10 |
| Annaduff | 7 |
| Fenagh | 4 |
| Rossinver | 14 |
| Oughteragh | 8 |
| Cloone | 9 |
| Cloonclare | 12 |
| Mohill | 5 |
| Killenummery | 3 |
| Inishmagrath | 9 |
| Killasnet | 6 |
| Drumreilly | 11 |
| Killargue | 6 |
| Drumlease | 3 |

*Source*: H.C. 1856, volume xxvii, Part I, The Twenty-Second report of the Commissioners of National education in Ireland for the year 1855, with appendices, vol. I, Appendix I, pp.318–323, List of 5,124 schools in operation on the 31 December 1855, Province of Connaught: County of Leitrim.

In his *Statistical Survey of County Leitrim*, published in 1802, McParlan had noted that the use of English was 'quite general' with very few of the older people unable to speak it. Also, when they were addressed in Irish, the children would 'always answer in English'.[40] This observation suggests that by the early nineteenth-century the English language was making inroads into native-speaking localities but a similar survey by Edward Wakefield published a decade later noted that in the Dromahaire area 'the poor all speak Irish', while in the area of the Leitrim mountains 'Irish is the common language of the district'. Wakefield's subsequent remark that 'schools have been established throughout the county and education is making rapid progress amongst them' also pointed to the probability that the expansion of schools teaching through the medium of English was contributing to the gradual demise of the native language.[41] Such expansion was accelerated by the introduction of the National System of Education in 1831. Some believe that this sounded the death knell for the language while others maintain that it was already slowly dying out. In the case of Leitrim, the census data for 1851 appears to offer support for both views. The data below relates to proficiency in Irish in Connacht in that year. The province had the highest number of native speakers in the country, at 50.8 per cent of the population:

**Table 10.31: Irish Speakers in Connacht as Percentage of 1851 Population**

|  | Irish Only | % | Irish and English | % | Total % |
|---|---|---|---|---|---|
| Mayo | 49,643 | 18.1 | 130,435 | 47.5 | 65.6 |
| Galway | 75,586 | 19.57 | 146,658 | 56.0 | 65.6 |
| Sligo | 10,584 | 8.2 | 38,644 | 30.1 | 38.3 |
| Roscommon | 1,326 | 0.8 | 44,970 | 25.9 | 26.7 |
| Leitrim | 144 | 0.1 | 14,859 | 13.3 | 13.4 |

*Source*: H.C. 1856, volume xxxi, 1851 Census of Ireland, p.xlvii.

Thus by 1851, Leitrim had the smallest proportion of Irish speakers in Connacht. Indeed the figures for the county were lower than the national average of 4.9 per cent for Irish speakers and 18.38 per cent for those speaking both Irish and English.[42] Of the total number of 15,003 who spoke the language to some degree, they were represented in the baronies as follows:

**Table 10.32: Irish Speakers in County Leitrim, 1851**

|  | Irish and English | Irish Only |
|---|---|---|
| Carrigallen | 997 | – |
| Dromahaire | 8,947 | 1 |
| Leitrim | 886 | – |
| Mohill | 824 | – |
| Rosslogher | 3,205 | 143 |
| TOTAL | **14,859** | **144** |

*Source*: H.C. 1856, volume xxxi, 1851 Census of Ireland: Table showing, in periods of ten years, the number and ages of males and females who speak Irish only, also those who speak Irish and English, p.565.

In those baronies in the south of the county – Carrigallen, Leitrim and Mohill – the language was almost wiped out. Indeed, between them, their number of speakers accounted for less than the total in Rossclogher. It is also interesting to note that these were the baronies which suffered the worst effects of the famine while Dromahaire and Rossclogher suffered to a significantly lesser degree.

Indicative of the serious decline in the use of the native tongue is the fact that of the 144 who claimed to speak only Irish, eleven were aged under thirty. This demise may be traced to a number of possibilities. There is little doubt that the Famine carried off many old people, the majority of whom would have spoken the language. At the same time, many of those who emigrated were probably in their thirties and forties. Under normal circumstances they could have been expected to have passed their knowledge of the language to their children. However, an important element may have been the influence of the recently-established national schools which had been set up in 1831. As noted in Chapter One, this initiative represented the first attempt by a British government to foster a non-denominational primary education system. One of the tenets of the system was that the children should learn to read and write in English and its chief opponent was Archbishop John MacHale of Tuam, a stout defender of the Irish language and Gaelic tradition. He refused to allow any national schools to be established in his archdiocese, as he believed they cultivated a love of all things English. Indeed, the report from the Mohill workhouse school which revealed that the children were receiving a 'thorough English education' appeared to justify this stance. However, as illustrated in Chapter One, many parents, not having received any education themselves, nevertheless wished to see their children learn to read and write, and were prepared to send them to such schools, regardless of the ethos therein. However, MacHale's fears appear to have been well-founded as within less than a generation, the language was dying out amongst the young people.

In relation to this study it is interesting to note that none of the posters requesting information from the public on recent outrages were in Irish. At the same time, and perhaps of more significance, threatening notices issued by the various agrarian organisations in the county were all in English. Linked to this was the fact that the various courts throughout the county operated through the means of that language and this is reflected by the fact that in an analysis of the court cases held from 1822 onwards, there was only one case, in 1836, in which a witness giving evidence required an interpreter.[43]

An innovative study by Garrett FitzGerald saw an attempt to gauge the number of speakers of Irish in the pre-Famine period from an analysis of those aged sixty and over in the 1911 census. In Leitrim there were 11,342 people in that category, of which 1,504 were Irish-speakers. This number represented 13.3 per cent of the age group and is almost identical with the figures for the county from the 1851 census (see Appendix Eleven).[44]

In analysing the data FitzGerald concluded that:

> ...save for a small isolated district near the mid-Leitrim/Cavan border, by 1851 Irish may have disappeared from the whole of an area some 25 to 30 miles wide, stretching from Carrick-on-Shannon eastwards to where the counties of Longford, Cavan and Meath meet at Lough Sheelin.[45]

At the same time there was a long strip of territory five to fifteen miles wide running forty miles north-east from near Ballaghadereen in County Roscommon to the border between north-west Cavan and Fermanagh which included the Iron Mountains east of Lough Allen. In this district Irish 'still remained the language of between 40% and 80% of the people'.[46] FitzGerald concluded that in those parts of Leitrim that contained 'important concentrations of Irish-speakers in the late eighteenth and early nineteenth centuries' but where a very low proportion of monoglot speakers was recorded in 1851 'the language had effectively disappeared amongst the younger population by the 1880s'.[47]

## POPULATION DECLINE, 1851–61

Between 1851 and 1861 the population of County Leitrim fell from 111,915 to 104,744, a decline of 7,171 (6.4 per cent). However, as with the earlier census, this figure masked a number of regional variations:

**Table 10.33: Population Change by Barony in County Leitrim, 1851–61**

| Barony | Population in 1851 | Population in 1861 | Decline | % |
|---|---|---|---|---|
| Carrigallen | 20,469 | 19,192 | 1,277 | 6.2 |
| Dromahaire | 28,577 | 27,741 | 816 | 2.9 |
| Leitrim | 22,515 | 19,590 | 2,925 | 13.0 |
| Mohill | 22,164 | 21,127 | 1,037 | 4.7 |
| Rossclogher | 18,210 | 17,694 | 516 | 2.8 |

*Source*: H.C. 1863, volume lv, 1861 Census of Ireland, County of Leitrim, p.112.

The level of variation within each denomination becomes apparent in an examination of the townland statistics:

**Table 10.34: Townland Population Change by Barony in County Leitrim, 1851-61**

| Barony | Number of Townlands | | |
|---|---|---|---|
| | Increase in Townland Population | Decrease in Townland Population | No Change |
| Carrigallen | 59 | 167 | 8 |
| Dromahaire | 166 | 197 | 13 |
| Leitrim | 90 | 245 | 11 |
| Mohill | 97 | 141 | 10 |
| Rossclogher | 69 | 151 | 7 |

*Source*: H.C. 1863, volume lv, 1861 Census of Ireland, County of Leitrim, pp.89–112.

Similarly, significant differences appear in the statistics for the various parishes:

**Table 10.35: Population Change by Parish in County Leitrim, 1851–61**

| Parish | Population in 1851 | Population in 1861 | Increase | Decrease | % |
|---|---|---|---|---|---|
| Annaduff | 3,167 | 3,092 | | 75 | 2.0 |

| | | | | | |
|---|---|---|---|---|---|
| Carrigallen | 5,940 | 5,522 | | 418 | 7.0 |
| Cloone | 12,872 | 12,820 | | 52 | 0.4 |
| Cloonclare | 9,303 | 8,759 | | 544 | 6.0 |
| Cloonlogher | 910 | 942 | 32 | | 3.5 |
| Drumlease | 3,655 | 3,383 | | 272 | 7.4 |
| Drumreilly | 7,628 | 7,766 | 138 | | 1.8 |
| Fenagh | 2,931 | 2,751 | | 180 | 6.0 |
| Inishmagrath | 6,632 | 6,713 | 81 | | 1.2 |
| Killenummery | 3,719 | 3,682 | | 37 | 1.0 |
| Killargue | 3,673 | 3,594 | | 79 | 2.0 |
| Kiltoghert | 12,779 | 10,861 | | 1,918 | 15.0 |
| Kiltubrid | 5,287 | 4,638 | | 649 | 12.0 |
| Killasnet | 4,708 | 4,314 | | 394 | 8.4 |
| Mohill | 10,699 | 9,256 | | 1,443 | 13.5 |
| Oughteragh | 7,023 | 6,399 | | 624 | 8.9 |
| Rossinver | 10,989 | 10,208 | | 781 | 7.0 |

*Source*: H.C. 1863, volume lv, 1861 Census of Ireland, County of Leitrim, pp.89–112.

From a total of townlands in seventeen parishes, 495 saw their population increase, in fifty-one there was no change, while the vast majority, 900, witnessed a decline. The figures per parish were as follows:

**Table 10.36: Population Change by Parish (Townland) in County Leitrim, 1851-61**

| | Number of Townlands | | |
|---|---|---|---|
| **Parish** | **Increase** | **No Change** | **Decline** |
| Annaduff | 31 | 4 | 27 |
| Carrigallen | 21 | 3 | 30 |
| Cloone | 35 | 3 | 69 |
| Cloonclare | 29 | 4 | 45 |
| Cloonlogher | 5 | – | 5 |
| Drumlease | 13 | – | 30 |
| Drumreilly | 38 | 3 | 50 |
| Fenagh | 21 | 1 | 36 |
| Inishmagrath | 65 | 5 | 67 |

| | | | |
|---|---|---|---|
| Killenummery | 18 | – | 26 |
| Killargue | 24 | 4 | 36 |
| Kiltoghart | 45 | 3 | 116 |
| Kiltubrid | 11 | 2 | 68 |
| Killasnet | 26 | 2 | 40 |
| Mohill | 64 | 9 | 92 |
| Oughteragh | 15 | 3 | 78 |
| Rossinver | 34 | 5 | 85 |

As with townlands and parishes the towns of the county returned contrasting results:

**Table 10.37: Population Change in County Leitrim Towns, 1851–61**

| Parish | Town | Population in 1851 | Population in 1861 |
|---|---|---|---|
| Carrigallen | Carrigallen | 387 | 392 |
| | Newtowngore | 193 | – |
| Oughteragh / Cloonclare | Ballinamore | 704 | 624 |
| Killasnet | Manorhamilton | 1,227 | 1,167 |
| Drumlease | Dromahaire | 346 | 331 |
| Inishmagrath | Drumkeeran | 400 | 426 |
| Annaduff | Drumsna | 384 | 339 |
| Kiltoghert | Carrick-on-Shannon | 1,100 | 1,403 |
| | Drumshanbo | 522 | 493 |
| | Jamestown | 212 | 174 |
| Cloone | Cloone | 123 | 135 |
| Mohill | Mohill | 1,217 | 1,123 |
| Cloonclare | Kiltyclogher | 321 | 427 |
| Rossinver | Kinlough | 217 | 231 |
| | Tullaghan | 114 | 130 |

*Source*: H.C. 1863, volume lv, 1861 Census of Ireland, County of Leitrim, pp.89–112.

Of the fifteen towns recorded in 1851, seven saw their populations increase while eight witnessed losses. As in 1851 the census enumerators stipulated that towns with less than twenty houses could no longer be deemed as such and were to be included as part of the nearest townland. Hence, Newtowngore (193 in 1851) in the parish of Carrigallen was included in the townland of Newtowngore which subsequently saw its population rise from 44 to 121.[48] Similarly, Keshcarrigan (117 in 1851), was now included in the townland of the same name which increased from 85 to 174 while Dromod's population (213 in 1851) was allocated to the townlands of Dromod Beg (45 to 161) and Dromod More (22 to 118).[49]

Between 1841 and 1851 twenty-two townlands exhibited no change in population. Given the much smaller population decline in the following decade it is no surprise that this number had increased to fifty-four (see Appendix Twelve). Further, of those eight townlands which lost their entire population between 1841 and 1851, four regained numbers as follows:

| Townland | Parish | Population in 1851 | Population in 1861 |
|---|---|---|---|
| Cornacreeve | Drumreilly | 0 | 5 |
| Moneynure | Kiltoghert | 0 | 5 |
| Mohill | Mohill | 0 | 44 |
| Shancurragh | Killasnet | 0 | 11 |

*Source*: H.C. 1863, volume lv, 1861 Census of Ireland, County of Leitrim, pp.90, 96, 102, 104, 107, 108, 109, 110.

Indeed, both Mohill and Shancurragh exceeded their 1841 population figures. However, the rest, Drummangarvagh, Cartron, Corduffhill and Tawnylust Barr, Upper, remained denuded of population. At the same time twenty-one town lands saw their numbers significantly reduced in the decade between 1851 and 1861, including fourteen which suffered losses of 100 per cent (see Appendix Thirteen).

The impact of such population loss on the landscape can be ascertained by examining the numbers of houses within the townlands concerned for each of the census returns. This has been done for those which contained no population by 1861 and are as follows:

| Townland | Parish | Number of Houses | | |
|---|---|---|---|---|
| | | 1841 | 1851 | 1861 |
| Manorhamilton | Cloonclare | – | 2 | – |

| Barragh Beg | Inishmagrath | – | 1 | – |
|---|---|---|---|---|
| Drumkeerin | | 5 | 14 | – |
| Lugmore | | 1 | 1 | – |
| Drumillion | Killargue | 2 | 2 | – |
| Drumlumman Glebe | | 7 | 1 | – |
| Aghintober | Annaduff | 1 | 1 | – |
| Crickeen | | – | 1 | – |
| Greagh | Kiltoghert | 2 | 1 | – |
| Leitrim | | – | 13 | – |
| Aghakilmore | Kiltubrid | 8 | 2 | – |
| Twigspark | Killasnet | 2 | 2 | 1 |
| Conwal, South | Rossinver | – | 12 | – |
| Sragarve | | 1 | 2 | 1 |

*Source*: H.C. 1863, volume lv, 1861 Census of Ireland, County of Leitrim, pp.89–112.

This table illustrates that, with the exception of two uninhabited houses in Twigspark and Sragarve, those townlands which had lost all their population by 1861 had also lost all their houses. This is most likely to have happened as a consequence of emigration, in which case the landlord presumably knocked the houses in order to increase the size of plots. Alternatively, the people may have been evicted from the land and their houses levelled. Either way, previously vibrant townlands containing 286 people living in fifty-five houses were reduced to a deafening silence by the forces of emigration and eviction.

Of the 65 townlands which witnessed a decline of 75 per cent or more (including those which lost 100 per cent) from 1841 to 1851, 37 of them saw a recovery in their population; five remained the same while 23 saw their populations continue to decline. Apart from the townlands of Mohill and Shancurragh (already noted) no area which increased on its 1851 figure came close to the population of 1841. However, one which did increase significantly was Drumparsons, in the parish of Kiltubrid which had declined from 46 persons (23 female and 23 male) to one female. By 1861 this figure had increased to 14 (9 females and 5 males).[50]

The 1861 census contains material which, without further information, baffles the historian. For example, the townland of Drumkeerin (parish of Inishmagrath) increased its population in the years from 1841 to 1851 from 18 to 50 but in the following decade this number disappeared completely.[51] Greaghnaglogh (parish of Inishmagrath) had a population of 185 in 1841, 161 in 1851 and 217 in 1861. In the same parish the townlands of Kiltyfeenaghty Glebe, Knockateean, Knockacoska, Lisadloney, Lisanorrus, Lugmeen, Moneencreave, Mullaghbawn, Ross, Rossbeg Glebe, Seltannaskeagh, Tullintowell, Tullyclevaun, Tullyveane and Turpaun, all exhibited population figures for 1861 which exceeded those of twenty years before.[52] Examples of similar statistics include Carrowcrin, Corglancey, Drumconor, Greaghnafarna and Tullynascreen in Killenummery;[53] Altavra, Belhavel, Killooman and Shancarrick in Killargue;[54] Curraghmartin, Drishoge and Drumsna in Annaduff;[55] Aghameeny, Carrickevy, Carricknabrack, Crey and Drumshanbo in Kiltoghert;[56] Aghacashlaun, Bunrevagh and Letterfine in Kiltubrid;[57] Aghadrumderg, Corraterriff, South, Drumoghty Beg Drumoula; Knockadrinan and Meelragh (Nagur) in Mohill[58] Cloontubbrid, Gortnalougher, and Lear in Cloone;[59] Cornagon and Garradice in Fenagh;[60] Ballyglass, Cullionboy, Fenagh, Mullies and Nure in Killasnet;[61] and Cloonawillin, Derryduff, Drumgane, Glack and Moneengaugagh in Rossinver.[62]

From a total of almost 1,500 townlands only three exhibited the same population statistics for each of the three census returns. These were Derreen (Southwell) in the parish of Kiltubrid with six each year; Drumregan in the parish of Mohill with sixty-nine and Sheean in the parish of Rossinver with ten in each of the census years.[63] However, this does not suggest that the Famine did not impact on such areas as, with the exception of Derreen, the numbers of males and females within each return fluctuated as follows:

| Townland | Parish | 1841 Population | | 1851 Population | | 1861 Population | |
|---|---|---|---|---|---|---|---|
| | | Male | Female | Male | Female | Male | Female |
| Derreen (Southwell) | Kiltubrid | 3 | 3 | 3 | 3 | 3 | 3 |
| Drumregan | Mohill | 38 | 31 | 35 | 34 | 45 | 24 |
| Sheean | Rossinver | 6 | 4 | 6 | 4 | 5 | 5 |

*Source*: H.C. 1863, volume lv, 1861 Census of Ireland, County of Leitrim, pp.103, 108, 112.

In Derreen (a small townland of twenty acres), the census reveals that there was only one house, inhabited by Myles Lee and his family, and the probability is that they survived the famine intact. Significantly, the value of Lees's land was greater than that of any of his neighbours in Derreen (Johnston) and Derreen (Lloyd) and suggests that he may have been able to afford the food prices which proved beyond the reach of others in the locality.[64] In 1841, Drumregan (140 acres) contained twelve houses, only one of which was not occupied. By 1851, all twelve were inhabited but ten years later, in spite of the population remaining the same, eleven houses were occupied. In Sheean (38 acres), the townland contained two inhabited houses in each of the three census years which points to two families in the area.

The available evidence points to the fact that the famine in Leitrim was more severe in the south of the county than in the north. A variety of mortality indices – baronial, parochial and workhouse – reveal that population loss in the south was substantially greater. In addition, a much greater number of private relief committees were established throughout the same area. Furthermore, of the three workhouses in the county, Manorhamilton was the only one not to see the appointment of paid public officials and evidence of the lesser impact in this area emerges in examining the rate-in-aid returns. This was a measure introduced by the British government in 1849 by which means poor law unions were taxed for the support of distressed unions in the west and south. Each of the three unions in Leitrim had to contribute to this fund but while Carrick-on-Shannon paid in £1,892/18 it received: £6,333. For its part the Mohill union contributed £1,786/2 and received £2,484 but Manorhamilton, despite paying £1,556/17, was not designated as a distressed union and therefore received no aid.[65] Indeed, throughout this period the union appeared to escape the worst of the crisis which overwhelmed those of Carrick-on-Shannon and Mohill. Trying to establish a reason or reasons for this is quite complex. Although it was the largest of the three at 157,159 acres (Mohill being 137,768 and Carrick-on-Shannon 132,516) Manorhamilton had the lowest population at 45,990. Mohill union had the highest (68,859) while Carrick-on-Shannon was slightly smaller at 67,077. The following table illustrates the number of landholders in each union and the size of their plots:

## Table 10.38: Land Holding in County Leitrim by Poor Law Union

| Union | Size of Holdings (in acres) | | | | | |
|---|---|---|---|---|---|---|
| | < 1 | 1–5 | 6–10 | 11–20 | 21–50 | 50–100 |
| Carrick-on-Shannon | 1,317 | 1,967 | 3,405 | 2,014 | 534 | 91 |
| Manorhamilton | 900 | 785 | 1,472 | 2,074 | 1,669 | 456 |
| Mohill | 1,692 | 2,066 | 3,407 | 2,741 | 799 | 79 |

*Source*: H.C., 1845, volume xxii, appendix to minute of evidence taken before her majesty's commissioners of inquiry into the state of the law and practice in respect to the occupation of land in Ireland, part iv. Appendix no. 94, return of persons holding land, etc, in Ireland, pp.280–3.

Analysis of these figures, in conjunction with population and total land area figures allows for some comparisons between the unions. The average acreage per landholder in Manorhamilton union was 19.7; in Carrick-on-Shannon 14 and in Mohill 12.6. The average acreage per head of population was 3.4 in Manorhamilton, 2 in Mohill and 1.97 in Carrick-on-Shannon. Evidently, therefore, population density in the Manorhamilton union was considerably less than the other two which, generally, returned similar figures. This is emphasised by the findings of the table above. In Carrick-on-Shannon and Mohill those possessing less than one acre of land was 14 per cent and 15.5 per cent respectively while in Manorhamilton it was only slightly less at 12 per cent. However, while in the latter only 10.5 per cent resided on plots from one to five acres, this figure was one-fifth both in Carrick-on-Shannon (21 per cent) and Mohill (19 per cent). This disparity continues in analysing the numbers living on land from six to ten acres. In Carrick-on-Shannon this figure represented more than one-third of the total of the union (36 per cent); in Mohill it was 31 per cent while in Manorhamilton it was less than one-fifth (19.7 per cent). For those occupying land from 11 to 20 acres the figures were generally similar for Manorhamilton (27.8 per cent) and Mohill (25 per cent) while Carrick-on-Shannon returned a figure of 21 per cent. However, it is significant that when commenting on payment of rates, in February 1848, Major Haliday noted that in the Mohill union, 'the actual poverty of a multitude of the tenants holding from 10 to 20 acres of land will make its complete collection impossible in several districts'.[66]

A marked difference between Manorhamilton and the other unions emerges in examining the numbers residing on land from 21 to 50 acres.

In Carrick-on-Shannon, this was 5.6 per cent of the total; in Mohill, 7 per cent, but in Manorhamilton this figure – 22.5 per cent – represented more than one-fifth of the entire union. Similarly, those in possession of 50 to 100 acres in both Carrick-on-Shannon (0.9 per cent) and Mohill (0.7 per cent) were negligible but in Manorhamilton they represented 6 per cent of the total. Another way of summarising the data is the fact that in Carrick-on-Shannon those possessing plots of less than ten acres represented 71 per cent of the union; in Mohill this figure was 65.5 per cent but in Manorhamilton it was 42 per cent. The importance of this was emphasised in comments made by Major Fitzgerald in February 1848. Maintaining that distress in the Manorhamilton union was most severe in the electoral division of Drumkeerin and least in Dromahaire, he argued that in relation to destitution 'as might be expected, the pressure is in direct ratio to the numbers of *small cottiers* [his italics]'.[67]

Such statistics help give an indication as to why the famine did not impact to the same extent in the Manorhamilton union as in the others. Although the average acreage per head of population was only slightly greater in Manorhamilton, in a county where prime prices were demanded, and received, for con-acre land this was a substantial difference. However, the most important aspect appears to be the fact that in Carrick-on-Shannon and Mohill unions huge numbers were forced to subsist on small plots of ground while the same pressure was not evident in Manorhamilton. At the same time, with more than one-fifth of the population of the latter union possessing between 21 and 50 acres, it can be surmised that such farmers were able to offer those in distress some employment and avoid the necessity of poor law relief. Crucially, it appears that the Manorhamilton union did not suffer to the same extent as Carrick-on-Shannon as a consequence of the Gregory Clause and hence was not witness to thousands of people desperately seeking aid and ultimately dying lonely deaths in bogs, ditches and lanes.

In a chapter which focuses on statistics it is easy to forget that every number represents a person – a mother, father, brother, sister, husband or wife. In fact, thousands of people born in the county between 1841 and 1846 never even officially existed and yet they lived in Leitrim and, like many other children, died, or were forced to emigrate with their families. While numbers of deaths and emigrants can be collated by the historian what cannot be assessed is the impact that the crisis had on those who survived. They left no testimonies or accounts of their experiences and one can only imagine the psychological impact on people who lived through the famine years. For example, how did the woman in Drumparsons, who watched her forty-five neighbours die, or leave, come to terms with her situation – the sole survivor in the townland? We will never know the answer to this question, and many more like it. All we have are statistics which reduce people to numbers and only scratch the surface of the human misery which engulfed the county in the Famine years.

# Chapter 11

# THE GENERAL EXTERMINATION OF THE PEOPLE

Names of those evicted from land in Gorvagh, County Leitrim, January 1860. Courtesy of Seamus Geraghty Collection, St George's Heritage Centre, Carrick-on-Shannon, County Leitrim.

B ETWEEN 1841 AND 1851 the population of Ireland declined
from 8,175,124 to 6, 552, 385, a fall of 19.8 per cent.[1] Six of the
thirty-two counties lost less than 15 per cent of their population and in
another six the decline ranged from 15–20 per cent. Of the remaining
twenty counties, nine lost from 20–25 per cent while eleven lost over 25
per cent in this period. With a loss of 28 per cent Leitrim was grouped
amongst the counties which suffered the greatest levels of loss. Indeed,
only Roscommon (31 per cent), Galway (29 per cent), Mayo (29 per cent)
Sligo (29 per cent) and Longford (29 per cent) surpassed Leitrim in this
respect.[2] In terms of excess mortality the statistics are very similar. Excess
deaths are those that occurred outside 'normal' death rates and historian
Joel Mokyr estimated that national excess mortality in the years 1846–
51 amounted to 1,082,000 persons if averted births (those which would
normally have taken place) are not counted, and to 1,498,000 if they are.
Examining the former figure from a provincial perspective illustrates that
excess mortality was greatest in Connacht, which accounted for 40.4 per
cent of the total, followed by Munster with 30.3 per cent, Ulster 20.7 per
cent and Leinster with 8.6 per cent.[3] The highest annual rates of excess
mortality per thousand of the population are reflected in the following
table:

**Table 11.1: Average Annual Rates of Excess Mortality by County,
1846–51 (Per Thousand)**

| County | Rate |
| --- | --- |
| Mayo | 58.4 |
| Sligo | 52.1 |
| Roscommon | 49.5 |
| Galway | 46.1 |
| Leitrim | 42.9 |
| Cavan | 42.7 |
| Cork | 32.0 |
| Clare | 31.5 |
| Fermanagh | 29.2 |
| Monaghan | 28.6 |

*Source*: James S. Donnelly, Jr, *The Great Irish Potato Famine* (Sutton Publishing Ltd, 2001), pp.176–7.

Thus, both in terms of actual percentage decline and estimated excess mortality, Leitrim emerges as one of the worst-affected counties in the country. It is also instructive to examine the county's plight in terms of its regional experience. The following table illustrates population loss in baronies contiguous with Leitrim:

**Table 11.2: Population Decline in Baronies Bordering on County Leitrim**

| Barony | County | Population Decline (%) |
|---|---|---|
| Tirhugh | Donegal | 14 |
| Magherboy | Fermanagh | 27 |
| Clanawley | Fermanagh | 28 |
| Tullyhaw | Cavan | 19 |
| Tullyhunco | Cavan | 28 |
| Granard | Longford | 26 |
| Longford | Longford | 29 |
| Ballintober North | Roscommon | 47 |
| Roscommon | Roscommon | 38 |
| Boyle | Roscommon | 28 |
| Tirerril | Sligo | 38 |
| Carbury | Sligo | 18 |

*Source*: H.C., 1852–53, volume xci, 1851 Census of Ireland, County of Longford, p.175; H.C., 1852–53, volume xcii, County of Cavan, p.103, County of Donegal, p.154, County of Fermanagh, p.228, County of Galway, p.418, County of Mayo, p.510, County of Roscommon, p.551 and County of Sligo, p.579.

Evidently, with the exception of the barony of Ballintubber North, the worst affected barony in Leitrim, Mohill, was one of the hardest hit in the region, sharing a population loss of 38 per cent. with Roscommon and Tirerril (County Sligo). The barony of Leitrim, with a decline of 31 per cent surpassed the figures for all the remaining neighbouring baronies. Hence, not only was south Leitrim the most severely affected part of the county, it was also one of the most severely affected areas in a north–west region which shared boundaries with Leinster and Ulster. Furthermore, contemporary comments suggest that conditions in the unions of Carrick-on-Shannon and Mohill, both situated in these baronies, were considerably worse than those of neighbouring counties. For example, when commenting on standard of clothing Poor Law Inspector, Major Haliday, maintained that in the Granard union in County Longford he noticed 'among the poorer peasantry whom I have passed on the roads a very perceptible superiority as to clothing to that of the similar classes in Leitrim'.[4] In similar vein, Captain Edmund Wynne made the following observations on the union of Boyle (County Roscommon):

> Many townlands exhibit strong marks of the march of the enemy, in the multitudes of ruined cottages or cabins, the absence of every description of cattle, and the neglected state of the land; yet these contain less destitution, and stand less in need of relief, than the most favoured townlands in the majority of the electoral divisions in this [Carrick-on-Shannon] union … The case of Boyle is not nearly so urgent as that of this union.[5]

Thus, in Wynne's estimation even the worst townlands in the Boyle union were still better circumstanced than any in Carrick-on-Shannon. The same could be said of the management of the district's workhouses. While the running of the Manorhamilton establishment appears to have been carried out in a reasonably efficient manner, with guardians taking an active interest in the affairs of the union, matters were altogether different in the south of the county. Although the Carrick-on-Shannon guardians attended board meetings regularly they appeared to be overwhelmed by the crisis which unfolded from October 1846 and on three occasions offered to resign. Indeed, as noted, in July 1847, they had actually suggested the appointment of paid guardians before eventually being replaced by the latter a few months later. However, this was not an unusual event and the boards of the Athlone, Ballina, Kanturk, Newcastle and Skibbereen unions all offered to resign at various stages.[6]

In Mohill, despite being under the chairmanship of Lord Leitrim, the guardians evinced little enthusiasm for enacting the poor law even prior to the onset of famine, their attendance had been poor. This prompted a local paper to comment that, 'it is remarkable that only when appointments are to be made or when personal friends are looking for situation or contract, anything like a full board may be expected'.[7]

Despite their ineptitude, upon being re-instated both boards appeared to suffer from selective amnesia and castigated the regimes of the vice-guardians. Even the press seemed to forget the obvious inability of the Carrick-on-Shannon board to conduct matters efficiently and the *Morning Chronicle* remarked how 'for some reason not clearly apparent ... the services of the local board of guardians of that union were summarily dispensed with'.[8]

Of course, it is easy to criticise the efforts of those who faced difficulties unimagined when the poor law was introduced. The fact was that, in the words of its architect George Nicholls, it was 'in its origins no more than a branch or offshoot of the English law'[9] and therefore totally inappropriate for the conditions of Ireland. Nonetheless, elected boards of guardians offered the first opportunity by interested parties to relinquish control from landlords and their agents and it can be argued that such 'local elections' represented a natural corollary of the demise of the Penal Laws in 1829 and a move towards representative democracy. The attempts to intimidate voters and influence voting patterns in the late 1830s reflected the importance of such contests and the relative success of Catholic candidates may well have been the template for the success of John Brady in the 1852 General Election. The presence of such members, alongside landlord's agents and those seeking a measure of social aggrandisement, merely reflected the eclectic composition of boards of guardians who were, for the most part, well-meaning and unpaid amateurs. Regular disagreements with the poor law commissioners simply reflected the fact that these were people who were not used to being told how to act or what to do and may well have contributed to the small attendances witnessed from the commencement of the poor law in Mohill. However, the guardians, as the name implies, were responsible for the supervision of thousands of people and although those in Carrick-on-Shannon and Mohill obviously despised the vice-guardians and the perceived 'interference' from central government which they epitomised, their own inability to effectively oversee the running of their respective unions demanded replacement by such paid officials. Indeed, it can be argued that without the intervention of the vice-guardians, there is little doubt that thousands more would have died. In Carrick-on-Shannon, the efforts of Captain Edmund Wynne were crucial in saving lives but this did not prevent an excoriation of his character by the board of guardians who subsequently attempted to portray him as a sexual predator both inside and outside the workhouse. This charge eventually led to the establishment of a House of Lords committee to examine the allegations and the evidence suggested that Wynne did take advantage of his position.

Nevertheless, some of the guardians appeared to expend more energy in pursuing Wynne than in seeking to address the spectre of hunger, disease and death in their midst.[10]

There is no doubt that the number of admissions to the county's workhouses from late 1846 onwards placed a severe strain on the ability of boards to cope. One of the difficulties with attempting to analyse workhouse data is that, as has been shown, so disorganised were the various officers that important administrative work was not carried out. Hence, while it is possible to obtain admission statistics for each workhouse from 1842 to 1846 neither Carrick-on-Shannon nor Mohill returned the necessary information for 1847. It is evident, though, that apart from the opening year of 1842 when a fever epidemic saw large numbers enter the workhouses in Carrick-on-Shannon and Mohill, numbers generally remained well below capacity:

**Table 11.3: Admissions to County Leitrim Workhouses, 1843–6**

|  | Number Admitted to March Each Year | | | |
| --- | --- | --- | --- | --- |
| Workhouse | 1843 | 1844 | 1845 | 1846 |
| Carrick-on-Shannon | 559 | 254 | 539 | 483 |
| Manorhamilton | 82 | 202 | 151 | 133 |
| Mohill | 721 | 228 | 298 | 247 |

*Source*: H.C., 1846, vol. xxxvi, Return of the number of paupers admitted into each workhouse in Ireland in the five years ending the 31st day of March 1846; and of the numbers of paupers that died in each workhouse in Ireland in each of those years; namely to the 31st day of March 1842, 1843, 1844, 1845 and 1846, respectively; distinguishing those who died from fever in each year.

Unfortunately, the only figures for 1847 are for Manorhamilton but they reveal that this number – 915 – was substantially greater than that for the total entries to the house since it opened. From 1848 statistics are available for each union and reveal the huge numbers in each workhouse:

**Table 11.4: Numbers Relieved in County Leitrim Workhouses, 1848–51**

|  | Number Relieved to September Each Year | | | |
| --- | --- | --- | --- | --- |
| Workhouse | 1848 | 1849 | 1850 | 1851 |
| Carrick-on-Shannon | 3,113 | 6,956 | 3,518 | 1,714 |

| | | | | |
|---|---|---|---|---|
| Manorhamilton | 1,701 | 4,761 | 2,152 | 1,376 |
| Mohill | 2,683 | 5,229 | 3,314 | 2,010 |

*Source*: First Annual Report of the Poor Law Commissioners for administering the laws for relief of the poor in Ireland, with appendices, Dublin, 1848, pp.196, 198–9; Third Annual Report, 1850, pp 82–3; Fourth Annual Report, 1851, pp.162, 164; Fifth Annual Report, 1852, pp.146,149.

Thus, the county's workhouses were the sole source of official relief for thousands of people into the early 1850s and it is therefore interesting to note how contemporary references suggest that, for some, the impact of the famine appears to have been limited. When a correspondent to a local paper alleged that clergymen lived 'in ease and comfort' the paper's editor disagreed and pointed to efforts made by them 'during the famine years of 1846-7'.[11] At the same time, the petition of the Mohill guardians in February 1850 complained about 'money expended by the officers of the government during the famine'[12] while, in August 1847, Father Thomas Maguire praised election candidate Edward King Tenison for his relief efforts 'during the time famine and fever had been committing ravages amongst the people'.[13] Significantly, all used the past tense when referring to the famine and by this usage implied that by the latter months of 1847 the crisis was over. This was very evidently not so but what such comments reveal is that in the county the very worst years of the famine were from the commencement of the second blight – August/September 1846 – up to the summer of 1847. It was during this twelve-month period that the public works were at their height, that thousands clamoured for entry to workhouses and that large-scale outdoor relief was organised under the auspices of the government. This was also the period in which graphic reports of death by starvation were reported. The fact that tens of thousands throughout the county relied on workhouse relief, outdoor rations and the support of multiple local efforts into the early 1850s simply reflects the unspeakable horror of this period.

Nevertheless, there are examples of people continuing to live as normal during the most severe period of distress. In September 1847, when government soup kitchens were being shut down, the Drumkeerin Free Mason's Lodge (warrant 187) was formed to eventually include, amongst others, justices of the peace, doctors, police, revenue officers and solicitors.[14] The records of Fenagh Catholic Church reveal that in that same year the average charge for a baptism was 2s 6d, although nine people were recorded as being unable to pay anything to the priest. However, on

29 April 1847 Patrick Heeran and his wife Anne (Gilroy) paid ten shillings for the baptism of their son, John and the following year paid five shillings for another baptism.[15] Heeran, as noted in chapter two, was a poor law guardian for the Mohill union. Such examples suggest that life during the famine period was more nuanced than some might think, a point made in an insightful article by historian Breandán Mac Suibhne who refers to the 'gray zone' of the Famine as being:

> …the demimonde of soupers and grabbers, moneylenders and meal-mongers, and those among the poor who had a full pot when neighbours starved, and the poorhouse bully who took the biscuit from the weak. It is where one finds the mother who denied one child food and fed another, a boy who slit the throat of two youths for a bag of meal and, indeed, rumoured and reported cases of cannibalism.[16]

In Leitrim this 'zone' was reflected in a number of ways: the mother who used money contributed for the purchase of a coffin for her child to instead buy food for herself; the father of 14-year-old James Foley who, having been discharged from the fever hospital in Killenummery, refused to allow him back into his home fearing his other children would contract fever with the result that James died[17]; large farmers and landlords' agents endeavouring to make sure their tenants would gain a place on the public works so that rent would be paid; the barony constables who waited on those on the works to be paid before taking their wages for cess; the workhouse officers – including medical staff – and administrators in Carrick-on-Shannon who sexually abused vulnerable and starving paupers under their supervision; two shopkeepers and a baker in Dromod 'who regulated the price of every article of food, taking it out of the power of the wretched inhabitants to obtain even the slightest relief'[18]; the fact that in Carrick the price of potatoes was, in the words of Captain Edmund Wynne, 'strange to say, forty per cent dearer in this market than they are at Ballaghaderreen, twenty miles distant'.[19] Finally, while reference has been made to the evictions carried out under the Gregory Clause Wynne made a brief, but telling, allusion to the fact that in order to receive outdoor relief 'land has been given up very generally; and where the landlord has refused to accept of it, it has been made over to a neighbour for a trifling consideration'.[20] Hence, friends and neighbours were willing to take advantage of those less fortunate in the grim struggle for survival and as one writer has noted, in such situations 'moral judgment may not then have been impossible but can scarcely have been easy, and today may seem utterly inappropriate'.[21]

Undoubtedly, the main beneficiaries during the famine period were those with workhouse contracts, all of whom, it appears, survived the crisis intact. Given the number of deaths it is no surprise that coffin-makers were in demand and despite the employment of a re-usable coffin in the Mohill workhouse for a number of months Thomas McTaggert was in regular receipt of union orders from 1847 until 1849.[22] Suppliers of food were particularly required throughout the period 1846–9 and in such a scenario those able to supply large amounts of meal benefitted greatly. This was particularly evident with the introduction of outdoor relief from 1848. For example, in Manorhamilton on 8 March 1849 Edward Bussell was paid £243 for providing meal to the workhouse and a further £76 for outdoor relief supplies.[23] In the other two unions, where outdoor relief was operated on a much greater scale, contractors received huge sums. In Mohill, the main meal contractor was Michael Murphy of Selton, Gorvagh and in the four weeks between 3 May and 2 June 1849 he was paid £1,586.[24] In Carrick-on-Shannon there were a variety of contractors, with seven bakers in the town providing bread to the workhouse, including Anne McDermott, Peter Keavy, Thomas Heslin and Pat Barrett, the latter also being responsible for providing a variety of other foodstuffs.[25] While there were a number of bakers in the area there appeared to be only one person capable of supplying the workhouse with water. The problems with water supply, consequent on the decision to site the building on a hill above the town, are well documented and as a consequence Margaret O'Dowd received regular orders for water from the period the house opened until at least the middle of 1850.[26]

O'Dowd benefitted from her ability to provide a unique service but others did so from being able to diversify. For example, coffin-maker William Cunningham was paid £6 by the Carrick-on-Shannon guardians on 13 June 1849 'for carriage of female emigrants to Mullingar'.[27] However, perhaps the best example of this, also in the Carrick-on-Shannon union, was Lancelot Lawder, Esq. On 1 January 1848 he received £100 for meal and at the end of that month was declared the sole supplier of meal for all nine relieving districts in the union. Hence, on 4 March he received £261 followed by £250 on 18 March. When the vice-guardians decided to acquire land for a new fever hospital adjacent to the workhouse they had to pay compensation to the sitting tenant – Lancelot Lawder – who received £30. On 30 September 1848 he was also appointed as the new rate collector for the Kiltubrid and Drumreilly electoral divisions.[28]

The urgent necessity for additional accommodation throughout 1847–9 proved beneficial to a number of individuals throughout the county. In the Manorhamilton union both James Geren and Christopher Wilson were able to rent buildings as auxiliary workhouses.[29] At the same time, in Carrick-on-Shannon the owners of the Jamestown Mill, its adjacent buildings and a number of buildings in Carrick itself benefitted from the need to obtain additional accommodation.[30] The willingness of owners to extract as much money as possible was illustrated by the rejection of an initial offer of £45 per year for three houses in the town; the owner holding out for, and obtaining, £60.[31]

While there is the suspicion that some contractors probably received favourable treatment from guardians, it was certainly the case in the Manorhamilton union. In October 1844 the poor law commissioners queried why contracts for supplying the workhouse were not advertised in the local press. The guardians replied that such would have involved 'needless expense' and that 'full care' had been taken to 'post and circulate handbills'.[32] However, the fact was that some of those on the board, such as members of the Armstrong and Nixon families, were facilitating their relatives to obtain contracts. This was noted by Temporary Poor Law Inspector, Major Fitzgerald, in February 1848 when stating, 'I perceive a strong tendency on the part of some of the guardians to play into the hands of favourite contractors, which it will be my duty to check and expose.' Having ascertained that meal contractors in Manorhamilton were operating what was effectively a cartel he eventually sourced meal in Sligo at a price of £8/15 per ton as against the local price of £11.[33] Of course, those who benefitted in such circumstances were simply taking advantage of economic conditions resulting from British government policy.

The official reaction to the initial crop failure of 1845 was limited to the importation of Indian meal and employment of those in need on works of 'public utility'. This outlet, in conjunction with increased entries to workhouses, may well have sufficed for a one-off event. The localised crop failure of 1839 had illustrated that such could be effectively dealt with if followed by a successful crop. However, the catastrophic failure of 1846, which witnessed the annihilation of the crop, demanded an innovative and immediate response. How aware was the government of conditions at a local level? Lord John Russell became Prime Minister on 30 June 1846 and one of his private secretaries was Colonel George Keppel who, as has been noted, owned land in the parishes of Kiltoghert and Mohill. On 18 December 1846 Keppel wrote to his agent, William Lawder, from Downing Street as follows:

> Mrs Keppel considering your last letter only an answer to mine tore it up as soon as read. This I regret because it contained information respecting the state of your neighbourhood which it is desirable the Government should be in possession of. Will you therefore, when you have leisure, furnish me with as many facts (isolated from all abstract speculation) as you from local knowledge can procure. In doing so you will confer a benefit on the Government who are most desirous of obtaining an accurate acquaintance with the condition of your unhappy country.[34]

If we assume that Lawder obliged then the information he supplied would strongly suggest that the British administration was aware of the impact of the famine, not only at parish level, but as it impacted on townlands in counties such as Leitrim. Yet, it persisted in limiting its actions to expanding public works while allowing thousands to seek refuge in overcrowded and disease-ridden workhouses. While some may argue that it was impossible to do much more in the face of such an overwhelming disaster, the comments of those in the Relief Commission to Loftus Tottenham in April 1846, during which they referred to the crop failure as 'a temporary inconvenience', reflected an underlying philosophy. This blind, rigid, unyielding adherence to the theoretical principles of political economy also maintained that poor rates should be collected in spite of the overwhelming evidence that this would prove almost impossible given the reduced nature of the population, both in terms of numbers and means. Furthermore, it infused the rules and regulations of the Relief Commission and impacted on local aid efforts. For example, members of the Cloone relief committee made known their anxiety about making a contribution to the independent Cloone Soup Shop in case the government would 'curtail their donation to the relief funds'.[35]

In January 1847, Acheson O'Brien, chairman of the Carrigallen relief committee, pointed out that the spread of disease was being exacerbated by lack of clothing for those employed on public works. In his reply, Sir Randolph Routh stated that if the funds of the relief committee were used to purchase bedding then clothing could be claimed but emphasised that 'neither objects are embraced by the instructions'.[36] This mentality was the subject of a stinging editorial in a local paper:

> A Party of English lawyers, merchants, manufacturers and landowners, assemble in a house in London to pass laws for a country of whose requirements they are ignorant; against whose wishes they are prejudiced; and whose prosperity might interfere with their private advantage. They add to their number a few Irishmen, some of whom are without knowledge, others of them without principle, and very few of them represent the feelings, express the wishes, or seek the interest of those whose representatives they are, by a legal quibble, called.
>
> This body of English ignorance and prejudice, supplemented by Irish place-hunting and incapacity, set to work to make laws for Ireland, and what is the result? Look first at the field spread by Providence for the exercise of their legislative abilities – A land of remarkable natural fertility; of broad rivers, wide lakes and capacious harbours; of minerals, coal-fields and peat-tracts; of strong, willing, idle hands, longing for something to do, and ready to go to the ends of the earth in search of where to toil. On this field, and with this material, what see we as the result of what calls itself legislation for Ireland? Oh! What the world scarce ever saw before. Workhouses from which industry is banished, in which old age rots, infancy is dwarfed, and childhood pines away; fruitful fields, deserted, untilled, untenanted; levelled houses, hamlets in which no voice is heard, and districts that are depopulated. The marks of a ruthless invader are on the land – not a foreign enemy – not a killing pestilence – but legislation.[37]

While such an attitude may have permeated the corridors of power those who experienced scenes of hunger and starvation had no doubt as to the extent of the tragedy unfolding before them. As has been noted, the engineers appointed by the Board of Works constantly urged the authorities to establish food depots in various parts of the county while James Cody, the employee of the Royal Agricultural Society, revealed the penury of the population consequent upon successive crop failures. The fact that eye-witnesses were motivated to act is perhaps exemplified by the revelation that three British Army regiments made contributions to local relief funds in Drumshanbo (£5-6-6), Mohill (£10) and Ballinamore (£2-14-3).[38]

Observers and those involved in aid efforts simply reflected what they saw and heard. They did not write with an eye to history or indulge in polemics and their comments leave little doubt as to where the blame lay. For example, in May 1847 Richard Clifford, Vicar of Oughteragh, wrote from Drumdarton in Aughnasheelin to the Society of Friends to complain about the strict parameters of the Temporary Relief Act, commenting 'it is the belief of the people that the government wish to starve them'.[39] Private relief efforts supported thousands outside this particular government measure but if the restrictions imposed under it could be regarded as harsh there is no doubt that those consequent upon the introduction of the Gregory Clause were seen as draconian, cruel and unnecessary and certainly not reflective of a government doing all it could to support starving thousands. It was doubtless after witnessing the effects of such in the Drumsna area that Emma Lawder, one of many women who played a leading role during this period, castigated the policy of the British government as resulting in 'the general extermination of the people'.[40]

This opinion was not that of a social radical or proto Irish nationalist. Her family, beneficiaries of the huge land confiscations of the seventeenth-century, were members of the Protestant Ascendancy, a social and political elite which, although a tiny minority of the population in the county, dominated all aspects of life. Hence, her comments are all the more salient but she was not the only one to share such thoughts and the *Impartial Reporter*, a newspaper very much supportive of the Union with Britain, was scathing in its assessment of the British government's relief efforts.

> A number equal to more than one half of the present inhabitants of Ireland has been swept off in four years; and as the mind wanders from one piled up graveyard to another, and from one desolated district to another, and we ask 'who slew all these?' what answer can be given? They died with plenty of food in the world – with plenty in the land. And what was the government, whose sole legitimate business is to watch over the prosperity of the people – what was

the government doing, while there was food to be had and the people starved? Were they employing that vast navy that wanders round the world, swallowing up the people's money – were they employing it to bring food that the people might live? Were they retrenching the vast expenditure, and sobering down the extravagant pomp of government, that means might be found to sustain life?... Extravagance was as great as ever, vain pomp was as costly as ever, public money was as wildly squandered as ever – while the millions of the people perished.[41]

Such witnesses to the catastrophic events which enveloped the county from 1845–53 had no doubt that the blame for the deaths of tens of thousands of people in Leitrim lay at the hands of the British administration. The consequence of its actions, and inaction, and the hopelessness and despair which followed was evident in the words of a local man when questioned as to the reason for the lack of agricultural activity in the spring of 1851. He answered, 'the people are gone: emigrated, in the poor house, dead…'[42]

# NOTES

## INTRODUCTION

1, 1 See A. T. Lucas, 'Nettles and Charlock as Famine Food' in *Breifne*, no 2, (1959), pp. 137–147; Rev. Terence P. Cunningham, 'The Great Famine in County Cavan' in *Breifne*, no. 8 (1966), pp. 413–438; James Grant, 'Local relief committees in Co. Cavan 1845–47' in *Breifne*, no. 31 (1995), pp. 553–566.

## CHAPTER ONE

1. Gustave De Beaumont, *Ireland: Social, Political, and Religious, with an introduction by Tom Garvin and Andreas Hess, edited and translated by W. C. Taylor* (Harvard University Press, 2006), p.130.
2. National Archives, Department of Education (hereafter, ED 1/49-50), Application of Mohervogue male and female school, March 1832.
3. Ibid., Application of Caraduff School, 19 July 1832.
4. H.C., 1836, volume xxxii, Appendix to First Report of Commissioners for inquiring into the Condition of the Poorer Classes in Ireland (hereafter Poor Enquiry), Appendix E, p.4.
5. Ibid., p.4.
6. Ibid.
7. Ibid.
8. Ibid.
9. Ibid., p.5.
10. Ibid.
11. Ibid.
12. Ibid.
13. Ibid.
14. Ibid.
15. Ibid., p.40.
16. Ibid.
17. Ibid.
18. Ibid., p.69.
19. Ibid.
20. Ibid.
21. Ibid.

22. Ibid., p.70.

23. Ibid., p.69.

24. Ibid., pp.69–70.

25. Ibid., p.70.

26. National Library of Ireland (hereafter, NLI), Leitrim Papers, 3026, Lough Rynn Weekly Return.

27. Poor Enquiry, Appendix E, p.69.

28. Ibid., p.70.

29. Ibid., p.102.

30. Ibid.

31. National Archives, Kew, London, Treasury Papers (Hereafter T), 91/199, A. Hogg, Curate, Cloone Parish to Berry Norris, 24 November 1835.

32. Ibid.

33. Ibid., Clements, Rynn, Mohill, to William Hyett, 12 December 1834.

34. Ibid., Berry Norris to William Hyett, Mohill, 30 November 1835.

35. Ibid., Robert Jones, Manorhamilton, to William Hyett, 30 November 1835.

36. Ibid., Statement of the charitable loans established in the County of Leitrim (1837).

37. Ibid., Richard Clifford, Drumshanbo to Berry Norris, 26 November 1835.

38. Ibid., R. Tate, Manorhamilton to F.R. Bertolacci, 29 October 1835.

39. NLI Ms 3829, Leitrim Papers.

40. Ibid.

41. NLI, p.4065, Lane-Fox Papers, Report on the Dromahaire Estate by David Stewart to John Parkinson, Esq., August 1843.

42. Ibid., Lane-Fox Papers, Report by D. Stewart, 25 June 1831.

43. Ibid., Report on the Dromahaire Estate by David Stewart to John Parkinson, Esq., August 1843. Analysis of available Catholic parish marriage registers illustrates that the majority of unions were conducted prior to Lent which in some cases led to multiple ceremonies on one day. For example, in Killenummery in 1842 there were fourteen marriages on 8 February while in the same month in 1846 there were three days on which four, five and six ceremonies took place. Similarly, in Cloone in 1843 there were four marriages on 27 February and three the following day. On 22 February 1841 there were five marriages in Kiltubrid and the same number in Kinlough on 8 February 1842. This pattern continued after the Famine and on 28 February 1854 there were three marriages in Kinlough. Five days earlier, in Kiltubrid, there had been five marriages and this number was repeated on 19 February 1855. See NLI, Catholic Parish Registers for Killenummery, Cloone, Kiltubrid and Kinlough.

44. NLI, p.4065, Lane-Fox Papers, Report on the Dromahaire Estate by David Stewart to John Parkinson, Esq., August 1843.

45. NLI, p.382a, Lane-Fox Papers, Memoranda as to Mr Fox's Irish Estates, 14 May 1845.

46. NLI, p.4065, Lane-Fox Papers, no date but c. 1833.

47. H.C., 1843, volume xxiv, Census of Ireland for the year 1851, General Table – Summary, pp.502–3.

48. H.C. 1845, volume xxii, Appendix to minutes of evidence taken before commissioners appointed to inquire into the occupation of land in Ireland, pp.274–5.

49. John Tunney, *Leitrim and the Great hunger: Poor Law, Famine and social decline in Co. Leitrim 1831–1851*, pp.10–15, unpublished, 1994.

50. National Archives (hereafter NAI), Outrage Papers, County Leitrim, 25 April 1836

51. Ibid., 12 November 1836.

52. Ibid., 30 September 1836.

53. Ibid., 19 June 1839.

54. Ibid., 19 November 1839.

55. Ibid., 15 October 1838.

56. Ibid., 28 September 1839.

57. Ibid., 29 August 1839.

58. Ibid., 6 March 1838.

59. Ibid., 27 March 1836.

60. Ibid., 6 April 1839.

61. Ibid., 6 June 1839.

62. Ibid., 17 January 1839.

63. Ibid., Kinlough, 13 January 1838.

64. NLI, p.4065, Lane-Fox Papers, Reward Paper, Dromahaire, 2 November 1833.

65. Ibid., Joshua Kell to 'My Dear Brother', 3 November 1833.

66. *Leitrim and Roscommon Gazette*, 19 October 1839.

67. Ibid., 28 January 1832.

68. Ibid., 4 February 1832.

69. Ibid.

70. Ibid., 6 November 1824.

71. Ibid., 4 February 1832.

72. NAI, ED 1/49-50, Application of Cashcarrigan female national school, November 1832.

73. Ibid., Application of Mohill Catholic Free School, 16 September 1832.

74. *Roscommon and Leitrim Gazette*, 29 December 1832.

75. NAI, Outrage Papers, County Leitrim, Andrew Hogg to Dublin Castle, 28 November 1836.

76. *Roscommon and Leitrim Gazette*, 17 December 1836.

77. Ibid., 5 March 1836.

78. Ibid., 30 May 1840.

79. Ibid., 2 May 1840.

80. NAI, Outrage Papers, County Leitrim, G. Montgomery, Inishmagrath Glebe to Major Warburton, 17 January 1836.

81. Ibid., George B. Gale, Drumkeerin, to Revenue Office, 15 January 1836.

82. Ibid., T. Howard, Carrick-on-Shannon, 10 March 1840. See also report of W. Frazer, Head Constable, 28 August 1840.
83. Ibid., John Stuart, Chief Constable, 18 June 1839.
84. Ibid., 10 March 1839.
85. Ibid., 13 June 1837.
86. Ibid., John Stuart, 29 September 1839.
87. Ibid., William Lynam, Mohill, to Under Secretary, Edward Lucas, 31 October 1841.
88. Ibid., 14 February 1836.
89. Ibid., 19 September 1837.
90. Ibid., 22 September 1841.
91. Ibid., 23 August 1838.
92. Ibid., 13 December 1838.
93. *Roscommon and Leitrim Gazette*, 14 January 1832.
94. Ibid., 28 January 1832.
95. NAI, Outrage Papers, County Leitrim, 19 November 1838.
96. Ibid., 26 October 1838.
97. Ibid.
98. Ibid., Nion Tucker, Head Constable, Ballinamore, 3 August 1840.
99. *Roscommon and Leitrim Gazette*, 20 January 1838.
100. Ibid., 12 May 1838.
101. Ibid., 20 January 1838.
102. NAI, Outrage Papers, County Leitrim, 25 October 1840.
103. Ibid.
104. Ibid., 17 March 1837.
105. Ibid., 14 January 1837.
106. Ibid., 24 May 1838.
107. Ibid., 27 November 1839.
108. H.C. 1825, volume viii, Fourth report from select committee on the state of Ireland, p.638.
109. NAI, Outrage Papers, County Leitrim. Reports of John Stuart, Mohill, 7 April 1839; Nion Tucker, Ballinamore, 23 February 1838; P.M. Feely, Kinlough, 9 December 1839; W. Evans, Dromahaire, 17 October 1839 and John Stuart, Carrick-on-Shannon, 16 June 1840.
110. Ibid., 5 September 1836.
111. Ibid., 4 November 1836.
112. *Roscommon and Leitrim Gazette*, 5 March 1836.
113. Ibid.
114. NAI, Outrage Papers, County Leitrim, 18 July 1837.
115. Ibid., 26 June 1841.
116. Ibid., 9 July 1838.
117. Ibid., T.D. Fitzgerald, Chief Constable, Dromahaire, 26 July 1839.
118. Ibid., William Meredith, Ballinamore, 18 February 1840.
119. Ibid. According to the 1841 census there were sixty-three musicians in the county of whom three were women. See H.C., 1843, volume xxiv, 1841

Census of Ireland, Table of occupations of persons above and under fifteen years of age, p.506.

# CHAPTER TWO

1. Church of Ireland Glebe House, Mohill, County Leitrim, Mohill Vestry Minute Book, 6 July 1763 and 25 March 1788.
2. Ibid., Cloone Vestry Minute Book, 27 March 1780.
3. Ibid., 3 May 1831.
4. Ibid., 1 April and 22 April 1834.
5. Ibid.
6. Ibid., 12 April 1841 and 12 April 1842.
7. *Roscommon and Leitrim Gazette*, 16 December 1837.
8. Hansard, House of Commons Debates, May 1837, vol. 38, col. 429.
9. *Roscommon and Leitrim Gazette*, 5 May 1838.
10. Ibid., 21 April 1838.
11. Ibid., 28 April 1838.
12. Ibid.
13. Ibid.
14. Ibid.
15. Ibid.
16. Ibid.
17. Ibid.
18. Ibid.
19. Ibid.
20. Ibid., 2 June 1838.
21. Ibid., 21 July 1838.
22. Ibid., 8 June 1839.
23. Ibid., 22 June 1839.
24. Ibid., 3 August 1839.
25. Ibid., 22 June 1839.
26. Ibid.
27. Ibid., 13 July 1839.
28. Ibid., 22 June 1839.
29. Ibid., 29 June 1839.
30. Ibid., 3 August 1839.
31. Ibid., 22 June 1839.
32. National Archives, Dublin (hereafter NAI), Outrage Papers, County Leitrim, 5 June 1839.
33. Ibid.
34. *Roscommon and Leitrim Gazette*, 29 June 1839.
35. NAI, Outrage Papers, County Leitrim, 9 June 1839.
36. *Roscommon and Leitrim Gazette*, 29 June 1839.
37. NAI, Outrage Papers, County Leitrim, 13 June 1839.

38. Ibid., 11 July 1839.
39. Ibid., 25 June 1839.
40. *Roscommon and Leitrim Gazette*, 17 August 1839.
41. John Robert Godley, *A letter on the subject of poor rates addressed to the landholders of the County of Leitrim* (Dublin, 1843).
42. Ibid.
43. Ibid.
44. National Library of Ireland, p.4065, Report on the Dromahaire Estate by David Stewart to John Parkinson, Esq., August 1843.
45. *Roscommon and Leitrim Gazette*, 20 July 1839.
46. National Archives, Kew, London, Home Office Papers, 100/258.
47. *Roscommon and Leitrim Gazette*, 14 September 1839.
48. Ibid.
49. Ibid., 28 September 1839.
50. Ibid.
51. Ibid.
52. Ibid.
53. Ibid., 5 October 1839.
54. Ibid., 21 December 1839.
55. Ibid., 26 October 1839.
56. Ibid., 28 September 1839.
57. Ibid., 5 October 1839.
58. NAI, Outrage Papers, County Leitrim, 28 September 1839.
59. Ibid., 11 July 1840.
60. *Roscommon and Leitrim Gazette*, 8 August 1840.
61. Ibid.
62. Ibid., 11 July 1840.
63. Ibid.
64. Ibid., 3 April 1841.
65. Ibid., 7 August 1841.
66. Ibid., 20 March 1841.
67. Ibid., 18 June 1842.
68. Leitrim County Library, Ballinamore (hereafter LCL), Manorhamilton board of guardians' rough minute book, BG 117/A/1, p.1.
69. Ibid., p.17.
70. Ibid., 7 June 1841, p.38.
71. Ibid., 17 June 1841, p.40.
72. Ibid., 11 April 1842, p.57 and 6 June 1842, p.59.
73. Ibid., 6 June 1842, p.60.
74. Ibid., 20 June 1842, p.61 and 4 July 1842, p.64.
75. Ibid., 18 August 1842, p.69.
76. Ibid., 1 September 1842, p.79.
77. Ibid., 18 May 1843, p.168.
78. Ibid., p.173, p.181 and p.184.

79. Ibid., 11 May 1843, p.163.
80. Ibid., pp.152, 161, 171, 175, 180, 186, 190, 193, 198, 201, 203, 206, 211, 215, 218, 222, 224, 233, 237, 241, 244, 247, 251, 255, 260, 268, 273, 276, 280, 283, 288.
81. Ibid., p.63, p.209, p.231 p.241.
82. Ibid., 26 October 1843, p.253.
83. Ibid., 2 November 1843, p.257.
84. Ibid., 28 September 1843, p.239.
85. Ibid., 16 February 1843, p.124.
86. Ibid., 17 August 1843, p.219; 21 September 1843, p.234; 2 November 1843, p.256 and 23 November 1843, p.269.
87. Ibid., 7 December 1843, p.278.
88. Ibid., 9 November 1843, p.262.
89. Ibid., 1 February 1844, p.309.
90. Ibid., 14 March 1844, p.330.
91. Ibid., 21 December 1843, p.285.
92. Ibid., 5 January 1844, p.305.
93. Ibid., 1 March 1844, p.335.
94. Ibid., 21 December 1843, p.287.
95. Ibid., 14 July 1844, p.402.
96. BG 117/AA/2, 15 August 1844, p.4.
97. Ibid., 12 September 1844.
98. Ibid., 31 October, 7 November, 14 November, 21 November, 28 November, 5 December, 12 December and 26 December 1844.
99. Ibid., 28 November 1844 and 19 December 1844.
100. Ibid., 2 January 1845.
101. Ibid., 9 January 1845.
102. Ibid., 20 March 1845.
103. Ibid., 15 May 1845.
104. Ibid., 24 April 1845 and 1 May 1845.
105. Ibid., 29 May 1845.
106. Ibid., 19 June 1845.
107. Ibid., 26 June 1845.
108. LCL, Mohill board of guardians' minute book, BG 122/A/1, 11 October 1839, p.3 and 12 March 1840, p.15.
109. Ibid., 26 January 1843, p.200.
110. Ibid., July 1840, p.249.
111. Ibid., pp.103–4.
112. *Roscommon and Leitrim Gazette*, 19 October 1839.
113. LCL, Mohill board of guardians' minute book BG 122/A/1, 12 March 1842, p.110.
114. Ibid., 28 March 1842, p.117.
115. Ibid., 25 May 1842, p.139.
116. *Roscommon and Leitrim Gazette*, 2 April 1842.

117. LCL, Mohill board of guardians' minute book BG 122/A/1, 15 June 1842, p.147 and 22 June 1842, p.149.
118. Ibid., 22 June 1842, p.151.
119. Ibid., 6 July 1842, p.155.
120. Ibid., 20 July 1842, p.163 and 27 July 1842, p.165.
121. *Roscommon and Leitrim Gazette*, 9 July 1842.
122. Ibid., 2 July 1842.
123. LCL, Mohill board of guardians' minute book, BG 122/A/1, 3 August 1842, p.170 and 4 August 1842, pp.175–6.
124. Ibid., 1 September 1842, p.191 and 8 September 1842, p.194.
125. Ibid., 15 September 1842, p.197and 19 September 1842, p.204.
126. Ibid., 6 October 1842, p.116.
127. Ibid., 8 October 1842, p.120.
128. Ibid., 20 October 1842, p.141 and 3 November 1842, p.144.
129. Ibid., pp.160, 163, 167, 179.
130. Ibid., 9 February 1843, p.268.
131. Ibid., 16 February 1843, p.273.
132. Ibid.
133. Ibid., 2 March 1843, p.280.
134. Ibid., 16 March 1843, p.288.
135. Ibid., 9 March 1843, p.284.
136. Ibid., 20 April 1843, p.310 and 4 May 1843, p.315.
137. *Roscommon and Leitrim Gazette*, 4 June 1842.
138. Ibid., 2 July 1842.
139. Ibid., 9 July 1842.
140. Ibid.
141. Ibid.
142. Ibid., 17 December 1842.
143. LCL, Mohill board of guardians' minute book BG 122/A/1, 13 April 1843, p.305.
144. Ibid.
145. Ibid., 25 May 1843 pp.335–6; 8 June, p.347 and 15 June 1843, p.347.
146. Ibid., BG 122/A/3 12 October 1843, p.747.
147. Ibid., pp.758, 787, 794.
148. Ibid., 11 January 1844, pp.809–810.
149. Ibid., 11 January 1844, p.807, 15 February, p.836, 22 February, p.841, 21 March, p.855, 11 April, p.874, 25 April, p.880, 16 May, p.890, 23 May, p.893 and 9 May, p.885.
150. Ibid., p.897.
151. Ibid., 6 June 1844, p.905.
152. Ibid., 30 May, p.898 and 6 June, p.903.
153. Ibid., 20 June 1844, p.911.
154. Ibid., 4 July, p.919, 932.
155. Ibid., pp.914, 923, 947.

156. Ibid., p.777.
157. Ibid., 25 March 1844, p.863.
158. Ibid., p.787.
159. Ibid., pp.791, 805, 812.
160. Ibid., pp.789, 816.
161. Ibid., pp.816–17.
162. Ibid., 26 December 1844, p.822.
163. Ibid., pp.827, 837, 838, 839, 846, 839.
164. Ibid., BG 122/A/4, pp.2, 14, 19, 45, 52.
165. Ibid., pp.26, 41, 43–4, 57.
166. Ibid., p.45.
167. Ibid., 5 June 1845, p.57 and 26 June 1845, p.64.
168. Ibid., pp.67–8, 76.
169. Ibid., 7 August 1845, p.92 and 18 September 1845, p.120.
170. Ibid., 10 July, p.70 and 4 September, p.105.
171. Ibid., 14 August, p.97.
172. *Roscommon and Leitrim Gazette*, 5 October 1839.
173. LCL, Carrick-on-Shannon board of guardians' minute book, BG 52/A/1, 6 July 1843, p.420.
174. *Roscommon and Leitrim Gazette*, 11 February 1840.
175. LCL, Carrick-on-Shannon board of guardians' minute book, BG 52/A/1, 15 June 1843, p.396 and 22 June 1843, pp.407–8.
176. Ibid., 6 July 1843, p.416.
177. Ibid., 22 June 1843, pp.408–9.
178. Ibid., 6 July 1843, p.420.
179. Ibid., p.429.
180. Ibid., 27 July 1843, pp.436–8 and 10 August 1843, pp.443–4.
181. Ibid., 10 August 1843, p.445; pp.447–8 and 24 August 1843, pp.468–9.
182. Ibid., 31 August 1843, p.464.
183. Ibid., 7 September 1843, pp.469–70.
184. Ibid., 21 September 1843, pp.481–2 and 19 October 1843, p507.
185. Ibid., 9 November 1843, p.531.
186. Ibid., p.529.
187. Ibid., 16 November 1843, p.537.
188. Ibid., p.536.
189. Ibid., 23 November 1843, p.542.
190. Ibid., 30 November 1843, p.550.
191. Ibid., p.551.
192. Ibid., pp.536, 549, 558, 563.
193. Ibid., 30 November 1843, p.551 and 14 December 1843, p.565.
194. Ibid., 28 December 1843, p.578.
195. Ibid., 14 December 1843, pp.565–6.
196. Ibid., 21 December 1843, p.571 and 11 April 1844, p.682.
197. Ibid., 25 January 1844, p.602.

198. Ibid., 1 February 1844, p.605.
199. Ibid., 15 February 1844, p.623.
200. Ibid., 7 March 1844, p.636.
201. Ibid., 14 March 1844, p.644.
202. Ibid., p.646.
203. Ibid., 21 March 1844, p.655.
204. Ibid., 28 March 1844, p.663.
205. Ibid., pp.666–7.
206. Ibid., 11 April 1844, pp.683–4.
207. Ibid., 21 March 1844, pp.657–8.
208. Ibid., 18 April 1844, p.690.
209. Ibid., p.691 and 2 May 1844, p.704.
210. Ibid., 8 June 1844, p.742 and pp.744–5.
211. Ibid., 15 June 1844, p.754.
212. Ibid., 9 May 1844, p.712 and 15 June 1844, pp.754–5.
213. Ibid., 29 June 1844, p.769.
214. Ibid., 13 July 1844, p.783.
215. Ibid., p.802.
216. BG 52/A/2, 24 August 1844, p.819.
217. Ibid., pp.757, 765, 772 and 28 September, p.852.
218. Ibid., 12 October 1844, p.868.
219. Ibid., 19 October 1844, p.872.
220. Ibid., 23 November 1844, p.910.
221. Ibid., 7 December 1844, p.925.
222. Ibid., 21 December 1844, p.940.
223. Ibid., 16 November 1844, pp. 899 and 903.
224. Ibid., pp. 916, 924, 934, 940 and 947.
225. Ibid., 21 December, p.947.
226. Ibid., 18 January 1845, p.965; 1 February 1845, p.979; 8 March 1845, p.1001; 14 June 1845, p.1100 and 25 October 1845, p.1223.
227. Ibid., 5 July 1845, p.1120 and 26 July 1845, p.1135.
228. Ibid., 4 January 1845, p.952; 1 February 1845, p.974; 3 May 1845 p.1045; 12 July 1845, p.1123; 2 August 1845, p.1139; 8 November 1845, p.1233 and 20 December 1845, p.1269.
229. Ibid., p.1023.
230. Ibid., p.1079.
231. Ibid., 31 May 1845, p.1086.
232. Ibid., 27 September 1845, p.1191 and 4 October 1845, p.1199.
233. Ibid., 26 July 1845, p.1136.
234. Ibid., July 1845, p.1136 and 16 August 1845, p.1149.
235. Ibid., 22 March, p.1020 and 10 May 1845, p.1059.
236. Ibid., 17 May 1845, p.1069–70.
237. Ibid., 24 May 1845, p.1078.
238. Ibid., 20 September 1845, p.1184.

239. Ibid., 4 October 1845, p.1197.
240. Ibid., 18 October 1845, pp.1213–14.
241. Ibid., 29 November 1845, p.1253.
242. Ibid., 27 December 1845, p.1276.

## CHAPTER THREE

1. *Roscommon and Leitrim Gazette,* 20 September 1845 and 27 September 1845.
2. Ibid., 27 September 1845.
3. Ibid., 25 October 1845.
4. National Archives Dublin (hereafter NAI), Relief Commission Papers (hereafter RLFC), 2/Z 14820, John Veevers to Richard Pennefather, 31 October 1845.
5. Ibid., RLFC 2/Z 14820, William Wray, Mohill, to Inspector General of Constabulary, 23 November 1845.
6. Ibid., RLFC 2/Z 16840, Denis Booth to Commission, 29 November 1845.
7. National Library of Ireland, p.4065 Lane-Fox Papers, Joshua Kell to George Lane-Fox, 12 December 1845.
8. HC 1846, volume xxxvii, correspondence explanatory of the measures adopted by her majesty's government for the Relief of Distress arising from the failure of the potato crop in Ireland, p.88.
9. Leitrim County Library, Ballinamore (hereafter LCL), Manorhamilton board of guardians rough minute book, BG 117/AA/2, 9 October 1845 and 13 November 1845.
10. LCL, Mohill board of guardians' minute book, BG 122/A/4, 6 November 1845 p.148;Carrick-on-Shannon board of guardians' minute book, BG 52/A/3, 15 November 1845, p.1239.
11. Ibid., Manorhamilton board of guardians' minute book, BG 117/AA/2, 4 December 1845.
12. Ibid., Mohill board of guardians' minute book, BG 122/A/4, 6 November 1845, pp.147–8. Carrick-on-Shannon board of guardians' minute book, BG 52/A/3, 15 November 1845, p.1239.
13. Carrick-on-Shannon board of guardians' minute book, BG 52/A/3, 27 December 1845, p.1278.
14. HC 1846, volume xxxvii, correspondence explanatory of the measures adopted by her majesty's government for the Relief of Distress arising from the failure of the potato crop in Ireland, p.492.
15. NAI, RLFC 3/1/2639, William Peyton to W. Stanley, 28 May 1846.
16. LCL, Mohill board of guardians' minute book, BG/122/A/4, pp.222–3.
17. Ibid., p.102, p.121; 13 November pp.149, 168.
18. Ibid., pp.110, 121, 127, 154, 164.
19. Ibid., p.163.

20. Ibid., 1 January 1846, p.170; 15 January 1846, p.181; 22 January 1846, p.190 and 22 January 1846, p.191.
21. Ibid., 5 February 1846, p.197.
22. Ibid., pp.192, 208, 209.
23. Ibid., p.206.
24. Ibid., p.221.
25. Ibid., pp.228, 235.
26. Ibid., Carrick-on-Shannon board of guardians' minute book, BG 52/A/3, 3 January 1846, p.1286.
27. Ibid., 17 January 1846, p.1298.
28. Ibid., 24 January 1846, p.1303 and 31 January 1846, p.1309.
29. Ibid., 14 February 1846, p.1327.
30. Ibid., p.1306 and 21 March 1846, p.1351.
31. Ibid., 25 May 1845, pp.1077, 1102.
32. Ibid., 21 March 1846, p.1353.
33. Ibid., 2 May 1846, p.1396.
34. Ibid., 28 March 1846, p.1356.
35. Ibid., p.1424.
36. Ibid., 13 June 1846, p.1431, 20 June 1846, p.1438 and 20 June 1846, p.1441.
37. Ibid., 8 August 1846, p.1470.
38. Ibid., 22 August 1846, p.1485.
39. HC 1846, volume xxxvii, correspondence explanatory of the measures adopted by her majesty's government for the Relief of Distress arising from the failure of the potato crop in Ireland, p.278.
40. Leitrim County Library, Ballinamore, Manorhamilton board of guardians' minute book, BG 117/AA/2, 12 February 1846.
41. Ibid., 4 December 1845, 26 March 1846 and 2 April 1846.
42. Ibid., 14 May 1846.
43. Ibid., 2 April 1846 and 7 May 1846.
44. Ibid., 14 May, 4 June, 25 June, 9 July, 30 July, 6 August and 20 August 1845.
45. Ibid., 9 April 1846, 23 April 1846, 23 July 1846 and 20 August 1846.
46. NAI, RLFC 3/1/873, Clements to Commissioners, 22 March 1846.
47. Ibid., RLFC 3/1/1407, Clements to Commissioners, 11 April 1846.
48. Ibid., RLFC 3/2/16/5.
49. Ibid., RLFC 3/1/1658, James Franks to Commissioners, 21 April 1846.
50. Ibid., RLFC 3/2/16/9, Montgomery to the Under Secretary, Castle, Dublin, 16 July 1846.
51. Ibid., RLFC 3/2/16/2, George M. Beresford and Rev. T. Maguire to Richard Pennefather, 31 May 1846.
52. Ibid., RLFC 3/2/16/2, Reply to George M. Beresford and Rev. T. Maguire, 25 June 1846.
53. HC 1846, volume xxxvii, correspondence explanatory of the measures adopted by her majesty's government for the Relief of Distress arising from the failure of the potato crop in Ireland, p.235.

54. Ibid., pp.236, 238, 240, 241, 242.
55. Ibid., pp.247–8.
56. Ibid., p.203.
57. Reprinted British Parliamentary Papers, volume 5, correspondence explanatory of the measures adopted by her majesty's government for the relief of distress arising from the potato crop in Ireland with similar correspondence commissariat [first part] and an index, 1846–47, pp.338, 354.
58. HC 1846, volume xxxvii, correspondence explanatory of the measures adopted by her majesty's government for the Relief of Distress arising from the failure of the potato crop in Ireland, pp.400–402.
59. Ibid., pp.401, 407.
60. Ibid., p.407.
61. Ibid.
62. Ibid., p.359.
63. NAI, RLFC 3/1/5248, Fr Felix MacHugh to W. Stanley, 7 August 1846.

## CHAPTER FOUR

1. Royal Irish Academy, Windele Mss 4/B/6/85 (i) William Forde to John Windele, 21 September 1846. One historian has commented that: 'Hugh O'Beirne was a professional fiddler who lived at Costrea, in the parish of Fenagh, near Ballinamore. Forde had the good fortune to meet him when he was in the locality in September and October 1846 and took down literally scores of Irish tunes from him. O'Beirne was a musician of quite exceptional taste and ability, and he was the largest single contributor to what Pigot calls the "splendid store" garnered by Forde on this tour.' See Donal O'Sullivan, *Carolan – The Life, Times and Music of an Irish Harper*, Celtic Music, 1958, p 139. I am grateful to Mary Conefrey, Leitrim County Library, for this reference.
2. Ibid, William Forde to John Windele, 12 October 1846.
3. National Archives, Dublin (hereafter NAI), Relief Commission Papers (hereafter RLFC), 5/16/01 Report of Denis Burke, 23 August 1846 and RLFC 5/16/02, report of T. Moreton, 30 August 1846.
4. Ibid., 5/16/07, report of W.F. Coghlan, 26 August 1846.
5. Ibid., 5/16/04, report of J.H. Bracken, 25 August 1846; RLFC 5/16/05, report of John Brown, 28 August 1846 and RLFC 5/16/08, report of William Wray, 22 August 1846.
6. Ibid., 5/16/03, report of W. Evans, 25 August 1846.
7. Ibid., 5/16/06, report of W. Evans, 23 August 1846.
8. Reprinted British Parliamentary Papers (hereafter BPP), volume 5, correspondence from July 1846 to January 1847 relating to the relief of the distress in Ireland, Commissariat, p.57.

9. BPP volume 6, correspondence from July 1846 to January 1847 relating to the measures adopted for the relief of distress in Ireland, Board of Works series, p.166.

10. Ibid., p.178.

11. Ibid., pp.186, 418.

12. Ibid., pp.175, 446.

13. Ibid., p.205.

14. Ibid., pp.276, 283.

15. Ibid., pp.318, 382.

16. Ibid., p.318.

17. BPP volume 7, correspondence from January to March 1847 relating to the measures adopted for the relief of the distress in Ireland, Board of Works series [second part], p.119.

18. BPP volume 6, correspondence from July 1846 to January 1847 relating to the measures adopted for the relief of distress in Ireland, Board of Works series, p.382.

19. Ibid., p.389.

20. Ibid., p.419.

21. Ibid. Rev. W.A. Percy, Rector of Kiltoghert, lived at Drumliffin Glebe and in 1852 suffered a personal tragedy. On 6 May he was hosting a party in his house to celebrate the birth of a child to the wife of Francis Tottenham of Keonbrook. At some stage during the day his young son, Digby, obtained a gun and accidentally shot and killed himself. Local tradition maintained that the door to the room in which the fatal accident took place was never again opened. See *Leitrim Journal*, 6 May 1852.

22. BPP volume 6, correspondence from July 1846 to January 1847 relating to the measures adopted for the relief of distress in Ireland, Board of Works series, p.164.

23. Ibid., p.445.

24. BPP volume 7, correspondence from January to March 1847 relating to the measures adopted for the relief of the distress in Ireland, Board of Works series [second part], pp.119–120.

25. Ibid., p.120.

26. Ibid., p.271.

27. Ibid., p.120.

28. NAI, Society of Friends Relief of Distress Papers (hereafter SOF), 2/506/37, form 26, 2 January 1847.

29. Ibid., 2/506/37, Form 16, 5 January 1847.

30. *Roscommon and Leitrim Gazette*, 26 September 1846 and 31 October 1846.

31. NAI, RLFC, 3/1/5237, Henry O'Brien, Carrigallen to Sir Randolph Routh, 7 August 1846; National Library of Ireland, Leitrim Papers, 3027.

32. Leitrim County Library, Ballinamore (hereafter LCL), Manorhamilton board of guardians' minute book, BG 117/AA/3, 22 October – 31 December 1846.

33. Ibid., 12 November 1846, 18 February 1847 and 25 February 1847.

34. Ibid., 21 January 1847.

35. Ibid., 19 November 1846.

36. Ibid., 24 December 1846.

37. Ibid., 28 January 1847, 4 February 1847, 18 March 1847, 6 May 1847 and 27 May 1847.

38. Ibid., 12 November 1847, 3 December 1847 and 24 December 1847.

39. Ibid., 3 December 1846.

40. Ibid., 22 April 1847, 13 May 1847 and 29 April 1847.

41. Ibid., 2 September 1847.

42. Ibid., 9 September 1847.

43. Leitrim County Library, Ballinamore, Mohill board of guardians' minute book, BG 122/A/4, p.259.

44. Ibid., p.261.

45. Ibid., 28 May, p.267 and 4 June, p.268.

46. Ibid., 25 June, p.279, 2 July, p.281, 9 July, p.281, 16 July, p.282, 23 July, p.283, 13 August, p.295, September, p.307, 10 September, p.308 and 24 September, p.314.

47. Ibid., 18 June, p.274, 30 July, p.284, 6 August, p.291, 20 August, p.296 and 30 July, pp.284–5.

48. Ibid., 30 July 1846, p.289.

49. Ibid., 20 August 1846, p.300.

50. Ibid., 8 October 1846, p.325.

51. Ibid., 24 September 1846, p.309 and 8 October 1846, p.326.

52. Ibid., 8 October 1846, pp.326–7.

53. Ibid., pp.307, 315, 333, 349, 360, 365.

54. Ibid., pp.333, 368.

55. Ibid., p.371.

56. Ibid., pp.393, 406.

57. Ibid., 2 January 1847, p.395.

58. Ibid., pp.395, 396, 403, 408, 411, 415.

59. Ibid, pp.430, 432.

60. Ibid., p.435.

61. Ibid., p.437 and 18 March 1847, p.440.

62. Ibid., p.443.

63. Ibid., 25 March 1847, p.442.

64. LCL, Mohill board of guardians' minute book, BG 122/A/5, 15 April 1847, pp.6, 9.

65. Ibid., pp.5, 9.

66. Ibid., pp.21, 26, 31.

67. Ibid., pp.34, 41.

68. Ibid., pp.56, 61, 66, 71, 76, 81, 86, 91, 96.

69. Ibid., 1 April 1847, pp.2–3.

70. Ibid., 5 August 1847, p.79.

71. Ibid., pp.5, 15, 55, 66.
72. Ibid., 29 April 1847, p.11 and 6 May 1847, p.17.
73. Ibid., p.21 and 15 May 1847, p.26.
74. Ibid., 29 April 1847, pp.13, 24.
75. LCL, Carrick-on-Shannon board of guardians' minute book, BG 52/A/3, 22 August 1846, p.1487.
76. Ibid., 22 August 1846, p.1487, 5 September 1846, pp.1497, 1499.
77. Ibid., 12 September 1846, p.1505.
78. Ibid., 19 September 1846, p.1511.
79. Ibid., p.1514.
80. Ibid.
81. Ibid., 17 October 1846, p.1542.
82. Ibid., 3 October 1846, p.1530.
83. Ibid., 10 October 1846, p.1536.
84. Ibid., 19 September 1846, p.1512.
85. Ibid., 10 October 1846, p.1536.
86. Ibid., 24 October 1846, p.1551.
87. Ibid., 17 October 1846, p.1544.
88. Ibid., 24 October 1846, p.1552.
89. Ibid., p.1553 and 31 October 1846, p.1559.
90. Ibid., 7 November 1846, p.1565.
91. Ibid.
92. Ibid., 11 November 1846, p.1572.
93. Ibid., 21 November 1846, p.1575 and 28 November 1846, p.1588.
94. Ibid., 11 November 1846, p.1580.
95. Ibid., 28 November 1846, p.1589.
96. Ibid., 5 December 1846, pp.1593, 1597, 11 November 1846, p.1572, 21 November 1846, p.1581 and 19 December 1846, p.1612.
97. Ibid., 12 December 1846, pp.1603–4.
98. Ibid., p.1604.
99. Ibid., 2 January 1847, pp.1621–2.
100. Ibid., BG 52/A/4, 6 February 1847, p.1.
101. Ibid., 30 January, p.1651 and 13 February, p.17.
102. Ibid., pp.32, 38 and 6 March 1847, p 48.
103. Ibid., 27 March 1847, pp.71, 77.
104. Ibid., p.71.
105. Ibid., 10 April 1847, p.91.
106. Ibid., p.18.
107. Ibid., 20 February 1847, pp.29–30.
108. Ibid., 13 February 1847, pp.11, 18.
109. Ibid., p.38.
110. Ibid., 19 June 1847, p.203.
111. Ibid., 27 February 1847, p.38, 27 March 1847, p.77 and 3 April, 1847, p.88.
112. Ibid., 10 April, 1847, pp.98–9.

113. Ibid., 17 April 1847, p.108.
114. Ibid., p.110.
115. Ibid., 17 April 1847, p.110.
116. Ibid., 24 April 1847, p.122 and 1 May 1847, p.132.
117. BG 52/A/3, 4 October 1846, p.1548 and 23 January 1847, p.1639.
118. Ibid., p.1650.
119. BG 52/A/4, p.76.
120. Ibid., p.88.
121. Ibid., p.89.
122. Ibid.
123. Ibid., 10 April pp.96, 98.
124. Ibid., 17 April 1847, pp.109–10 and 19 June 1847, p.201.
125. Ibid., 17 April 1847, p.107.
126. Ibid., 24 April, p.122 and 1 May 1847, p.130.
127. Ibid., 8 May 1847, p.143.
128. Ibid., 22 May 1847, p.162 and 5 June 1847, p.182.
129. Ibid., 5 June 1847, p.184.
130. Ibid., 12 June 1847, p.190.
131. Ibid., 3 April 1847, p.81.
132. Ibid., pp.225, 235, 245, 255, 263, 273, 283, 293, 303, 313, 323, 337.
133. Ibid., 3 July 1847, pp.222–3.
134. Ibid., 10 July 1847, pp.230–3.
135. Ibid., p.333.
136. Ibid.
137. Ibid., 3 July 1847, p.222.
138. Ibid., 17 July 1847, p.242.
139. Ibid., 31 July 1847, p.261.
140. Ibid., p.255.
141. Ibid., 7 August 1847, p.263.
142. Ibid., p.271, 14 August 1847, p.279, 21 August 1847, p.291.
143. NAI, RLFC 3/2/16/26, Andrew Hogg to Sir Randolph Routh, 4 February 1847 and 13 February 1847.
144. Ibid., 3/2/15/16, George Shaw to Sir Randolph Routh, 23 February 1847.
145. Ibid., 3/2/16/12, N.L. Tottenham, Manorhamilton, to Sir Randolph Routh, 25 September 1846.
146. Ibid., 3/2/16/12, Reply to above, 26 September 1846.
147. Ibid., 3/2/16/5, Father Henry O'Brien to William Stanley, 12 March 1847.
148. Ibid., 3/2/16/19, Arthur Birchill to W. Stanley, 9 November 1846.
149. Ibid., 3/2/16/21, George Beresford to William Stanley, 17 April 1847 and 3/2/16/35, John Dickson, Kinlough, Ballyshannon to Sir Randolph Routh, 26 April 1847.
150. National Archives, Kew, Treasury Papers, 91/199, George Shaw to F.R. Bertolacci, 24 March 1846.

151. Royal Irish Academy (hereafter RIA), Irish Relief Association (hereafter IRA) File 24 Q 27, form 34, 30 November 1846.
152. Ibid., File 24 Q 27, form 24, 4 December 1846.
153. NAI, RLFC 3/2/16/26, Andrew Hogg to Sir Randolph Routh, 10 December 1846.
154. *Roscommon and Leitrim Gazette*, 14 November 1846.
155. RIA, IRA, File 24 Q 27, form 178, 26 December 1846.
156. Ibid., File 24 Q 27, form 191, 30 December 1846.
157. NAI, RLFC 2/1/11818, Pat Browne to Colonel Duncan McGregor, 22 February 1847.
158. BPP volume 7, correspondence from January to March 1847 relating to the measures adopted for the relief of the distress in Ireland, Board of Works series [second part], p.85.
159. Ibid., p.270.
160. *Transactions of the Central Relief Committee of the Society of Friends during the Famine in Ireland in 1846 and 1847, with an index by Rob Goodbody*, de Búrca, 1996, pp.145–6.
161. Ibid., p.146.

## CHAPTER FIVE

1. Reprinted British Parliamentary Papers (hereafter BPP), volume 7, correspondence from January to March 1847 relating to the measures adopted for the relief of the distress in Ireland, Board of Works series [second part], p.211.
2. National Archives, Dublin (hereafter NAI), Society of Friends Relief of Distress Papers (hereafter SOF), box 2/506/37, form 2, George Shaw, 30 December 1846.
3. Royal Irish Academy (hereafter RIA), Irish Relief Association (hereafter IRA), 24 Q 27, form 228, John Lawder and Francis Reynolds PP, 5 January 1847.
4. NAI, SOF box 2/506/37, form 26, 2 January 1847.
5. Ibid., form 16, 5 January 1847.
6. RIA, IRA, 24 Q 27, form 220, Rev James La Touche, 5 January 1847.
7. NAI, SOF box 2/506/37, form 71, Penelope Johnston, 12 January 1847.
8. Ibid., form 54, Clements, Hyde and Veevers, Mohill, 15 January 1847.
9. Ibid., 2/506/19, Arthur Hyde, Mohill, 21 January 1847.
10. Ibid., 2/506/37, form 54, Clements, Hyde and Veevers, Mohill, 15 January 1847.
11. Ibid., W. Percy, Thomas Rutherford and Thomas Fitzgerald, Carrick-on-Shannon, 15 January 1847.
12. RIA, IRA 24 Q 28, form 371, Archdeacon John Strean, Killucan, Elphin, 23 January 1847.
13. Ibid., form 446, Francis Nesbitt and Francis Kane, Dromod, 30 January 1847.

14. Ibid., 24 Q 29, form 633, John Hudson, Glenlough Parish, 8 February 1847.
15. NAI, SOF box 2/506/37, form 182, W. Percy, Ballinamore, 2 February 1847.
16. Ibid., 2/506/19, Connolly, Crieve to Committee, 2 February 1847.
17. Ibid., 2/506/37, form 217, Robert King, Kilmore, 6 February 1847.
18. Ibid., form 217, Robert King, Kilmore, 6 February 1847.
19. Ibid., form 304, William Noble, Drumshanbo, 16 February 1847.
20. RIA, IRA 24 Q 28, form 486, H. Heslin, W.C. Peyton and B. McKeon, Drumshanbo, 9 February 1847.
21. Ibid., 24 Q 29, form 693, Rev J.H. Hoope, Mohill, 12 February 1847.
22. NAI, SOF box 2/506/37, form 371, James A. Thompson Aughey, 22 February 1847.
23. Ibid., form 370, Francis Kane, Drumsna, 24 February 1847.
24. RIA, IRA 24 Q 29, form 838, J.M. Kirkwood, Woodbrook Lodge, Tumna Carrick-on-Shannon, 24 February 1847. An interesting perspective on mid-nineteenth century Irish society was offered by Kirkwood's comment that she did not wish to have her application made known because, 'as a female, I should rather not have my name made public'.
25. NAI, SOF box 2/506/37, form 379, Cairncross Thomas Cullen, Glenade, Manorhamilton, 25 February 1847.
26. Ibid.
27. Ibid.
28. Ibid., form 392, James McGauran PP, Killasnet, Lurganboy, Manorhamilton, 26 February 1847.
29. Ibid., form 393, William Whyte, Dromahaire, 27 February 1847.
30. Ibid., form 160, Nicholas Loftus Tottenham, Glenfarne Hall, Manorhamilton, 30 January 1847.
31. Ibid., form 418, George D Mansfield, Kiltubrid, Cashcarrigan, 2 March 1847.
32. RIA, IRA 24 Q 31, form no. 24, Rev Andrew Hogg, Cloone, 15 March 1847.
33. Ibid., 24 Q 29, form no. 850, Rev William W. Wynne, 16 March 1847.
34. NAI, SOF box 2/506/19, Henry Irwin, Eastersnow, 27 March 1847.
35. Ibid., 2/506/37, no. 563 Marianne Cullen, Corry, Drumkeerin, 29 March 1847.
36. BPP, volume 7, correspondence from January to March 1847 relating to the measures adopted for the relief of the distress in Ireland, Board of Works series [second part], p.211.
37. NAI, SOF box 2/506/37, form 561, John Hudson, Glenlough, Sligo, 8 March 1847.
38. Ibid., Letter enclosed to committee from Nicholas Tottenham, Glenfarne Hall, 30 March 1847.
39. Ibid., 2/506/19, George Shaw, Annaduff, 9 March 1847.
40. Ibid., George Shaw, Annaduff, 29 March 1847.

41. RIA, IRA 24 Q 31, form 178, Rev John Richardson, Drumkeerin, 1 April 1847.
42. NAI, SOF box 2/506/19, George D. Mansfield, Kiltubrid, 3 April 1847.
43. RIA, IRA 24 Q 30, form 929, Nicholas Tottenham, Manorhamilton, 3 April 1847.
44. NAI, SOF box 2/506/37, B130, William Noble, Prospect, Drumshanbo, 22 April 1847.
45. Ibid., B345 John R. Dickson, Woodville, Bundoran, 6 April 1847.
46. Ibid., B188 John Thomas Warren, Aughavas, Carrigallen, 30 April 1847.
47. RIA, IRA 24 Q 30, form 1026, Henry O'Brien, Killegar, 1 May 1847; NAI, SOF, Box 2/506/37, B186, Henry O'Brien, Killegar, 1 May 1847.
48. NAI, SOF, 2/506/37, B187, John O'Brien, Drumrahan, Mohill, 3 May 1847.
49. Ibid., B 184, Thomas Cullen, Corry, Drumkeerin, 30 April 1847.
50. Ibid., box 2/506/19, no number, Letitia Veevers, Mohill, 23 April 1847.
51. Ibid., box, 2/506/37, B131 George Peyton, Driney House, Cashcarrigan, 26 April 1847.
52. RIA, IRA 24 Q 30, form 1020, Denis Booth and George Shaw, Drumsna, 26 April 1847.
53. Ibid.
54. NAI, SOF, box 2/506/19, George D. Mansfield, Kiltubrid, Cashcarrigan, 10 May 1847.
55. Ibid., William Noble, Drumshanbo, 5 April 1847.
56. Ibid., no. 2201, Letitia F. Nisbett, Dromod, 21 June 1847.
57. Ibid., SOF 2/506/36, no. 2309, Elizabeth Peyton, Driney, House, Cashcarrigan, 23 June 1847.
58. Ibid., SOF 2/506/20, G.H. Peyton, Driney House, Cashcarrigan, to committee, 3 July 1847.
59. Ibid., Penelope Johnston, Kinlough House, Bundoran, 30 June 1847; box 2/506/37, form 122, 28 December 1847.
60. Ibid., box 2/506/36, no number, William Noble, Drumshanbo, 5 April 1847.
61. Ibid., no number, George De La Poer Beresford, Fenagh, 17 April 1847; no number, George D. Mansfield, Cashcarrigan, 27 April 1847.
62. Ibid., no number, J.M. Kirkwood, Woodbrook Lodge, Carrick-on-Shannon, no date.
63. Ibid., no number, Anne Devenish, Rush Hill, Carrick-on-Shannon, 22 April 1847.
64. Ibid., no. 2269, Mary Johnston, Aghacashill, Cashcarrigan, 24 June 1847; box 2/506/37, form 127, 27 December 1847.
65. Ibid., 2/506/36, no 1556, Annadelia Slack, Annadale, Drumshanbo, 20 May 1847; no number, Hannah M. Peyton, Driney House, Cashcarrigan, 29 April 1847, 2/506/37, form 108, Annadelia Slack, Annadale, Cashcarrigan, 30 December 1847; additional letter (no. 505), 13 April 1848.

66. Ibid., box 2/506/20, Penelope Johnston, Kinlough House, Bundoran, 30 June 1847; box 2/506/36, no. 379, T. K. Little, Castle, Mohill, no date; 2/506/37, B 515 Alicia Crofton, Lakefield, Mohill, 4 June 1847; box 2/506/36, no number, Thomasine Sophia Saunderson, Keadue, 19 May 1847; box 2/506/36, no. 2439, John Fisher, Carrigallen, 29 June 1847; box 2/506/36, no. 1849, M.J. Peyton, Springfield, Carrick-on-Shannon, 18 May 1847.

67. Ibid., SOF box 2/506/37, form 7, J.M. Kirkwood, Woodbrook Lodge, Carrick-on-Shannon, 23 December 1847.

68. Ibid., form 151, Matilda Shanly, Riversdale, Ballinamore, 27 December 1847.

69. Ibid., form 156, Rev. George Shaw, Annaduff Glebe, Drumsna, 29 December 1847.

70. Ibid., no number, Jane Isabel Banks, Rose Bank, Dromahaire, 31 December 1847.

71. National Archives, Kew, London (hereafter TNA), Treasury Papers (hereafter T), 91/199, G. Shaw to F.R. Bertolacci, 15 March 1847.

72. Ibid.

73. Ibid., G. Shaw to F.R. Bertolacci, 1 April 1847.

74. Ibid., Lord Clements to Lewis A. Jones, 26 April 1847.

75. Ibid., Lord Clements to governors of the Irish Reproductive Loan Fund, 26 April 1847.

76. Ibid., John Duckworth to Lord Clements, 20 April 1847 and Guy Lloyd to Lord Clements, 24 April 1847.

77. T91/232, Statement by the governors of the Irish Reproductive Loan Fund.

78. Ibid.

79. T91/232 and T91/233, Rev. W. Wynne, Vicarage, Drumkeerin to Committee, 1 May 1847 and William Macartney to Committee, 15 April 1847.

80. NAI, SOF box 2/506/37, B260, Richard Clifford, Drumdarton, Ballinamore, 6 May 1847.

81. Ibid., 2/506/20, Penelope Johnston, Kinlough House, Bundoran, 30 June 1847.

82. TNA, T91/233, W. Wray, Mohill to Committee, 13 April 1847.

83. Ibid., Neon Tucker to Committee, 16 April 1847.

84. Ibid., Proctor, Ballinamore, 23 April 1847.

85. Ibid., T91/232, Distribution of loans made by the Irish Reproductive Loan Fund.

86. NAI, SOF box 2/506/37, B488, Francis Kane, Drumsna, 29 May 1847.

87. Ibid., 2/506/20, George Beresford, Fenagh, 22 June 1847.

88. Ibid.

89. Ibid., SOF Box 2/506/7, Francis Reynolds, Parish Priest, Abbey View, Fenagh, 13 August 1847.

90. Ibid., Box 2/506/37, B306 James E. Hoope, Mohill, 4 May 1847.

91. Ibid.
92. Ibid., B260½, John W. Evers, Mohill, 7 May 1847.
93. RIA, IRA 24 Q 30, no. 1155, George Hindes, Vicar, Killargue, 3 June 1847.
94. NAI, SOF box 2/506/37, B158, R. Kerr, Ballyshannon, 3 May 1847.
95. Ibid., 2/506/16, J Strean, Bundoran, Ballyshannon, to committee 17 August 1847.
96. Ibid., box 2/506/37, B252, Peter Dawson, PP Kiltoghert, Carrick-on-Shannon, 5 May 1847.
97. Ibid., B409, Jane Isabel Banks, Carrick-on-Shannon, 18 May 1847.
98. Ibid., SOF 2/506/20, Jane Corbett, Carrick-on-Shannon, 19 May 1847 and Elizabeth Forster to Dear Friend, Earlham Road, Norwich, 21 May 1847.
99. Ibid., B460, Mary Johnston, Aghacashill, Cashcarrigan, 24 May 1847; B461, Annadelia Slack, Annadale, 24 May 1847.
100. Ibid., 2/506/19, George Shaw, Annaduff Glebe, 7 May 1847.
101. Ibid., box 2/506/37, B462, W. Lawder, 20 May 1847.
102. Ibid., box 2/506/20, W. Lawder, Carrigallen, 3 June 1847.
103. Ibid., F. Hamilton, Eastersnow, Boyle, 26 May 1847.
104. Ibid.
105. Ibid., box 2/506/36, B537, Jane Ellis, Brooklawn, Ballinamore, 4 June 1847.
106. Ibid., B515, Alicia Crofton, Lakefield, Mohill, 4 June 1847.
107. Ibid., Box 2/506/20, B561, Mary Ann Noble, Prospect, Drumshanbo, 7 June 1847 and reply from committee, 21 June 1847.
108. Ibid., George Shaw, Annaduff Glebe, Drumsna, to committee, 7 June 1847.
109. Ibid., Ellen Lawder, Fenagh, to committee, 14 June 1847.
110. Ibid., Edward Keogh, Cloonaff, Drumsna, County Roscommon, 18 June 1847.
111. Ibid., Loftus Tottenham, Glenfarne Hall, Manorhamilton, 19 June 1847.
112. Ibid., Richard Clifford, Oughteragh, 22 June 1847.
113. Ibid., box 2/506/36, B685, Catherine Godley, Killargue, 25 June 1847.
114. Ibid., box 2/506/20, Francis Kane, Drumsna, 25 June 1847.
115. Ibid., Jane Isabella Banks, Carrick-on-Shannon, 29 June 1847.
116. Ibid., box 2/506/36, B736, George Hindes, Killargue Glebe, Dromahaire, 7 July 1847.
117. Ibid., B560, Anne Percy, Garadice, Ballinamore, June 1847 (no precise date).
118. Ibid.
119. RIA, IRA 24 Q 30, form 1193, J. Peyton, Springfield, Croghan, 25 June 1847.
120. NAI, SOF box 2/506/36, form 1190, Margaritta Kirkwood, Lakeview, Carrick-on-Shannon, no date but letter received 12 July 1847.
121. Ibid., box 2/506/37, B185, George Beresford, Fenagh Glebe, to committee, 29 April 1847 and RLFC 3/2/16/21, George Beresford to William Stanley, 17 April 1847.
122. NAI, SOF, box 2/506/37, B874, Richard Conolly, Newtownforbes, 14 August 1847.

123. Ibid., box 2/506/7, George D. Mansfield, Kiltubrid, Cashcarrigan, to committee, 3 August 1847.
124. Ibid., box 2/506/36, B881, Matilda Shanly, Riversdale, Ballinamore, 31 August 1847.
125. Ibid., box 2/506/16, George Beresford, Fenagh Glebe, Carrick-on-Shannon, to committee, 16 August 1847 and reply 19 August 1847.
126. Ibid., E Lawder, Mough House, Fenagh, Carrick-on-Shannon, 19 August 1847 and reply 26 August 1847.
127. Ibid., John Strean, Bundoran, Ballyshannon, to committee 17 August 1847 and reply 21 August 1847.
128. Ibid., 2/506/16, Denis Booth, Drumsna, to committee, 16 August 1847.
129. Ibid., box 2/506/7, Emily Auchmuty, Kilmore House, Drumsna, to committee, 30 August 1847.
130. TNA, T91/199, Captain John Duckworth to F.R. Bertolacci, 27 July 1847.

## CHAPTER SIX

1. Peter Gray, *The Making of the Irish Poor Law, 1815–43*(Manchester University Press, 2009), pp.333–4.
2. National Archives, Dublin (hereafter, NAI), Society of Friends Relief of Distress Papers (hereafter, SOF), box 2/506/7, J.M. Kirkwood, Woodbrook Lodge, Carrick-on-Shannon, to committee, August 1847.
3. Ibid., 2/506/7, Jane Ellis, Ballinamore, to committee, 28 August 1847 and reply from committee, 30 August 1847.
4. Ibid., 2/506/8, Francis Kane, Drumsna, to committee, 11 September 1847 and reply, 15 September 1847.
5. Ibid., 2/506/8, Denis Booth, Drumsna, to committee, 28 September 1847 and reply, 30 September 1847.
6. Ibid., 2/506/9, Emma Lawder, Longfield, Drumsna, to committee, 3 October 1847 and reply, 9 October 1847.
7. Ibid., 2/506/9, Emily Auchmuty, Kilmore House, Drumsna, to committee, 9 October 1847.
8. Ibid., 2/506/8, James Kirkwood, Killukin Committee Room, Carrick-on-Shannon, to committee, 17 September 1847.
9. Ibid., 2/506/10, Belinda Hanley and Mary Conry, Rushport, Drumsna, to committee, 3 November 1847 and Jane Ireland, Drumsna, to committee, 5 November 1847.
10. Ibid., Penelope Johnston, Kinlough House, Bundoran, to committee, 29 November 1847 and reply, 8 December 1847.
11. Ibid., John B Hogg, Cartron, Drumsna, to committee, 29 November 1847 and reply, 3 December 1847.
12. Ibid., G.H.C. Peyton, Driney House, Carrick-on-Shannon, to committee, 16 November 1847 and reply 20 November 1847.

13. Ibid., Emma Lawder, Longfield, Drumsna, 1 December 1847 and reply 18 December 1847.
14. Leitrim County Library, Ballinamore (hereafter LCL), Carrick-on-Shannon board of guardians' minute book, BG 52 /A/4, p.270.
15. Ibid., 14 August, pp.273, 280.
16. Ibid.
17. Ibid., 13 November 1847, p.388.
18. Ibid, p.397.
19. Ibid.
20. NAI, SOF 2/506/10, George Shaw, Annaduff Glebe, Drumsna, to committee, 16 November 1847.
21. Ibid., Edward Keogh, Parish Priest, Drumsna to committee, 13 November 1847.
22. Ibid.
23. Reprinted British Parliamentary Papers (hereafter BPP), volume 2, Papers relating to proceedings for the relief of the distress and state of the unions and workhouse in Ireland, Fifth Series 1848, p.137.
24. Ibid., p.137.
25. Ibid., pp.137–8.
26. Ibid., p.138.
27. Ibid.; LCL, BG 52/A/4 18 December 1847, p.446.
28. BPP, volume 2, Papers relating to proceedings for the relief of the distress and state of the unions and workhouse in Ireland, Fifth Series 1848, p.139.
29. Ibid.
30. Ibid.
31. Ibid.
32. LCL, BG 52/A/4, 20 November 1847, p.398 and p.404.
33. Ibid., 20 November 1847, pp.398–405.
34. BPP, volume 2, Papers relating to proceedings for the relief of the distress and state of the unions and workhouse in Ireland, Fifth Series 1848, p.140.
35. Ibid., p.145 and LCL, BG 52/A/4, p.414 and 4 December 1847, p.418.
36. Ibid., 4 December 1847, pp.418, 426.
37. Ibid., 11 December 1847, pp.435–6.
38. Ibid., 18 December, 1847, p.439, 445.
39. Ibid., 24 December 1847, p.448.
40. Ibid., p.453.
41. BPP, volume 2, Papers relating to proceedings for the relief of the distress and state of the unions and workhouse in Ireland, Fifth Series 1848, p.146.
42. Ibid., p.150.
43. Ibid., p.154.
44. Ibid., p.146.
45. Ibid., p.153.
46. Ibid., p.147.
47. Ibid.

48. The National Archives, Kew, Home Office Papers, 45/2472, Edward Wynne to W. Stanley, 4 January 1848.
49. LCL, BG 52/A/4, 24 December 1847, pp.449, 454–6.
50. BPP volume 2, Papers relating to proceedings for the relief of the distress and state of the unions and workhouses in Ireland, Fourth Series 1847, p.113.
51. Ibid., p.114.
52. Ibid., p.113.
53. Ibid.
54. Ibid.
55. BPP, volume 2, Papers relating to proceedings for the relief of the distress and state of the unions and workhouse in Ireland, Fifth Series 1848, p.154.
56. Ibid., p.159.
57. Ibid., p.160.
58. Ibid.
59. Ibid., p.161.
60. BPP, volume 3, Papers relating to proceedings for the relief of the distress and state of unions and workhouses in Ireland, Sixth Series, pp.717–18.
61. Ibid., pp.724–5.
62. Ibid., p.725.
63. LCL, BG 52/A/5, 5 February 1848, p.A 15.
64. Ibid., 12 February 1848, p.A 25.
65. Ibid., 26 February, 1848, p.A 46.
66. Ibid., 11 March 1848, p.A 66.
67. Gray, *The Making of the Irish Poor law, 1815–43*, pp.333–4.
68. LCL, BG 52/A/5, 3 January 1848, p.470.
69. Ibid., 29 January 1848, p.A1.
70. BPP, volume 3, sixth series, p.733.
71. LCL, BG 52/A/5, 4 March 1848, p.A53.
72. BPP, volume 3, Papers relating to proceedings for the relief of the distress and state of unions and workhouses in Ireland, sixth series, p.727.
73. LCL, BG 52/A/5, 3 January 1848, p.469.
74. Ibid., 12 February 1848, p.A 29.
75. Ibid., 26 February 1848, p.A 50.
76. Ibid., 11 March 1848, p.A 69.
77. BPP, volume 3, Papers relating to proceedings for the relief of the distress and state of unions and workhouses in Ireland, sixth series, p.753.
78. BG 52/A/5, 19 February 1848, p.A37, 25 March 1848, p.A88 and 1 April 1848, p.A98.
79. BPP, volume 3, Papers relating to proceedings for the relief of the distress and state of unions and workhouses in Ireland, sixth series, p.748.
80. Ibid., pp.756–7.
81. Ibid., p.749.
82. LCL, BG 52/A/5, 29 January 1848, p.A9 and 1 January 1848, p.466.

83.  BPP, volume 3, Papers relating to proceedings for the relief of the distress and state of unions and workhouses in Ireland, sixth series, p.742.

84.  Ibid., p.751.

85.  LCL, BG 52/A/5, 5 January 1848 p.44.

86.  BPP, volume 3, Papers relating to proceedings for the relief of the distress and state of unions and workhouses in Ireland, sixth series, p.754.

87.  Ibid., pp.721–2.

88.  Ibid., p.722.

89.  Ibid., p.728.

90.  LCL, BG 52/A/6, 27 June 1849, p.1263.

91.  BPP, volume 3, Papers relating to proceedings for the relief of the distress and state of unions and workhouses in Ireland, sixth series, p.75.

92.  NAI, SOF box 2/506/22, George Shaw, Drumsna, to committee 14 January 1848. Appendix (A) to First Annual Report of the Commissioners of Irish Poor Laws, No.vii, Statement of advances and other relief afforded by the British Relief Association, pp.113-4.

93.  BPP, volume 3, Papers relating to proceedings for the relief of the distress and state of unions and workhouses in Ireland, sixth series, p.722.

94.  Ibid., p.726.

95.  Ibid., p.727.

96.  LCL, BG 52/A/5, 18 March 1848, p.A80 and 29 April 1848, p.A 138. Its location is determined by a reference in the minute books to 'Rev. Mr Sweeny's communication applying for the Roman Catholic Chaplainship to the auxiliary workhouse at the bridge'. See BG 52/A/6, 19 September 1849, p.1381. This building subsequently became the town police barracks.

97.  BPP, volume 3, Papers relating to proceedings for the relief of the distress and state of unions and workhouses in Ireland, sixth series, p.723.

98.  LCL, BG 52/A/5, 5 February 1848, p.A 1712 and February 1848, p.A 29.

99.  Ibid., 26 February 1848, p.A 50.

100. Ibid., 4 March 1848, p.A 60.

101. Ibid., 6 May 1848, p.A 157.

102. BPP, volume 3, Papers relating to proceedings for the relief of the distress and state of unions and workhouses in Ireland, sixth series, p.721.

103. Ibid., p.737.

104. LCL, BG 52/A/5, 3 June 1848, p.A 198 and p.A201.

105. BPP, volume 3, sixth series, p.747.

106. LCL, BG 52/A/5, p.A 70.

107. Ibid., p.A 117.

108. BPP, volume 3, Papers relating to proceedings for the relief of the distress and state of unions and workhouses in Ireland, sixth series, p.734.

109. LCL, BG 52/A/5, 13 May, p.A 165; 3 June, p.A199, 10 June, p.A209, 17 June, p.A220, 1 July, p.A239 and 22 July, p.A280.

110. Ibid., pp.A 134, A 224, A 226.

111. Ibid., 12 August, p.A 299.

112. Ibid., 29 April, p.A 142 and 29 July p.A.290.
113. Ibid., 12 August, p.A 299 and 29 August, p.324.
114. Ibid., pp.A 210, A 220, A 230, A 240, A 250.
115. Ibid., 5 December 1846, p.1604.
116. Ibid., 18 March 1848, p.A 79.
117. Ibid., 3 June 1848, p.A 201.
118. Ibid., 22 April 1848, p.A 126.
119. Ibid., 6 May 1848, p.A154; 3 June 1848, p.A 202; 7 October 1848, p.A 377 and 16 December 1848, p.C 18.
120. Ibid., 6 May 1848, p.150.
121. Ibid., 3 June 1848, p.A201.
122. Ibid., 17 June 1848, p.A218.
123. LCL, Mohill board of guardians' minute book, BG 122/A/5, pp.81, 84.
124. Ibid., pp.106, 109.
125. Ibid., 6 May, p.19.
126. Ibid., 3 June, p.39.
127. Ibid., 17 June, p.46 and 5 August, p.76.
128. Ibid., pp.36, 41, 46, 51, 56, 61, 66, 71, 76, 81, 86, 91, 96, 101, 106.
129. Ibid., 14 October, p.133.
130. Ibid., 30 September, p.116.
131. Ibid., 11 November, p.154, 18 November, p.159 and 25 November, p.168.
132. BPP volume 2, papers relating to proceedings for the relief of distress and the state of the unions and workhouses in Ireland, fourth series 1847–48, p.116.
133. Ibid.
134. Ibid., p.117.
135. Ibid., pp.117, 124.
136. NAI, SOF 2/506/10, Matilda Shanly, Riversdale, Ballinamore, to committee, 10 November 1847.
137. BPP volume 2, papers relating to proceedings for the relief of distress and the state of the unions and workhouses in Ireland, fourth series 1847–48, p.123.
138. Ibid., p.120.
139. Ibid., pp.124–5.
140. Ibid., p.121.
141. LCL, BG 122/A/5, 23 November 1847, p.160.
142. BPP volume 2, papers relating to proceedings for the relief of distress and the state of the unions and workhouses in Ireland, fourth series 1847–48, p.119.
143. LCL, BG 122/A/5, p.176.
144. Ibid., p.229.
145. Ibid., p.230.
146. Ibid., 16 December, pp.181–183.
147. Ibid., p.184.

148. Ibid., 30 December 1847, p.196.
149. BPP volume 2, Papers relating to proceedings for the relief of distress and the state of the unions and workhouses in Ireland, fourth series 1847–48, p.233.
150. Ibid., p.195.
151. Ibid., p.233.
152. BPP volume 2, Papers relating to proceedings for the relief of distress and state of the unions and workhouses in Ireland, fifth series 1848, p.173.
153. Ibid.
154. Ibid., p.174.
155. LCL, BG 122/A/5, 30 December 1847, p.201.
156. BPP volume 2, Papers relating to proceedings for the relief of distress and state of the unions and workhouses in Ireland, fifth series1848, p.176.
157. Ibid., p.181.
158. Ibid., p.185.
159. Ibid.
160. Ibid., p.184.
161. Ibid.
162. Ibid., p.185.
163. Ibid.
164. Ibid., p.186.
165. Ibid., p.198.
166. Ibid., p.191.
167. BPP, volume 3, Papers relating to proceedings for the relief of distress and state of unions and workhouses in Ireland, sixth series, p.433.
168. Ibid., p.440.
169. BPP, volume 2, Papers relating to proceedings for the relief of distress and state of the unions and workhouses in Ireland, fifth series, p 187.
170. Ibid., p.190.
171. Ibid., pp.193–4.
172. Ibid., p.196.
173. Ibid., p.198.
174. Ibid., p.201.
175. Ibid.
176. Ibid., p.203.
177. Ibid.
178. Ibid.
179. BPP, volume 3, Papers relating to proceedings for the relief of distress and state of unions and workhouses in Ireland, sixth series, p.426.
180. Ibid., p.429.
181. Ibid.
182. Ibid., p.430.
183. Ibid., p.432.
184. Ibid.

185. Ibid., p.435.
186. Ibid., p.436.
187. Ibid., p.444.
188. Ibid., pp.436–7.
189. BPP, volume 4, Papers relating to proceedings for the relief of distress and the state of unions and workhouses in Ireland, seventh series 1848, appendix ix, p.cxi.
190. LCL, Manorhamilton board of guardians' minute book, BG 117/AA/3, 16 September 1847.
191. Ibid., 7 October 1847.
192. Ibid., 14 October 1847.
193. Ibid., 25 November 1847.
194. Ibid., 11 May 1848.
195. Ibid., 18 November 1847.
196. Ibid., 6 January 1848.
197. Ibid., BG 117/A/2, p 108, 22 June 1848.
198. Ibid., 25 March, 30 March and 20 April 1848.
199. Ibid., 21 March 1848.
200. Ibid., 27 April 1848.
201. Ibid., 20 April 1848.
202. Ibid., p. 71, 18 May 1848.
203. NAI, SOF, Box 2/506/37, Clothing form 148, 1 January 1848.
204. Ibid., Clothing form 485, Clare Dickson, Woodville, Bundoran, 10 April 1848.
205. Ibid., Clothing form 110, 4 January 1848.
206. Ibid., Clothing form 86, 4 January 1848.
207. Ibid., Clothing form 250, 6 January 1848.
208. Ibid., Clothing form 150, 6 January 1848.
209. Ibid., Clothing form 109, 8 January 1848.
210. Ibid., Clothing form 431, Richard Clifford, Drumdarton, Ballinamore, 24 March 1848.
211. Ibid., box 2/506/22, Margaritta Kirkwood, Lakeview, Carrick-on-Shannon, 9 April 1848.
212. Ibid., box 2/506/37, Clothing form 285, 25 January 1848.
213. Ibid., box 2/506/22, Letitia Veevers, Mohill, to committee 19 January 1848.
214. Ibid., box 2/506/37, form 346 Thomas Hayes, Mohill, to committee, 16 February 1848.
215. Ibid., box 2/506/22, Dromod, 1 March 1848.
216. Ibid., box 2/506/7, Nicholas Tottenham to committee, 27 January 1848.
217. Ibid., Andrew Hogg, Cloone to Todhunter, 28 January 1848.
218. Ibid., box 2/506/38, G.H.C. Peyton, Driney House, Cashcarrigan, 1848 (no month).
219. Ibid., box 2/506/7 John Lawder, Drumsna, to committee 22 February 1848.
220. Ibid., William Parke to Todhunter, 2 March 1848.

221. Ibid., N.L. Tottenham, Glenfarne Hall, to Todhunter, 24 March 1848.
222. Ibid., George Shaw, Annaduff Glebe, 1 April 1848.
223. Ibid., George Shaw, Annaduff Glebe, 28 March 1848.
224. Ibid., Penelope Johnston, Kinlough House, Bundoran, to committee, 24 April 1848 and 27 April 1848.
225. Ibid., John W. Lawder to Todhunter, 11 May 1848.
226. Ibid., Mary Johnston, Aghacashill, Cashcarrigan, to committee, 7 April 1848.
227. Ibid., box 2/506/38, 29 April 1848 and 12 August 1848.
228. Ibid., box 2/506/8, George De La Poer Beresford, Fenagh Glebe, 30 June 1848; Francis Kane, Annaduff, Drumsna, 9 June 1848.
229. Ibid., box 2/506/23, Emma Lawder, Longfield, Drumsna, 23 July 1848.
230. Ibid., box 2/506/8, James Cody, Mohill, 2 July 1848 and 19 July 1848.
231. Ibid., 2/506/22, J Feld, 2 May 1848.
232. Ibid., box 2/506/22, Emma Lawder, Lowfield, Drumsna, 25 April 1848.
233. Ibid.
234. Ibid., box 2/506/23, Mary Johnston, Aghacashill, Cashcarrigan, 17 June 1848.
235. Ibid., box 2/506/22, Emily Auchmuty, Kilmore House, Drumsna, 10 May 1848.
236. Ibid., box 2/506/23, J.M. Kirkwood, Woodbrook Lodge, 6 June 1848.
237. Ibid., box 2/506/7, Letitia Veevers, Mohill, 3 April 1848.
238. Ibid., box 2/506/8, James Cody, Mohill, 1 August 1848.

## CHAPTER SEVEN

1. National Archives, Dublin (hereafter NAI), Society of Friends Relief of Distress Papers (hereafter SOF), box 2/506/8, James Cody Mohill, to committee, 16 August 1848.
2. Reprinted British Parliamentary Papers (hereafter BPP), volume 4, Papers relating to proceedings for the relief of the distress and state of the unions and workhouses in Ireland, seventh series 1848, pp.45–6.
3. Ibid., p.23.
4. NAI, SOF 2/506/8, John Lawder Longfield, Drumsna, 17 August 1848.
5. Ibid., John Lawder Longfield, Drumsna, 1 August 1848.
6. Ibid., J.M. Kirkwood, Woodbrook, Carrick-on-Shannon, 26 June 1848.
7. Ibid., J.M. Kirkwood, Woodbrook, Carrick-on-Shannon, 5 August 1848.
8. Ibid., box 2/506/23, Ursula Hamilton, Estersnow Glebe, 2 August 1848.
9. Ibid., George Shaw, Annaduff Glebe, 3 August 1848.
10. Ibid., box 2/506/8, J. M. Kirkwood, Woodbrook, Carrick-on-Shannon, 5 August 1848.
11. Ibid., box 2/506/23, George Shaw, Annaduff, Drumsna, 20 November 1848.
12. BPP, volume 4, Papers relating to proceedings for the relief of the distress and state of the unions and workhouses in Ireland, seventh series 1848, pp.22, 52.

13. Leitrim County Library, Ballinamore (hereafter LCL), Manorhamilton board of guardians' minute book, BG 117/A/2, 27 July 1848, p.124.

14. BPP, volume 4, Papers relating to proceedings for the relief of the distress and the state of unions and workhouses in Ireland, seventh series 1848, appendix ix, p.cx.

15. LCL, Manorhamilton board of guardians' minute book, BG 117/A/2, p.200.

16. Ibid., 7 September, 1848, p.172 and 3 August 1848, p.133.

17. Ibid., 31 August 1848, p.164.

18. Ibid., 14 September 1848, p.174.

19. Ibid., 21 September 1848, p.182.

20. Ibid., 26 October 1848, pp.211, 212.

21. Ibid., 21 September 1848, p.182.

22. Ibid., pp.71, 78, 86, 92, 95, 101, 111, 116, 133, 138, 158, 164, 169, 174.

23. Ibid., 14 September 1848, p.174 and 28 September 1848, p.188.

24. Ibid., pp.186, 190, 196, 200, 207, 213, 220, 225, 231, 238, 240, 247, 250, 256, 260, 265, 268.

25. Ibid., 28 December 1848, p.258.

26. Ibid., 4 January 1849, p.264.

27. Ibid., 1 February 1849, p.283.

28. Ibid., pp.264, 269, 275, 287, 298, 310.

29. Ibid., 8 March 1849, p.313.

30. Ibid., p.331.

31. BPP, volume 4, Papers relating to proceedings for the relief of the distress and state of the unions and workhouses in Ireland, eighth series 1849, p.41.

32. NAI, SOF 2/506/9, Penelope St George, Mount Prospect, to committee, 23 January 1849.

33. Ibid., Penelope St George to committee, 7 March 1849.

34. Ibid., 2/506/38, Penelope St George to committee, 2 April 1849.

35. Ibid., 2/506/9, Penelope St George to committee, 3 May 1849.

36. Ibid., 2/506/10, Penelope St George to committee, 7 September 1849.

37. LCL, Manorhamilton board of guardians' minute book, BG 117/A/3, 5 April 1849, p.11 and 12 April 1849, p.14.

38. Ibid., 19 April 1849, pp.23, 27.

39. Ibid., 10 May 1849, p.56.

40. Ibid., p.132.

41. Ibid., pp.11, 22, 32, 42, 52, 62, 72, 82, 92, 102, 112, 122, 132, 142, 152, 162, 172, 182, 192, 202, 212, 222, 232, 240, 252.

42. Ibid., pp.82, 92, 102, 112, 122, 132, 142, 152, 162.

43. Ibid., pp.162, 172, 182, 192, 202, 212.

44. Ibid., pp.82, 132, 212.

45. Ibid., 20 September, p.237.

46. Ibid.

47. Ibid., 18 October 1849, p.272, 279.

48. Ibid., 15 November 1849, p.315.
49. Ibid., 6 December 1849, pp.356–7.
50. Ibid., 23 December 1849, p.275.
51. Ibid., 29 December 1849, p.388.
52. Ibid., 27 December 1849, p.379.
53. Ibid., p.247.
54. LCL, Mohill board of guardians' minute book, BG 122/A/6, pp.3, 10–11.
55. Ibid., 25 November 1848 and 9 December 1848.
56. Ibid., 25 November 1848, p.25.
57. Ibid., 7 December 1848, p.39.
58. Ibid., 23 December 1848, p.55.
59. Ibid.
60. Ibid., 28 December 1848, p.65.
61. Ibid., p.69.
62. Ibid.
63. Ibid., p.86.
64. BPP, volume 4, Papers relating to proceedings for the relief of the distress and state of union workhouses in Ireland, eighth series 1849, p.44.
65. Ibid.
66. NAI, SOF, 2/506/9, Letitia Veevers, Mohill, 15 March 1849.
67. LCL, Mohill board of guardians' minute book, BG 122/A/6, 10 February 1849, pp.131, 139.
68. Ibid., p.209.
69. Ibid., 12 April 1849, p.211.
70. Ibid., p.209.
71. Ibid., 10 May 1849, p.248.
72. Ibid., pp.234, 244, 253, 263.
73. Ibid., 3 May 1849, p.240 and 23 June 1849, p.290; NAI, SOF 2/506/9, William James Slacke, Newtowngore, Ballinamore, to committee, 19 January 1849.
74. LCL, Mohill board of guardians' minute book, BG 122/A/6, 10 February 1849, 26 May 1849, p.263 and 21 June 1849, p.204.
75. NAI, SOF 2/506/9, Andrew Hogg, Cloone, to committee, 9 May 1849.
76. LCL, Mohill board of guardians' minute book, BG 122/A/6, 7 June 1849, p.278.
77. Ibid., 28 April 1849, p.223, 2 June 1849, p.263 and 30 June 1849, p.293.
78. Ibid., 21 April, p.213 and 30 June 1846, p.293.
79. Ibid., 5 May 1849, p.238 and 28 September 1849, p.428.
80. Ibid., 1 September 1849, p.393, 7 September 1849, p.400 and 29 September 1849, p.433.
81. Ibid., BG 122/A/7, 2 November 1849, no pagination from hereon.
82. Ibid., 16 November 1849.
83. Ibid., 23 November 1849 and 14 December 1849.
84. NAI, SOF 2/506/10, Ellen Lawder, Mough, Fenagh, to committee, 10 November 1849.

85. LCL, Carrick-on-Shannon board of guardians' minute book, BG 52/A/5, 22 July 1848, p.A 271 and 29 July 1848, p.A 291.
86. Ibid., 16 September 1848, p.A 349 and 30 September 1848, p.A 367.
87. Ibid., 21 October 1848, p.A 390.
88. Ibid., p.A 394.
89. BG 52/A/6, 4 November 1848, p.A 410 and p.A 417; 18 November 1848, p.A 434; 2 December 1848, p.A 453 and 24 February 1849, p.C 118.
90. 11 November 1848, p.A 420 and p.A 426.
91. 18 November 1848, p.A 430, p.A 433, p.A 434.
92. 16 December 1848, p.C 12 and p.C 19.
93. BPP, volume 4, Papers relating to proceedings for the relief of the distress and state of union workhouses in Ireland, eighth series 1849, p.47.
94. LCL, Carrick-on-Shannon board of guardians' minute book, BG 52/A/6, 6 January 1849, p.C 42.
95. Ibid., 30 December 1848, p.C 39.
96. Ibid., 20 January 1849, p.C 62 and 3 February 1849, p.C 82.
97. Ibid., p.C 89.
98. Ibid., 10 March 1849, p.C 136.
99. Ibid., 3 February 1849, p.C 89 and 10 February 1849, p.C 99.
100. Ibid., 19 March 1849, p.C 161.
101. Ibid., pp.C 52, C 62, C 72, C 82, C 92, C 102, C 112, C 122, C 132, C 142, C 152, C 164, C 174, C 184, C 194, C 204, C 214.
102. BPP, volume 4, Papers relating to proceedings for the relief of the distress and state of union workhouses in Ireland, eighth series 1849, p.47.
103. LCL, Carrick-on-Shannon board of guardians' minute book, BG 52/A/6, 3 February 1849, p.C 82 and 10 March 1849, p.C 132.
104. Ibid., 10 February 1849, p.C 97.
105. Ibid., pp.C 48, C 58, C 68, C 78, C 88, C 98, C 108, C 118, C 128, C 138, C 160, C 171.
106. NAI, SOF 2/506/23, J. Kirkwood, Woodbrook, Carrick-on-Shannon, to committee, 12 March 1849.
107. LCL, BG 52/A/6, 24 February 1849, p.C120. See *London Times*, 7 September 1850.
108. LCL, Carrick-on-Shannon board of guardians' minute book, BG 52/A/6, 19 March 1849, p.C 152, 16 April 1849, p.C 194 and 4 July 1849, p.1266.
109. Ibid., 16 April 1849, p.C 200; pp.C 210, C 220, C 230, C 240, 1212, 1222, 1232, 1242, 1251, 1262, 1272.
110. Ibid., 30 May 1849, p.1221; 27 June 1849 p.1261; 25 July 1849, p.1301 and 15 August 1849, p.1331.
111. Ibid., 9 April 1849, p.C 184; 16 April 1849, p.C 194; 23 April 1849, p.C 204; 30 April 1849, p.C 214 and 30 April 1849, p.C 214.
112. Ibid., 18 July 1849, p.1286.
113. Ibid., pp.1326, 1336, 1346, and 26 September 1849, p.1386.
114. Ibid., 13 June 1849, p.1243.

115. Ibid., 20 June 1849, p.1250.
116. Ibid., 4 July 1849, p.1270; 11 July 1849, p.1280; 18 July 1849, p.1290 and 25 July 1849, p.1300.
117. NAI, SOF 2/506/38, William Parke, Clogher House, Drumsna, to committee, 10 January 1849 and 16 March 1849.
118. Ibid., 2/506/38, George Shaw to committee, 18 March 1849.
119. Ibid., 2/506/9, J. M. Kirkwood, Carrick-on-Shannon, 16 June 1849.
120. Ibid., George Shaw to committee, 22 June 1849 and 30 June 1849; 2/507/3, G. Shaw to committee, 14 August 1849.
121. Ibid., SOF, 2/506/10, Margaretta Kirkwood, Lakeview, Carrick-on-Shannon, 2 July 1849.
122. LCL, Carrick-on-Shannon board of guardians' minute book, BG 52/A/6, 25 July 1849, p.1302.
123. Ibid., 26 September 1849, p.1388.
124. Ibid., 19 September 1849, p.1380.
125. By late August a deal had been concluded between the union and the owner, Mrs Walsh. See BG 52/A/6, 15 August 1849, p.1334; 29 August 1849, p.1349; 26 September 1849, p.1391.
126. NAI, SOF, 2/506/10, Matthew O'Connor, Lough Allen Island, Drumshanbo, to committee, 16 November 1849.

# CHAPTER EIGHT

1. Reprinted British Papers (hereafter BPP), volume 4, Papers relating to proceedings for the relief of the distress and state of union workhouses in Ireland, eighth series 1849, pp.45–62.
2. *Roscommon and Leitrim Gazette*, 16 March 1850 and *Morning Chronicle* quoted in *Roscommon and Leitrim Gazette*, 17 August 1850.
3. *Roscommon and Leitrim Gazette*, 6 April 1850.
4. Ibid., 5 January 1850.
5. Ibid.
6. Ibid., 2 March 1850.
7. *Morning Chronicle*, quoted in *Roscommon and Leitrim Gazette*, 17 August 1850.
8. *Roscommon and Leitrim Gazette*, 13 July 1850, 27 July 1850 and 3 August 1850.
9. The National Archives, Kew, (hereafter TNA), Home Office Papers (hereafter HO), 45/3366 Captain Haymes, Carrick-on-Shannon, 24 March 1850, and 7 April 1850.
10. Ibid., Captain Haymes, Mohill, 24 March 1850.
11. National Archives, Dublin (hereafter NAI), Society of Friends Relief of Distress Papers (hereafter SOF), Matthew O'Connor to committee, 21 November 1850.

12. *Leitrim Journal*, 13 February 1851.
13. Ibid., 10 April 1851.
14. Ibid., 7 August 1851.
15. Ibid., 28 August 1851.
16. TNA, HO 45/3366, Captain Haymes, Carrick-on-Shannon, 24 March 1850.
17. *Leitrim Journal*, 18 August 1853 and 22 September 1853.
18. Ibid., 1 September 1853.
19. Leitrim County Library, Ballinamore (hereafter LCL), Carrick-on-Shannon board of guardians' minute book, BG 52/A/7, 5 June 1850, p.418, 420.
20. Ibid., pp.422–3.
21. Ibid., 3 July 1850, pp.460, 463.
22. Ibid., p.469.
23. Ibid., p.467.
24. Ibid., 10 July 1850, p.479.
25. Ibid., 7 August 1850, pp.514, 522; 4 September 1850, pp.522, 560.
26. Ibid., 16 October 1850, p.622.
27. Ibid., 28 August 1850, p.549.
28. Ibid., p.555.
29. Ibid., 11 September 1850, p.574 and 25 September 1850, p.598.
30. Ibid., 23 October 1850, p.642.
31. Ibid., 29 May 1850, p.410 and 13 November 1850, p.675.
32. Ibid., 18 July 1850, p.736.
33. Ibid., 20 November 1850, p.686 and 27 November 1850, p.698.
34. Ibid., BG 52/A/8, 1 February 1851, p.202; 3 May 1851, p.61; 5 July 1851, p.169; 2 August 1851, p.217 and 6 September 1851, p.276.
35. Ibid., BG52/A/9, 7 February 1852, p.616 and 6 March 1852, p.680; BG 52/A/10, p.1003.
36. Ibid., BG 52/A/11, 29 January 1853, p.305; BG 52/A/12, 19 November 1853, p.97.
37. *Impartial Reporter*, 15 August 1850.
38. LCL, Mohill, board of guardians' minute book, BG 122/A/9, 23 August 1851, p.238; 30 August 1851, p.246; 6 September 1851, p.254; 13 September 1851, p.262; 20 September 1851, p.270; 27 September 1851, p.278 and 4 October 1851, no pagination.
39. Ibid., BG 122/A/9, 21 February 1852, no pagination.
40. Ibid., 6 March 1852, no pagination; BG 122/A/10, 27 March 1852, p.1; 24 July, p.257; 31 July p.273; 7 August, p.289; 14 August, p.305; 21 August, p.321 and 4 September, p.337.
41. Ibid., BG 122/A/11, no pagination; BG 122/A/12, 4 June 1853, p.81 and 24 September 1853, p.288.
42. *Impartial Reporter*, 1 May 1851.
43. LCL, Manorhamilton board of guardians' minute book, BG 117/A/5, 8 February 1851, p.237 and 5 October 1850, p.25.

44. Ibid., BG 117/A/6, 12 July 1851, p.129 and 4 October 1851, p.321.
45. Ibid., BG 117/A/7, 28 February 1852, p.177.
46. Ibid., 4 September 1852, p.229.
47. Ibid., BG 117/A/8, 29 January 1853, p.451; BG 117/A/9, 9 July 1853, p.479.
48. *Roscommon and Leitrim Gazette*, 7 December 1850.
49. Ibid., 14 December 1850.
50. *Leitrim Journal*, 7 August 1851 and 11 September 1851.
51. Ibid., 31 July 1851 and 25 December 1851.
52. Ibid., 18 September 1851.
53. Ibid., 29 April 1852.
54. Ibid., 20 May 1852.
55. Ibid., 20 July 1854.
56. Ibid., 17 August 1854.
57. Ibid., 20 September 1855 and 25 October 1855.
58. Ibid., 19 July 1855 and 16 August 1855.
59. Ibid., 7 November 1850.
60. Ibid., 6 March 1851.
61. Ibid., 1 May 1851.
62. Ibid., 15 May 1851.
63. Ibid., 6 October 1853 and 16 February 1854.
64. Ibid., 7 November 1850.
65. Ibid., 19 December 1850.
66. Ibid., 30 August 1855 and 21 April 1851.
67. Ibid., 11 May 1854.
68. Ibid., 28 November 1850 and 20 March 1851.
69. Ibid., 27 November 1851.
70. Ibid., 12 December 1850.
71. *Impartial Reporter*, 8 May 1851.
72. Public Record Office, Belfast, Turner Papers, D 4123/5/5/37, Josias Rowley to Colonel George Keppel, May 1849.
73. Ibid.
74. Ibid.
75. *Impartial Reporter*, 23 November 1854.
76. *Leitrim Journal*, 9 November 1854, 16 November 1854 and 23 November 1854; *Impartial Reporter*, 23 November 1854.
77. *Leitrim Journal*, 25 January 1855.
78. Ibid., 20 September 1855. Apparently, similar scenes were evident in the town of Sligo where crowds assembled at the market cross and 'the greatest enthusiasm seemed to prevail'. See *Leitrim Journal*, 20 September 1855.
79. *Leitrim Journal*, 20 May 1852.
80. Ibid., 6 May 1852 and 24 June 1852.
81. Ibid., 1 July 1852.
82. Ibid.

83. *Roscommon and Leitrim Gazette*, 14 August 1847.
84. Ibid.
85. *Leitrim Journal*, 13 February 1851.
86. Ibid., 6 February 1851.
87. Ibid., 3 August 1854.
88. Ibid., 31 March 1853.
89. Ibid., 15 April 1852.
90. Ibid., 7 September 1854.
91. Ibid., 11 January 1855.
92. Ibid., 5 August 1852.
93. Ibid., 24 February 1853.
94. Ibid., 4 November 1852.
95. Ibid.
96. Ibid., 11 November 1852.
97. Ibid., 25 December 1851.
98. Ibid., 15 January 1852.
99. Ibid., 31 March 1853.
100. 32nd Report of the Irish Society (established 1818), contained in NAI, SOF box 2/507/3.
101. Ibid.
102. *Leitrim Journal*, 4 December 1851.
103. Ibid., 17 February 1853.
104. Ibid., 24 February 1853, 17 March 1853, 24 March 1853 and 23 November 1854.
105. Ibid., 9 January 1851.
106. Ibid., 25 September 1851.
107. Ibid., 29 January 1852.
108. Ibid., 16 January 1851.
109. Ibid., 10 June 1852.
110. Ibid.
111. Ibid., 15 December 1853.
112. NAI, Outrage Papers, County Leitrim, John Stuart, Chief Constable, Mohill, 22 January 1839.
113. *Impartial Reporter*, 4 December 1851.
114. *Leitrim Journal*, 17 April 1851.
115. Ibid., 29 December 1853.
116. Ibid., 12 January 1854.
117. Ibid., and 14 June 1855.
118. Ibid., 27 February 1851.
119. Ibid.
120. Ibid., 7 August 1851.
121. Ibid., 12 December 1850.

# CHAPTER NINE

1. *Roscommon and Leitrim Gazette*, 5 January 1850.
2. *Leitrim Journal*, 4 September 1851.
3. *Roscommon and Leitrim Gazette*, 7 September 1850 and *Leitrim Journal*, 11 December 1851.
4. *Leitrim Journal*, 17 April 1851.
5. National Library of Ireland (hereafter NLI), Leitrim Papers, 3027.
6. Ibid.
7. Public Record Office, Belfast (hereafter PRONI), Turner Papers, D 4123/5/5/2, George Keppel to William Lawder, 13 May 1846.
8. Ibid., D 4123/5/5/8, George Keppel to William Lawder, 1 September 1846.
9. Ibid., D 4123/5/5/11, Susan Keppel to William Lawder, 6 October 1846.
10. Ibid., D 4123/5/5/12, Susan Keppel to William Lawder, 15 October 1846.
11. Ibid.
12. Ibid., D 4123/5/5/8, Colonel Keppel to William Lawder, 1 September 1846.
13. Ibid., D 4123/5/5/15, Denis Booth to Colonel George Keppel, 11 November 1846.
14. Ibid., D 4123/5/5/26, George Keppel to William Lawder, 27 November 1846.
15. Ibid., D 4123/5/5/18, George Keppel to William Lawder, 20 November 1846.
16. Ibid., D 4123/5/5/16, George Keppel to William Lawder, 13 November 1846.
17. Ibid.
18. Ibid., D 4123/5/5/18, George Keppel to William Lawder, 20 November 1846.
19. Ibid., D 4123/5/5/36, Mary Ann Walsh to William Lawder, 18 December 1846.
20. Ibid., D 4123/5/5/19, George Keppel to William Lawder, 9 December 1846.
21. PRONI, Madden Papers, D 3465/H/4B, Robert O'Brien to Robert Burrowes, 29 July 1848.
22. Ibid., Robert O'Brien to Robert Burrowes, 31 August 1848 and 9 September 1848.
23. Ibid., Robert O'Brien to Robert Burrowes, 29 July 1848.
24. Ibid.
25. Ibid., Robert O'Brien to Robert Burrowes, 31 August 1848.
26. Ibid.
27. Ibid., Robert O'Brien to William Cochrane, 2 October 1848.
28. Ibid.
29. Ibid., William Cochrane to Dear Madam [probably Mrs Madden], 3 October 1848.
30. Ibid.

31.  Ibid., Robert O'Brien to Robert Burrowes, 9 September 1848.
32.  Ibid., Robert Burrowes to Robert O'Brien, 30 September 1848.
33.  Ibid., Robert O'Brien to William Cochrane, 23 June 1849.
34.  Ibid., Robert O'Brien to William Cochrane, 4 November 1849.
35.  Ibid., Robert O'Brien to William Cochrane, 10 November 1849.
36.  Ibid., Robert O'Brien to William Cochrane, 21 September 1850.
37.  Ibid., Robert O'Brien to Mrs Madden, 23 May 1851.
38.  Ibid., Robert O'Brien to Mrs Madden, 15 May 1852.
39.  Reprinted British Parliamentary Papers, volume 4, Papers relating to proceedings for the relief of the distress and state of the unions and workhouses in Ireland, seventh series 1848, p.46.
40.  *Leitrim Journal*, 16 January 1851.
41.  Ibid., 7 August 1851.
42.  H.C., 1881, Volume lxxvii, Return 'by the Provinces and Counties (compiled from Returns made to the Inspector General, Royal Irish Constabulary), of Cases of Evictions which have come to the knowledge of the Constabulary in each of the years from 1849 to 1880, inclusive', p.3.
43.  Catholic Diocesan Archives, Cullen Papers, 332/4/I/17, Memorial of Hugh McGolrick and others of Greenane, near Dromahaire, parish of Drumlease and County Leitrim, to Cullen, 25 July 1854.
44.  Ibid.
45.  Ibid., 332/8/I/57, Bat McSharry to Most Revd. Dr Cullen, Stonepark, 10 November 1855.
46.  National Archives, Dublin, (hereafter NAI), Society of Friends Relief of Distress Papers (hereafter SOF), 2/506/10, John B. Hogg, Cartron, Drumsna, to committee, 29 November 1847.
47.  PRONI, Turner Papers, D 4123/5/5/33, George Keppel to William Lawder, 26 June 1850.
48.  NLI, O'Beirne Papers, 8647(4), Ferdinand Keon to Francis O'Beirne, 19 October 1850.
49.  *Impartial Reporter*, 28 February 1850.
50.  National Archives of Scotland (hereafter NAS), Argyll Justiciary Court: Processes, SC54/17/2/53/3.
51.  National Archives, Kew, London, Colonial Office Papers, 384/16, North America: Irish applicants, ff.34, 46, 65, 157, 413, 494, 505, 545, and 691.
52.  NLI, Leitrim Papers, 33834 (4).
53.  *Roscommon and Leitrim Gazette*, 28 March 1840.
54.  Ibid., 11 July 1840.
55.  *Leitrim Journal*, 17 April 1851.
56.  Ibid.
57.  Ibid., 18 September 1851.
58.  Ibid.
59.  Ibid., 16 October 1851.
60.  Ibid., 15 April 1852.

61. Ibid., 16 March 1854.
62. Ibid., 14 April 1853.
63. Ibid., 2 January 1851.
64. NAI, Outrage Papers, County Leitrim, 1852.
65. *Leitrim Journal*, 31 March 1853.
66. NAI, SOF, 2/506/9, Francis Gibbons, Mohill, to committee, 17 February 1849.
67. Ibid., Francis Gibbons, Mohill, to committee, 11 May 1849.
68. Ibid., Francis Gibbons, Mohill, to committee, 14 May 1849.
69. Ibid., 2/506/23, Francis Gibbons, Mohill, to committee, 10 June 1849 and 13 June 1849.
70. Ibid., Francis Gibbons, Mohill, to committee, 30 July 1849 and reply 4 August 1849; 2/506/10, Francis Gibbons, Mohill, to committee, 5 August 1849.
71. HC 1843, volume xxiv, Report of the Census Commissioners, Ireland, p xxvi and p xxvii.
72. 1851 Census of Scotland.
73. Ibid.,1851 Census of England.
74. Ibid., 1851 Census of England.
75. Ibid., 1851 Census of Channel Islands.
76. Ibid., 1851 Census of Scotland.
77. Ibid., 1851 Census of England.
78. NAS, Crown Office precognitions, 1847, AD14/47/613.
79. Ibid., Crown Office precognitions, 1850, AD14/50/217.
80. Ibid., Crown Office precognitions, 1853, AD14/53/390.
81. Ibid., Crown Office precognitions, 1855, AD14/55/263.
82. Ibid., Crown Office precognitions, 1857, AD14/57/31.
83. Central Library, Paisley, Poor Law Records, statement 2681 (2).
84. NAI, MFGS 51/002 Carrick-on-Shannon Prison Records 1849, pp.202–5.
85. *Leitrim Journal*, 16 January 1851.
86. NAI, MFGS 51/002 Carrick-on-Shannon Prison Records 1849, pp.203–4.
87. *Leitrim Journal*, 20 October 1853.
88. Ibid., 8 December 1853.

# CHAPTER TEN

1. *Impartial Reporter*, 10 July 1851.
2. Cloonclare baptisms commence, 29 April 1841. For the year 1846 baptisms in Killenummery end in July and the register then recommences in April 1847 when two baptisms are recorded for that year – 16 April and 25 October. The pages for 1848 are almost indecipherable with one baptism recorded on 10 June, two others on which the date is unclear and 11 in November. Aughavas baptisms commence in May 1845 while Fenagh baptisms commence in April 1843 until end of March 1845. There is then a gap until January 1847.

3. Mohill marriages begin 18 November 1845.
4. Marriages in Killenummery end after August 1846 and recommence in November 1848. There are no marriages recorded in Cloone in 1846 until August of that year and this is followed by three marriages in 1847 with no dates given. The Kiltubrid registers are very irregular with marriages noted in 1841 and then nothing until 1847. Aughavas marriages commence on 28 August 1845. There are no marriages recorded in Fenagh for the years 1841–44 and 1847. Kinlough marriages are first recorded from November 1840.
5. *Freeman's Journal*, 11 May 1847, 13 May 1847 and 15 May 1847; National Archives, Dublin, Society of Friends Relief of Distress Papers, box 2/507/3, Report of the General Central Relief Committee for All Ireland from its formation on 29 December 1846 to 31 December 1847.
6. *Freeman's Journal*, 5 May 1847
7. H.C. 1856, vol. xxx, 1851 Census of Ireland [Workhouses, Auxiliary workhouses and Workhouse Hospitals], p.108–9.
8. Ibid., p.109.
9. Ibid., p.108.
10. H.C. 1856, vol xxix, 1851 Census of Ireland. Report of tables of deaths, pp.370–1.
11. Ibid., pp.378–9.
12. Reprinted British Parliamentary Papers, volume 3, sixth series, p.426.
13. Ibid., p.437.
14. H.C. 1856, vol. 29, 1851 Census of Ireland. Table showing the committals, receptions into hospitals and deaths in the several prisons, 1831 to 1851, p.396 and p.398.
15. Ibid., p.394.
16. Ibid., pp.395–6.
17. H.C. 1852–53, volume xcii, 1851 Census of Ireland, County of Leitrim, pp.102–3.
18. Ibid., p.110.
19. Ibid., pp.89–90.
20. Ibid., pp.90–1.
21. Ibid., pp.91–2.
22. Ibid., pp.93–4.
23. Ibid., pp.94–5.
24. Ibid., pp.95–7.
25. Ibid., pp.97–8.
26. Ibid., pp.100–3.
27. Ibid., pp.103–4.
28. Ibid., p.106.
29. Ibid., pp.106, 108.
30. Ibid., p.109.
31. Ibid., pp.109–110.

32.  Ibid., pp.110–112.
33.  Ibid., p.99.
34.  H.C. 1856,volume xxxi, 1851 Census of Ireland, general report, p.xii.
35.  Ibid.
36.  Ibid., p.xv.
37.  Ibid., p.xxiii.
38.  H.C.1856,vol.xxvii,Part I,TheTwenty-Second report of the Commissioners of National education in Ireland for the year 1855, with appendices, vol. I, Appendix viii, p.365, Table showing the number of National schools in operation and the number of children on the rolls for the half years ending 31 March and 30 September 1855.
39.  Ibid.
40.  James McParlan, *Statistical Survey of the County Leitrim*, Dublin, 1802, p.85.
41.  Edward Wakefield – *An account of Ireland Statistical and political, volume 2,* London 1812, p.747.
42.  H.C. 1856, volume xxxi, 1851 Census of Ireland, p.xlvii.
43.  *Roscommon and Leitrim Gazette*, 16 July 1836.
44.  Garret FitzGerald, 'Irish-speaking in the pre–Famine period: A study based on the 1911 Census data for people born before 1851 and still alive in 1911', in *Proceedings of the Royal Irish Academy, Volume 103 C, Number 5, 2003*, p.281.
45.  Ibid., p.201.
46.  Ibid.
47.  Ibid., p.204.
48.  H.C. 1863, volume lv, 1861 Census of Ireland, County of Leitrim, p.90.
49.  Ibid., pp.104–5.
50.  Ibid., p.103.
51.  Ibid., p.96.
52.  Ibid., pp.96–7.
53.  Ibid., pp.97–8.
54.  Ibid., pp.98–9.
55.  Ibid., pp.99–100.
56.  Ibid., pp.101–2.
57.  Ibid., pp.103–4.
58.  Ibid., pp.107–8.
59.  Ibid., pp.105–6.
60.  Ibid., p.106.
61.  Ibid., pp.109–110.
62.  Ibid., pp.111–2.
63.  Ibid., pp.103,108, 112.
64.  Griffith's Valuation, County Leitrim, Union of Mohill, p.107.
65.  H.C.1852,volume xlvi ,(1) Accounts 'showing the total sum assessed as "Rate in aid" on each union in Ireland, under the Act 12Vict. C. 24, distinguishing the amount assessed under each of the orders of the commissioners for

administering the Laws for Relief of the Poor in Ireland, bearing date the 13th day of June 1849 and the 23rd day of December 1850 respectively; showing also the Total sum, down to the 31st day of December 1851, paid by each union to the credit of the "General Rate in Aid Account" in the Bank of Ireland, and the amount remaining to be paid over on that date on account of the total sum assessed on each Union:' (2) 'And, showing the total sum appropriated to each Union out of the "general Rate in Aid Fund" down to the 31st day of December 1851, specifying the purposes to which the several amounts were appropriated; showing also the amount remaining unappropriated on that date of the Total sum assessed as Rate in aid on the several unions', pp.127, 129.

66.  BPP, volume 3, Papers relating to proceedings for the relief of distress and the state of the unions and workhouses in Ireland [sixth series] 1847–8, p.412.

# CONCLUSION

1.  James Donnelly, Jr, *The Great Irish Potato Famine*(Sutton Publishing Ltd, 2001), p.169.
2.  Ibid and H. C., 1852–53, volume xci, 1851 Census of Ireland, County of Longford, p.175; H.C., 1852–53, volume xcii, County of Galway, p.418, County of Mayo, p.510, County of Roscommon, p.551, County of Sligo, p.579.
3.  James Donnelly, Jr, *The Great Irish Potato Famine*, p.176.
4.  Reprinted Parliamentary Papers (hereafter, BPP), volume 4, Papers relating to proceedings for the relief of the distress and state of the unions and workhouses in Ireland, eighth series, 1849, p.134.
5.  Ibid., volume 3, sixth series, Papers relating to proceedings for the relief of distress and the state of the unions and workhouses in Ireland [sixth series] 1847–8, p.730, Wynne to commissioners, 19 February 1848.
6.  Christine Kinealy, *This Great Calamity – The Irish Famine 1845–52*(Gill & MacMillan, 1994), p.211.
7.  *Roscommon and Leitrim Gazette*, 18 May 1850.
8.  *Morning Chronicle* quoted in *Roscommon and LeitrimGazette*,17 August 1850.
9.  George Nicholls, *A History of the Irish Poor Law*(New York, 1967), p.v.
10.  See H.C., 1850 (725), Minutes, Appendix and Report from the Select Committee of the House of Lords appointed to investigate and report upon the allegations and charges contained in the petition of the board of guardians of the union of Carrick-on-Shannon, complaining of the management and misconduct of the late vice-guardians of the said union.
11.  *Leitrim Journal*, 3 April 1851.
12.  *Roscommon and Leitrim Gazette*, 2 March 1850.
13.  Ibid., 14 August 1847.

14. *Impartial Reporter*, 19 February 1852.
15. National Library of Ireland, Parish of Fenagh baptism register, p.4239.
16. Breandán Mac Suibhne, 'A Jig in the Poorhouse', in *Dublin Review of Books*, Issue 32, April 8 2013, p.1.
17. BPP, volume 3, pp.416–7.
18. BPP, volume 7, correspondence from January to March 1847 relating to the measures adopted for the relief of the distress in Ireland, Commissariat Series [second part], p.77–8.
19. BPP, volume 3, sixth series, p.755.
20. Ibid., p.741.
21. Breandán Mac Suibhne, 'A Jig in the Poorhouse', in *Dublin Review of Books*, issue 32, April 8 2013, p.2.
22. Leitrim County Library, Ballinamore (hereafter LCL), Mohill board of guardians' minute book, BG 122/A/5, 1 April 1847, p.2, Thomas McTaggert £7 for coffins; 20 May 1847, p.27, Thomas Mc Taggart £20 for coffins and BG 122/A/6, 28 June 1849, p.296, Thomas Mc Taggert £1/7/6; Carrick-on-Shannon board of guardians' minute book, BG 52/A/4, 20 February 1847 p.27; 27 March 1847, p.78, W. Cunningham £15; 24 December 1847, William Cunningham, 37/10 for coffins; BG52/A/5, 26 February 1848, p.A 50, William Cunningham, £15 for coffins; 18 March 1848, p.A 75, W Cunningham, £33 for coffins; 15 April 1848, p.A 116, W. Cunningham, £30 for coffins; 1 July 1848, p.A 238, William Cunningham, £10/10 for coffins; 22 July 1848, p.A 278, William Cunningham, £8/16/3 for coffins; 21 October 1848, p.A 394, William Cunningham, £40 for coffins; BG 52/A/6, 16 December 1848, p.C16, William Cunningham, £16/17/4 for coffins; 13 January 1849, William Cunningham, £13/19 for coffins.
23. LCL, Manorhamilton board of guardians' minute book, BG 117/A/2, p.314.
24. LCL, Mohill board of guardians minute book, BG 122/A/6, 3 May 1849, p.236, Murphy, £196 for Indian meal for outdoor relief; 10 May 1849, p 246, Murphy, £298 for Indian meal for outdoor relief; 26 May 1849, p.266, Murphy, £442 for Indian meal for outdoor relief; 2 June 1849, p 276, Murphy, £650 for Indian meal for outdoor relief.
25. LCL, Carrick-on-Shannon board of guardians' minute book, BG 52/A/4, 20 February 1847, p.27, Pat Barrett; 24 July, p.248, Pat Barrett, £8/11/8 for bread and groceries; 31 July, p.258, Pat Barrett, £20 for same; 21 August, p.286, £30 to Pat Barrett for bread, Indian meal and groceries; 18 September 1847, p.326, £30 to Pat Barrett for same; 16 October 1847, p.351, £18 to Pat Barrett for groceries; 11 December 1847, p.431, £23 to Pat Barrett for bread and groceries; BG 52/A/5, 18 March 1848, p.A 75, £100 to Pat Barrett for bread and groceries.
26. LCL, Carrick-on-Shannon board of guardians' minute, BG 52/A/4, 27 February 1847, p.39, £10 to Margaret O'Dowd for water; 29 May 1847, p.172, more than £17 to 'widow Dowd'; 16 October 1847, p.351, £12/18

to Margaret O'Dowd for water; BG 52/A/6, 13 January 1849, £10/18/7 to Margaret O'Dowd for water; 26 June 1850, p.454, £8/12 to Margaret O'Dowd for water.

27. LCL, Carrick-on-Shannon board of guardians' minute, BG 52/A/6, p.463.
28. LCL, BG 52/A/5, 4 March, p.A 55; 18 March p A 75; 27 May 1848, p.A 183 and 30September 1848, p.A 370.
29. LCL, Manorhamilton board of guardians' minute, BG 117/A/3, p 237, 20 September 1849.
30. LCL, Carrick-on-Shannon board of guardians' minute book, BG 52/A/4, 19 June 1847, p.203; BG 52/A/5, 16 September 1848, p.A 349.
31. LCL, BG 52/A/6, 2 December 1848, p.A 453.
32. LCL, Manorhamilton board of guardians' minute, BG 117/AA/2, 3 October 1844.
33. BPP, volume 3, pp.417–21.
34. Public Records Office, Belfast, D 4123/5/1/21, Turner Papers, Colonel George Keppel to William Lawder, 18 December 1846.
35. BPP, volume 7, correspondence from January to March 1847 relating to the measures adopted for the relief of the distress in Ireland, Board of Works series [second part], p.12.
36. Ibid., p.207.
37. *Leitrim Journal*, 2 October 1851.
38. National Archives, Dublin (hereafter NAI), Relief Commission Papers, (hereafter, RLFC), 3/2/16/28; RLFC, 3/2/16/3 and RLFC, 3/2/16/19. The captain of the 41st Regiment and his detachment gave £5/6/6 to the Drumshanbo relief fund while a donation of £10 was made to the Mohill Benevolent Relief Society by a captain in the 32nd regiment and the officers and men of the 33rd detachment. The captain of the 33rd regiment gave £2 while each of the non-commissioned officers and privates of the same regiment contributed 1½ days' pay each – a total of £2/14/3 – to the Ballinamore relief fund.
39. NAI, Society of Friends Relief of Distress Papers, box 2/506/37, B260, Richard Clifford, Drumdarton, Ballinamore, to committee, 6 May 1847.
40. Ibid., box, 2/506/10, Emma Lawder, Longfield, Drumsna, to committee, 1 December 1847.
41. *Impartial Reporter*, 10 July 1851.
42. Ibid., 8 May 1851.

# APPENDICES

## APPENDIX ONE

### Protestant Population in County Leitrim in 1834

| Parish | Established Church | Percentage of Population | Total Population |
|--------|------|------|------|
| Carrigallen | 2,150 | 28 | 7,809 |
| Drumlease | 621 | 16 | 3,901 |
| Inishmagrath | 483 | 6 | 8,310 |
| Killargue | 395 | 9 | 4,411 |
| Cloonclare | 2,024 | 21 | 9,494 |
| Cloonlogher | 108 | 8 | 1,294 |
| Killasnet | 791 | 20 | 3,887 |
| Oughteragh | 1,117 | 13 | 8,449 |
| Rossinver | 1,044 | 7 | 14,088 |
| Drumreilly | 752 | 8 | 9,663 |
| Annaduff | 583 | 9 | 6,119 |
| Cloone | 942 | 5 | 20,279 |
| Fenagh | 113 | 3 | 4,337 |
| Killenummery | 659 | 15 | 4,279 |
| Kiltoghert | 2,091 | 12 | 17,093 |
| Kiltubrid | 366 | 5 | 6,729 |
| Mohill | 1,590 | 9 | 17,311 |
| TOTAL | 15,829 | 11 | 147,453 |

*Source:* HC 1835, vol. xxxiii, Commission of Public Instruction, Ireland, Class I – Rectories and Vicarages, pp.30a, 34a, 36a, 42a, 44a, 52a, 54a, 56a, 58a, 60a.

(There were also fifty-six Presbyterians and eight designated as 'other' in the parish of Carrigallen.)

# APPENDIX TWO

**Electoral Divisions in County Leitrim**
**Ballyshannon Union**

| Electoral Division | Population In 1841 |
|---|---|
| Glenade | 4,234 |
| Kinlough | 4,646 |
| **Total:** | **8,880** |

**Carrick-on-Shannon Union, County Leitrim**

| | |
|---|---|
| Ck-on-Shannon | 5,695 |
| Drumshanbo | 6,000 |
| Drumreilly | 3,735 |
| Drumsna | 3,028 |
| Keshcarrigan | 4,932 |
| Kiltubrid | 3,949 |
| Leitrim | 4,244 |

**County Roscommon**

| | |
|---|---|
| Aughrim | 4,469 |
| Creeve | 2,827 |
| Elphin | 5,363 |
| Gilstown | 4,600 |
| Kilglass | 5,759 |
| Killukin | 3,863 |
| Kilmore | 5,164 |
| Tumna | 3,449 |
| **Total:** | **67,077** |

**Mohill Union**

| | |
|---|---|
| Mohill | 7,990 |
| Aughavas | 4,779 |
| Annaduff | 6,469 |
| Annaveagh | 5,627 |
| Ballinamore | 6,970 |
| Carrigallen | 4,763 |
| Cloone | 7,038 |
| Drumreilly | 3,700 |
| Eslin | 3,095 |
| Fenagh | 4,374 |
| Newtowngore | 3,337 |
| Oughteragh | 4,714 |
| Rinn | 6,003 |
| **Total:** | **68,859** |

**Manorhamilton Union**

| | |
|---|---|
| Manorhamilton | 8,074 |
| Cloonlogher | 2,451 |
| Dromahaire | 4,182 |
| Drumkeerin | 5,923 |
| Inishmagrath | 3,712 |
| Killenummery | 4,605 |
| Killargue | 3,616 |
| Kiltyclogher | 4,728 |
| Lurganboy | 4,011 |
| Rossinver | 4,686 |
| **Total:** | **45,988** |

*Source*: Reprinted British Parliamentary Papers, volume 8, Distress (Ireland), Supplementary appendix to the seventh, and last, report of the Relief Commissioners, pp.28, 33, 67 and 68.

## APPENDIX THREE

## 32nd Report of the Irish Society, Statistical table for 1850

| | Numbers of Each | |
|---|---|---|
| Categories | Dromahaire | Drumshanbo |
| Number of Schools Inspected | 26 | 17 |
| Spellers Passed | 395 | 70 |
| Readers Passed | 201 | 10 |
| Translators of Gospel | 75 | 12 |
| Translators of Bible | 38 | 4 |
| Repetitioners Passed | – | – |
| Total Pupils Passed | 709 | 96 |
| Total Under Instruction | 1,633 | 336 |
| Pupils Under 15 Years of Age | 169 | 43 |
| Pupils from 15–50 Years of Age | 518 | 51 |
| Females | 191 | 27 |
| Pupils Above 50 Years | 22 | 2 |

*Source*: National Archives, Dublin, Society of Friends Relief of Distress Papers, box 2/507/3.

## APPENDIX FOUR

### Encumbered Estates Sales in County Leitrim, 1850–1855

| | |
|---|---|
| **Owner** | John D. Brady |
| **Petitioner** | Romney Foley |
| **Barony** | Leitrim |
| **Lands** | Keonbrook (including house), Ballytrily and Gortnagullion |
| **Extent** | 550 acres |

| | |
|---|---|
| **Owner** | Cairncross Cullen |
| **Petitioner** | William Williams Brown |
| **Barony** | Dromahaire and Rossclogher |
| **Extent** | 40 townlands |

| | |
|---|---|
| **Owner** | Robert Robinson |
| **Petitioner** | Joseph Bennett |
| **Barony** | Leitrim |
| **Lands** | Plot of ground and premises formerly called the Old Infirmary. Plot lately known as the Old Post Office in Carrick-on-Shannon with the four new dwelling houses hereon held by lease from Charles Manners St George. |

| | |
|---|---|
| **Owner** | Rev John Williamson, John Williamson and David Williamson |
| **Petitioner** | John Tate |
| **Barony** | Rossclogher |
| **Lands** | Eames's Tenement, Connolly's Tenement, Algeo's Tenement, Rea's Tenement and O'Donnell's Tenement in Manorhamilton. |

| | |
|---|---|
| **Owner** | William O'Brien, Esq., Mohill |
| **Petitioner** | William George Newman |
| **Barony** | Mohill |
| **Lands** | Drumregan, Lismackniff and Kiltifea |
| **Extent** | 327 acres |

| | |
|---|---|
| **Owner** | John Charles Doveton |
| **Petitioner** | Same |
| **Barony** | Rossclogher |
| **Lands** | Mantiagh, Conwall, Carrovegh, Aughahow, Gorteenachurry |
| **Extent** | 2,063 acres |
| **Purchaser** | Initially bought by William A Cosgrave, Frederick Flood and John Robinson for a total of £3,220 but later purchased as one lot by Flood for the same amount. |

| | |
|---|---|
| **Owner** | Alex Berry |
| **Barony** | Carrigallen |
| **Lands** | Killyhurk (close to town of Carrigallen) |
| **Extent** | 327 acres |

| | |
|---|---|
| **Owner** | John Missett |
| **Petitioner** | |
| **Barony** | Leitrim |
| **Lands** | Ground, house and premises in Carrick-on-Shannon (Main Street) |

| | |
|---|---|
| **Owner** | Westby H. Percival |
| **Petitioner** | Thomas Sandes |
| **Barony** | Carrigallen |
| **Lands** | Drumconra, Drumlea, Ardunsaughan, Derrygoan, Carrickmakeegan, Cuilmore |
| **Extent** | 2,338 acres |

| | |
|---|---|
| **Owner** | Elizabeth McMorry, James McTernan, John Clarke |
| **Petitioner** | Thomas Croker |
| **Barony** | Rosclogher |
| **Lands** | Fivepoundland (parish of Killasnet) |
| **Extent** | 36 acres |

| | |
|---|---|
| **Owner** | John Parke |
| **Petitioner** | John Parke |
| **Barony** | Rosclogher |
| **Lands** | Gortaclary |

| | |
|---|---|
| **Owner** | William George Percy |
| **Petitioner** | George Faris |
| **Barony** | Carrigallen |
| **Lands** | Lisnatullagh |

| | |
|---|---|
| **Owner** | Francis Nesbitt |
| **Petitioner** | Maxwell Hamilton |
| **Barony** | Mohill |
| **Lands** | Aughery, Dromodmore, Dromodbeg, Dromod town, Drumlum, Derrywillow, Faltass, Furnace, Gortinea, Killyfad, Mohereven, castle, demesne and lands of Derrycarne and islands |
| **Extent** | 2,646 |
| **Purchaser** | Charles T. Ward, Esq., Aughry House |

| | |
|---|---|
| **Owner** | Acheson O'Brien |
| **Petitioner** | John King |
| **Barony** | Carrigallen |
| **Lands** | Mansion house, offices and demesne lands of Drumsilla |
| **Extent** | 2,276 acres |

| | |
|---|---|
| **Owner** | |
| **Petitioner** | |
| **Barony** | |
| **Lands** | Glenaniff estate |
| **Extent** | |
| **Purchaser** | Robert St George Johnston, Kinlough House and 7, Mountjoy Square East, Dublin |

| | |
|---|---|
| **Owner** | W. Waller and John Lynch (assignee) |
| **Petitioner** | Robert Stevenson and Margaret Spear |
| **Barony** | Carrigallen |
| **Lands** | Lessiagh and Drumkeelwick |
| **Extent** | 229 acres |
| **Purchaser** | Patrick Kiernan |
| **Price** | £2,150 |

| | |
|---|---|
| **Owner** | John Hamilton Peyton, Bernard Peyton and Christopher Hume Lawder (assignee) |
| **Petitioner** | Charles Robert Peyton |
| **Barony** | Leitrim |
| **Lands** | Cartown, Carhowna, Caldra, Port, etc |

| | |
|---|---|
| **Owner** | Gerald Francis Walsh (a minor) and Mary Anne Walsh (widow) |
| **Petitioner** | John Seymour and William Digby Seymour MP |
| **Barony** | Leitrim and Mohill |
| **Lands** | Gubron, Leaminish, Kilmacsherrell, Boneal, Kiltyfanon, Drumany (O'Brien), Drumany (Tanants), Stralongford, Tullylackamore, Pattore, Kiltohart |
| **Extent** | 2,257 acres |
| **Purchaser** | Mr McFadden and Mr Nolan |
| **Price** | £13,925 |

| | |
|---|---|
| **Owner** | Michael Jones, Cregg House, Sligo |
| **Petitioner** | Michael Jones |
| **Barony** | Carrigallen |
| **Lands** | Drumbibe estate (close to Ballinamore) comprising 13 townlands |
| **Extent** | 2,124 acres |

| | |
|---|---|
| **Purchaser** | John Brady M P |
| **Price** | £12,650 |

| | |
|---|---|
| **Owner** | Joseph Johnston, Robert Johnston and Joseph Francis Johnston (a minor) |
| **Petitioner** | John Ennis, John Peyton and Thomas Kiernan |
| **Barony** | Leitrim |
| **Lands** | Kilnagross, Annaghkeentamore, Annaghselerny, Knockacullen, Mullaghgarrow, Gortnavane, Aughacashel, Caldra, Derreen Upper and Derreen Lower |
| **Extent** | 3,837 acres |

*Source*: *Roscommon and Leitrim Gazette*, 13 July 1850, 3 August 1850; *Leitrim Journal,* 13 February 1851, 6 March 1851, 27 March 1851, 1 May 1851, 3 July 1851, 12 June 1851, 18 September 1851, 2 October 1851, 11 December 1851, 11 March 1852, 16 July 1852, 12 May 1853, 18 August 1853, 25 August 1853, 19 January 1854, 16 February 1854, 18 May 1854, 29 June 1854, 12 April 1855, 10 May 1855, 13 September 1855.

# APPENDIX FIVE

## Population Change by Parish (Townland)

| | Number of Townlands | | |
|---|---|---|---|
| **Parish** | **Increase** | **No Change** | **Decline** |
| Annaduff | 3 | – | 59 |
| Carrigallen | 8 | 2 | 56 |
| Cloone | 3 | – | 105 |
| Cloonclare | 17 | 1 | 64 |
| Cloonlogher | 1 | – | 8 |
| Drumlease | 7 | 1 | 35 |
| Drumreilly | 13 | 1 | 80 |
| Fenagh | 9 | 2 | 48 |
| Inishmagrath | 21 | 3 | 114 |
| Killenummery | 9 | – | 35 |
| Killargue | 11 | 2 | 54 |
| Kiltoghart | 14 | 3 | 145 |
| Kiltubrid | 4 | 1 | 75 |
| Killasnet | 12 | 2 | 56 |
| Mohill | 3 | 2 | 161 |
| Oughteragh | 18 | – | 79 |

| Rossinver | 18 | 2 | 108 |
|---|---|---|---|

*Source*: H.C. 1852–53, volume xcii, 1851 Census of Ireland, County of Leitrim, pp.89–112.

## APPENDIX SIX

## Townland Population Loss by Percentage

| Parish | Number of Townlands | | | | | | | | | |
|---|---|---|---|---|---|---|---|---|---|---|
| | 0–10 | 11–20 | 21–30 | 31–40 | 41–50 | 51–60 | 61–70 | 71–80 | 81–90 | 91–100 |
| Annaduff | 1 | 5 | 5 | 5 | 10 | 13 | 5 | 10 | 4 | 1 |
| Carrigallen | 5 | 10 | 10 | 18 | 6 | 4 | 1 | 1 | 1 | – |
| Cloone | 5 | 5 | 20 | 29 | 26 | 11 | 5 | 2 | 2 | – |
| Cloonclare | 14 | 15 | 12 | 9 | 8 | 2 | 2 | – | 1 | 1 |
| Cloonlogher | 3 | 1 | 1 | 1 | 1 | – | – | 1 | – | – |
| Drumreilly | 14 | 18 | 19 | 11 | 10 | 3 | 1 | 3 | – | 1 |
| Fenagh | 2 | 9 | 7 | 11 | 9 | 5 | 2 | 3 | 1 | – |
| Drumlease | 9 | 8 | 8 | 6 | 3 | 1 | – | – | – | – |
| Inishmagrath | 9 | 21 | 12 | 12 | 18 | 14 | 12 | 5 | 5 | 2 |
| Killenummery | 7 | 5 | 7 | 7 | 6 | 3 | – | – | – | – |
| Killargue | 5 | 10 | 12 | 11 | 12 | 2 | – | 1 | 1 | – |
| Kiltoghert | 10 | 28 | 27 | 20 | 18 | 16 | 13 | 9 | 2 | 2 |
| Kiltubrid | 10 | 15 | 17 | 14 | 6 | 10 | 1 | – | 1 | 1 |
| Killasnet | 5 | 14 | 13 | 11 | 6 | 3 | 1 | 1 | 1 | 1 |
| Mohill | 5 | 15 | 27 | 30 | 24 | 21 | 18 | 11 | 5 | 5 |
| Oughteragh | 10 | 19 | 14 | 13 | 6 | 9 | 3 | 3 | 1 | – |
| Rossinver | 18 | 28 | 33 | 8 | 7 | 11 | – | 1 | 1 | 0 |

*Source*: H.C. 1852–53, volume xcii, 1851 Census of Ireland, County of Leitrim, pp.89–112.

## APPENDIX SEVEN

## Townland Decline Compared to County Average (28%)

| Parish | Number of Townlands at or Below County Average | Number of Townlands Above County Average |
|---|---|---|
| Annaduff | 11 | 48 |

| | | |
|---|---|---|
| Carrigallen | 25 | 31 |
| Cloone | 30 | 75 |
| Cloonclare | 41 | 23 |
| Cloonlogher | 5 | 3 |
| Drumlease | 25 | 10 |
| Drumreilly | 51 | 29 |
| Fenagh | 18 | 31 |
| Inishmagrath | 42 | 72 |
| Killenummery | 19 | 16 |
| Killargue | 27 | 27 |
| Kiltoghert | 65 | 80 |
| Kiltubrid | 42 | 33 |
| Killasnet | 32 | 24 |
| Mohill | 47 | 114 |
| Oughteragh | 43 | 35 |
| Rossinver | 79 | 28 |

*Source*: H.C. 1852–53, volume xcii, 1851 Census of Ireland, County of Leitrim, pp.89–112.

## APPENDIX EIGHT

### Majority Population Loss (Number of Townlands and Percentage)

| Parish | Number of Townlands | % of Total | Population Decline (%) |
|---|---|---|---|
| Annaduff | 13 | 24 | 51–60 |
| Carrigallen | 18 | 32 | 31–40 |
| Cloone | 29 | 28 | 31–40 |
| Cloonclare | 15 | 23 | 11–20 |
| Cloonlogher | 3 | 38 | 0–10 |
| Drumlease | 9 | 26 | 0–10 |
| Drumreilly | 19 | 24 | 21–30 |
| Fenagh | 11 | 22 | 31–40 |
| Inishmagrath | 21 | 19 | 11–20 |
| Kiltoghert | 28 | 19 | 11–20 |
| Kiltubrid | 17 | 23 | 21–30 |

| Killasnet | 14 | 25 | 11–20 |
|---|---|---|---|
| Mohill | 30 | 19 | 31–40 |
| Oughteragh | 19 | 24 | 11–20 |
| Rossinver | 33 | 31 | 21–30 |

*Source*: H.C. 1852–53, volume xcii, 1851 Census of Ireland, County of Leitrim, pp.89–112.

## APPENDIX NINE

## Townlands in Which No Population Change Occurred

| Townland | Parish | Population in 1841 | Population in 1851 |
|---|---|---|---|
| Derrylahan | Carrigallen | 6 | 6 |
| Sonnagh | | 63 | 63 |
| Kinnara Glebe | Drumlease | 27 | 27 |
| Cuiltia | Drumreilly | 49 | 49 |
| Braudphark | Inishmagrath | 11 | 11 |
| Fingreagh, Lower | | 14 | 14 |
| Rossbeg Glebe | | 21 | 21 |
| Belhavel | Killargue | 20 | 20 |
| Killargue | | 69 | 69 |
| Costrea | Fenagh | 74 | 74 |
| Aghakilconnell | Kiltoghert | 47 | 47 |
| Fahymore | | 8 | 8 |
| Newbrook | | 45 | 45 |
| Derreen (Southwell) | Kiltubrid | 6 | 6 |
| Garradice | Fenagh | 32 | 32 |
| Drumregan | Mohill | 69 | 69 |
| Selton | | 35 | 35 |
| Tullintaggart | Cloonclare | 16 | 16 |
| Gorteenaguinnell | Killasnet | 105 | 105 |
| Twigspark | | 14 | 14 |
| Drumcolla | Rossinver | 25 | 25 |
| Sheean | | 10 | 10 |

*Source*: H.C. 1852–53, volume xcii, 1851 Census of Ireland, County of Leitrim, pp.89–112.

## APPENDIX TEN

### Townland Decline of 75% or More

| Townland | Parish | Population in 1841 | Population in 1851 | % Decline |
|---|---|---|---|---|
| Cornacreeve | Drumreilly | 10 | 0 | 100 |
| Mullaghfadda | Inishmagrath | 61 | 3 | 95 |
| Drumloona | Carrigallen | 90 | 17 | 81 |
| Killydrum | | 96 | 24 | 75 |
| Acres | Cloone | 65 | 8 | 88 |
| Aghoo | Drumreilly | 62 | 15 | 76 |
| Camagh | Oughteragh | 66 | 15 | 77 |
| Liscuilfea | | 81 | 15 | 81 |
| Tullylackan-beg | | 22 | 5 | 77 |
| Skreeny, Little | Cloonclare | 90 | 13 | 86 |
| Boggaun | Cloonlogher | 324 | 76 | 76 |
| Kilgarriff | Drumreilly | 109 | 22 | 80 |
| Corglass | Inishmagrath | 31 | 6 | 81 |
| Curraghs, South | | 62 | 12 | 81 |
| Derrycullinanbeg | | 20 | 3 | 85 |
| Drummangarvagh | | 8 | 0 | 100 |
| Falty | | 108 | 20 | 81 |
| Lurga | | 28 | 3 | 98 |
| Liscuillew, Lower | | 115 | 29 | 75 |
| Barlear | Killargue | 61 | 14 | 77 |
| Drumlumman Glebe | | 45 | 6 | 87 |
| Derryoughter | Annaduff | 49 | 9 | 82 |
| Dristernan | | 122 | 31 | 75 |
| Drumkeerin | | 40 | 7 | 82.5 |
| Foxborough | | 25 | 4 | 84 |
| Corrachoosaun | Fenagh | 141 | 28 | 80 |
| Drumcattan | | 105 | 25 | 76 |
| Laragh | | 81 | 10 | 88 |

| | | | | |
|---|---|---|---|---|
| Coaughrim | Kiltoghert | 74 | 6 | 92 |
| Cornamucklagh | | 41 | 8 | 80 |
| Correen | | 121 | 29 | 76 |
| Corryolus | | 78 | 19 | 76 |
| Derrintober | | 87 | 19 | 78 |
| Lisnabrack | | 29 | 7 | 76 |
| Moneynure | | 6 | 0 | 100 |
| Tawneycurry | | 67 | 12 | 82 |
| Aghakilmore | Kiltubrid | 44 | 8 | 82 |
| Drumparsons | | 46 | 1 | 98 |
| Bunnymore, Lower | Mohill | 78 | 5 | 94 |
| Cartron | | 46 | 0 | 100 |
| Cornageeha | | 52 | 11 | 79 |
| Drumgownagh | | 151 | 10 | 93 |
| Laheen, North | | 84 | 9 | 89 |
| Antfield | Annaduff | 111 | 28 | 75 |
| Drumlom | | 153 | 35 | 77 |
| Dromodmore | | 245 | 22 | 91 |
| Fedaro | | 35 | 4 | 89 |
| Trean | Cloone | 165 | 28 | 83 |
| Aghnahunshin | Mohill | 53 | 6 | 89 |
| Annaghderg, Lower | | 94 | 22 | 77 |
| Cloonlaughill | | 13 | 3 | 77 |
| Corduffhill | | 19 | 0 | 100 |
| Cormore | | 40 | 8 | 80 |
| Corracoffy | | 122 | 24 | 80 |
| Drumkilleen | | 75 | 13 | 83 |
| Kildoo | | 39 | 7 | 82 |
| Liscloonadea | | 152 | 20 | 87 |
| Mullaghrigny | | 42 | 10 | 76 |
| Tullybradan | | 37 | 9 | 76 |
| Mohill | | 15 | 0 | 100 |
| Tawnylust Barr, Upper | Cloonclare | 31 | 0 | 100 |
| Shancurragh | Killasnet | 6 | 0 | 100 |
| Skreeny | | 39 | 5 | 87 |

| Cloodrevagh | Rossinver | 38 | 6 | 84 |
|---|---|---|---|---|
| Duncarbry | | 290 | 62 | 79 |

*Source*: H.C. 1852–53, volume xcii, 1851 Census of Ireland, County of Leitrim, pp.89–112.

## APPENDIX ELEVEN

## District Electoral Divisions in County Leitrim Showing Numbers of Irish Speakers Aged 60+ in 1911

| Division | Population | 60+ | Irish-Speaking | % |
|---|---|---|---|---|
| Yugan | 871 | 163 | 131 | 80 |
| Mahanagh | 1,426 | 270 | 171 | 63 |
| St Patrick's | 695 | 131 | 83 | 63 |
| Glenfarn | 608 | 107 | 64 | 60 |
| Arigna | 408 | 77 | 45 | 58 |
| Aghalateeve | 267 | 62 | 31 | 50 |
| Killargue | 622 | 118 | 56 | 47 |
| Drumreilly East | 383 | 72 | 31 | 43 |
| Aghanlish | 693 | 160 | 67 | 42 |
| Cloonclare | 762 | 134 | 49 | 37 |
| Drumreilly West | 542 | 101 | 37 | 37 |
| Garvagh | 985 | 165 | 58 | 35 |
| Kiltyclogher | 1,299 | 229 | 79 | 34 |
| Munakill | 860 | 151 | 41 | 27 |
| Tullaghan | 1,130 | 261 | 67 | 26 |
| Glenaniff | 641 | 122 | 30 | 25 |
| Glenboy | 364 | 64 | 15 | 23 |
| Killenummery | 865 | 145 | 27 | 19 |
| Drumkeerin | 1,271 | 240 | 44 | 18 |
| Aughavas | 866 | 166 | 29 | 17 |
| Belhavel | 1,090 | 183 | 31 | 17 |
| Ballinamore | 1,386 | 225 | 35 | 16 |

| | | | |
|---|---|---|---|
| Manorhamilton | 2,161 | 380 | 56 | 15 |
| Corriga | 625 | 120 | 17 | 14 |
| Glenade | 569 | 109 | 14 | 13 |
| Ballaghameehan | 867 | 166 | 20 | 12 |
| Sramore | 765 | 146 | 18 | 12 |
| Lisgillock | 565 | 92 | 10 | 11 |
| Oughterard | 662 | 107 | 11 | 10 |
| Aghavoghill | 247 | 57 | 5 | 9 |
| Dromahaire | 1,629 | 274 | 25 | 9 |
| Kinlough | 935 | 216 | 19 | 9 |
| Cloonlogher | 987 | 166 | 13 | 8 |
| Stralongford | 500 | 81 | 6 | 7 |
| Glencar | 653 | 125 | 8 | 6 |
| Gubacreeny | 785 | 181 | 10 | 6 |
| Carrick-on-Shannon | 2,061 | 361 | 17 | 5 |
| Cashel | 482 | 79 | 3 | 4 |
| Cloone | 1,191 | 192 | 7 | 4 |
| Cloverhill | 1,125 | 182 | 7 | 4 |
| Lurganboy | 707 | 135 | 6 | 4 |
| Melvin | 500 | 115 | 4 | 3 |
| Drumshanbo | 1,114 | 208 | 5 | 2 |
| Garadice | 1,024 | 166 | 3 | 2 |
| Carrigallen East | 476 | 91 | 1 | 1 |
| Aghacashel | 288 | 54 | 0 | 0 |
| Barnameenagh | 641 | 120 | 0 | 0 |
| Carrigallen West | 839 | 161 | 8 | 0 |
| Gortermone | 784 | 150 | 0 | 0 |
| Greaghlass | 887 | 144 | 0 | 0 |
| Kiltubrid | 555 | 104 | 1 | 0 |

*Source*: Garret FitzGerald, 'Irish-speaking in the pre-Famine period: A study based on the 1911 Census data for people born before 1851 and still alive in 1911,' *Proceedings of the Royal Irish Academy*, Volume 103 C, Number 5, 2003, pp.251–3.

# APPENDIX TWELVE

## Townlands in Which No Population Change Occurred

| Townland | Parish | Population in 1851 | Population in 1861 |
|----------|--------|-------------------|-------------------|
| Drumercross | | 26 | 26 |
| Drumergoole | Carrigallen | 25 | 25 |
| Killahuke | | 252 | 252 |
| Longfield | | 32 | 32 |
| Corriga | Cloone | 145 | 145 |
| Gorteen | | 83 | 83 |
| Corralahan | Drumreilly | 5 | 5 |
| Curraghatawy | | 89 | 89 |
| Glennanbeg | | 3 | 3 |
| Sranadarragh | | 91 | 91 |
| Boggaun | Oughteragh | 33 | 33 |
| Drumkeen | | 73 | 73 |
| Tomoloskan | | 35 | 35 |
| Tullylackan Beg | | 5 | 5 |
| Briscloonagh | Cloonclare | 146 | 146 |
| Cronastauk | | 68 | 68 |
| Lurgan | | 24 | 24 |
| Skreeny | | 7 | 7 |
| Derreens | Inishmagrath | 26 | 26 |
| Derrycullinabeg | | 3 | 3 |
| Derrynalurgan | | 6 | 6 |
| Moneenatieve | | 93 | 93 |
| Geskanagh Glebe | Killargue | 27 | 27 |
| Greaghnagon | | 31 | 31 |
| Sweetwood, Little | | 52 | 52 |
| Tawnylea | | 67 | 67 |
| Drumsna | Annaduff | 46 | 46 |

| | | | |
|---|---|---|---|
| Glebe | Fenagh | 11 | 11 |
| Lisdauky | Kiltoghert | 58 | 58 |
| Portaneoght | | 9 | 9 |
| Sallaghan | | 13 | 13 |
| Derreen (Southwell) | Kiltubrid | 6 | 6 |
| Drumadykey | | 10 | 10 |
| Bunnymore, Lower | Mohill | 5 | 5 |
| Cornageeha | | 11 | 11 |
| Lisdrumgivel, Lower | | 23 | 23 |
| Cuilmore | Annaduff | 28 | 28 |
| Doora | | 30 | 30 |
| Drumcree | | 43 | 43 |
| Drummeen | Cloone | 73 | 73 |
| Sunnaghbeg | | 94 | 94 |
| Annaghderg, Upper | Mohill | 21 | 21 |
| Cloonbonaigh, South | | 165 | 165 |
| Corrascoffy | | 24 | 24 |
| Curragha | | 69 | 69 |
| Drumregan | | 69 | 69 |
| Gubagraffy | | 34 | 34 |
| Glebe | Killasnet | 157 | 157 |
| Meenaphuill | | 25 | 25 |
| Aghaderrard, West | Rossinver | 65 | 65 |
| Derrynahimmirk | | 93 | 93 |
| Drumnacolla | | 25 | 25 |
| Sheean | | 10 | 10 |
| Tullyderrin | | 36 | 36 |

*Source*: H.C. 1863, volume lv, 1861 Census of Ireland, County of Leitrim, pp.89–112.

## APPENDIX THIRTEEN

## Townland Decline of 75% or More

| Townland | Parish | Population in 1851 | Population in 1861 | % Decline |
|---|---|---|---|---|
| Aghoo, West | Oughteragh | 82 | 11 | 87 |
| Creevy | | 35 | 2 | 94 |
| Manorhamilton | Cloonclare | 21 | 0 | 100 |
| Barragh Beg | | 10 | 0 | 100 |
| Drumkeerin | Inishmagrath | 50 | 0 | 100 |
| Lugmore | | 9 | 0 | 100 |
| Drumillion | | 16 | 0 | 100 |
| Drumlumman Glebe | Killargue | 6 | 0 | 100 |
| Aghintober | | 5 | 0 | 100 |
| Crickeen | Annaduff | 4 | 0 | 100 |
| Mountcampbell | | 28 | 2 | 92 |
| Tully | Fenagh | 78 | 18 | 77 |
| Greagh | | 4 | 0 | 100 |
| Leitrim | Kiltoghert | 75 | 0 | 100 |
| Tawnycurry | | 12 | 2 | 83 |
| Townparks | | 345 | 43 | 87.5 |
| Aghakilmore | Kiltubrid | 8 | 0 | 100 |
| Bunny More, Upper | Mohill | 39 | 3 | 92 |
| Twigspark | Killasnet | 14 | 0 | 100 |
| Conwal, South | Rossinver | 56 | 0 | 100 |
| Sragarve | | 8 | 0 | 100 |

*Source*: H.C. 1863, volume lv, 1861 Census of Ireland, County of Leitrim, pp.89–112.

# SELECT BIBLIOGRAPHY

## MANUSCRIPT SOURCES

**Leitrim County Library, Ballinamore**
Carrick-on-Shannon board of guardians' minute books
Manorhamilton board of guardians' minute books
Mohill board of guardians' minute books
Killegar Papers

**Famine Attic, St Patrick's Hospital, Carrick-on-Shannon**
Transcriptions of Carrick-on-Shannon board of guardians' minute books

**Church of Ireland Glebe House, Mohill, County Leitrim**
Cloone vestry minute books
Mohill vestry minute books
Birth, death and marriage registers of County Leitrim Church of Ireland
parishes

**Kiltoghert Parish Office, Carrick-on-Shannon**
Birth, death and marriage registers for the parish of Kiltoghert

**St George's Heritage Centre, Carrick-on-Shannon**
Seamus Geraghty Collection

**Catholic Diocesan Archives, Dublin**
Cullen Papers

**National Archives, Dublin**
Department of Education Papers
Outrage Papers
Prison Records
Relief Commission Papers
Society of Friends Relief of Distress Papers

## National Library, Dublin
Lane-Fox Papers
Leitrim Papers
O'Beirne Papers
Waldron Papers
Catholic Parish Registers

## Public Records Office, Belfast
Madden Papers
Turner Papers

## Royal Irish Academy, Dublin
Records of the Irish Relief Association
Windele Mss

## Central Library, Paisley, Scotland
Poor Law Records

## National Archives of Scotland
Argyll Justiciary Court: Processes
Crown Office precognitions

## National Archives, Kew, London
Colonial Office Papers
Home Office Papers
Treasury Papers

# NEWSPAPERS

*Freeman's Journal*

*Impartial Reporter*

*Leitrim Journal*

*London Times*

*Roscommon and Leitrim Gazette*

# PARLIAMENTARY PAPERS

H.C. 1825, volume viii, Fourth report from select committee on the state of Ireland.

H.C., 1836, volume xxxii, Appendix to First Report of Commissioners for inquiring into the Condition of the Poorer Classes in Ireland.

Hansard, House of Commons Debates, May 1837, 38.

H.C., 1843, volume xxiv, Census of Ireland for the year 1841.

H.C. 1845, volume xxii, Appendix to minutes of evidence taken before commissioners appointed to inquire into the occupation of land in Ireland.

H.C. 1846, volume xxxvii, Correspondence explanatory of the measures adopted by her majesty's government for the Relief of Distress arising from the failure of the potato crop in Ireland.

H.C. 1852, volume xlvi, Rate in Aid (Ireland).

H.C. 1856, volume xxix, Census of Ireland for the year 1851. Report of tables of Deaths.

H.C. 1856, volume xxx, Census of Ireland for the year 1851 [Workhouses, Auxiliary workhouses and Workhouse Hospitals].

H.C. 1856, volume xxix, Census of Ireland for the year 1851. Table showing the committals, receptions into hospitals and deaths in the several prisons, 1831 to 1851.

H.C. 1852-53, volume xcii, Census of Ireland for the year 1851, County of Leitrim.

H.C. 1856, volume xxxi, Census of Ireland for the year 1851, general report.

H.C. 1856, volume xxvii, Part I, The Twenty-Second report of the Commissioners of National education in Ireland for the year 1855, with appendices, vol. I.

H.C. 1856, volume xxxi, Census of Ireland for the year 1851.

H.C. 1863, volume lv, Census of Ireland for the year 1861, County of Leitrim.

H.C., 1881, volume lxxvii, Return 'by the Provinces and Counties (compiled from Returns made to the Inspector General, Royal Irish Constabulary), of Cases of Evictions which have come to the knowledge of the Constabulary in each of the years from 1849 to 1880, inclusive'.

Reprinted British Parliamentary Papers, volume 2, Papers relating to proceedings for the relief of the distress and state of the unions and workhouse in Ireland, Fifth Series, 1848.

Reprinted British Parliamentary Papers, volume 2, papers relating to Proceedings for the relief of the Distress and State of the Unions and Workhouses in Ireland, Fourth Series, 1847.

Reprinted British Parliamentary Papers, volume 3, Papers relating to proceedings for the relief of the distress and state of unions and workhouses in Ireland, sixth series.

Reprinted British Parliamentary Papers, volume 4, Papers relating to proceedings for the relief of the distress and the state of unions and workhouses in Ireland, seventh series, 1848.

Reprinted British Papers, volume 4, Papers relating to proceedings for the relief of the distress and state of union workhouses in Ireland, eighth series, 1849.

Reprinted British Parliamentary Papers, volume 5, Correspondence from July 1846 to January 1847 relating to the relief of the distress in Ireland, Commissariat.

Reprinted British Parliamentary Papers, volume 5, Correspondence explanatory of the measures adopted by her majesty's government for the relief of distress arising from the potato crop in Ireland with similar correspondence commissariat [first part] and an index, 1846–47.

Reprinted British Parliamentary Papers, volume 6, correspondence from July 1846 to January 1847 relating to the measures adopted for the relief of distress in Ireland, Board of Works series.

Reprinted British Parliamentary Papers, volume 7, correspondence from January to March 1847 relating to the measures adopted for the relief of the distress in Ireland, Board of Works series [second part].

## CONTEMPORARY PUBLICATIONS

Godley, John Robert, *A letter on the subject of poor rates addressed to the landholders of the County of Leitrim* (Dublin, 1843).

McParlan, James, *Statistical Survey of the County Leitrim* (Dublin, 1802).

Nicholls, George, *A History of the Irish Poor Law* (London, 1856).

Wakefield, Edward, *An account of Ireland, statistical and political, vols. 1 and 2* (London, 1812).

# BOOKS

De Beaumont, Gustave, *Ireland: Social, Political, and Religious, with an introduction by Tom Garvin and Andreas Hess, edited and translated by W.C. Taylor* (Harvard University Press, 2006).

Donnelly, Jr, James, *The Great Irish Potato Famine* (Sutton Publishing, 2001).

Gray, Peter, *The Making of the Irish Poor Law, 1815–43* (Manchester University Press, 2009).

Kelly, Liam, *Kiltubrid, County Leitrim: Snapshots of a parish in the 1890s, (Maynooth Studies in Local History)*, 2005.

Kinealy, Christine, *This Great Calamity – The Irish Famine 1845–52* (Gill and MacMillan, 1994).

MacAtasney, Gerard, *Leitrim and the Great Hunger -- a 'temporary inconvenience'?* (Carrick-on-Shannon, 1997).

O'Flynn, T.M., *A history of Leitrim* (1938).

Ó Duigneáin, Proinnsios, *North Leitrim in Famine Times, 1840–50* (Drumlin Publications, 1987).

O'Sullivan, Donal, *Carolan – The Life, Times and Music of an Irish Harper* (London, 1958).

Slevin, Fiona, *By hereditary virtues – a history of Lough Rynn* (Coolabawn Publishing, 2006).

*Transactions of the Central Relief Committee of the Society of Friends during the Famine in Ireland in 1846 and 1847, with an index by Rob Goodbody* (de Búrca, 1996).

# ARTICLES

Garret FitzGerald, 'Irish-speaking in the pre-Famine period: A study based on the 1911 Census data for people born before 1851 and still alive in 1911', in *Proceedings of the Royal Irish Academy, Volume 103 C, Number 5, 2003*.

David Fitzpatrick, 'Class, family and rural unrest in nineteenth-century Ireland', in P.J. Drudy (ed.), *Irish Studies, volume 1* (Cambridge 1981).

David Fitzpatrick, 'Famine, entitlements and seduction: Captain Edmond Wynne in Ireland, 1846-1851', in *The English Historical Review, volume cx, no. 437, June 1995*.

Dermot McCabe and Cormac Ó Gráda, 'Better off thrown behind a ditch': Enniskillen Workhouse during the Great Famine, working paper series // UCD Centre for Economic Research, No. 09/26, 2009.

Liam McNiffe, 'The 1852 Leitrim Election', in *Breifne Journal, volume v., number 18, 1977–8.*

Breandán Mac Suibhne, 'A Jig in the Poorhouse', in *Dublin Review of Books*, Issue 32, April 8 2013.

Liam Ó Caithnia, 'Hugh O'Beirne, The Fiddler of Ballinamore', in *Leitrim Guardian*, 1978.

Cormac Ó Gráda, Yardsticks for workhouses during the great famine, working paper series // UCD Centre for Economic Research, No. 2007/08, 2007.

Tom Rogers, Linda Fibiger, L.G. Lynch and Declan Moore, 'Two glimpses of nineteenth-century institutional burial practice in Ireland: a report on the excavation of burials from Manorhamilton Workhouse, Co. Leitrim, and St Brigid's Hospital, Ballinasloe, Co. Galway', in *The journal of Irish archaeology, volume xv, 2006.*

## ONLINE SOURCES

Ancestry.com: *1851 Scotland Census, 1851 England Census, 1851 Wales Census, 1851 Channel Islands Census.*

Irish Landed Estates Database: *http://www.nuigalway.ie/mooreinstitute/*

## UNPUBLISHED THESES

Jennifer Kelly, *An Outward Looking Community? Ribbonism & Popular Mobilisation in Pre-Famine Leitrim, 1836–1846,* 2003.

John Tunney, *Leitrim and the Great hunger: Poor Law, Famine and Social Decline in Co. Leitrim, 1831–1851,* 1994.

# INDEX